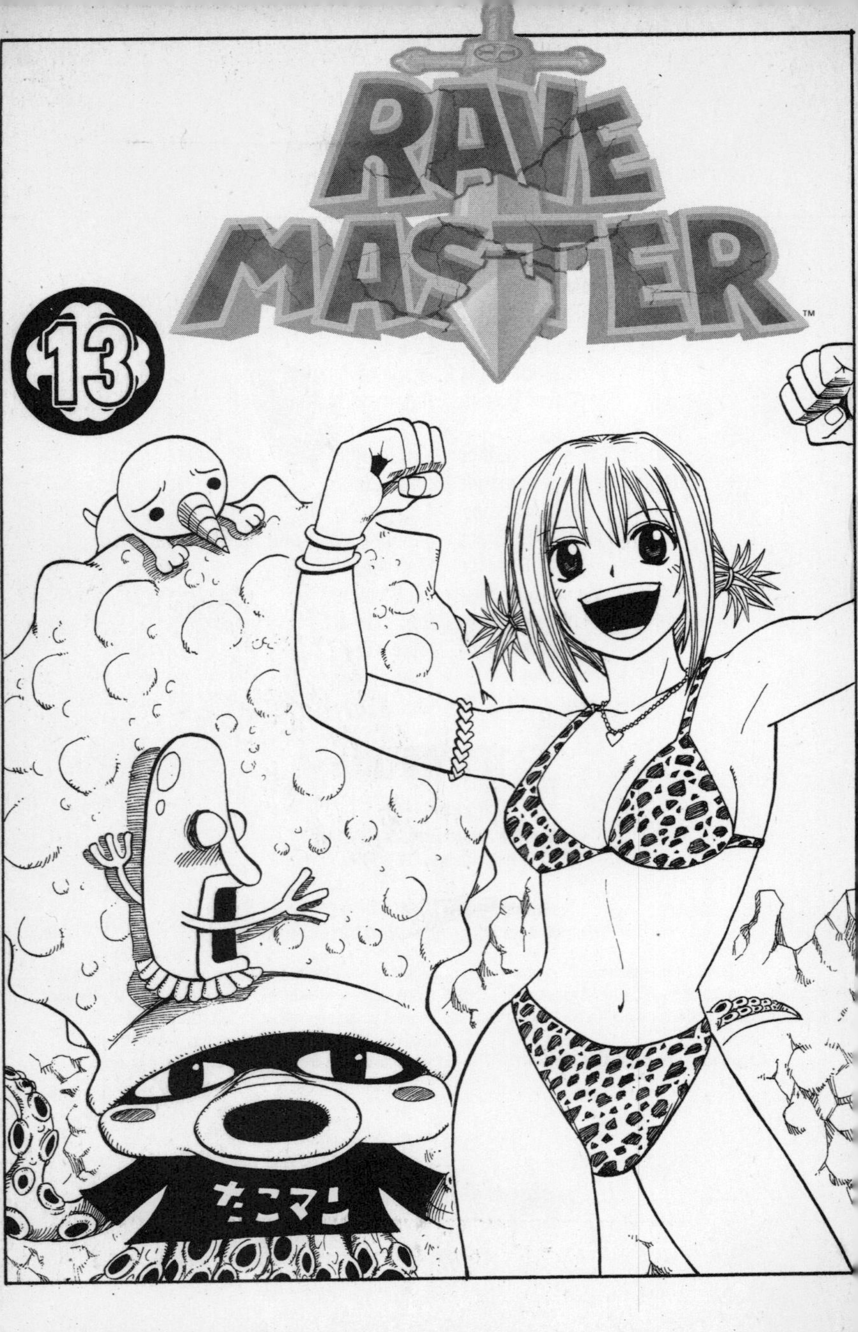
RAVE MASTER™
13
たこマン

Rave Master Vol. 13
Created by Hiro Mashima

Translation - Jeremiah Bourque
English Adaptation - Jake Forbes
Copy Editor - Troy Lewter
Retouch and Lettering - Eva Han
Production Artist - Jason Milligan
Cover Design - Raymond Makowski

Editor - Tim Beedle
Digital Imaging Manager - Chris Buford
Pre-Press Manager - Antonio DePietro
Production Managers - Jennifer Miller and Mutsumi Miyazaki
Art Director - Matt Alford
Managing Editor - Jill Freshney
VP of Production - Ron Klamert
Editor-in-Chief - Mike Kiley
President and C.O.O. - John Parker
Publisher and C.E.O. - Stuart Levy

A 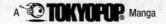 Manga

TOKYOPOP Inc.
5900 Wilshire Blvd. Suite 2000
Los Angeles, CA 90036

E-mail: info@TOKYOPOP.com
Come visit us online at www.TOKYOPOP.com

ISBN: 1-59532-018-0

First TOKYOPOP printing: February 2005
10 9 8 7 6 5 4 3 2 1
Printed in the USA

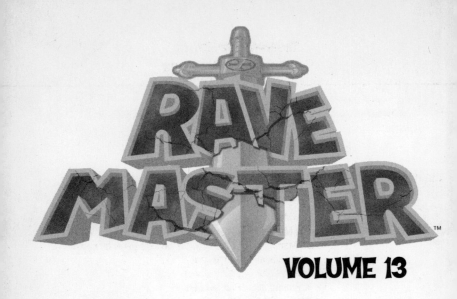

VOLUME 13

Story and Art by

HIRO MASHIMA

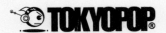

HAMBURG // LONDON // LOS ANGELES // TOKYO

THE STORY SO FAR...

Haru and his companions have been to Symphonia and back in their search for the missing **Rave Stones** and the elusive **Star Memory**, but it was not an easy journey. Confronted by the five living members of the brutal Oracion Six, they likely would have perished were it not for a last minute save by the elemental master, **Sieg Hart**. Now an **archmage**, Sieg Hart soundly defeated the Oracion Six, who fled while warning Haru's team that they'd soon meet again. It's a warning that Haru had better take seriously, for the Oracion Six are now taking orders from a new King--**Lucia Raregroove**, the son of their former leader Gale Raregroove.

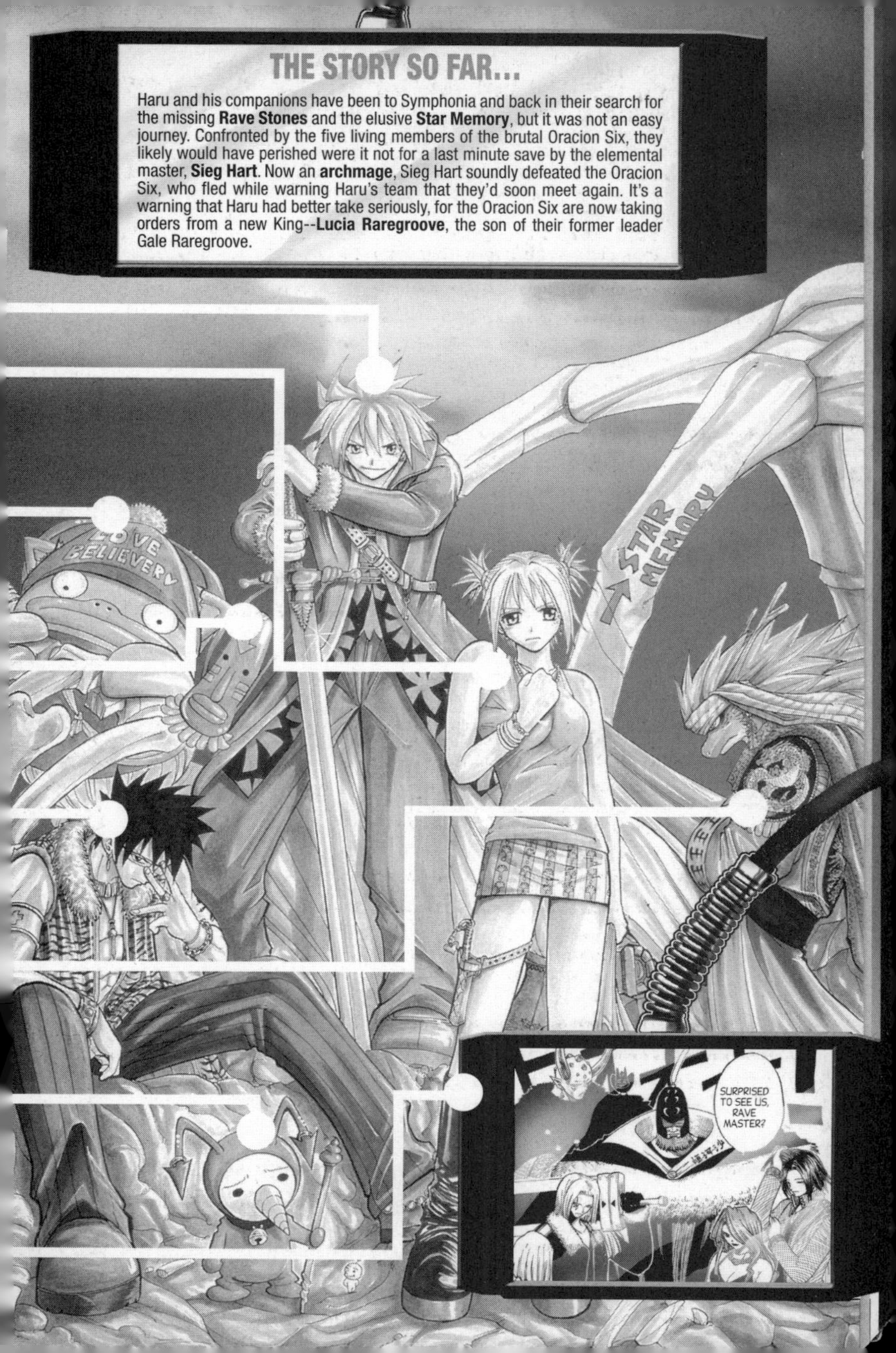
LOVE BELIEVER
STAR MEMORY
SURPRISED TO SEE US, RAVE MASTER?

THE RAVE MASTER CREW

HARU GLORY

A small-town boy turned savior of the world. As the **Rave Master** (the only one capable of using the holy weapon RAVE), Haru set forth to find the missing Rave Stones and defeat Demon Card. He fights with the **Ten Powers Sword,** a weapon that takes on different forms at his command. With Demon Card seemingly out of the way, Haru now seeks the remaining two Rave Stones in order to open the way to Star Memory.

ELIE

The girl without memories. Elie joined Haru on his quest when he promised to help her find out about her past. She's cute, spunky and loves gambling and shopping in equal measures. Locked inside of her is the power of **Etherion.**

RUBY

A "penguin-type" sentenoid, Ruby loves rare and unusual items. After Haru saved him from Pumpkin Doryu's gang, Ruby agreed to sponsor Haru's team in their search for the ultimate rare treasures: the Rave Stones!

GRIFFON KATO (GRIFF)

Griff is a loyal friend, even if he is a bit of a coward. His rubbery body can stretch and change shape as needed. Griff's two greatest pleasures in life are mapmaking and peeping on Elie.

MUSICA

A **"Silverclaimer"** (an alchemist who can shape silver at will) and a former street punk who made good. He joined Haru for the adventure, but now that Demon Card is defeated, does he have any reason to stick around?

LET

A member of the Dragon Race, he was formerly a member of the Demon Card's Five Palace Guardians. He was so impressed by Haru's fighting skills and pureness of heart that he made a truce with the Rave Master. After passing his Dragon Trial, he gained a human body, but his blood is still Dragon Race.

PLUE

The **Rave Bearer,** Plue is the faithful companion to the Rave Master. In addition to being Haru's guide, Plue also has powers of his own. When he's not getting Haru into or out of trouble, Plue can be found enjoying a sucker, his favorite treat.

THE ORACION SIX

Demon Card's six generals. Haru defeated Shuda after finding the Rave of Wisdom. The other five generals were presumed dead after King destroyed Demon Card Headquarters.

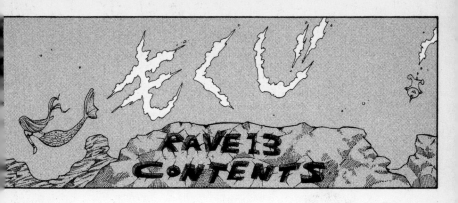

RAVE 13
CONTENTS

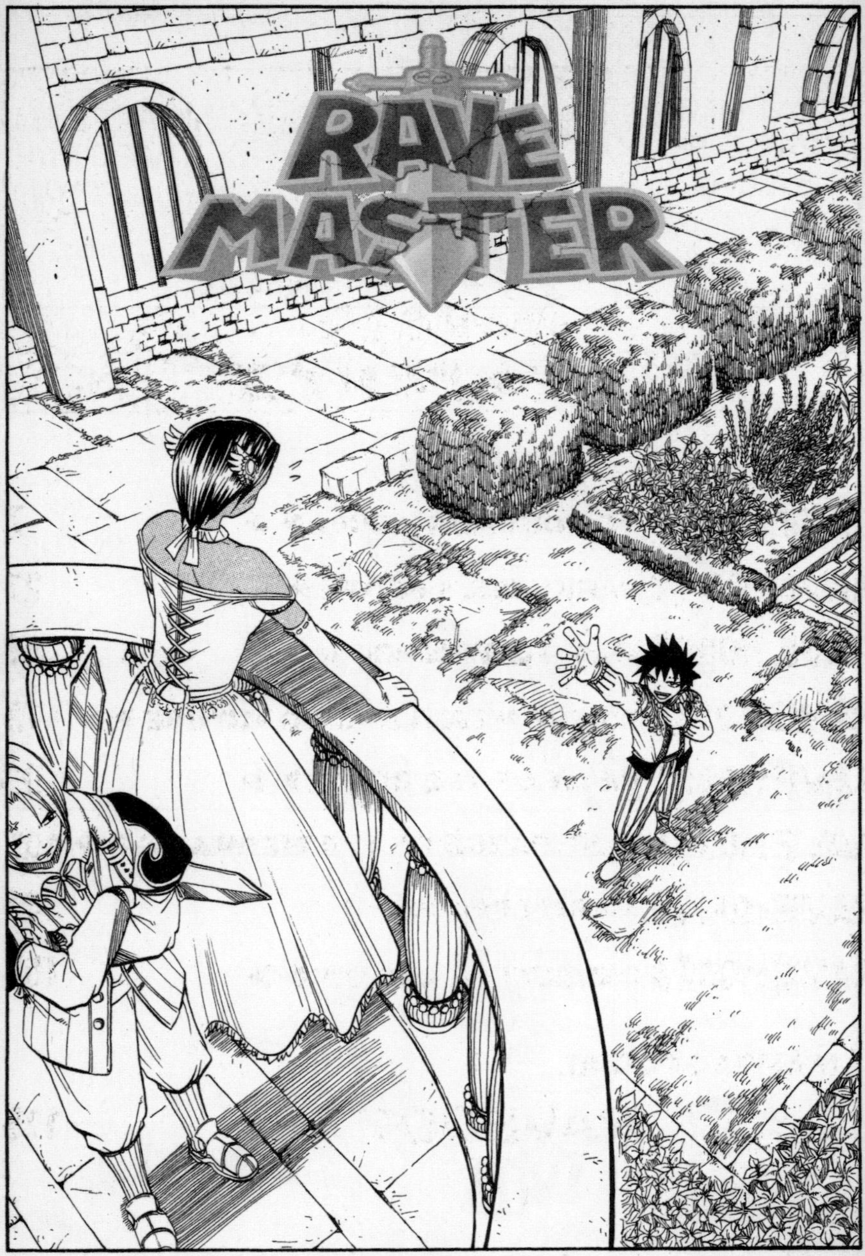
RAVE MASTER

RAVE:98 ✠ TO SOUTHERNBURG!

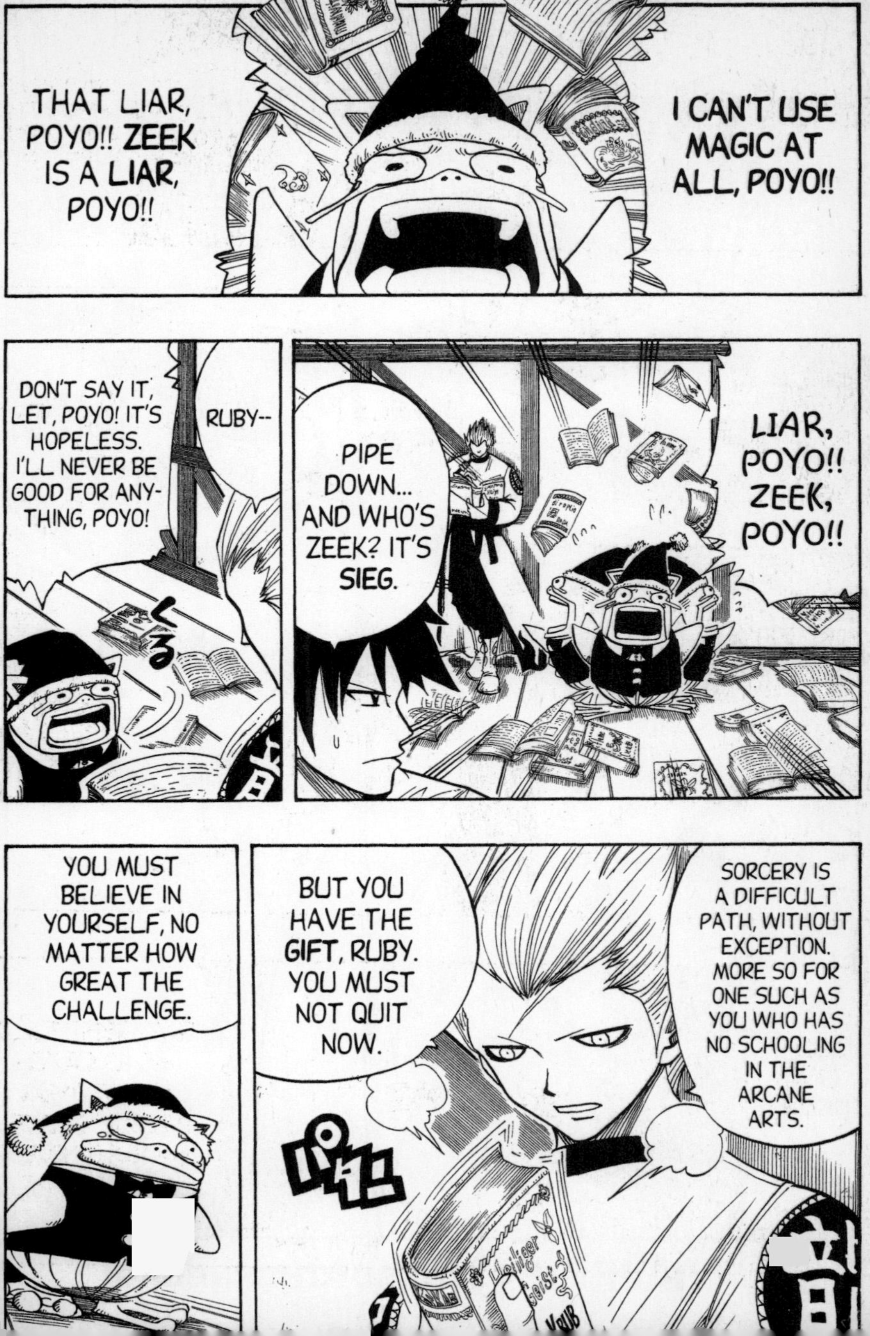
I CAN'T USE MAGIC AT ALL, POYO!!
THAT LIAR, POYO!! ZEEK IS A LIAR, POYO!!
LIAR, POYO!! ZEEK, POYO!!
PIPE DOWN... AND WHO'S ZEEK? IT'S SIEG.
RUBY--
DON'T SAY IT, LET, POYO! IT'S HOPELESS. I'LL NEVER BE GOOD FOR ANYTHING, POYO!
SORCERY IS A DIFFICULT PATH, WITHOUT EXCEPTION. MORE SO FOR ONE SUCH AS YOU WHO HAS NO SCHOOLING IN THE ARCANE ARTS.
BUT YOU HAVE THE GIFT, RUBY. YOU MUST NOT QUIT NOW.
YOU MUST BELIEVE IN YOURSELF, NO MATTER HOW GREAT THE CHALLENGE.

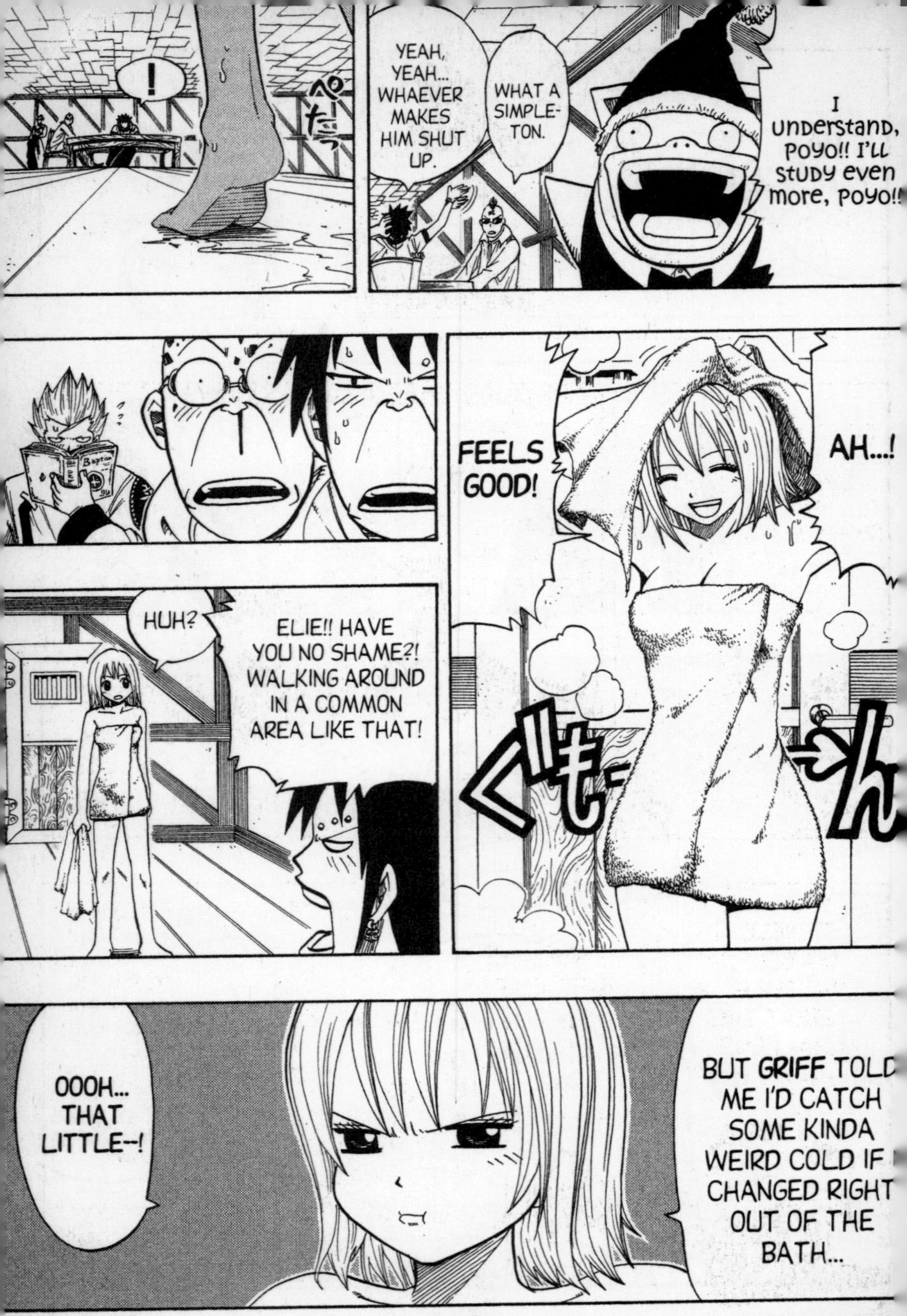
I understand, Poyo!! I'll study even more, Poyo!!
WHAT A SIMPLE-TON.
YEAH, YEAH... WHAEVER MAKES HIM SHUT UP.
!
AH...!
FEELS GOOD!
ELIE!! HAVE YOU NO SHAME?! WALKING AROUND IN A COMMON AREA LIKE THAT!
HUH?
BUT GRIFF TOLD ME I'D CATCH SOME KINDA WEIRD COLD IF CHANGED RIGHT OUT OF THE BATH...
OOOH... THAT LITTLE--!

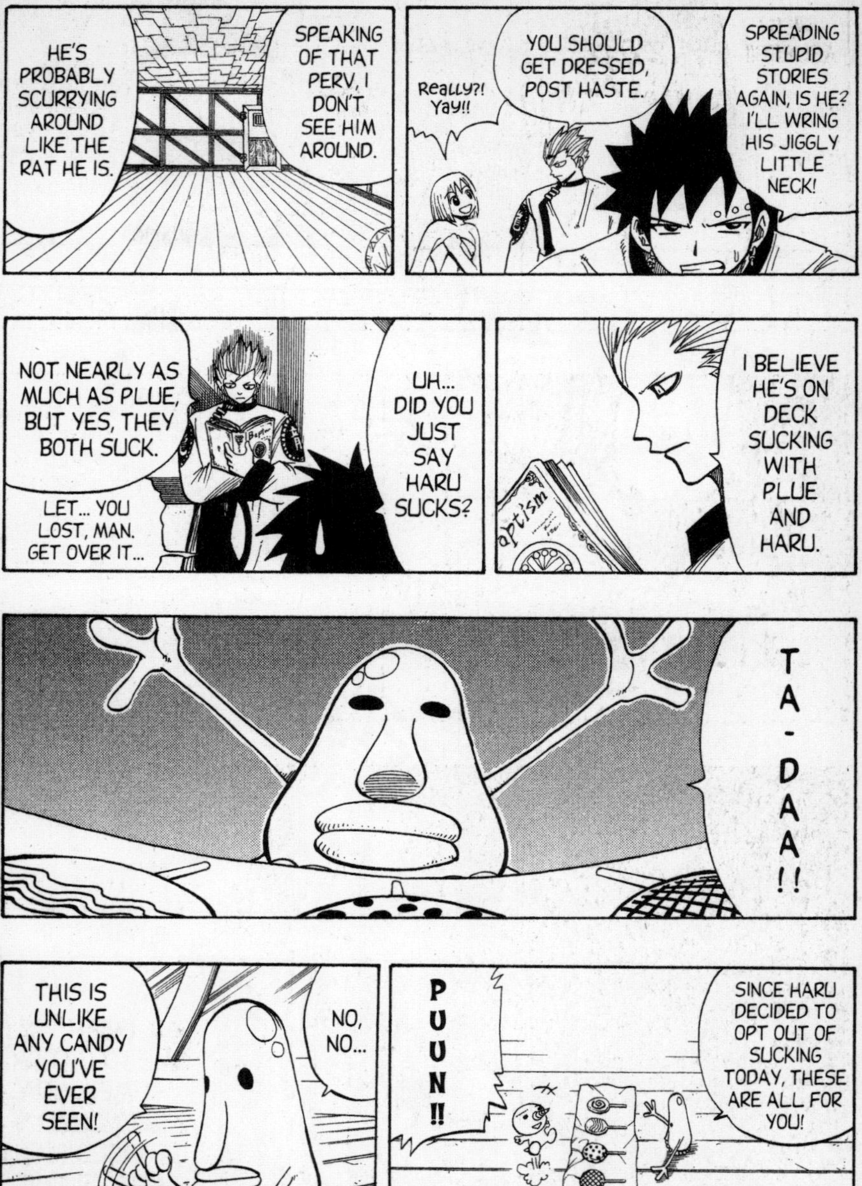
SPREADING STUPID STORIES AGAIN, IS HE? I'LL WRING HIS JIGGLY LITTLE NECK!
YOU SHOULD GET DRESSED, POST HASTE.
Really?! Yay!!
SPEAKING OF THAT PERV, I DON'T SEE HIM AROUND.
HE'S PROBABLY SCURRYING AROUND LIKE THE RAT HE IS.
I BELIEVE HE'S ON DECK SUCKING WITH PLUE AND HARU.
UH... DID YOU JUST SAY HARU SUCKS?
NOT NEARLY AS MUCH AS PLUE, BUT YES, THEY BOTH SUCK.
LET... YOU LOST, MAN. GET OVER IT...
TA-DAA!!
SINCE HARU DECIDED TO OPT OUT OF SUCKING TODAY, THESE ARE ALL FOR YOU!
PUUN!!
NO, NO...
THIS IS UNLIKE ANY CANDY YOU'VE EVER SEEN!

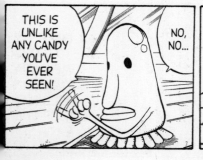

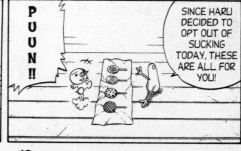

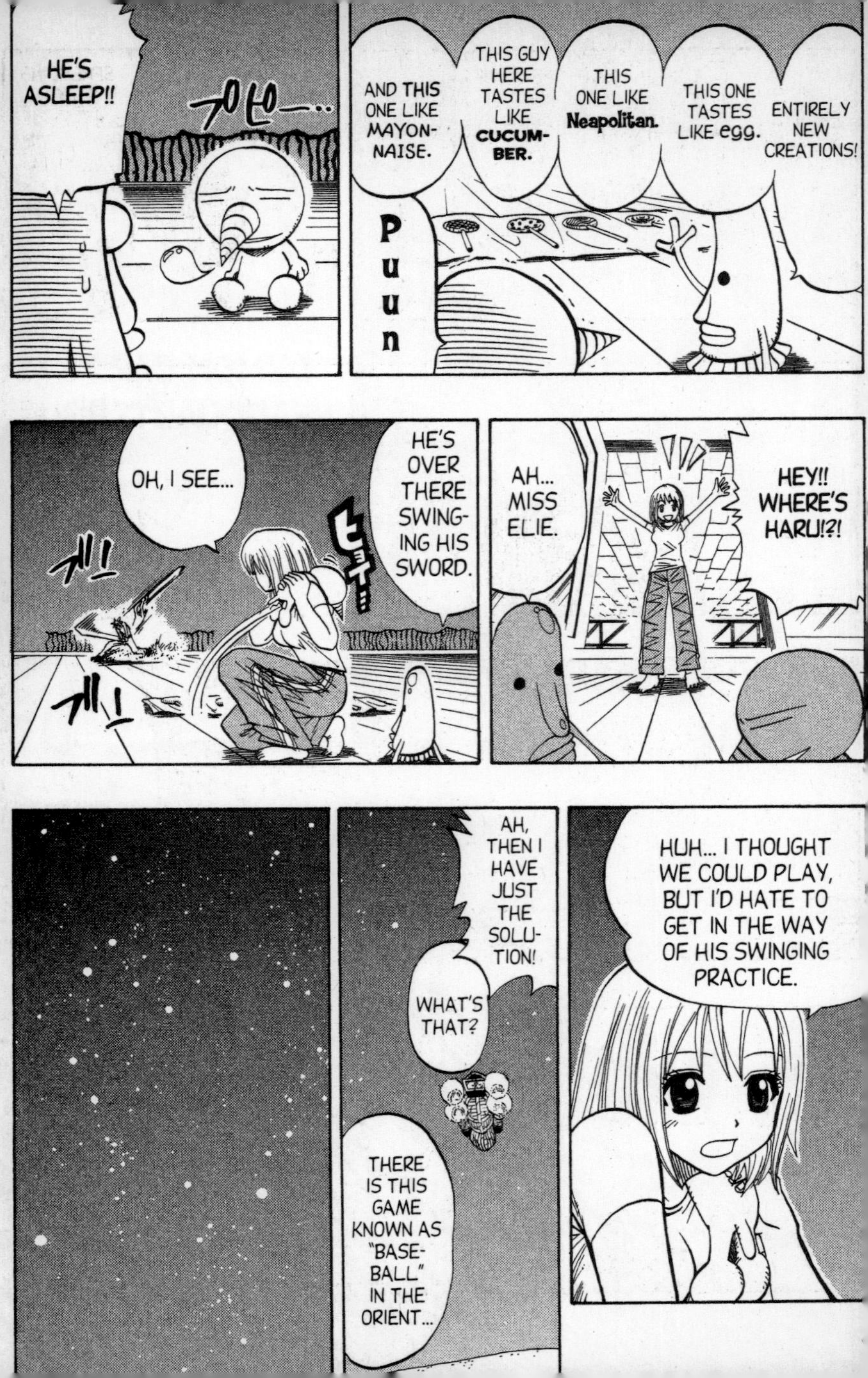
ENTIRELY NEW CREATIONS!
THIS ONE TASTES LIKE egg.
THIS ONE LIKE Neapolitan.
THIS GUY HERE TASTES LIKE CUCUMBER.
AND THIS ONE LIKE MAYONNAISE.
Puun
HE'S ASLEEP!!
HEY!! WHERE'S HARU!?!
AH... MISS ELIE.
HE'S OVER THERE SWINGING HIS SWORD.
OH, I SEE...
HUH... I THOUGHT WE COULD PLAY, BUT I'D HATE TO GET IN THE WAY OF HIS SWINGING PRACTICE.
AH, THEN I HAVE JUST THE SOLUTION!
WHAT'S THAT?
THERE IS THIS GAME KNOWN AS "BASEBALL" IN THE ORIENT...

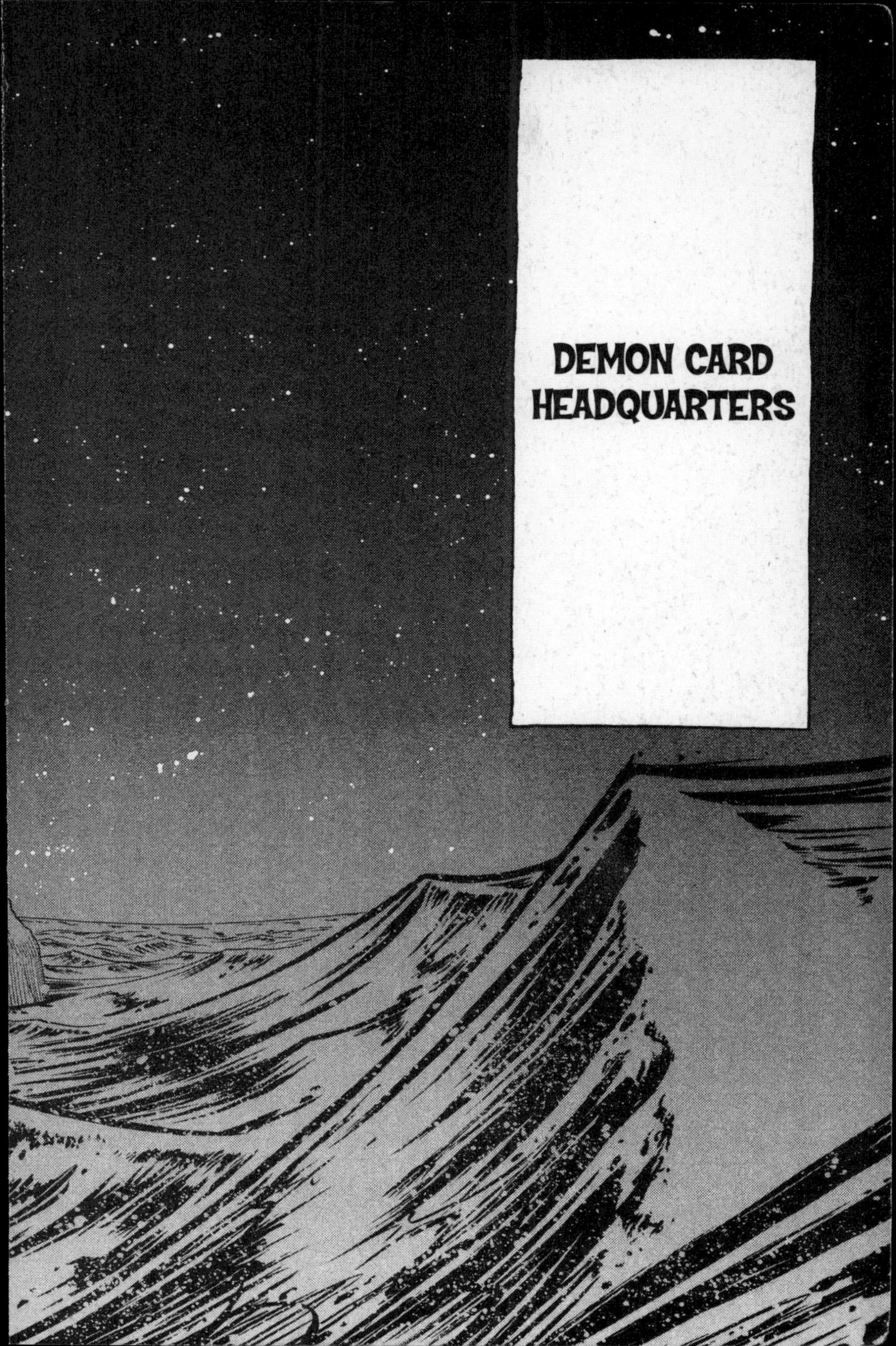
DEMON CARD HEADQUARTERS

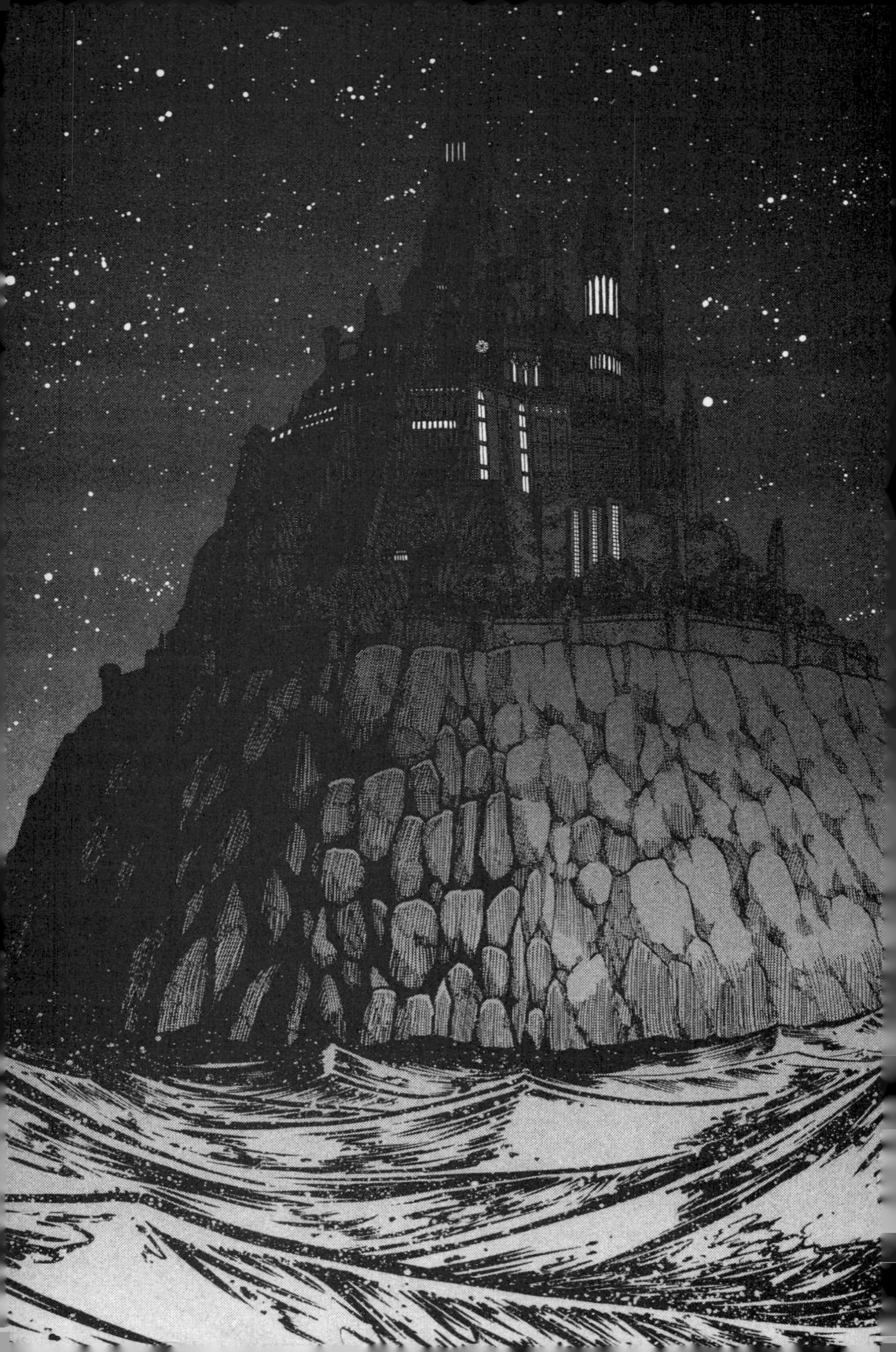

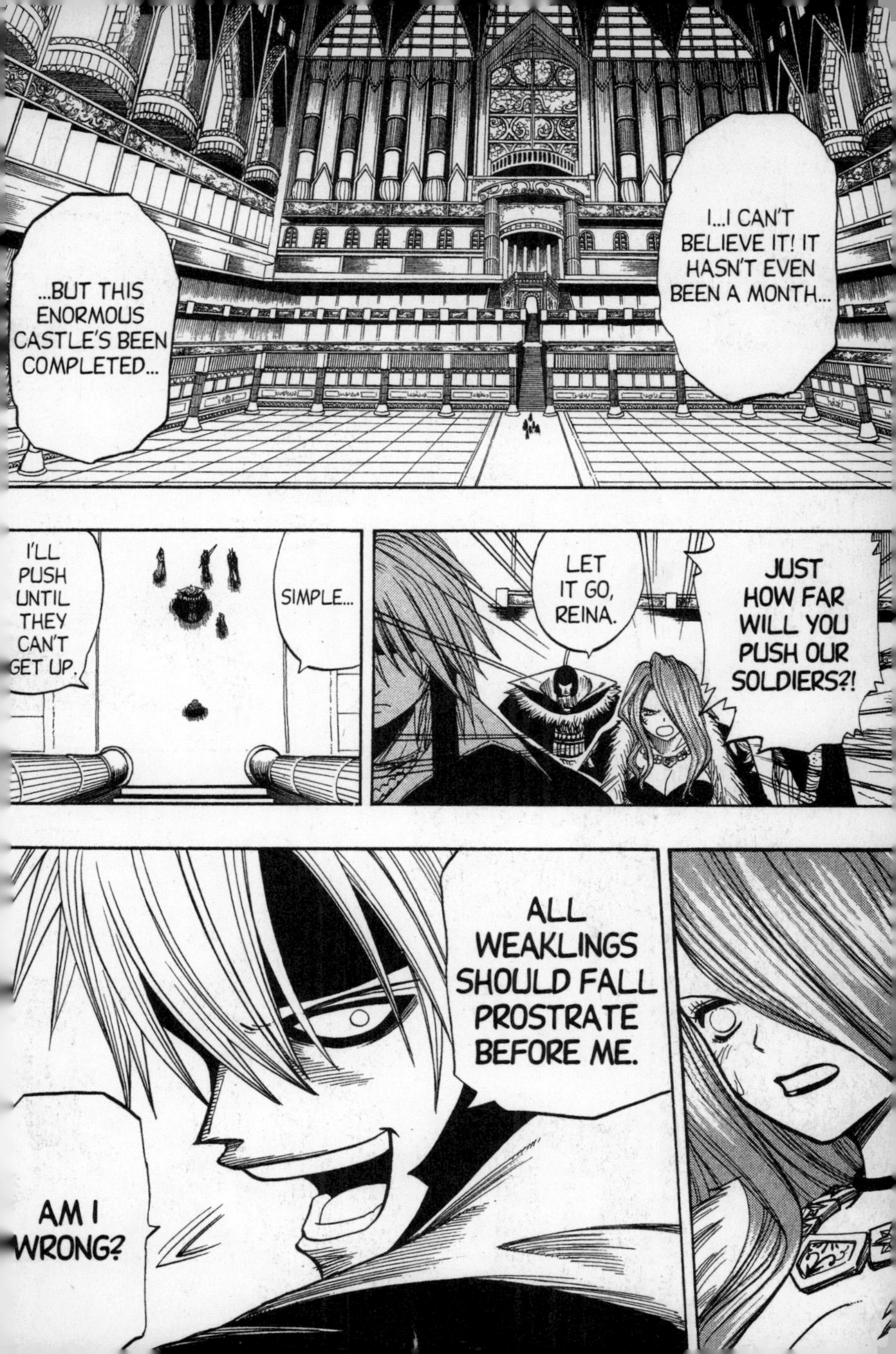
I...I CAN'T BELIEVE IT! IT HASN'T EVEN BEEN A MONTH...
...BUT THIS ENORMOUS CASTLE'S BEEN COMPLETED...
JUST HOW FAR WILL YOU PUSH OUR SOLDIERS?!
LET IT GO, REINA.
SIMPLE...
I'LL PUSH UNTIL THEY CAN'T GET UP.
ALL WEAKLINGS SHOULD FALL PROSTRATE BEFORE ME.
AM I WRONG?

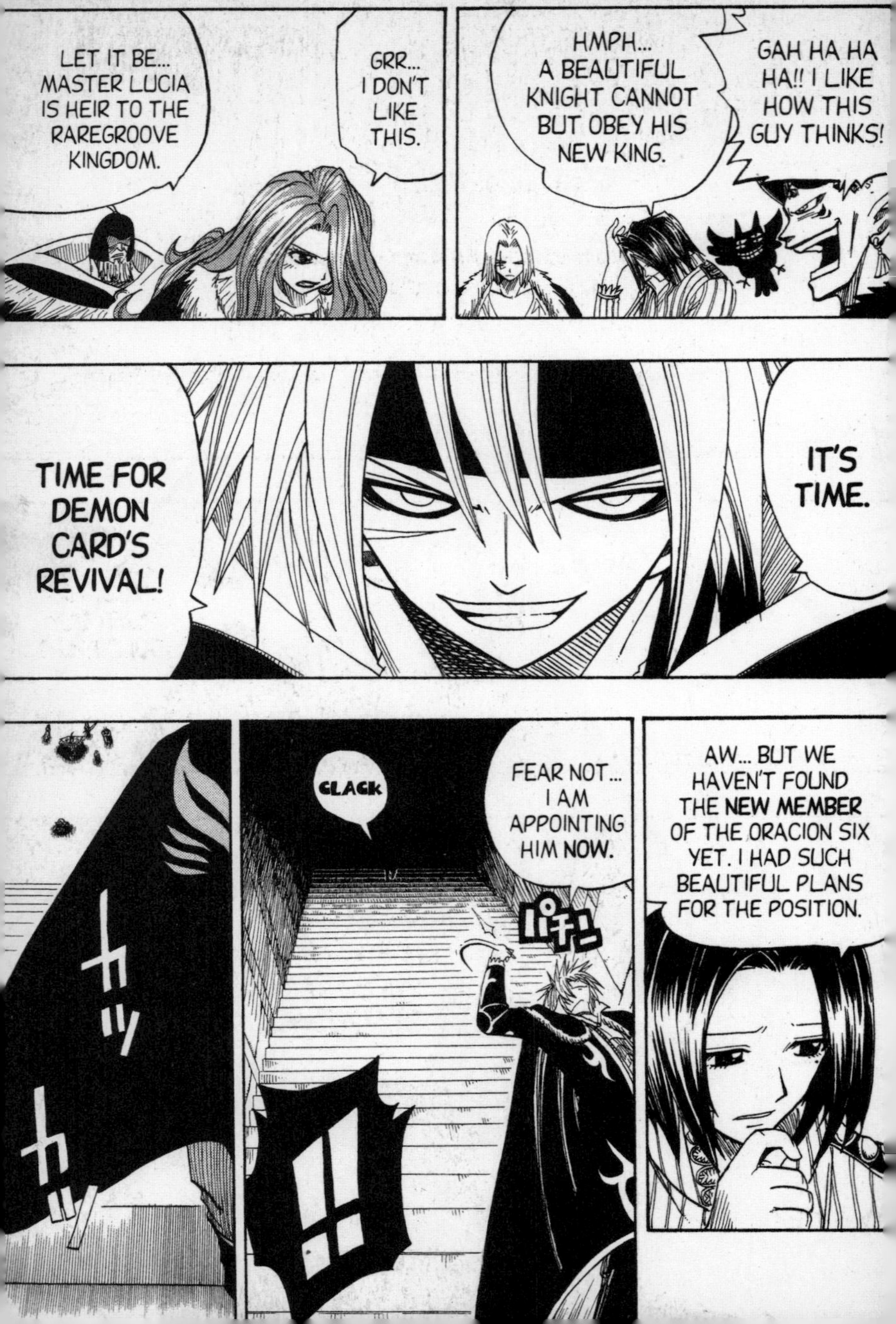
GAH HA HA HA!! I LIKE HOW THIS GUY THINKS!
HMPH... A BEAUTIFUL KNIGHT CANNOT BUT OBEY HIS NEW KING.
GRR... I DON'T LIKE THIS.
LET IT BE... MASTER LUCIA IS HEIR TO THE RAREGROOVE KINGDOM.
IT'S TIME.
TIME FOR DEMON CARD'S REVIVAL!
AW... BUT WE HAVEN'T FOUND THE NEW MEMBER OF THE ORACION SIX YET. I HAD SUCH BEAUTIFUL PLANS FOR THE POSITION.
FEAR NOT... I AM APPOINTING HIM NOW.
パチン
CLACK
!!
カッ
カッ
カッ

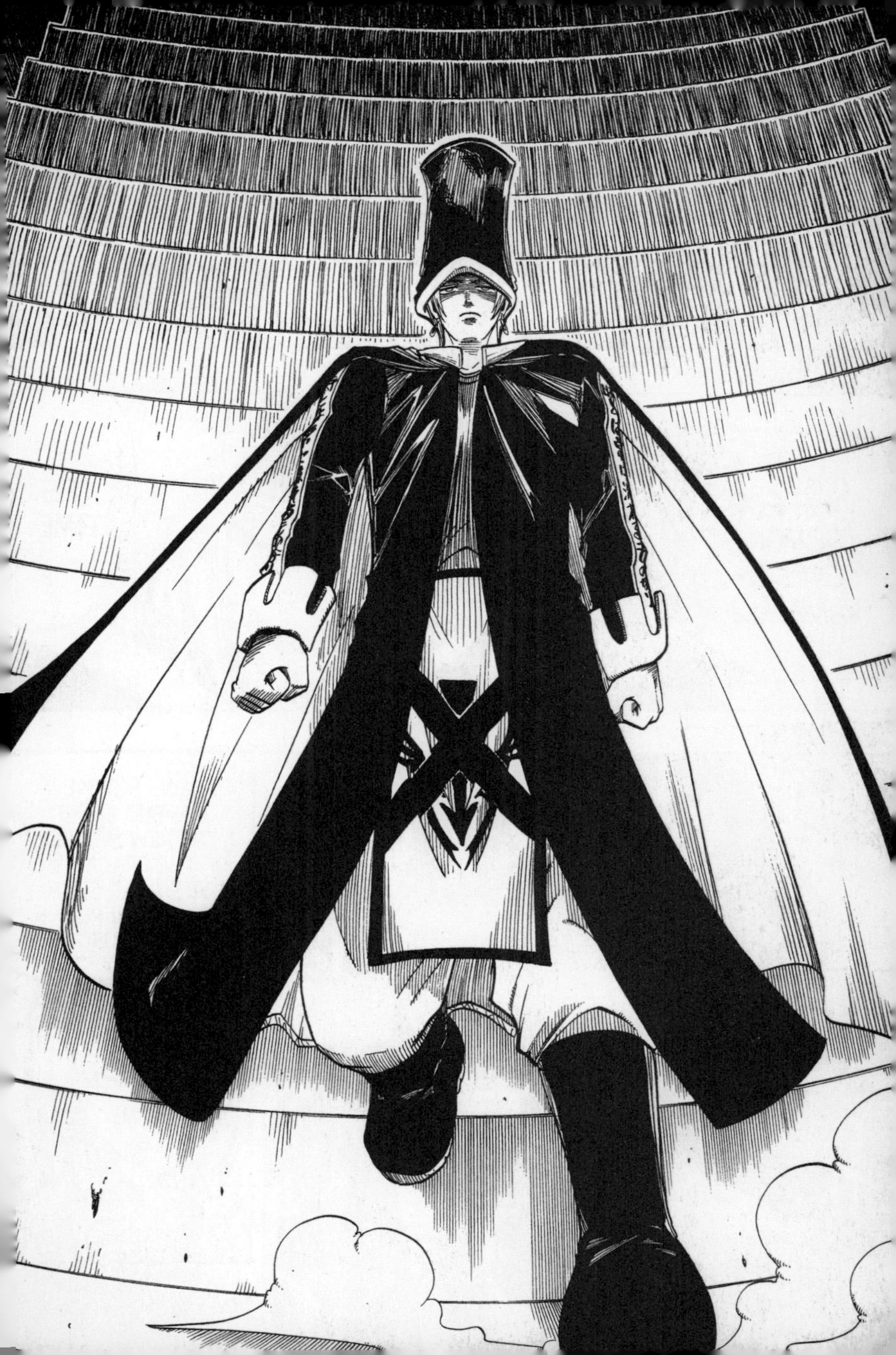

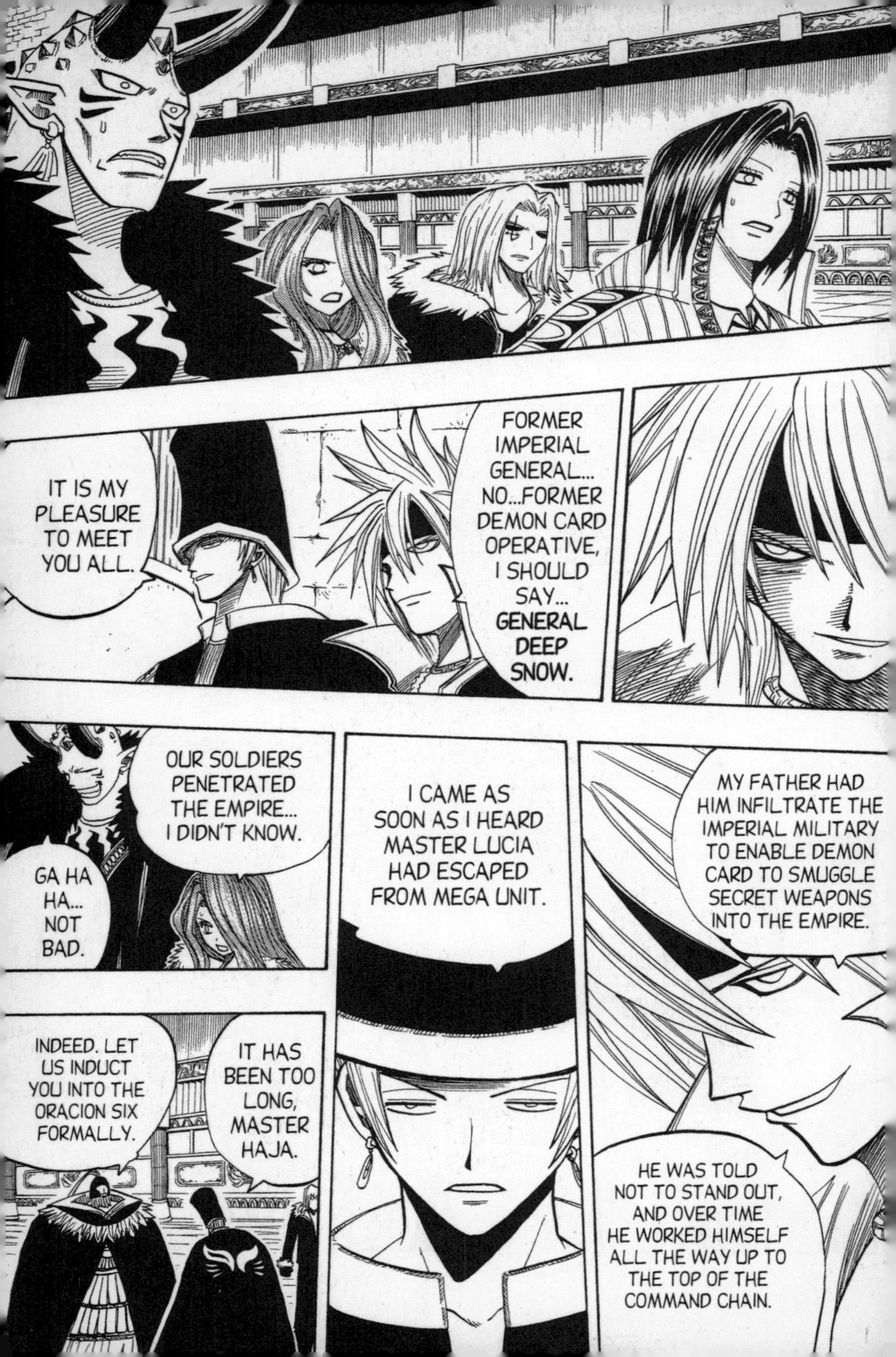
FORMER IMPERIAL GENERAL... NO...FORMER DEMON CARD OPERATIVE, I SHOULD SAY... **GENERAL DEEP SNOW.**
IT IS MY PLEASURE TO MEET YOU ALL.
MY FATHER HAD HIM INFILTRATE THE IMPERIAL MILITARY TO ENABLE DEMON CARD TO SMUGGLE SECRET WEAPONS INTO THE EMPIRE.
HE WAS TOLD NOT TO STAND OUT, AND OVER TIME HE WORKED HIMSELF ALL THE WAY UP TO THE TOP OF THE COMMAND CHAIN.
I CAME AS SOON AS I HEARD MASTER LUCIA HAD ESCAPED FROM MEGA UNIT.
OUR SOLDIERS PENETRATED THE EMPIRE... I DIDN'T KNOW.
GA HA HA... NOT BAD.
IT HAS BEEN TOO LONG, MASTER HAJA.
INDEED. LET US INDUCT YOU INTO THE ORACION SIX FORMALLY.

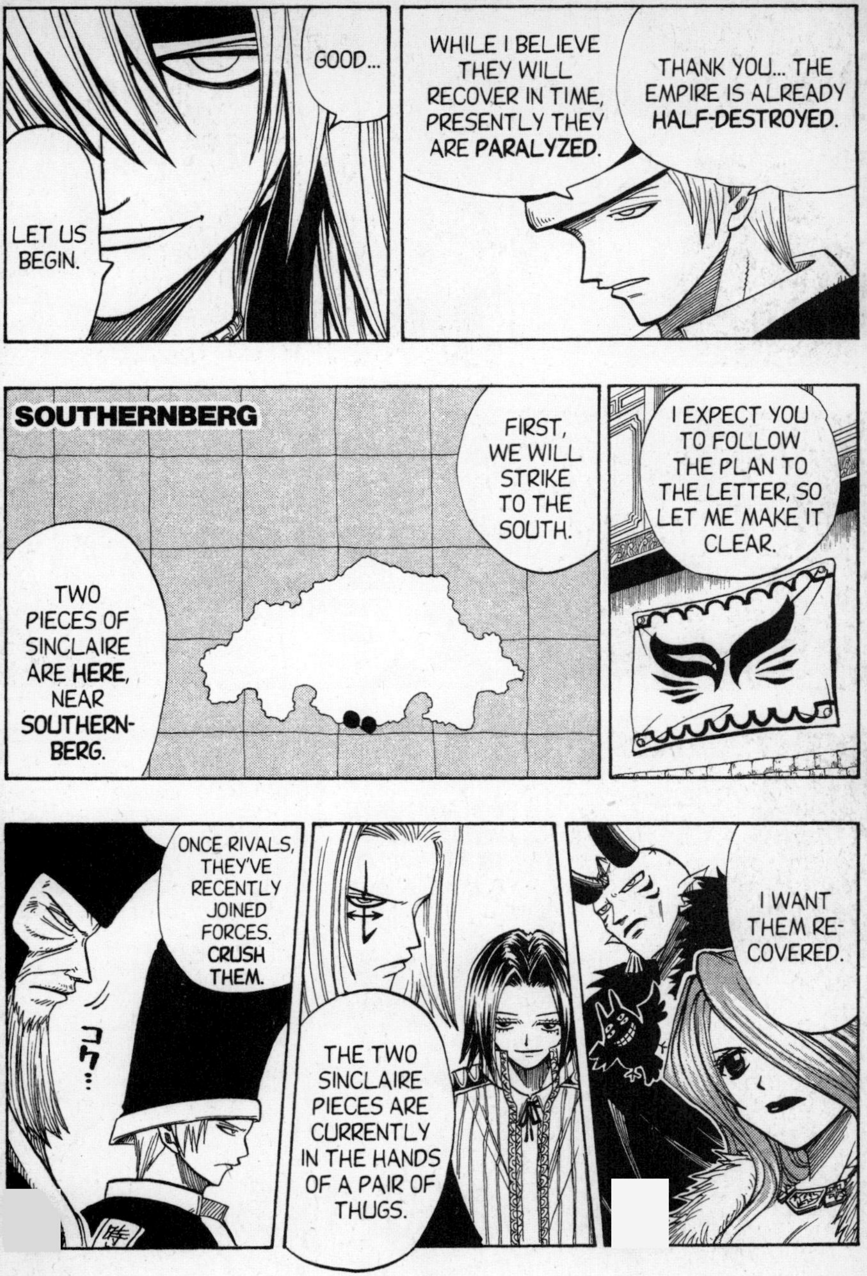
THANK YOU... THE EMPIRE IS ALREADY HALF-DESTROYED.
WHILE I BELIEVE THEY WILL RECOVER IN TIME, PRESENTLY THEY ARE PARALYZED.
GOOD...
LET US BEGIN.
I EXPECT YOU TO FOLLOW THE PLAN TO THE LETTER, SO LET ME MAKE IT CLEAR.
FIRST, WE WILL STRIKE TO THE SOUTH.
SOUTHERNBERG
TWO PIECES OF SINCLAIRE ARE HERE, NEAR SOUTHERN-BERG.
I WANT THEM RE-COVERED.
THE TWO SINCLAIRE PIECES ARE CURRENTLY IN THE HANDS OF A PAIR OF THUGS.
ONCE RIVALS, THEY'VE RECENTLY JOINED FORCES. CRUSH THEM.
コク…

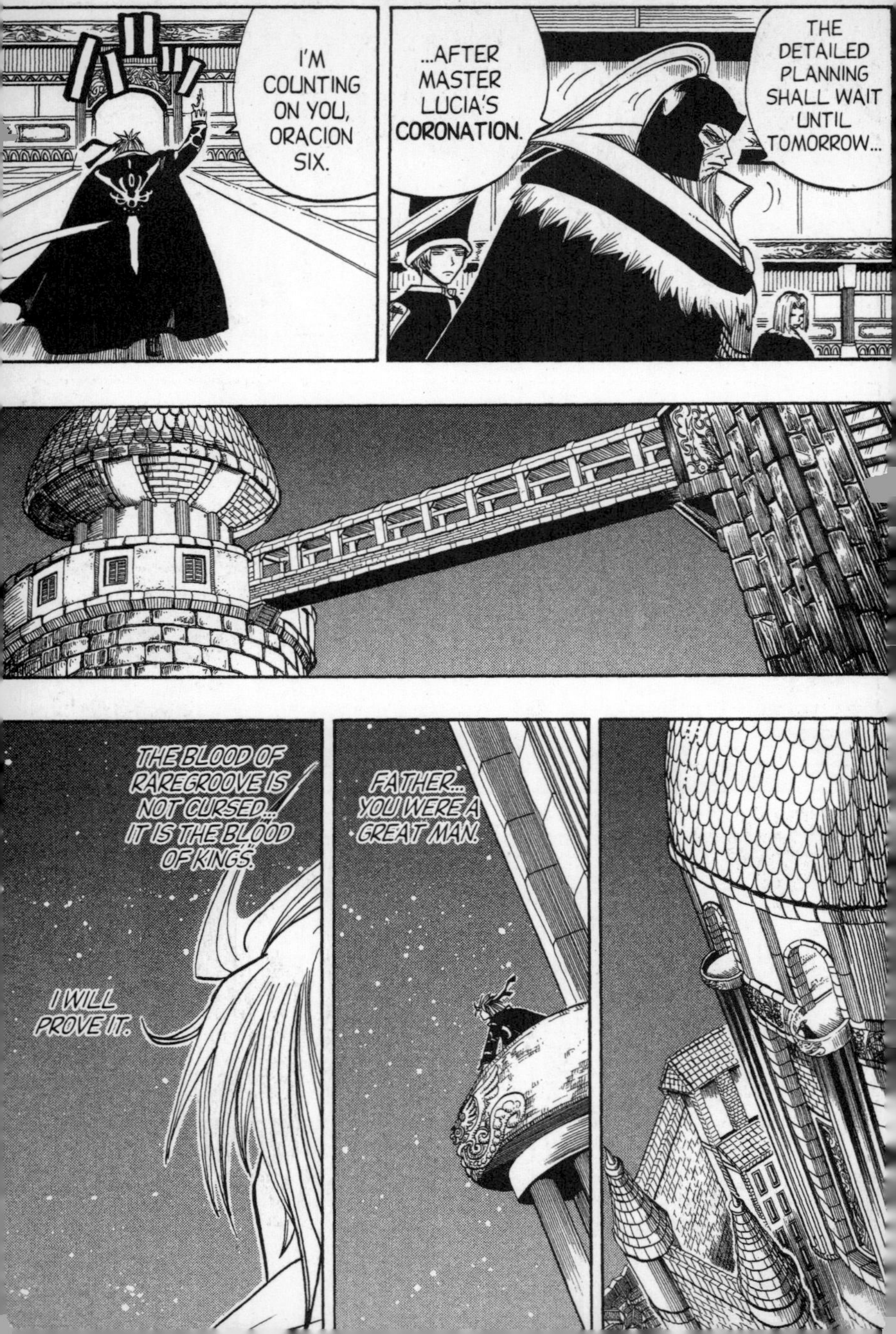
THE DETAILED PLANNING SHALL WAIT UNTIL TOMORROW...
...AFTER MASTER LUCIA'S CORONATION.
I'M COUNTING ON YOU, ORACION SIX.
FATHER... YOU WERE A GREAT MAN.
THE BLOOD OF RAREGROOVE IS NOT CURSED... IT IS THE BLOOD OF KINGS.
I WILL PROVE IT.

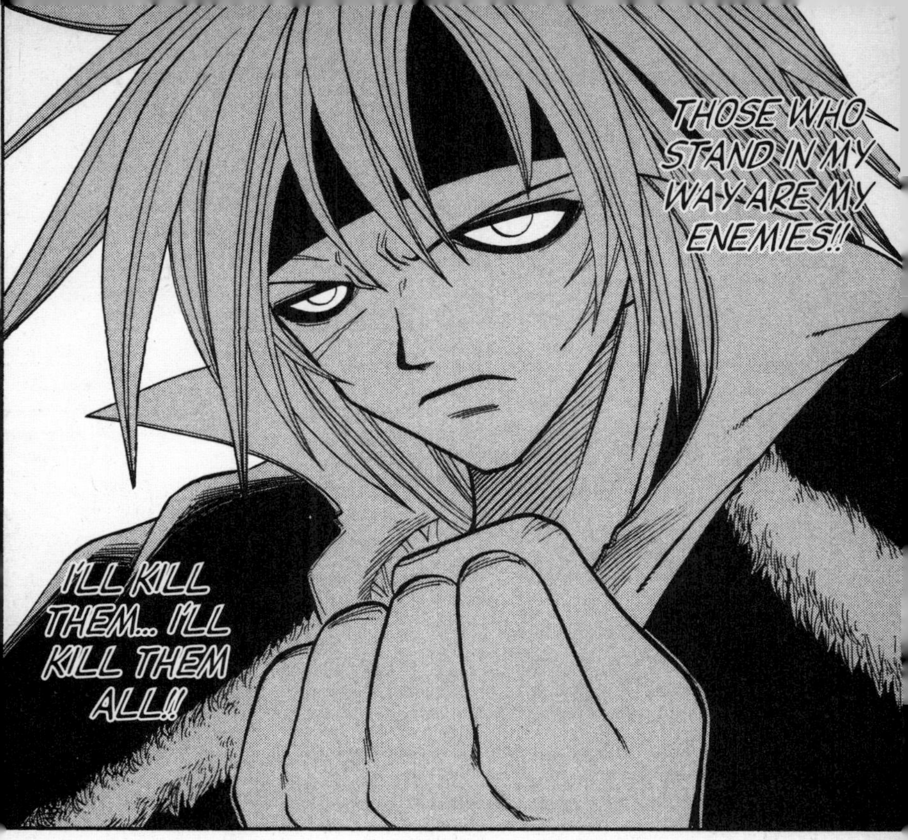
THOSE WHO STAND IN MY WAY ARE MY ENEMIES!!
I'LL KILL THEM... I'LL KILL THEM ALL!!
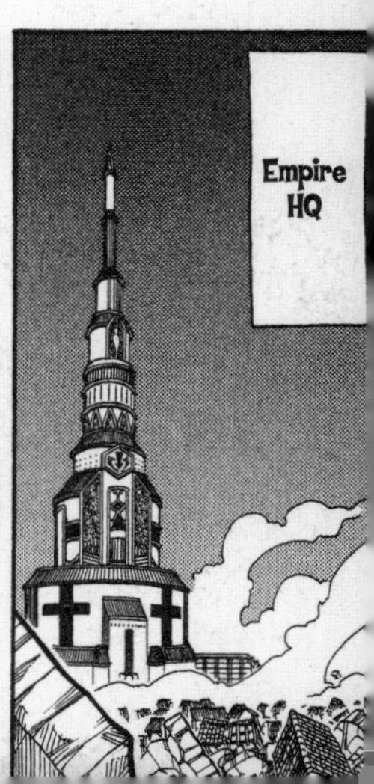
Empire HQ
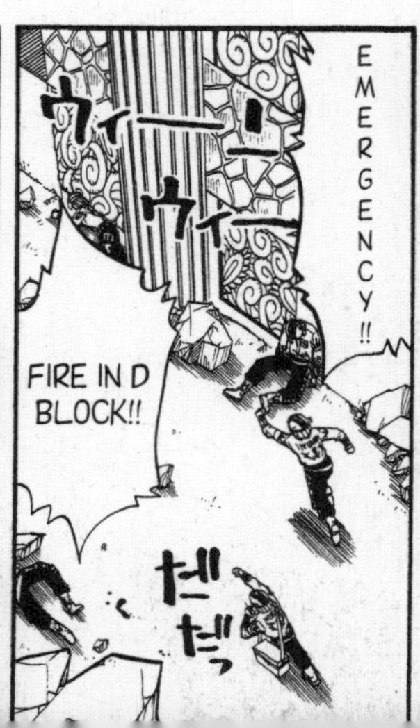
EMERGENCY!!
ウィーー
ウィーー
FIRE IN D BLOCK!!
だっ
だっ
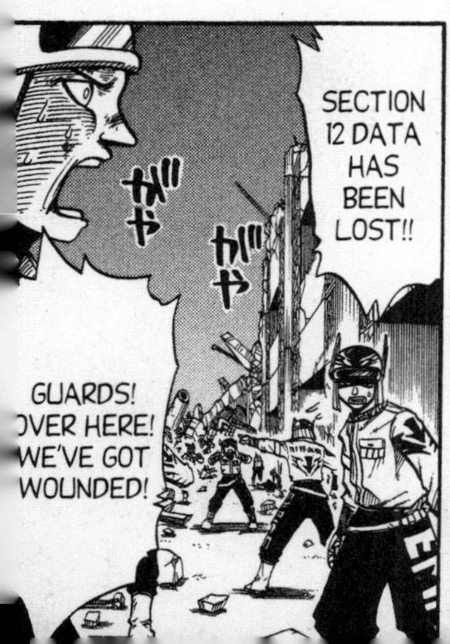
SECTION 12 DATA HAS BEEN LOST!!
ガヤ
ガヤ
GUARDS! OVER HERE! WE'VE GOT WOUNDED!

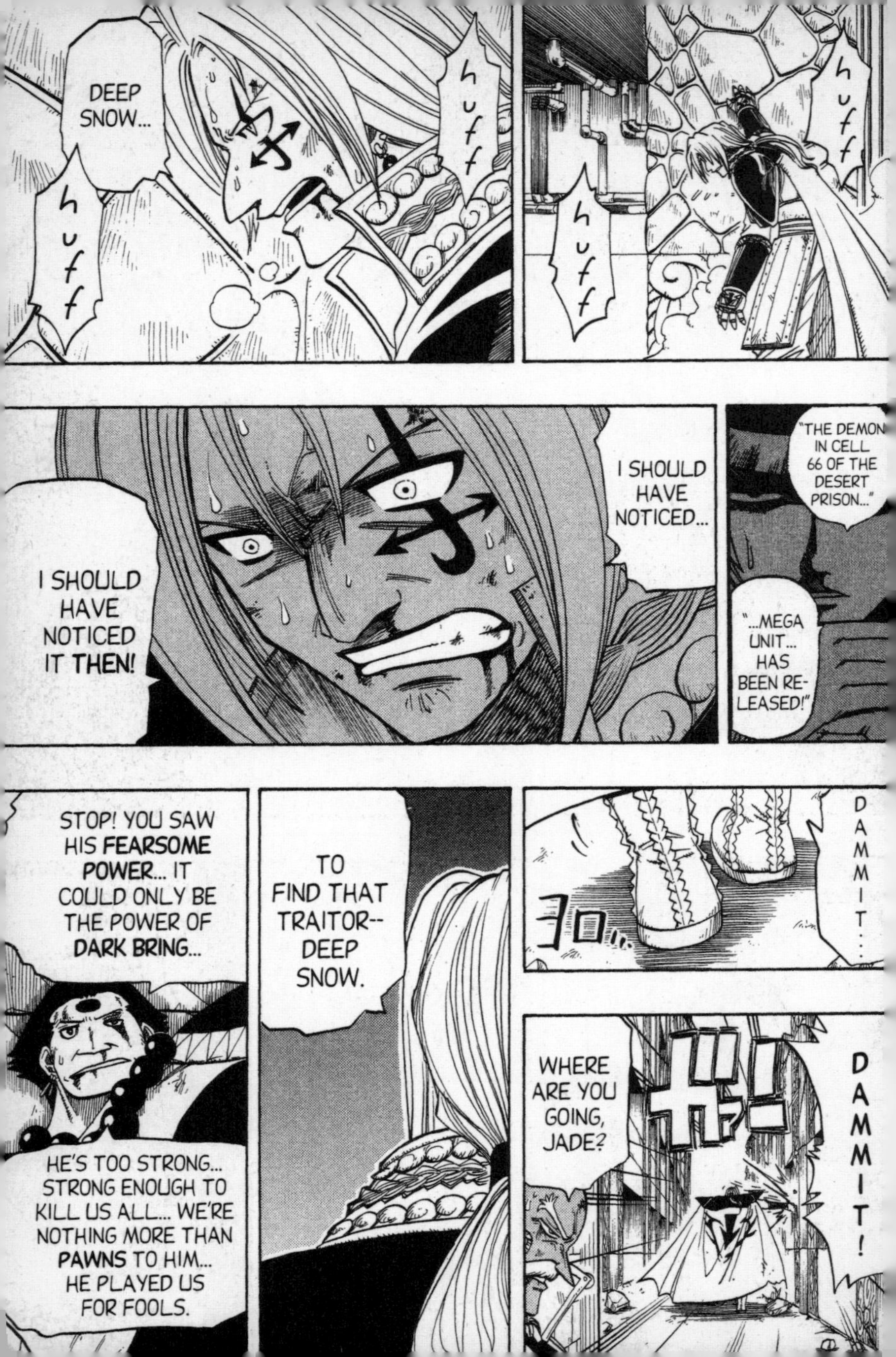
huff
huff
huff
DEEP SNOW...
huff
"THE DEMON IN CELL 66 OF THE DESERT PRISON..."
"...MEGA UNIT... HAS BEEN RE-LEASED!"
I SHOULD HAVE NOTICED...
I SHOULD HAVE NOTICED IT THEN!
DAMMIT...
ヨロ...
WHERE ARE YOU GOING, JADE?
DAMMIT!
TO FIND THAT TRAITOR-- DEEP SNOW.
STOP! YOU SAW HIS FEARSOME POWER... IT COULD ONLY BE THE POWER OF DARK BRING...
HE'S TOO STRONG... STRONG ENOUGH TO KILL US ALL... WE'RE NOTHING MORE THAN PAWNS TO HIM... HE PLAYED US FOR FOOLS.

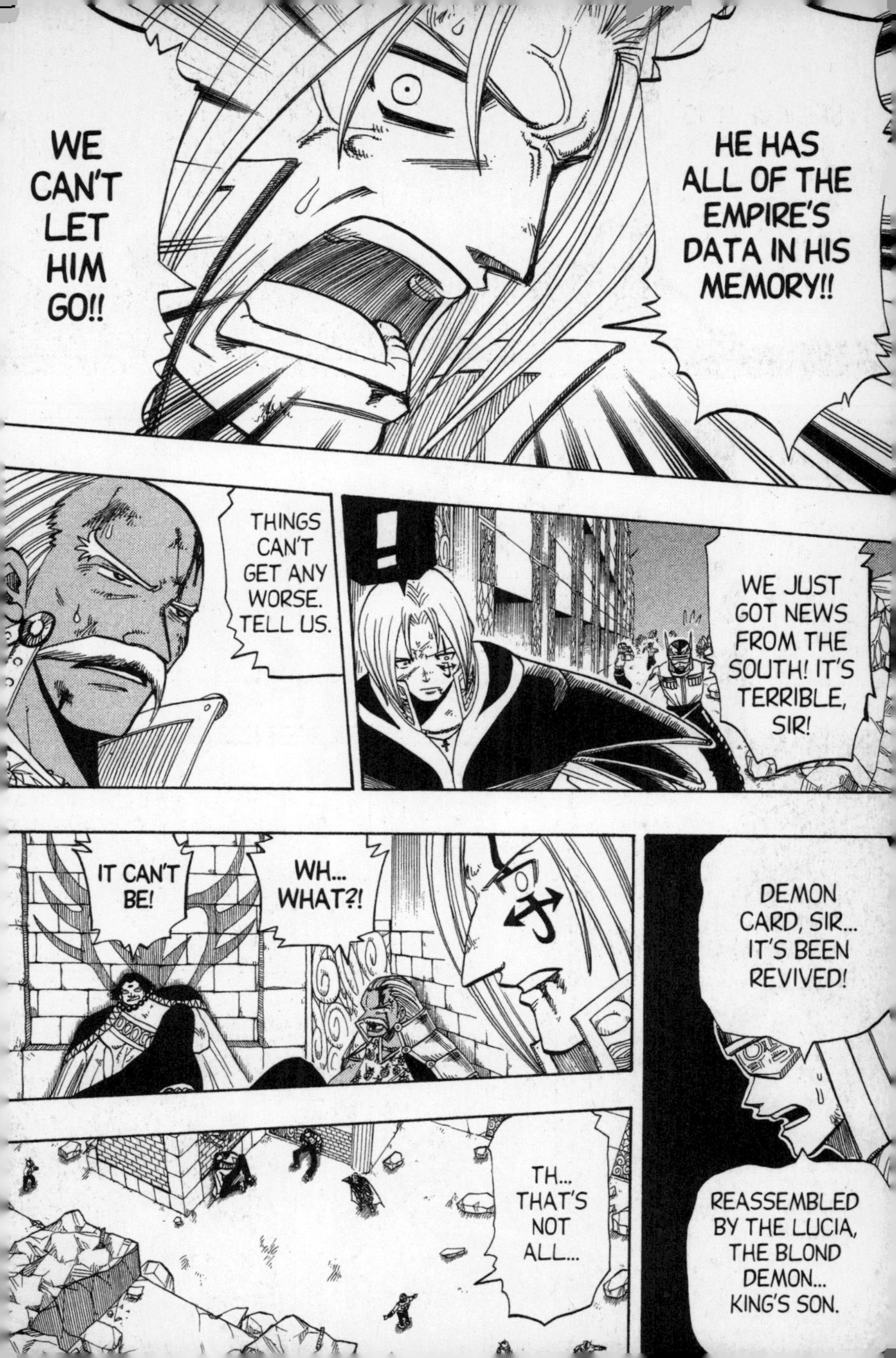
HE HAS ALL OF THE EMPIRE'S DATA IN HIS MEMORY!!
WE CAN'T LET HIM GO!!
!
WE JUST GOT NEWS FROM THE SOUTH! IT'S TERRIBLE, SIR!
THINGS CAN'T GET ANY WORSE. TELL US.
DEMON CARD, SIR... IT'S BEEN REVIVED!
REASSEMBLED BY THE LUCIA, THE BLOND DEMON... KING'S SON.
WH... WHAT?!
IT CAN'T BE!
TH... THAT'S NOT ALL...

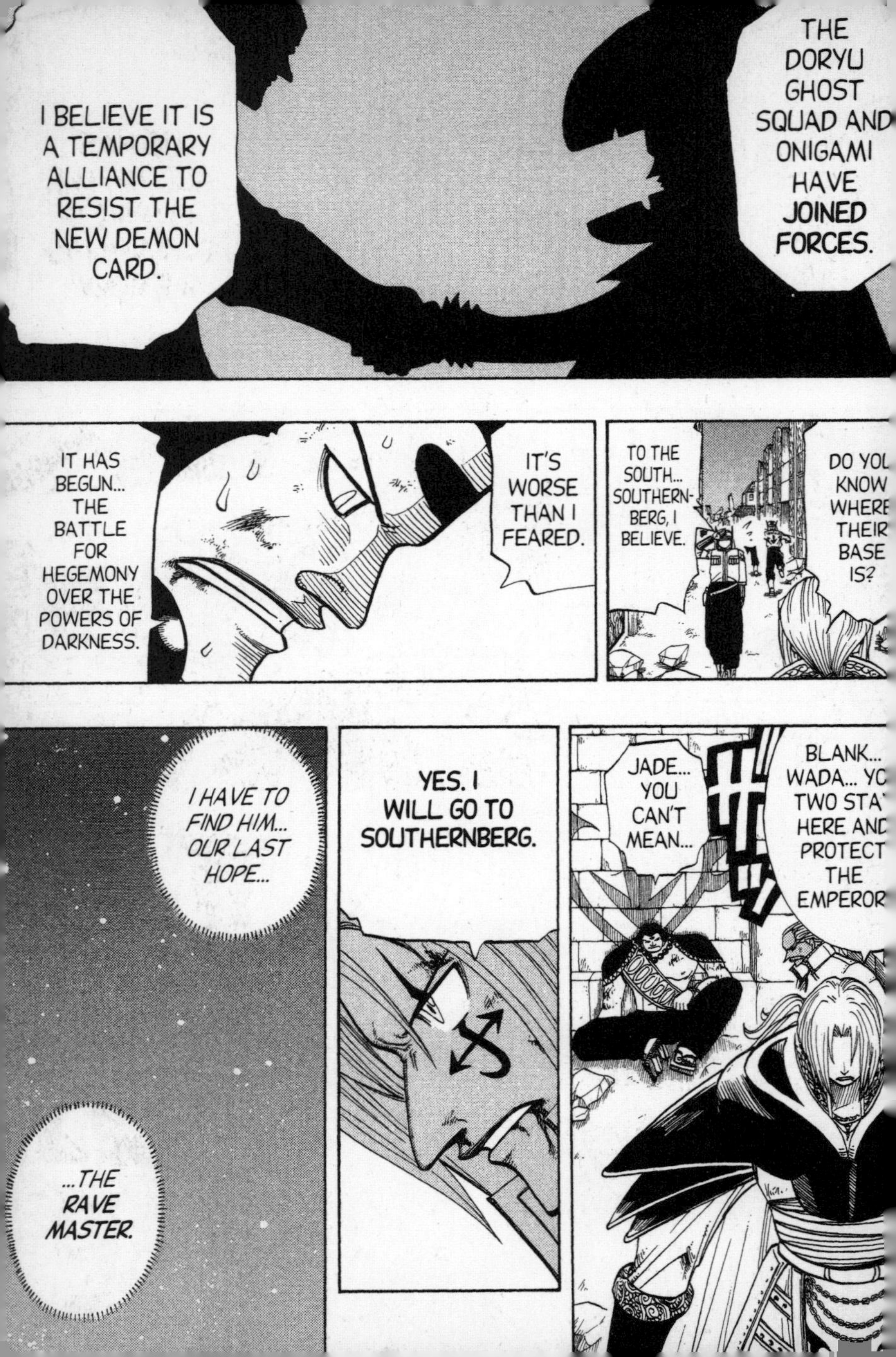
THE DORYU GHOST SQUAD AND ONIGAMI HAVE JOINED FORCES.
I BELIEVE IT IS A TEMPORARY ALLIANCE TO RESIST THE NEW DEMON CARD.
DO YOU KNOW WHERE THEIR BASE IS?
TO THE SOUTH... SOUTHERN-BERG, I BELIEVE.
IT'S WORSE THAN I FEARED.
IT HAS BEGUN... THE BATTLE FOR HEGEMONY OVER THE POWERS OF DARKNESS.
BLANK... WADA... YO TWO STA HERE AND PROTECT THE EMPEROR
JADE... YOU CAN'T MEAN...
YES. I WILL GO TO SOUTHERNBERG.
I HAVE TO FIND HIM... OUR LAST HOPE...
...THE RAVE MASTER.

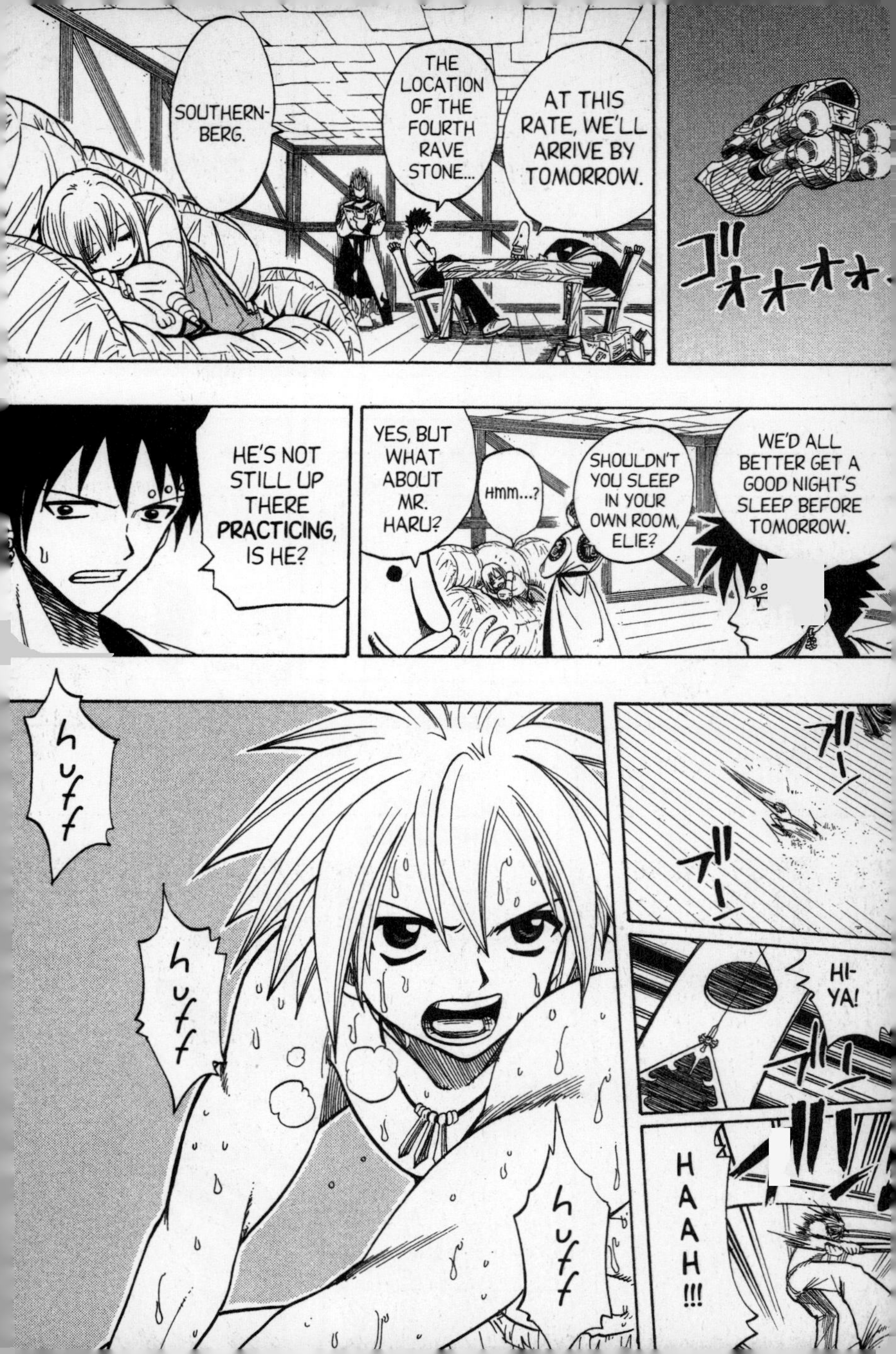
ゴオオオオ
AT THIS RATE, WE'LL ARRIVE BY TOMORROW.
THE LOCATION OF THE FOURTH RAVE STONE...
SOUTHERN-BERG.
WE'D ALL BETTER GET A GOOD NIGHT'S SLEEP BEFORE TOMORROW.
SHOULDN'T YOU SLEEP IN YOUR OWN ROOM, ELIE?
HMM...?
YES, BUT WHAT ABOUT MR. HARU?
HE'S NOT STILL UP THERE PRACTICING, IS HE?
ブー
ブー
HI-YA!
HAAAH!!!
huff
huff
huff

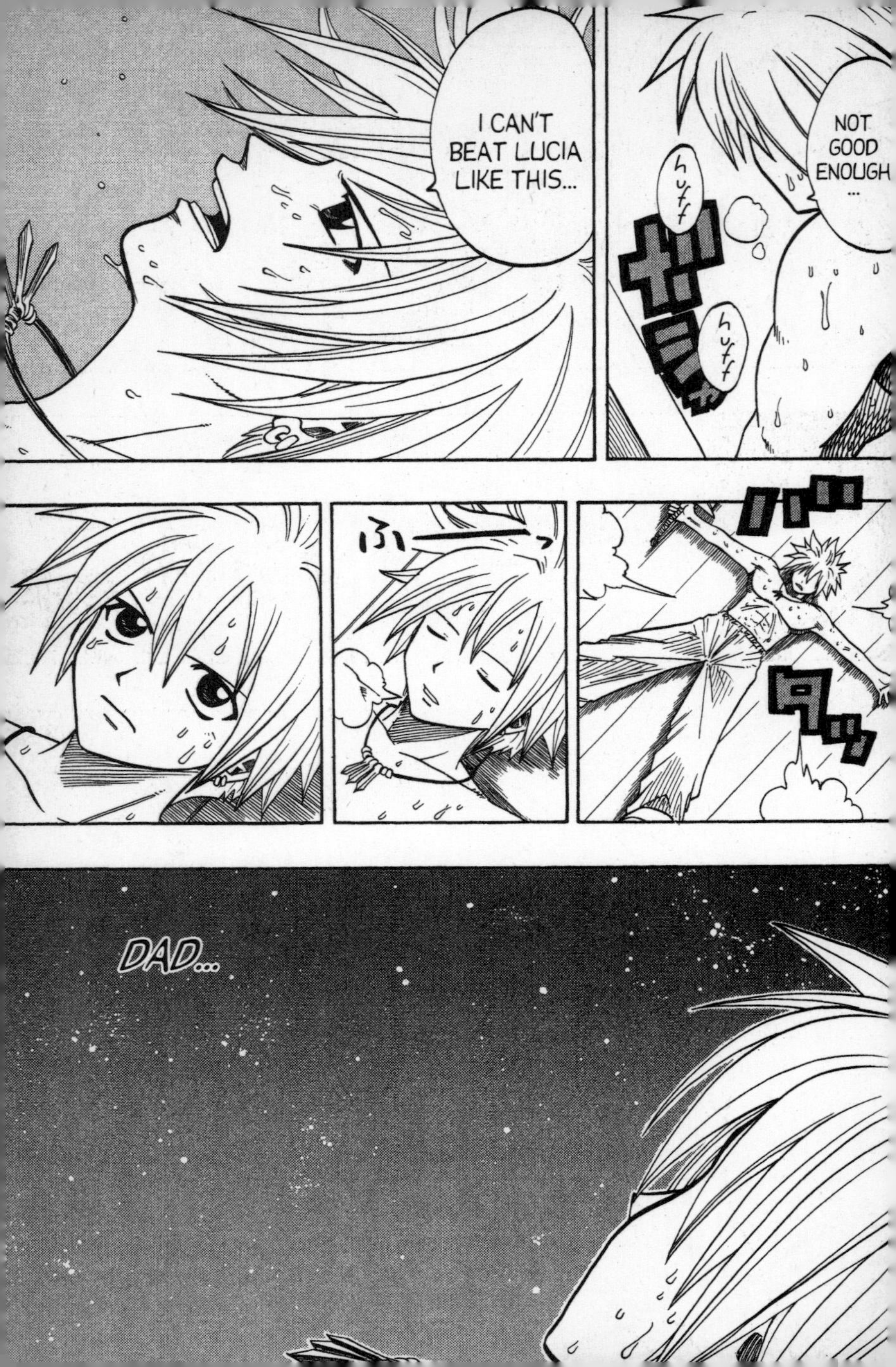
NOT GOOD ENOUGH ...
huff
huff
I CAN'T BEAT LUCIA LIKE THIS...
バッ
タッ
ふーーっ
DAD...

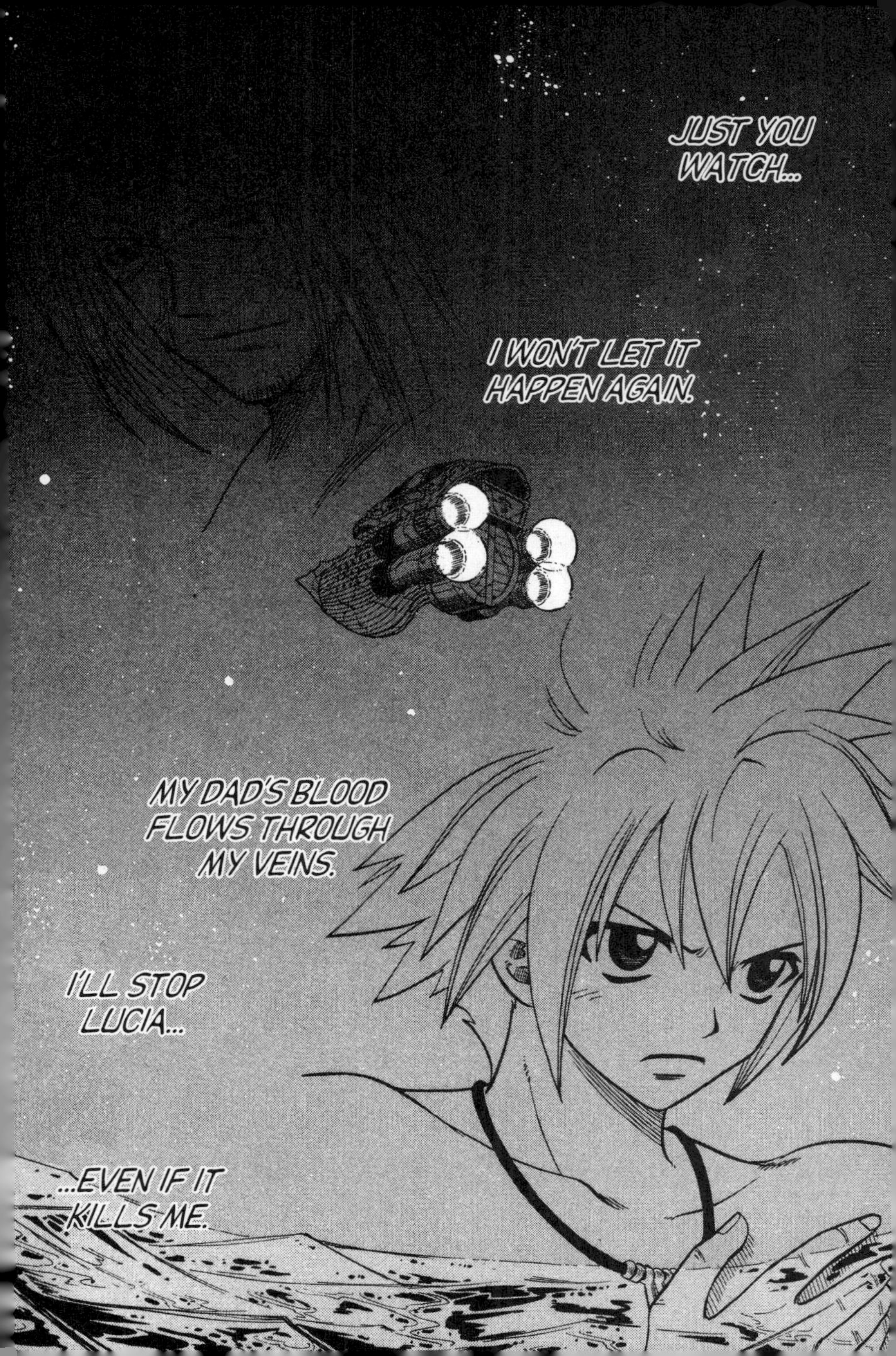
JUST YOU WATCH...
I WON'T LET IT HAPPEN AGAIN.
MY DAD'S BLOOD FLOWS THROUGH MY VEINS.
I'LL STOP LUCIA...
...EVEN IF IT KILLS ME.

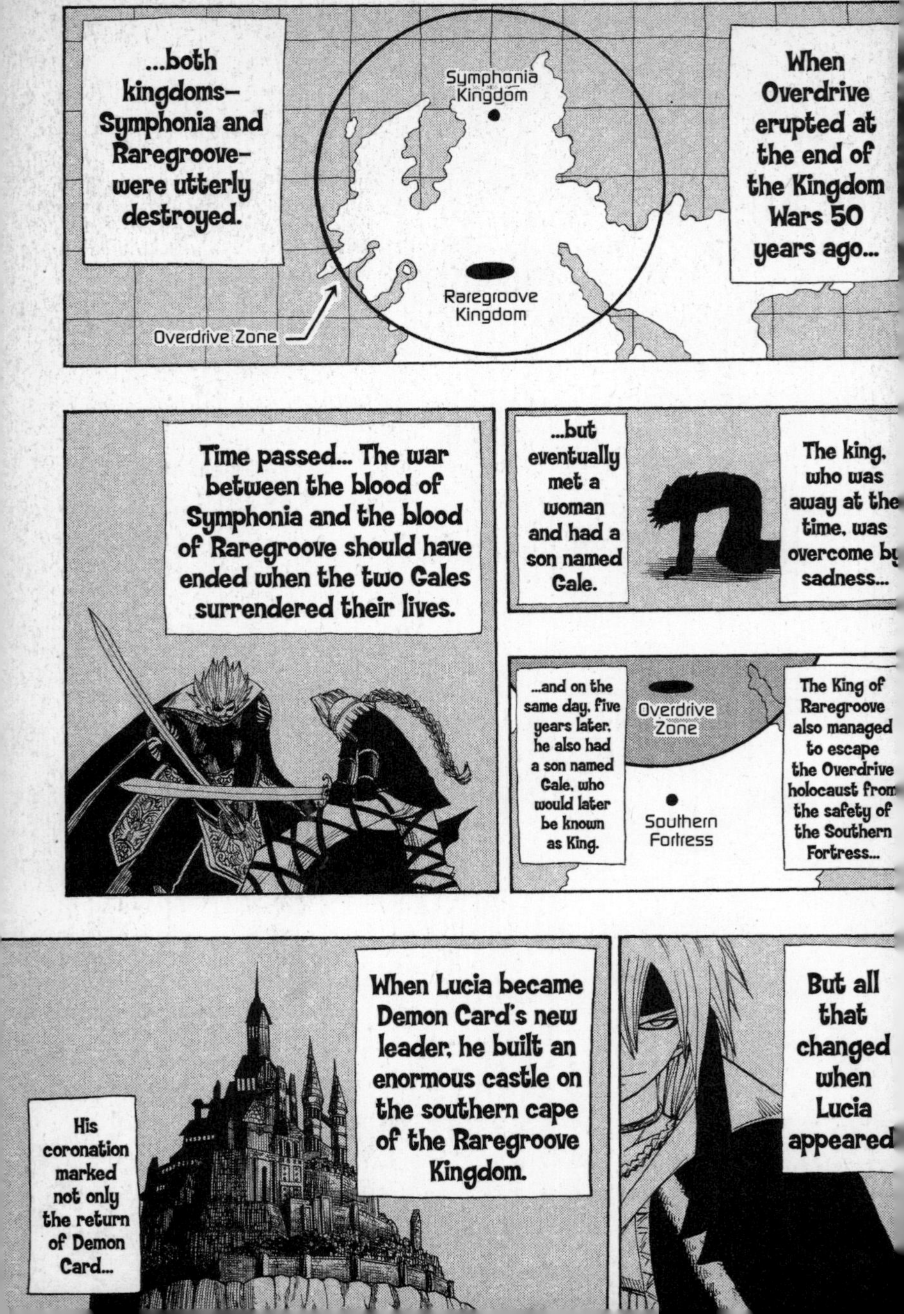
When Overdrive erupted at the end of the Kingdom Wars 50 years ago...
Symphonia Kingdom
Raregroove Kingdom
Overdrive Zone
...both kingdoms—Symphonia and Raregroove—were utterly destroyed.
The king, who was away at the time, was overcome by sadness...
...but eventually met a woman and had a son named Gale.
The King of Raregroove also managed to escape the Overdrive holocaust from the safety of the Southern Fortress...
Overdrive Zone
Southern Fortress
...and on the same day, five years later, he also had a son named Gale, who would later be known as King.
Time passed... The war between the blood of Symphonia and the blood of Raregroove should have ended when the two Gales surrendered their lives.
But all that changed when Lucia appeared.
When Lucia became Demon Card's new leader, he built an enormous castle on the southern cape of the Raregroove Kingdom.
His coronation marked not only the return of Demon Card...

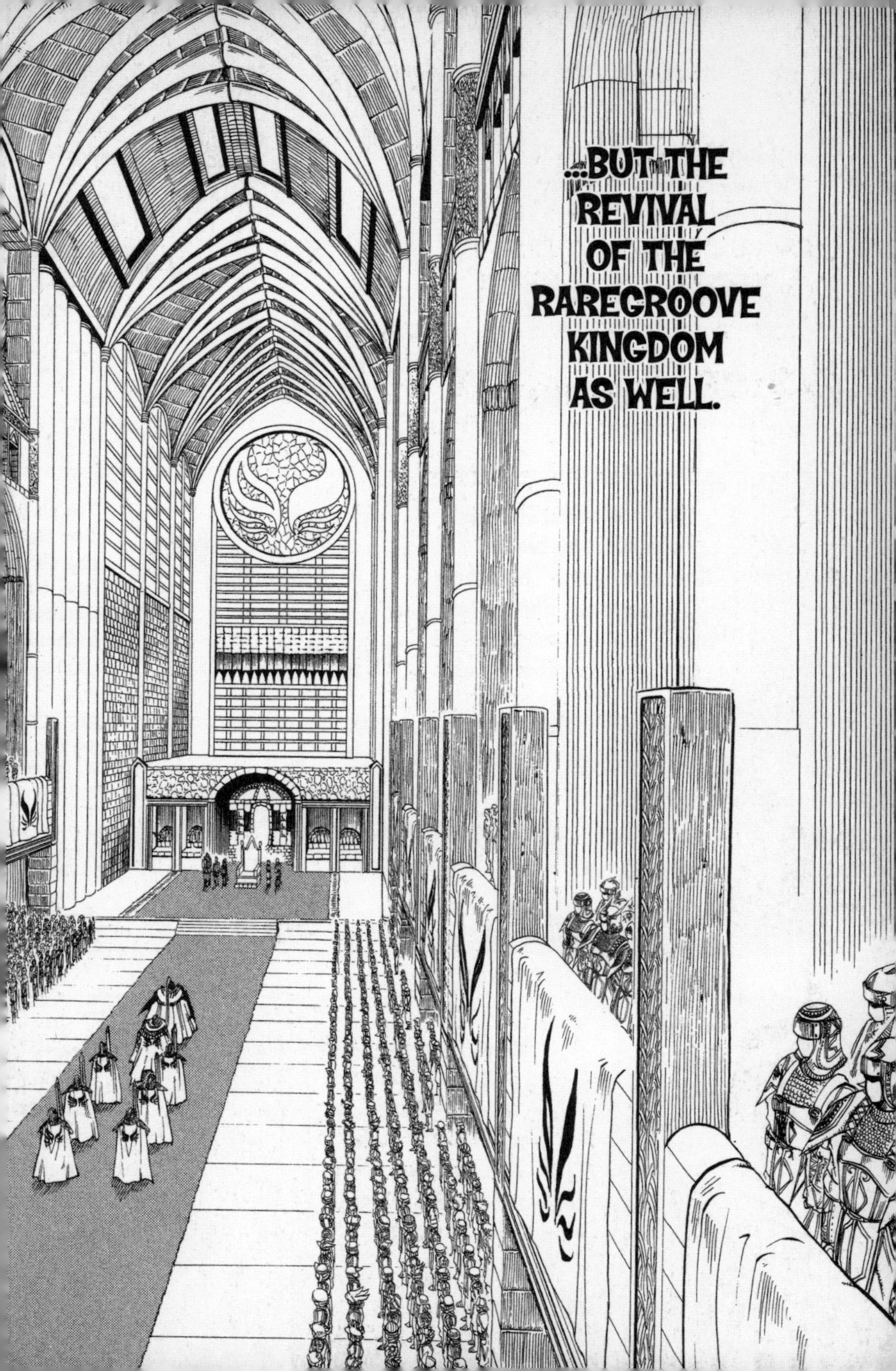
...BUT THE REVIVAL OF THE RAREGROOVE KINGDOM AS WELL.

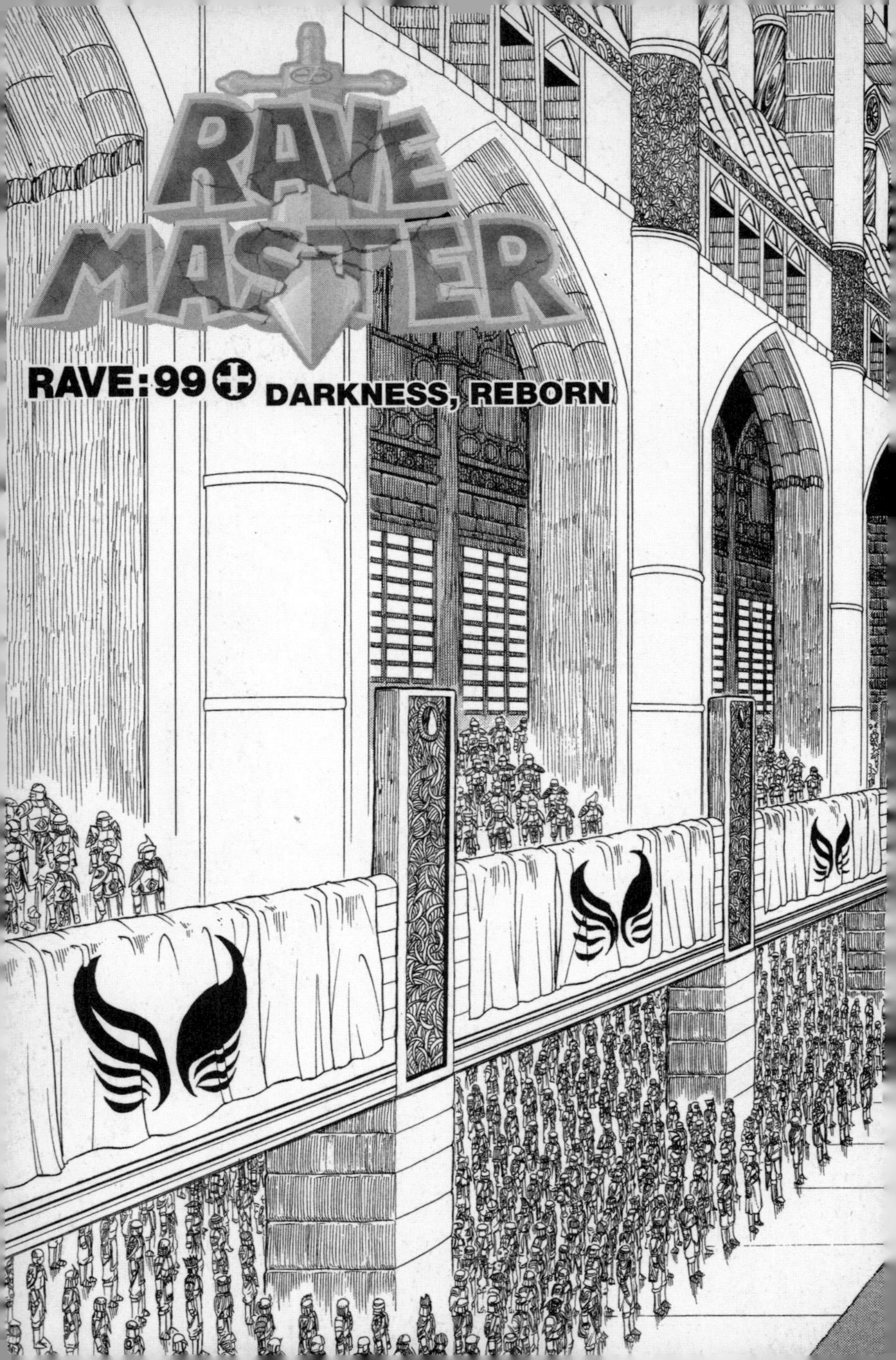
RAVE MASTER
RAVE:99 DARKNESS, REBORN

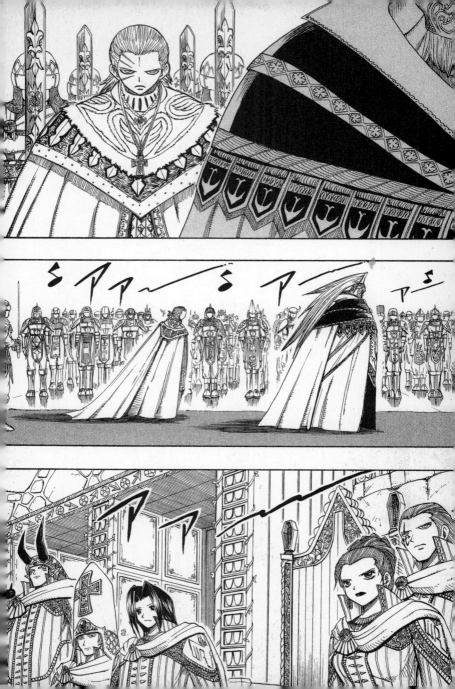

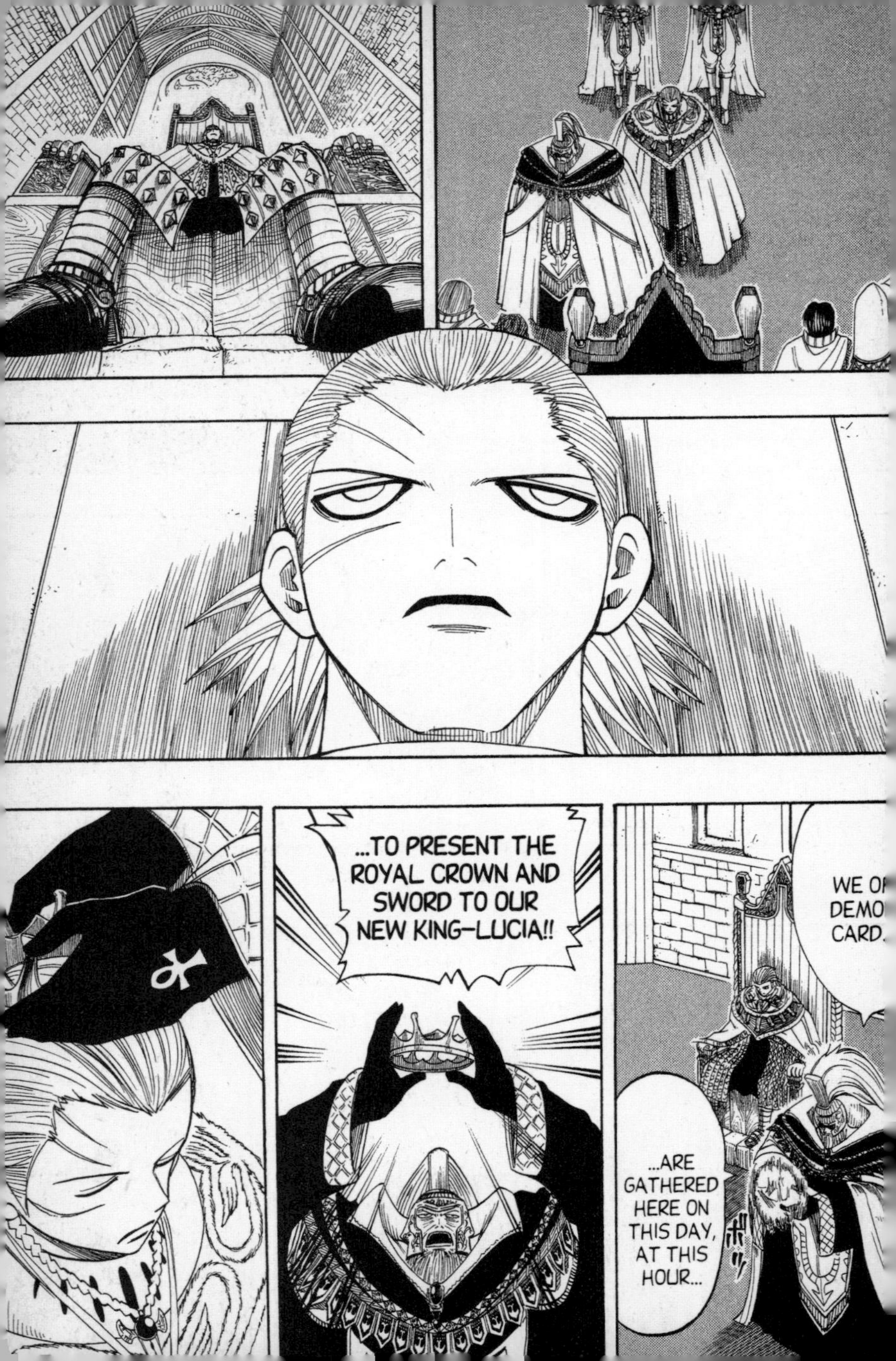
WE OF DEMO CARD.
...ARE GATHERED HERE ON THIS DAY, AT THIS HOUR...
...TO PRESENT THE ROYAL CROWN AND SWORD TO OUR NEW KING—LUCIA!!

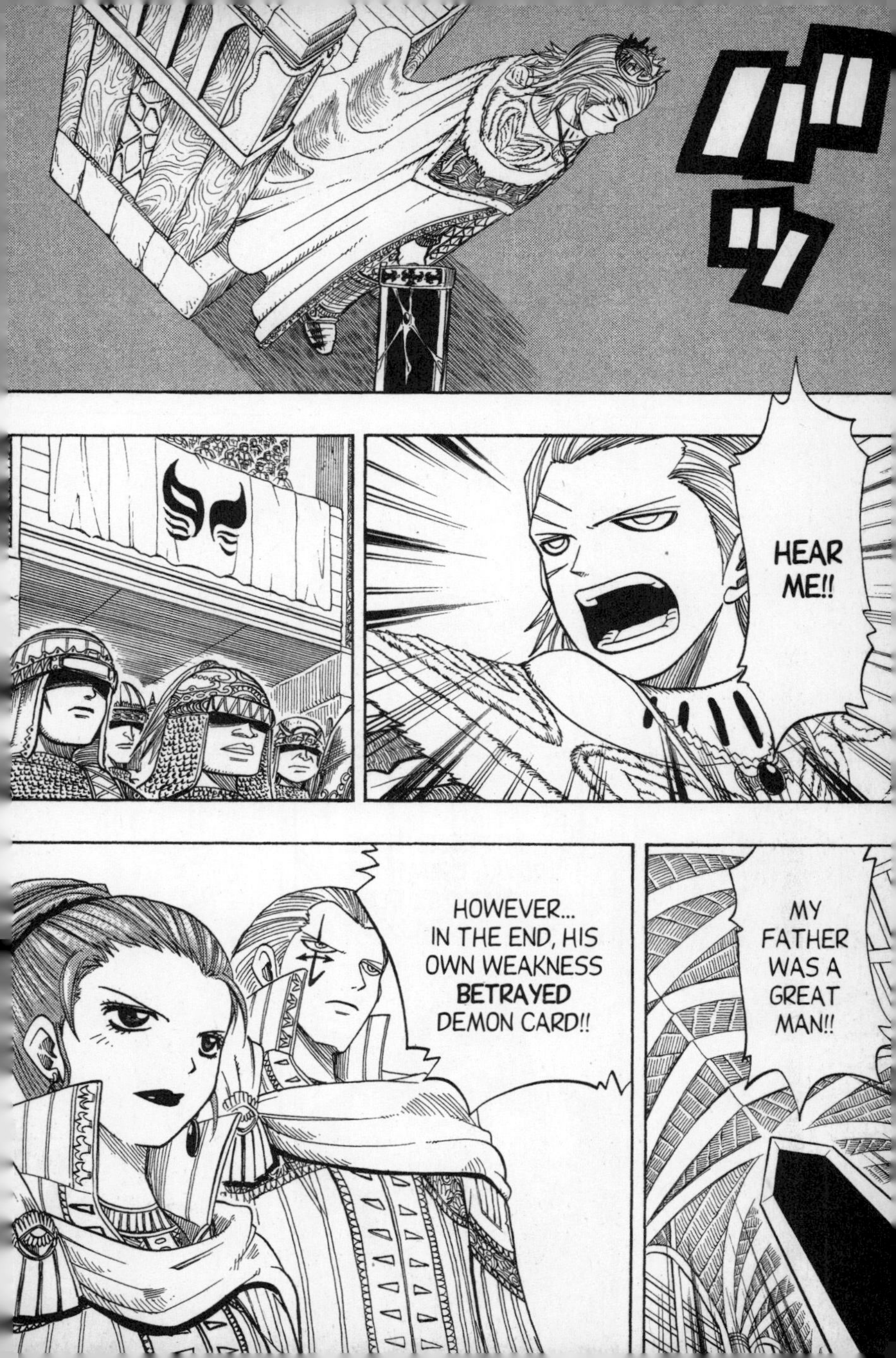
バッ
HEAR ME!!
MY FATHER WAS A GREAT MAN!!
HOWEVER... IN THE END, HIS OWN WEAKNESS **BETRAYED** DEMON CARD!!

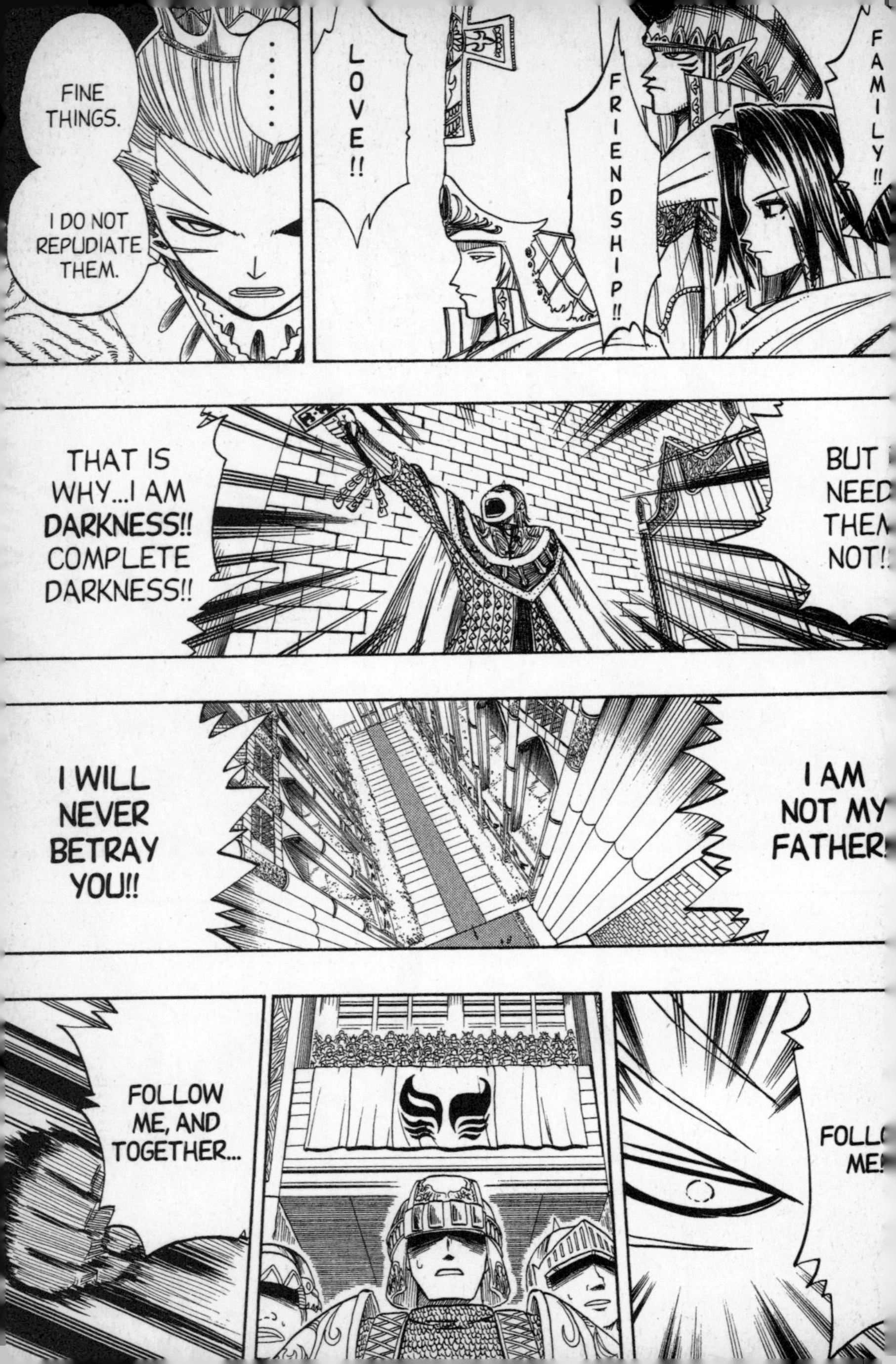
FAMILY!!
FRIENDSHIP!!
LOVE!!
......
FINE THINGS.
I DO NOT REPUDIATE THEM.
BUT I NEED THEM NOT!!
THAT IS WHY...I AM **DARKNESS!!** COMPLETE DARKNESS!!
I AM NOT MY FATHER!
I WILL NEVER BETRAY YOU!!
FOLLOW ME!
FOLLOW ME, AND TOGETHER...

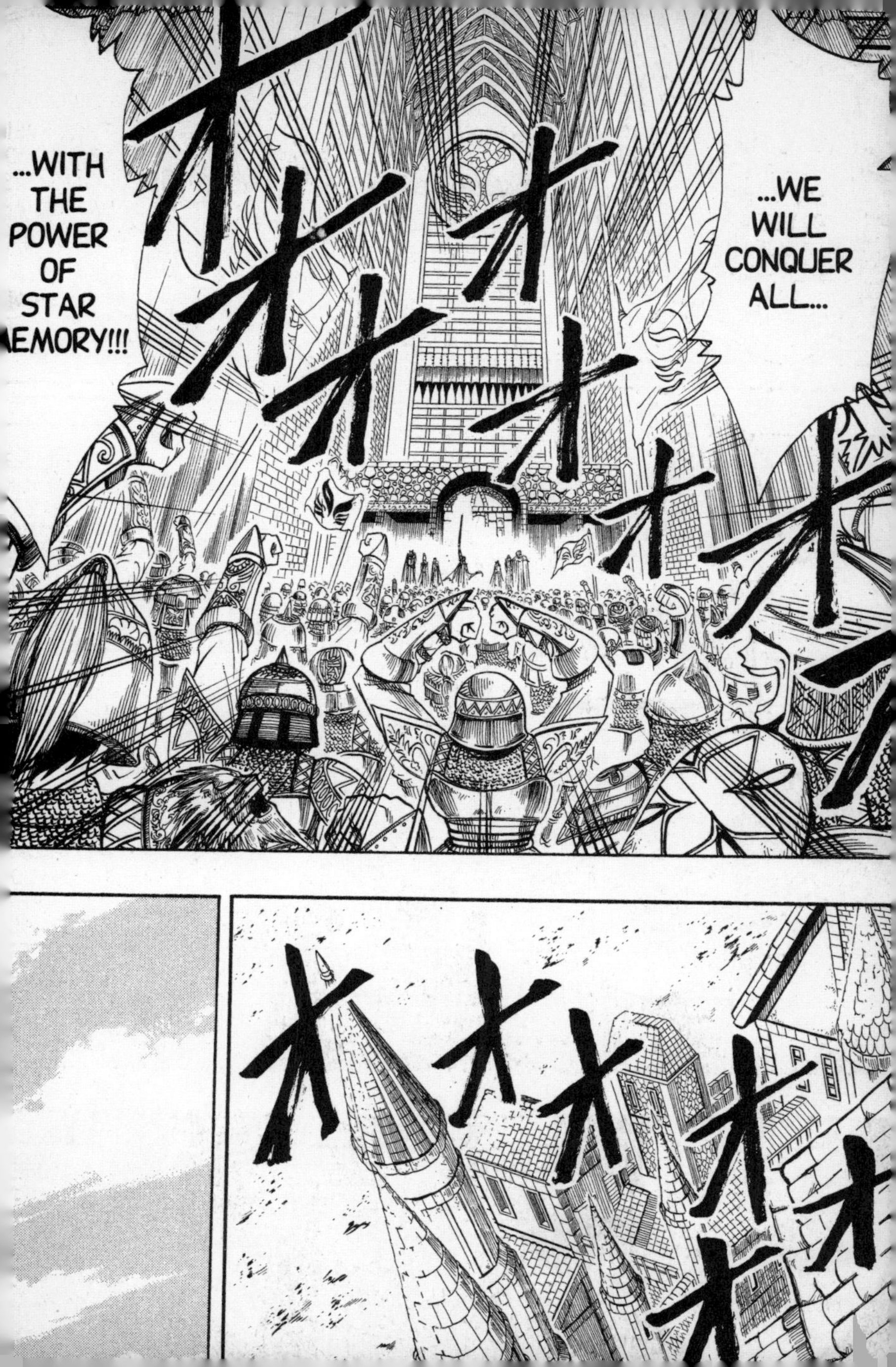
...WE WILL CONQUER ALL...
...WITH THE POWER OF STAR MEMORY!!!
オオオオオオオオ
オオオオオ

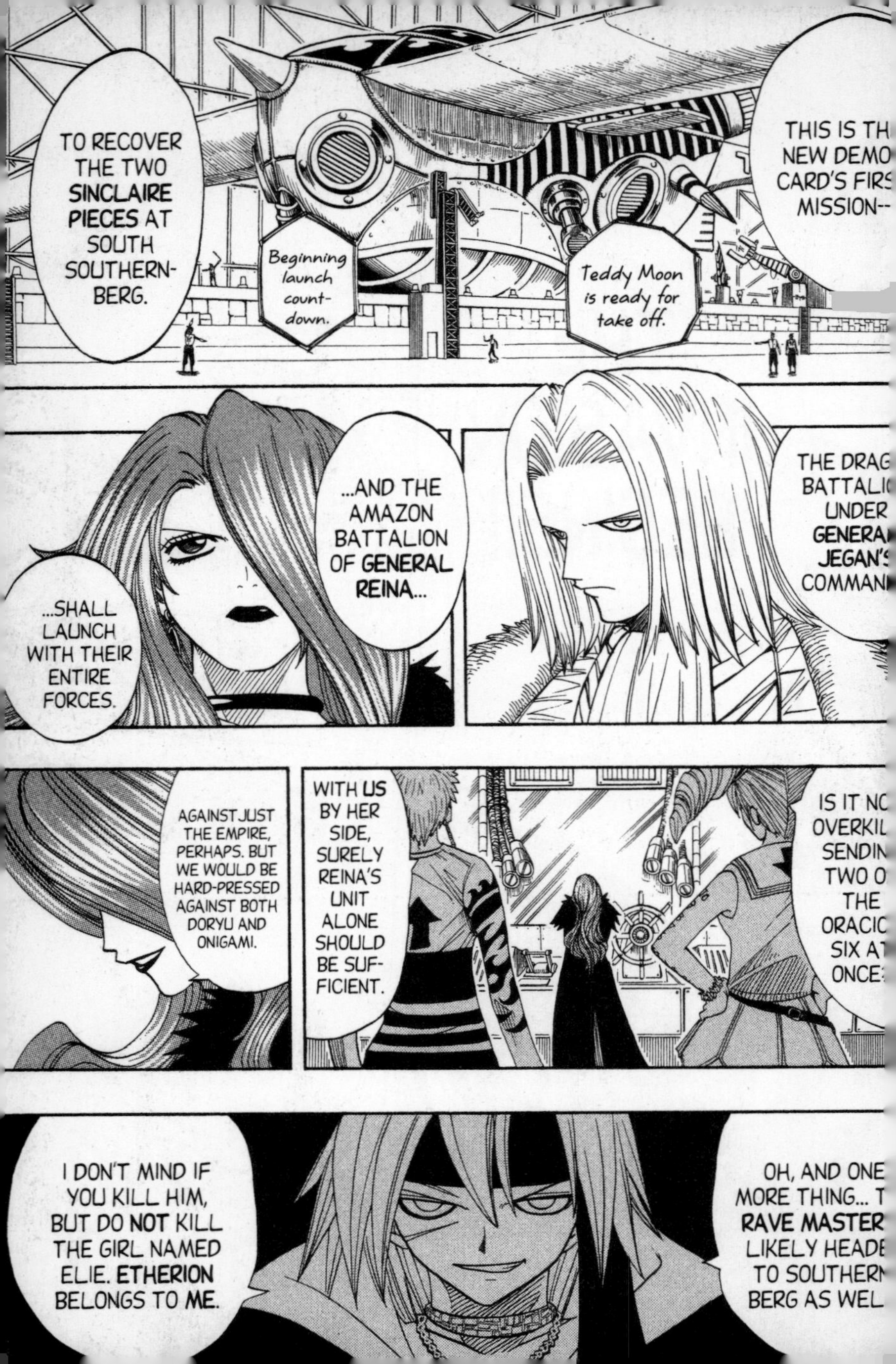
THIS IS TH NEW DEMO CARD'S FIRS MISSION--
TO RECOVER THE TWO SINCLAIRE PIECES AT SOUTH SOUTHERNBERG.
Teddy Moon is ready for take off.
Beginning launch countdown.
THE DRAG BATTALIO UNDER GENERA JEGAN'S COMMAN
...AND THE AMAZON BATTALION OF GENERAL REINA...
...SHALL LAUNCH WITH THEIR ENTIRE FORCES.
IS IT NO OVERKIL SENDIN TWO O THE ORACIO SIX AT ONCE
WITH US BY HER SIDE, SURELY REINA'S UNIT ALONE SHOULD BE SUFFICIENT.
AGAINST JUST THE EMPIRE, PERHAPS. BUT WE WOULD BE HARD-PRESSED AGAINST BOTH DORYU AND ONIGAMI.
OH, AND ONE MORE THING... T RAVE MASTER LIKELY HEADE TO SOUTHERNBERG AS WEL
I DON'T MIND IF YOU KILL HIM, BUT DO NOT KILL THE GIRL NAMED ELIE. ETHERION BELONGS TO ME.

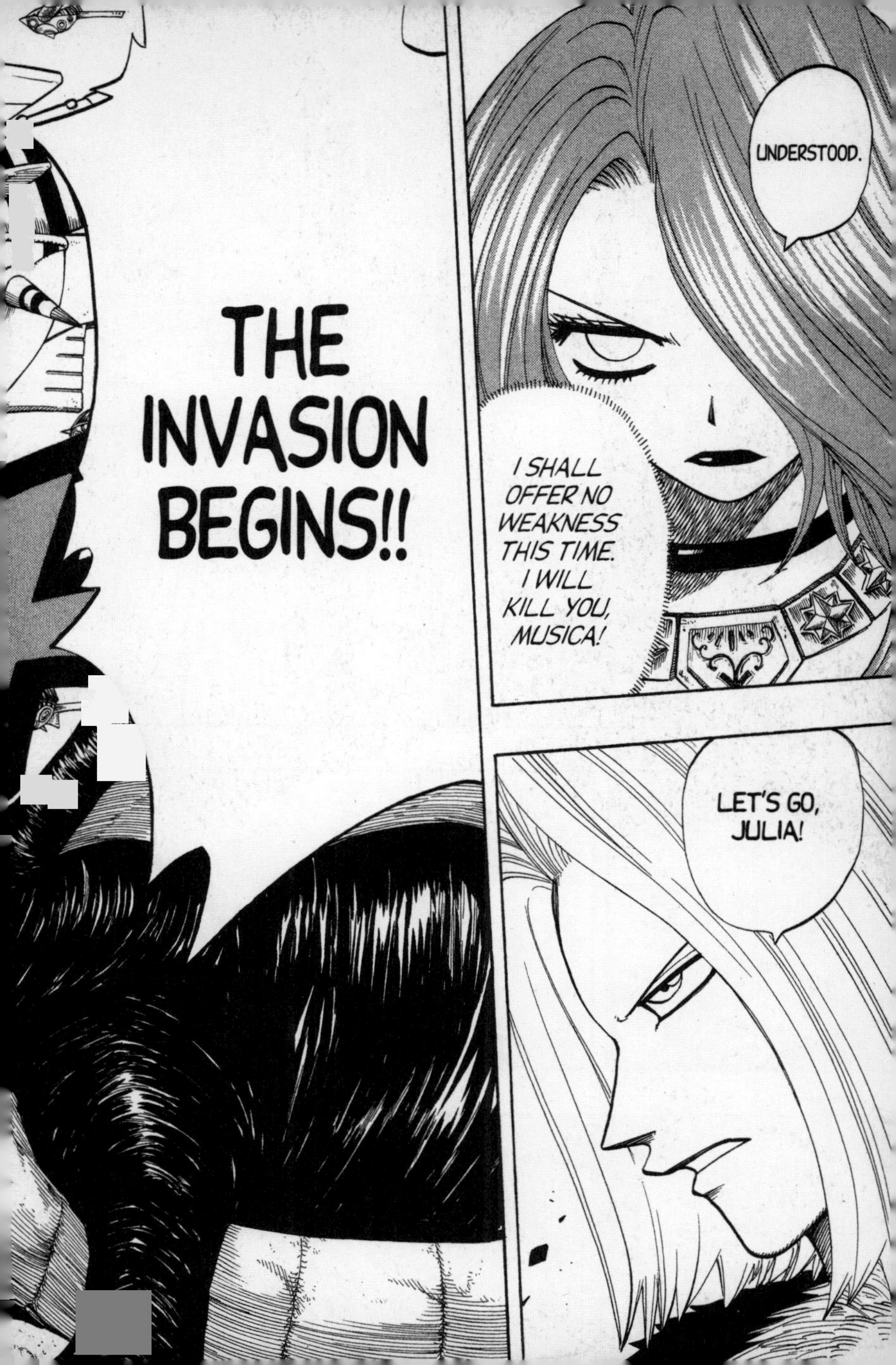
UNDERSTOOD.
I SHALL OFFER NO WEAKNESS THIS TIME. I WILL KILL YOU, MUSICA!
LET'S GO, JULIA!
THE INVASION BEGINS!!

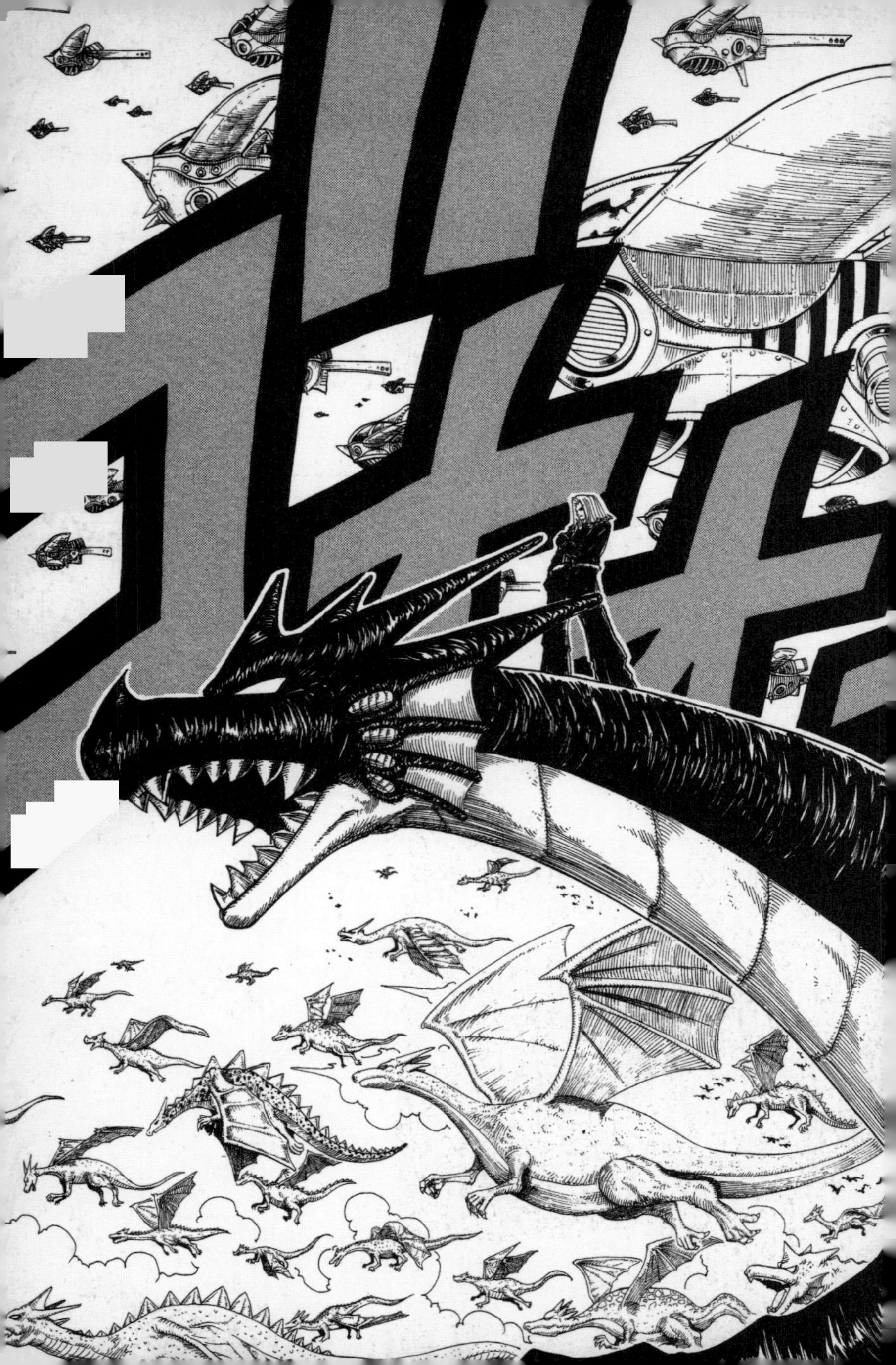

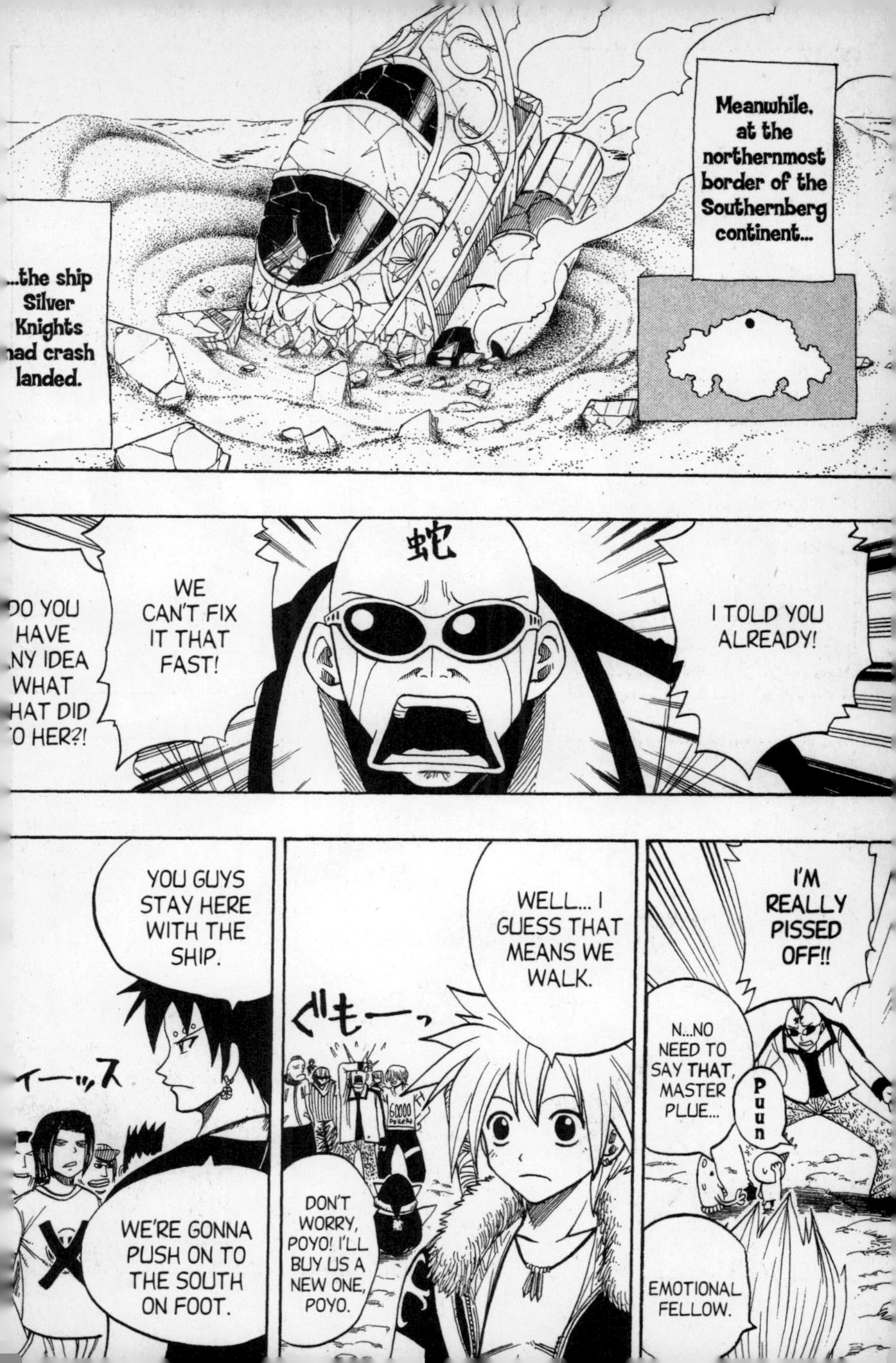
Meanwhile, at the northernmost border of the Southernberg continent...
...the ship Silver Knights ad crash landed.
I TOLD YOU ALREADY!
蛇
WE CAN'T FIX IT THAT FAST!
DO YOU HAVE NY IDEA WHAT HAT DID O HER?!
I'M REALLY PISSED OFF!!
N...NO NEED TO SAY THAT, MASTER PLUE...
Puun
EMOTIONAL FELLOW.
WELL... I GUESS THAT MEANS WE WALK.
ぐもーっ
DON'T WORRY, POYO! I'LL BUY US A NEW ONE, POYO.
YOU GUYS STAY HERE WITH THE SHIP.
イーッス
WE'RE GONNA PUSH ON TO THE SOUTH ON FOOT.

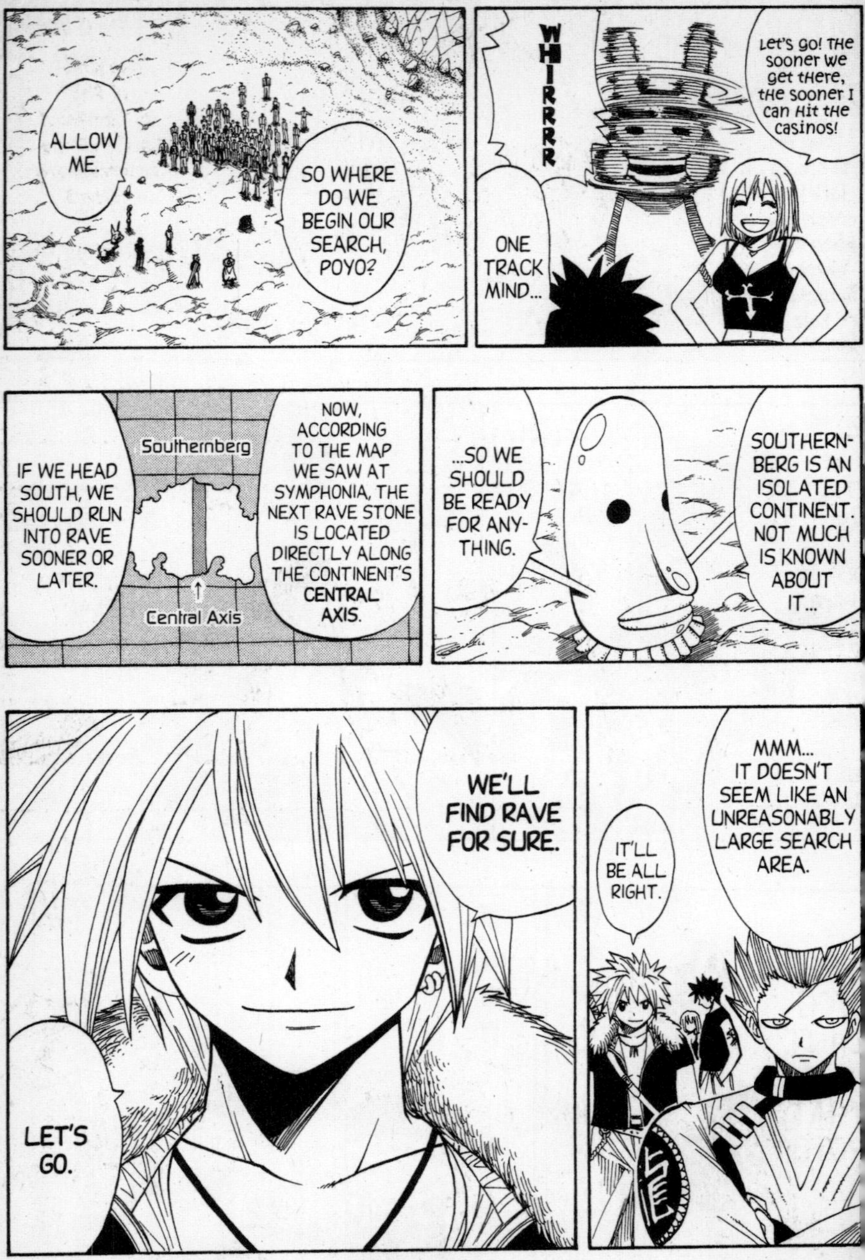
Let's go! The sooner we get there, the sooner I can hit the casinos!
WHIRRRR
ONE TRACK MIND...
SO WHERE DO WE BEGIN OUR SEARCH, POYO?
ALLOW ME.
SOUTHERN-BERG IS AN ISOLATED CONTINENT. NOT MUCH IS KNOWN ABOUT IT...
...SO WE SHOULD BE READY FOR ANY-THING.
NOW, ACCORDING TO THE MAP WE SAW AT SYMPHONIA, THE NEXT RAVE STONE IS LOCATED DIRECTLY ALONG THE CONTINENT'S **CENTRAL AXIS.**
Southernberg
↑
Central Axis
IF WE HEAD SOUTH, WE SHOULD RUN INTO RAVE SOONER OR LATER.
MMM... IT DOESN'T SEEM LIKE AN UNREASONABLY LARGE SEARCH AREA.
IT'LL BE ALL RIGHT.
WE'LL FIND RAVE FOR SURE.
LET'S GO.

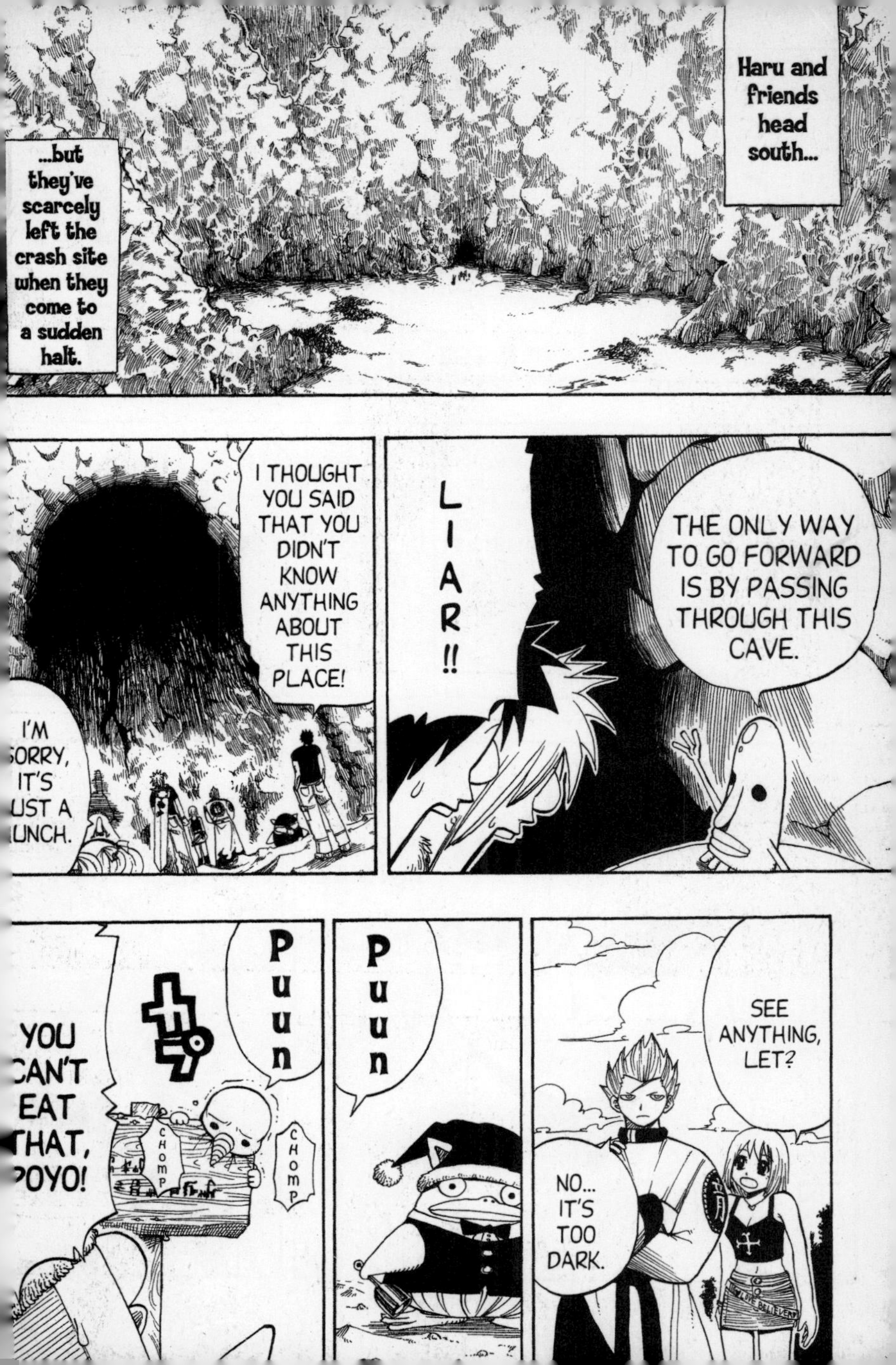

Haru and friends head south...
...but they've scarcely left the crash site when they come to a sudden halt.
THE ONLY WAY TO GO FORWARD IS BY PASSING THROUGH THIS CAVE.
LIAR!!
I THOUGHT YOU SAID THAT YOU DIDN'T KNOW ANYTHING ABOUT THIS PLACE!
I'M SORRY, IT'S JUST A HUNCH.
SEE ANYTHING, LET?
NO... IT'S TOO DARK.
Puun
CHOMP
Puun
CHOMP
YOU CAN'T EAT THAT, POYO!

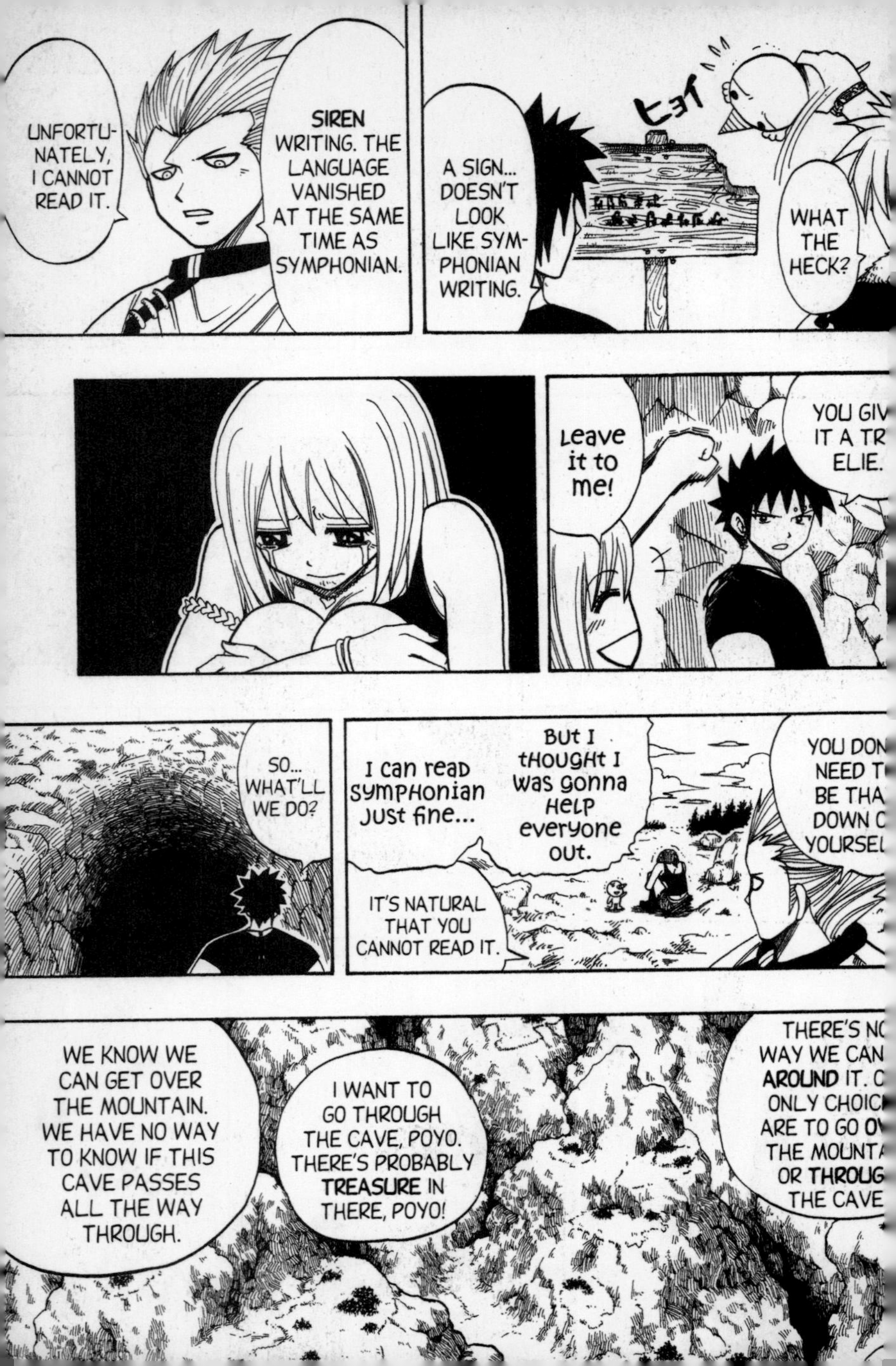

ヒョイ
WHAT THE HECK?
A SIGN... DOESN'T LOOK LIKE SYMPHONIAN WRITING.
SIREN WRITING. THE LANGUAGE VANISHED AT THE SAME TIME AS SYMPHONIAN.
UNFORTUNATELY, I CANNOT READ IT.
YOU GIV IT A TR ELIE.
Leave it to me!
YOU DON NEED T BE THA DOWN O YOURSEL
But I thought I was gonna help everyone out.
I can read Symphonian just fine...
IT'S NATURAL THAT YOU CANNOT READ IT.
SO... WHAT'LL WE DO?
THERE'S NO WAY WE CAN AROUND IT. O ONLY CHOIC ARE TO GO OV THE MOUNTA OR THROUG THE CAVE
I WANT TO GO THROUGH THE CAVE, POYO. THERE'S PROBABLY TREASURE IN THERE, POYO!
WE KNOW WE CAN GET OVER THE MOUNTAIN. WE HAVE NO WAY TO KNOW IF THIS CAVE PASSES ALL THE WAY THROUGH.

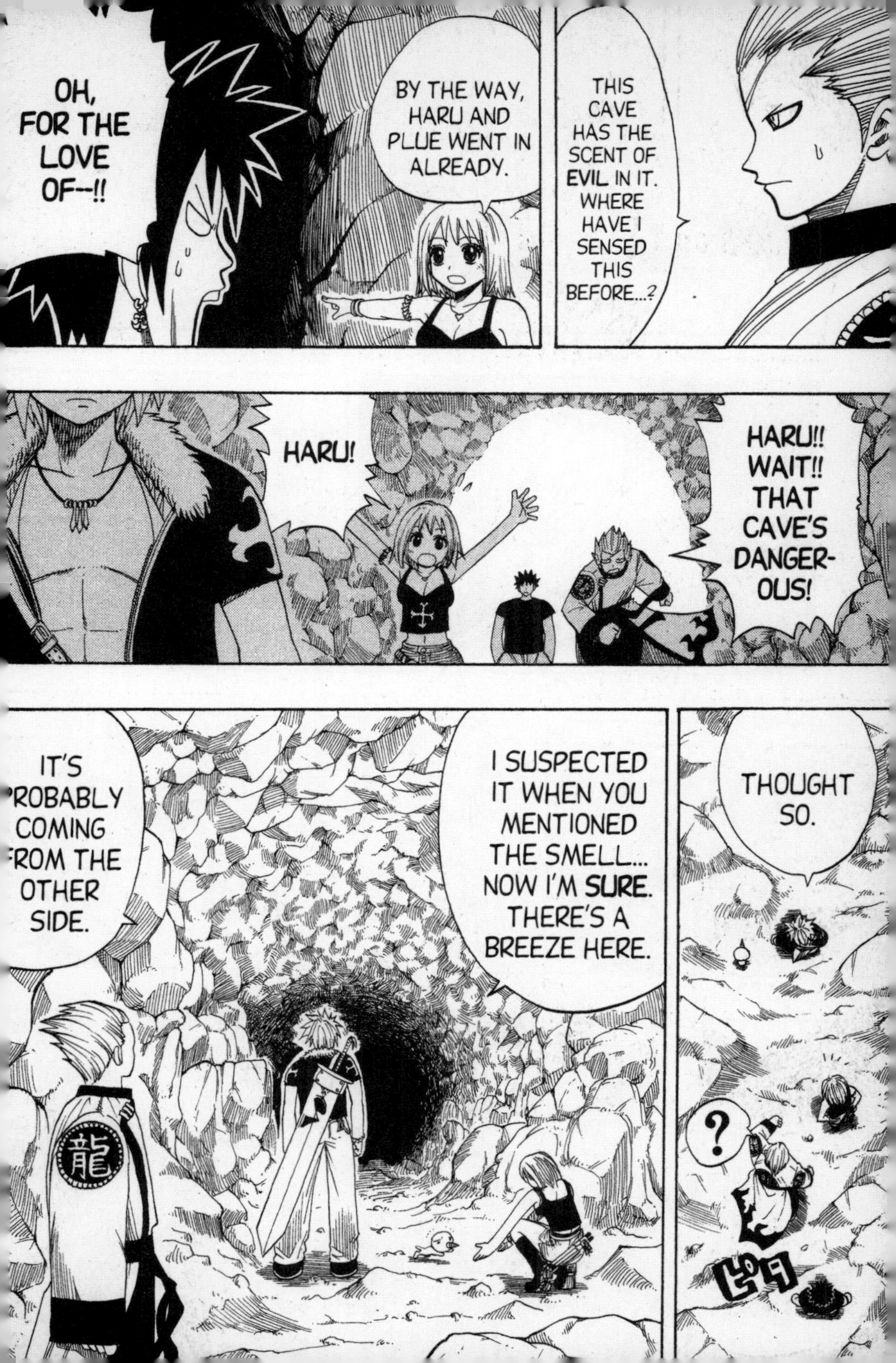

THIS CAVE HAS THE SCENT OF EVIL IN IT. WHERE HAVE I SENSED THIS BEFORE...?
BY THE WAY, HARU AND PLUE WENT IN ALREADY.
OH, FOR THE LOVE OF--!!
HARU!! WAIT!! THAT CAVE'S DANGER-OUS!
HARU!
THOUGHT SO.
?
ピタ
I SUSPECTED IT WHEN YOU MENTIONED THE SMELL... NOW I'M SURE. THERE'S A BREEZE HERE.
IT'S PROBABLY COMING FROM THE OTHER SIDE.

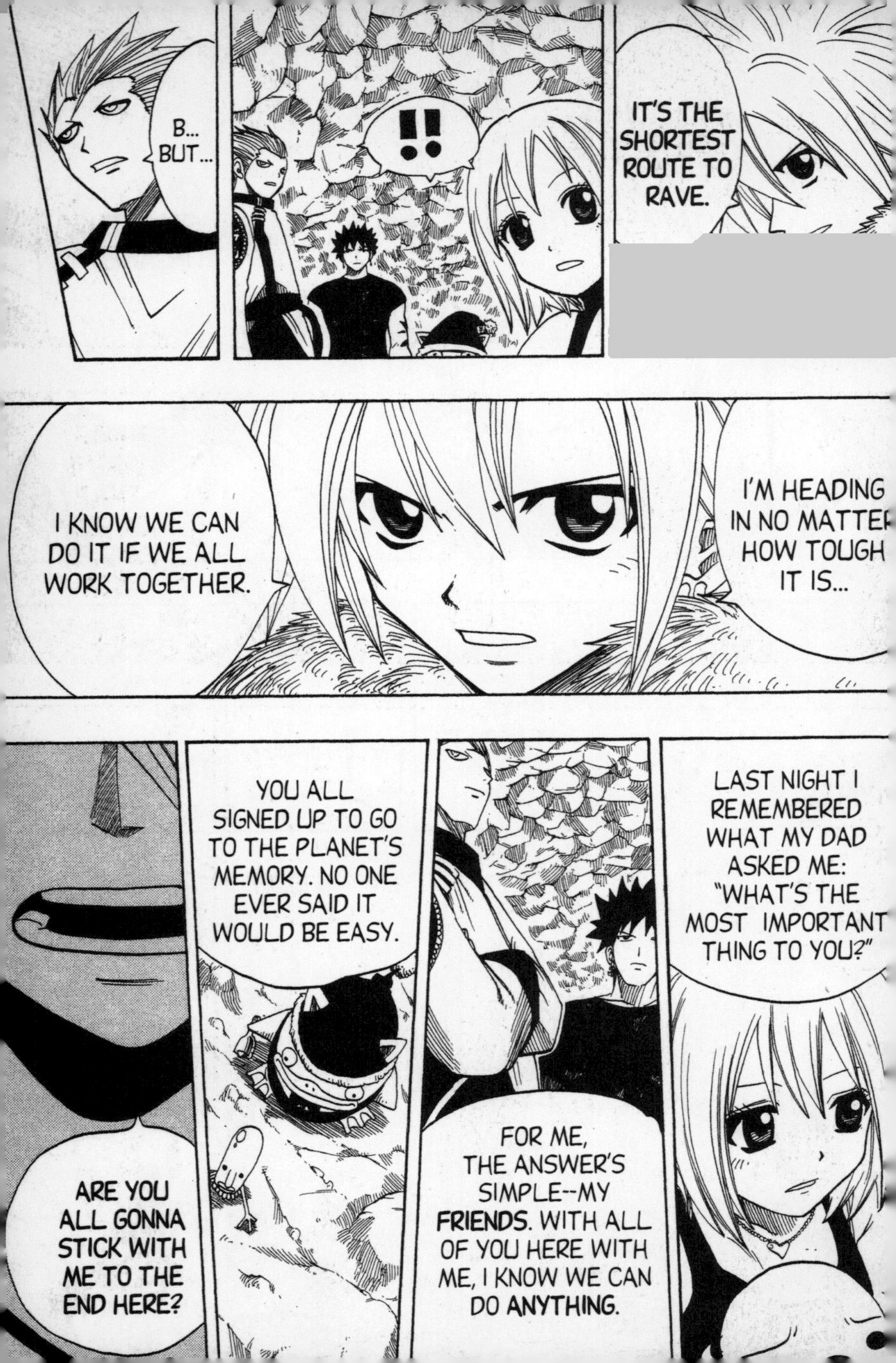
IT'S THE SHORTEST ROUTE TO RAVE.
!!
B... BUT...
I'M HEADING IN NO MATTER HOW TOUGH IT IS...
I KNOW WE CAN DO IT IF WE ALL WORK TOGETHER.
LAST NIGHT I REMEMBERED WHAT MY DAD ASKED ME: "WHAT'S THE MOST IMPORTANT THING TO YOU?"
FOR ME, THE ANSWER'S SIMPLE--MY FRIENDS. WITH ALL OF YOU HERE WITH ME, I KNOW WE CAN DO ANYTHING.
YOU ALL SIGNED UP TO GO TO THE PLANET'S MEMORY. NO ONE EVER SAID IT WOULD BE EASY.
ARE YOU ALL GONNA STICK WITH ME TO THE END HERE?

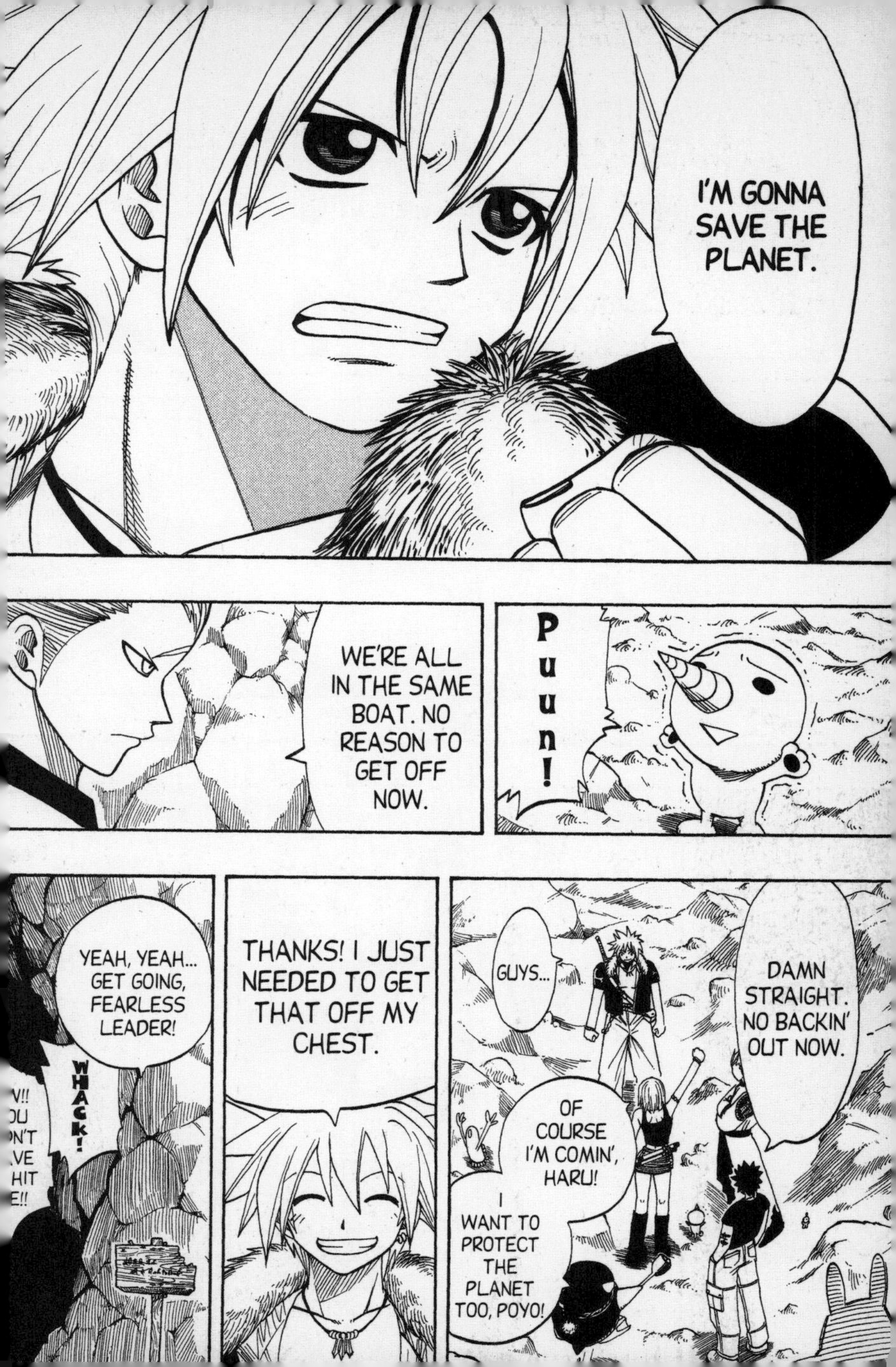
I'M GONNA SAVE THE PLANET.
Puun!
WE'RE ALL IN THE SAME BOAT. NO REASON TO GET OFF NOW.
DAMN STRAIGHT. NO BACKIN' OUT NOW.
GUYS...
OF COURSE I'M COMIN', HARU!
I WANT TO PROTECT THE PLANET TOO, POYO!
THANKS! I JUST NEEDED TO GET THAT OFF MY CHEST.
YEAH, YEAH... GET GOING, FEARLESS LEADER!
WHACK!

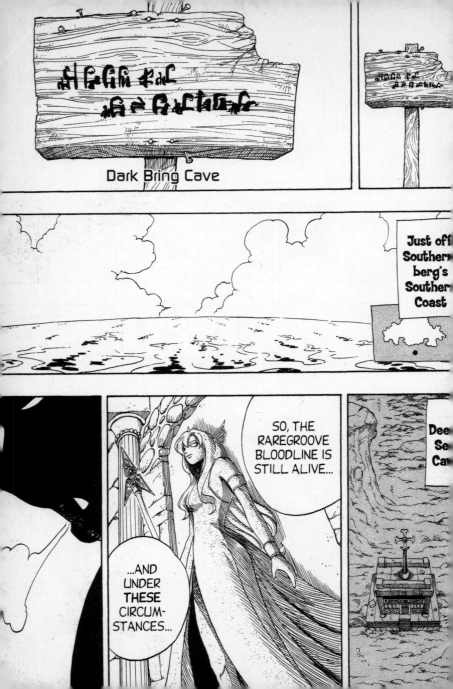

Dark Bring Cave

Just off Southern berg's Southern Coast

SO, THE RAREGROOVE BLOODLINE IS STILL ALIVE...

...AND UNDER THESE CIRCUM-STANCES...

Dee Se Ca

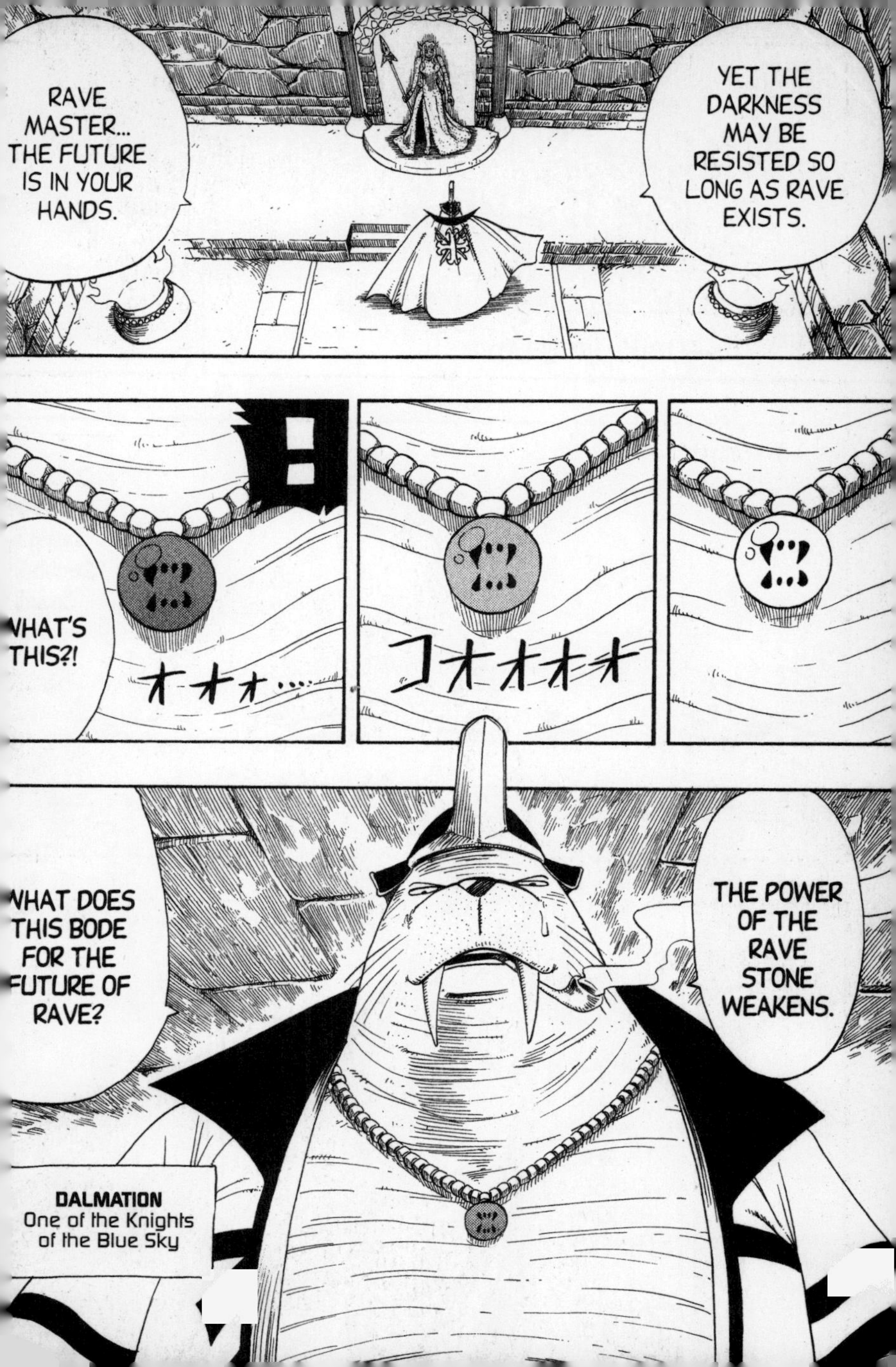

YET THE DARKNESS MAY BE RESISTED SO LONG AS RAVE EXISTS.
RAVE MASTER... THE FUTURE IS IN YOUR HANDS.
コオオオオ
WHAT'S THIS?!
オオォ....
THE POWER OF THE RAVE STONE WEAKENS.
WHAT DOES THIS BODE FOR THE FUTURE OF RAVE?
DALMATION
One of the Knights of the Blue Sky

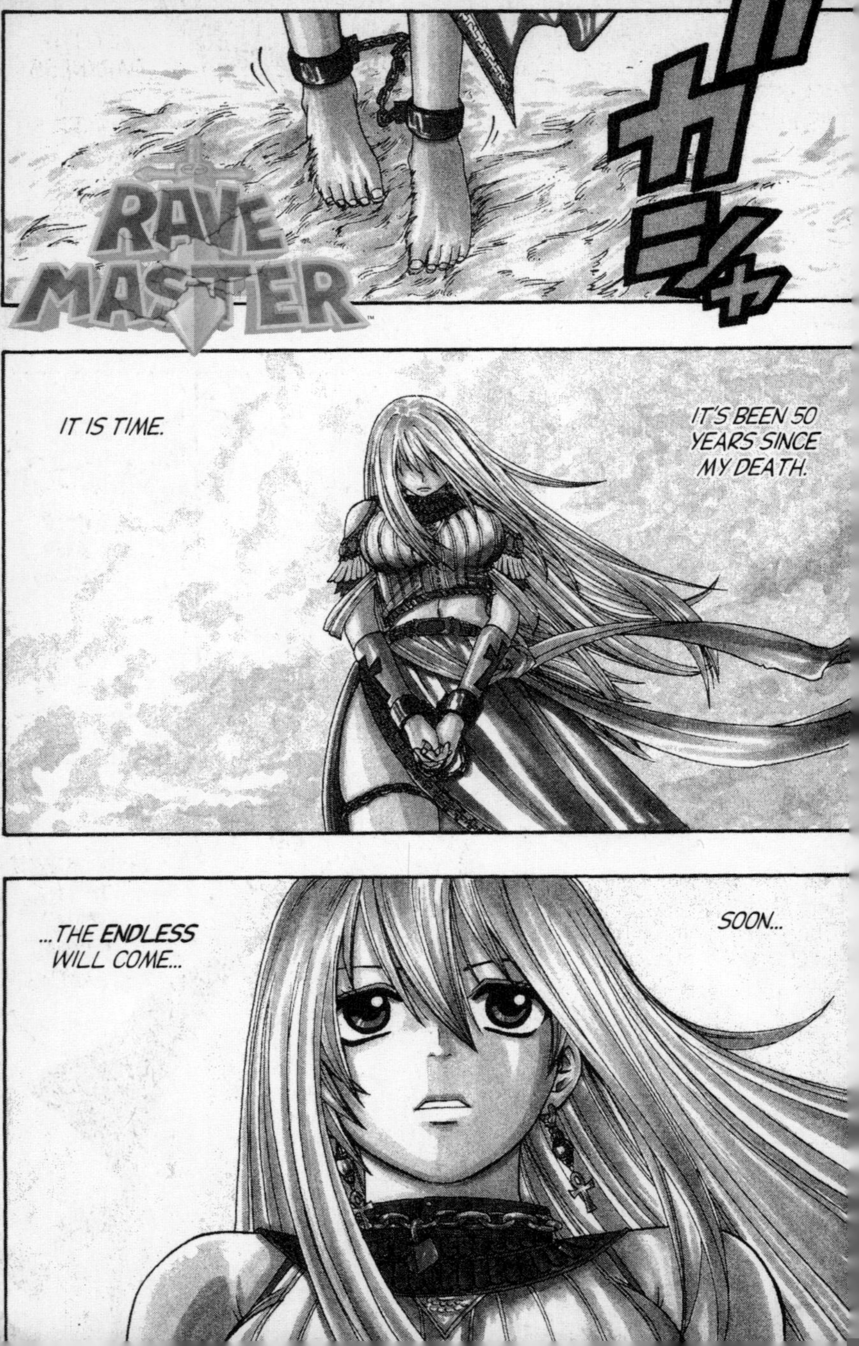
RAVE MASTER
IT'S BEEN 50 YEARS SINCE MY DEATH.
IT IS TIME.
SOON...
...THE ENDLESS WILL COME...

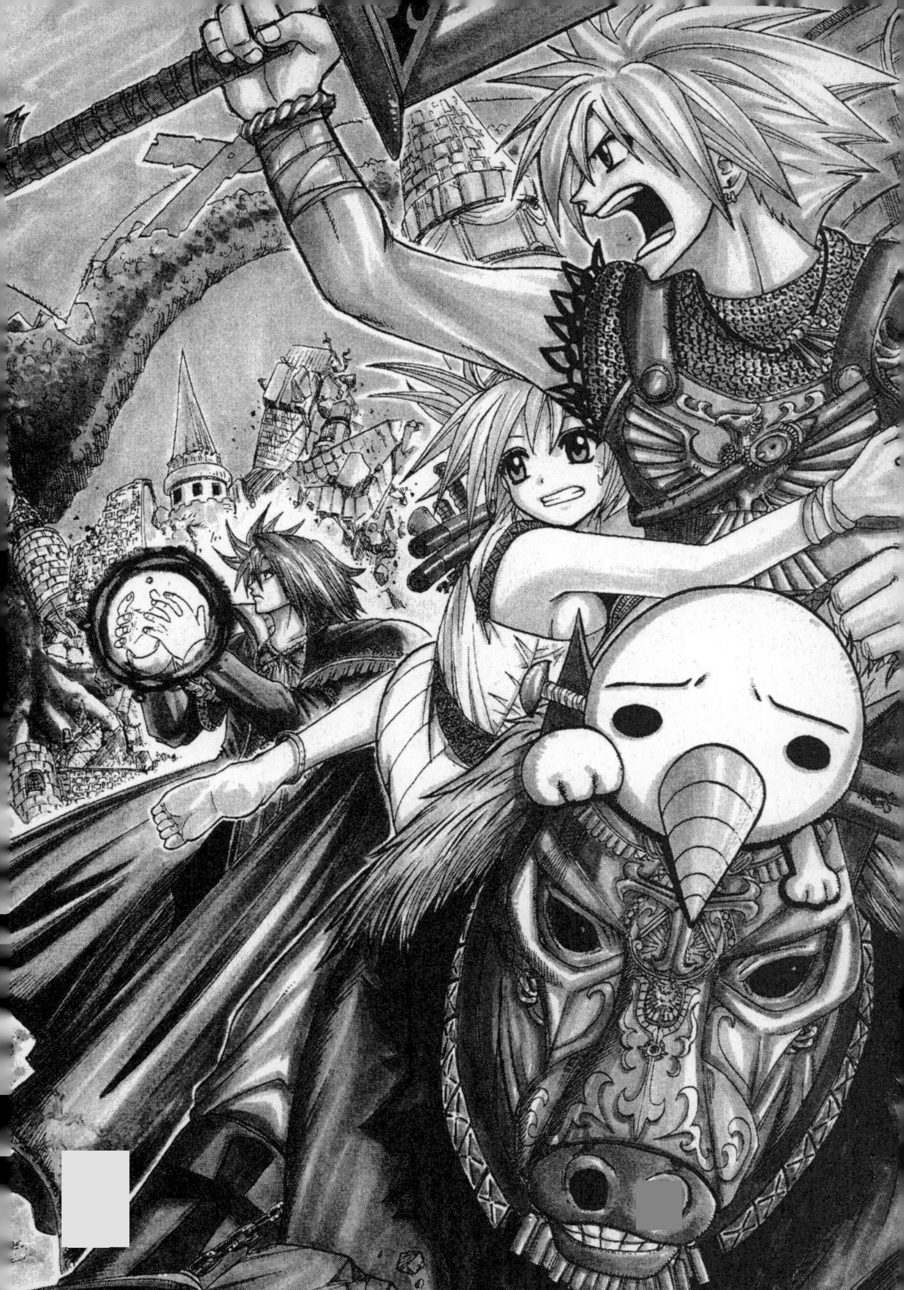

RAVE: 100 ✠ TIME TO SYNCHRO

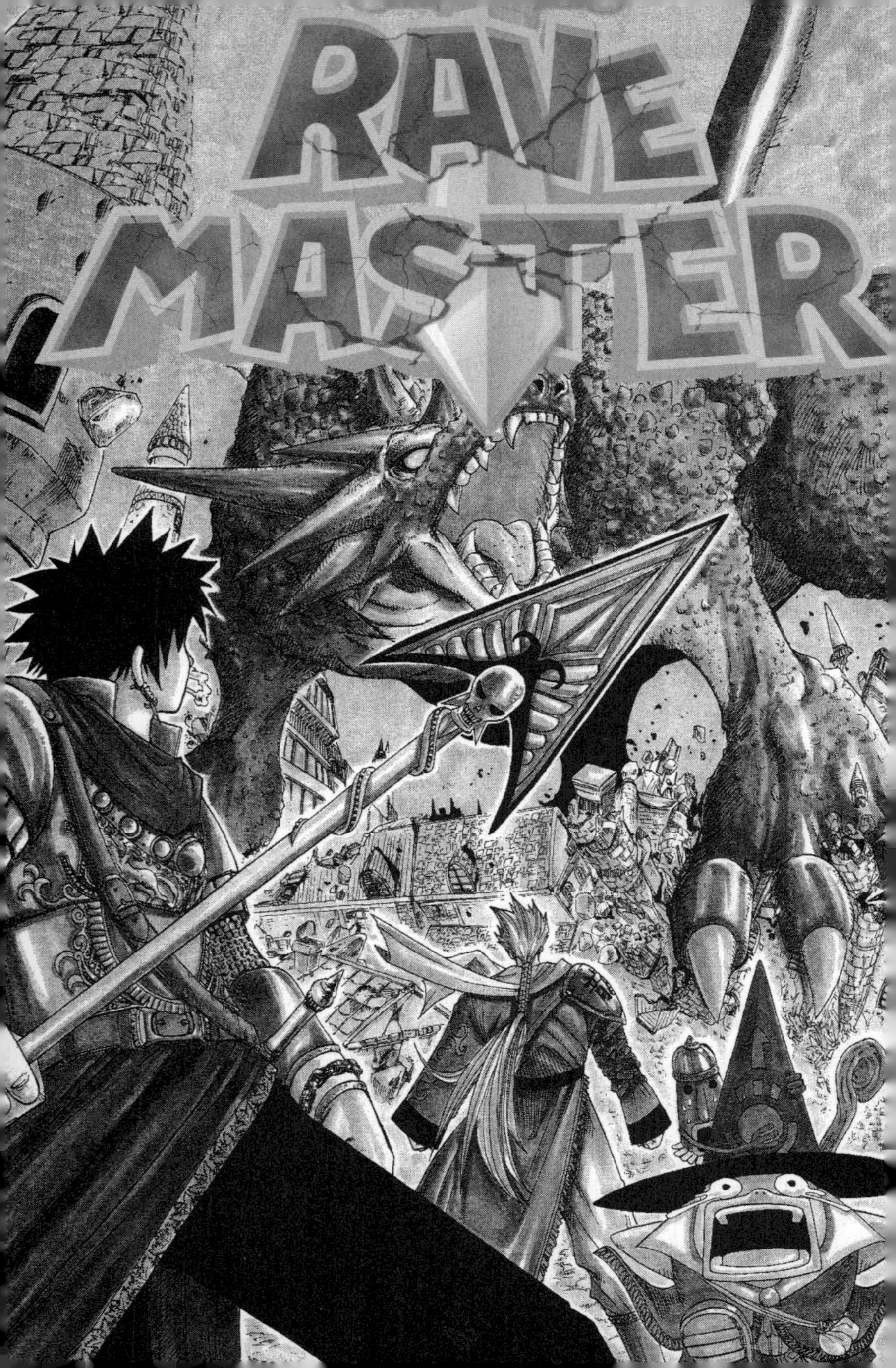
RAVE MASTER

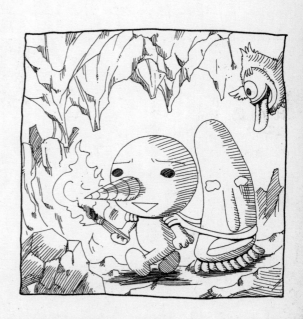

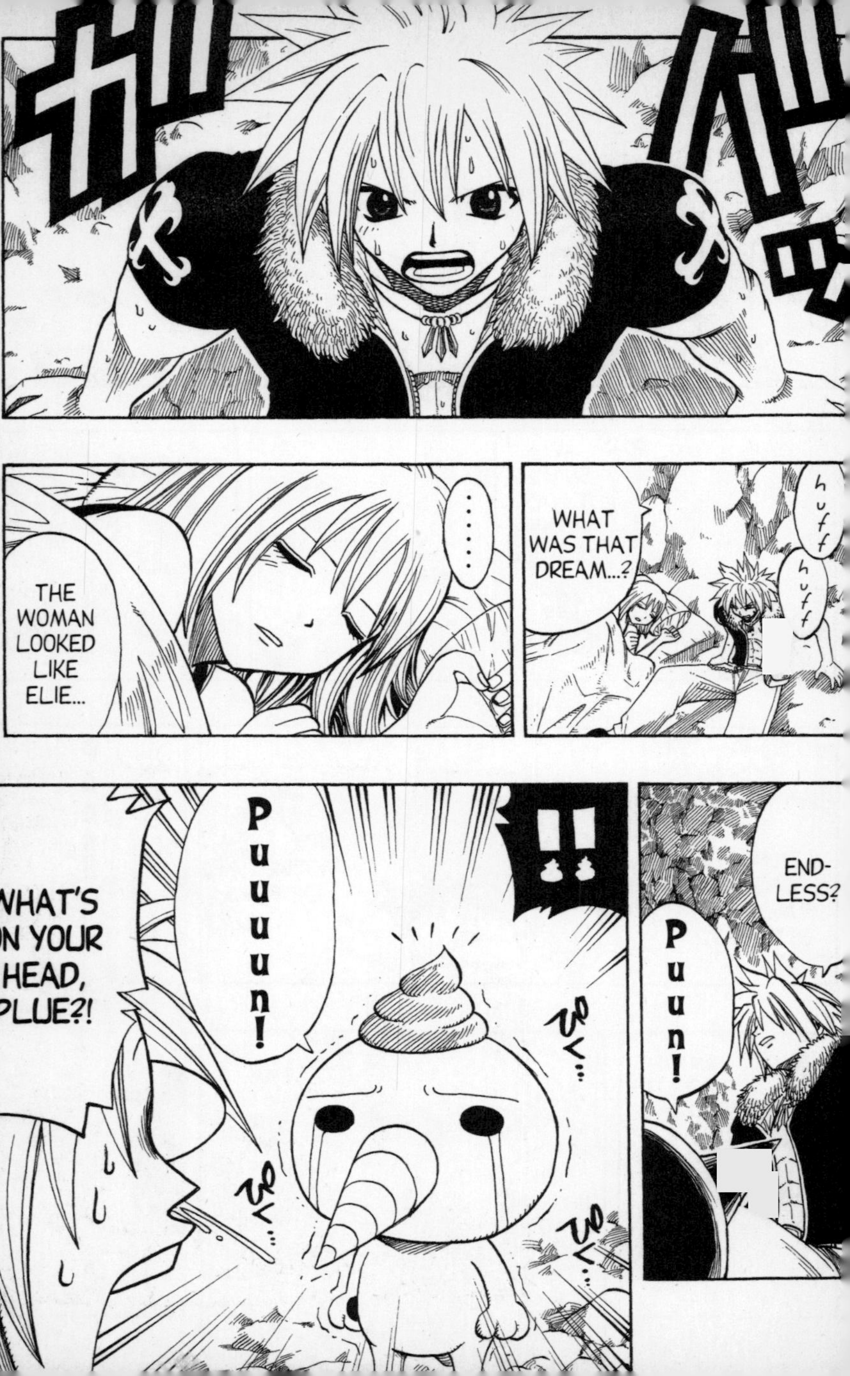
huff
huff
WHAT WAS THAT DREAM...?
......
THE WOMAN LOOKED LIKE ELIE...
END-LESS?
Puun!
!!
Puuuun!
WHAT'S ON YOUR HEAD, PLUE?!

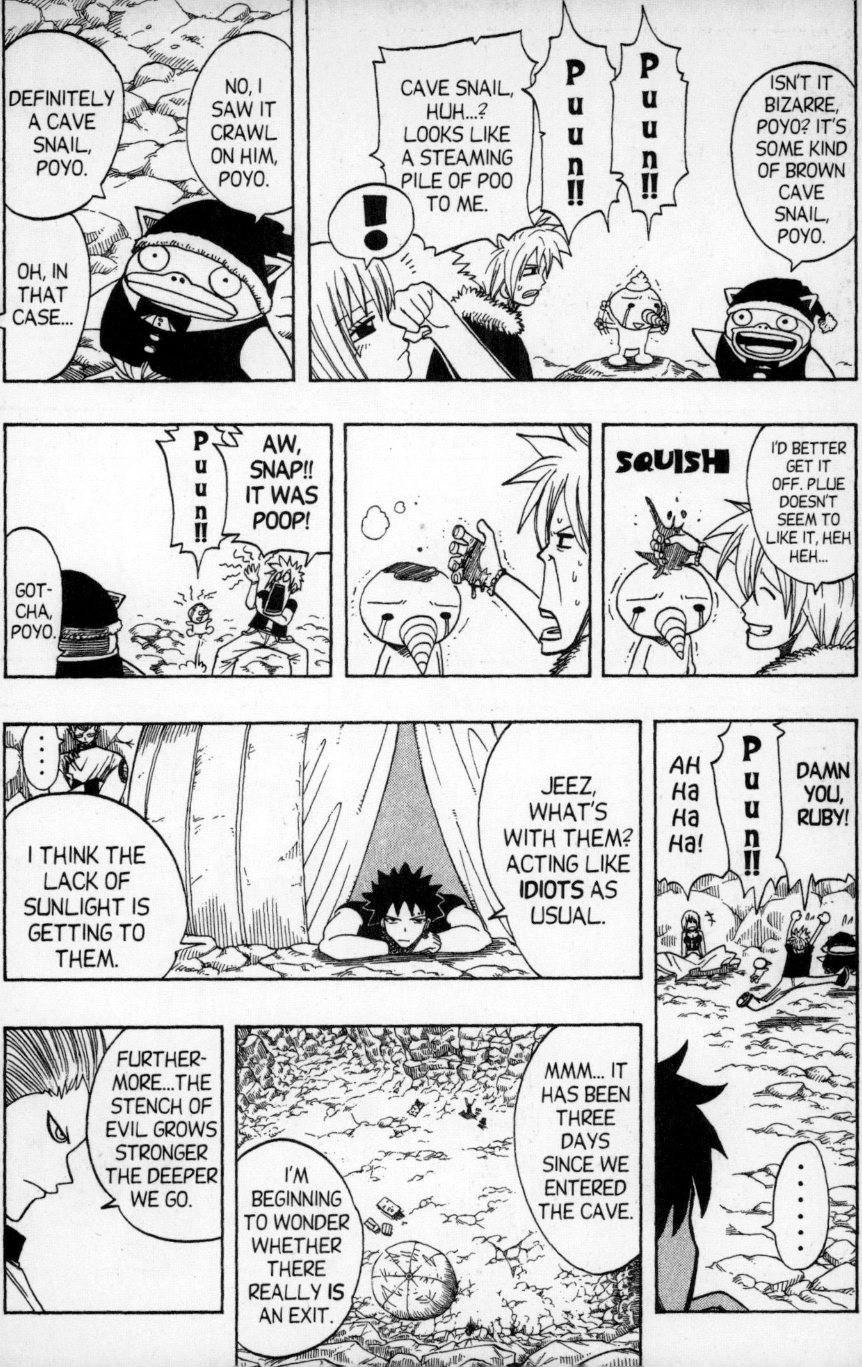
ISN'T IT BIZARRE, POYO? IT'S SOME KIND OF BROWN CAVE SNAIL, POYO.
Puun!!
Puun!!
CAVE SNAIL, HUH...? LOOKS LIKE A STEAMING PILE OF POO TO ME.
!
NO, I SAW IT CRAWL ON HIM, POYO.
DEFINITELY A CAVE SNAIL, POYO.
OH, IN THAT CASE...
I'D BETTER GET IT OFF. PLUE DOESN'T SEEM TO LIKE IT, HEH HEH...
SQUISH
AW, SNAP!! IT WAS POOP!
Puun!!
GOT-CHA, POYO.
DAMN YOU, RUBY!
Puun!!
AH Ha Ha Ha!
......
JEEZ, WHAT'S WITH THEM? ACTING LIKE IDIOTS AS USUAL.
I THINK THE LACK OF SUNLIGHT IS GETTING TO THEM.
....
MMM... IT HAS BEEN THREE DAYS SINCE WE ENTERED THE CAVE.
I'M BEGINNING TO WONDER WHETHER THERE REALLY IS AN EXIT.
FURTHER-MORE...THE STENCH OF EVIL GROWS STRONGER THE DEEPER WE GO.

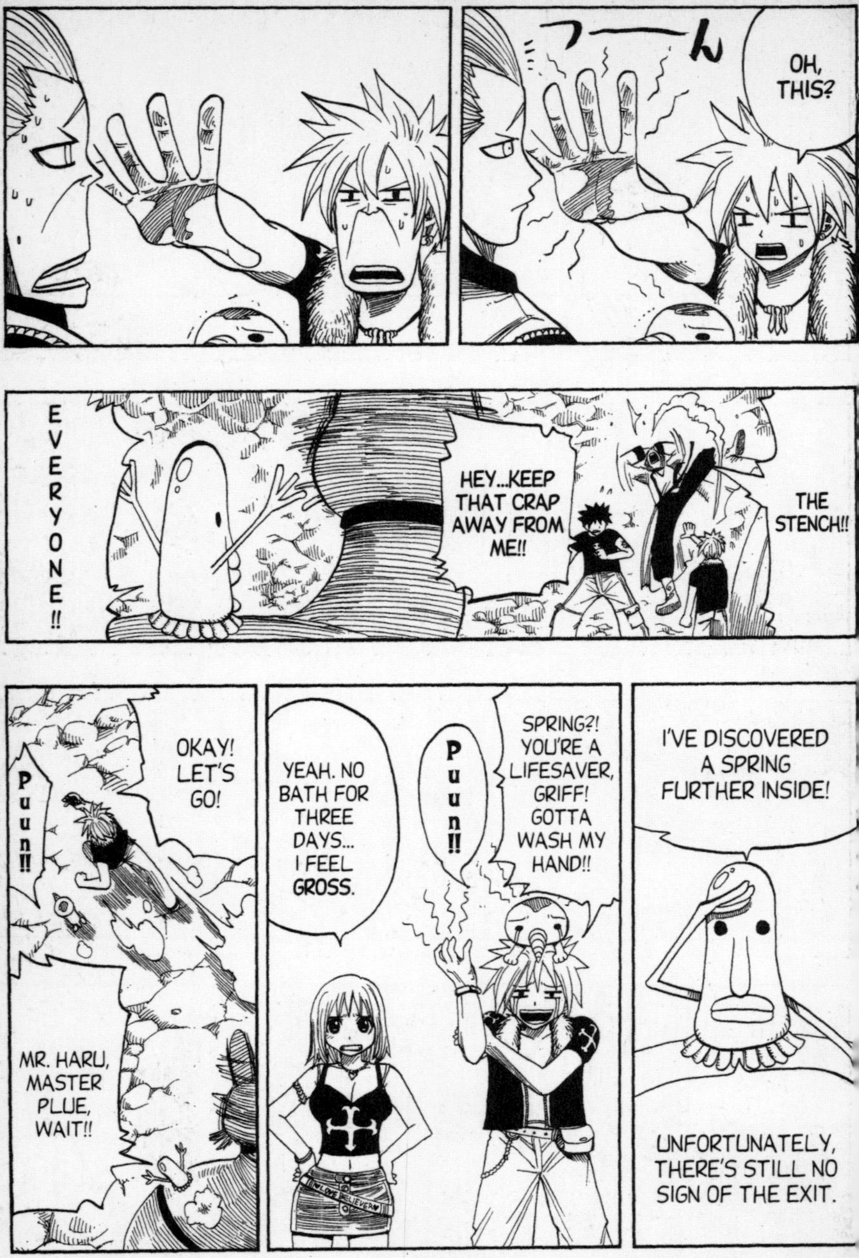
フーん
OH, THIS?
THE STENCH!!
HEY...KEEP THAT CRAP AWAY FROM ME!!
EVERYONE!!
I'VE DISCOVERED A SPRING FURTHER INSIDE!
UNFORTUNATELY, THERE'S STILL NO SIGN OF THE EXIT.
SPRING?! YOU'RE A LIFESAVER, GRIFF! GOTTA WASH MY HAND!!
Puun!!
YEAH. NO BATH FOR THREE DAYS... I FEEL GROSS.
LOVE BELIEVER
OKAY! LET'S GO!
Puun!!
MR. HARU, MASTER PLUE, WAIT!!

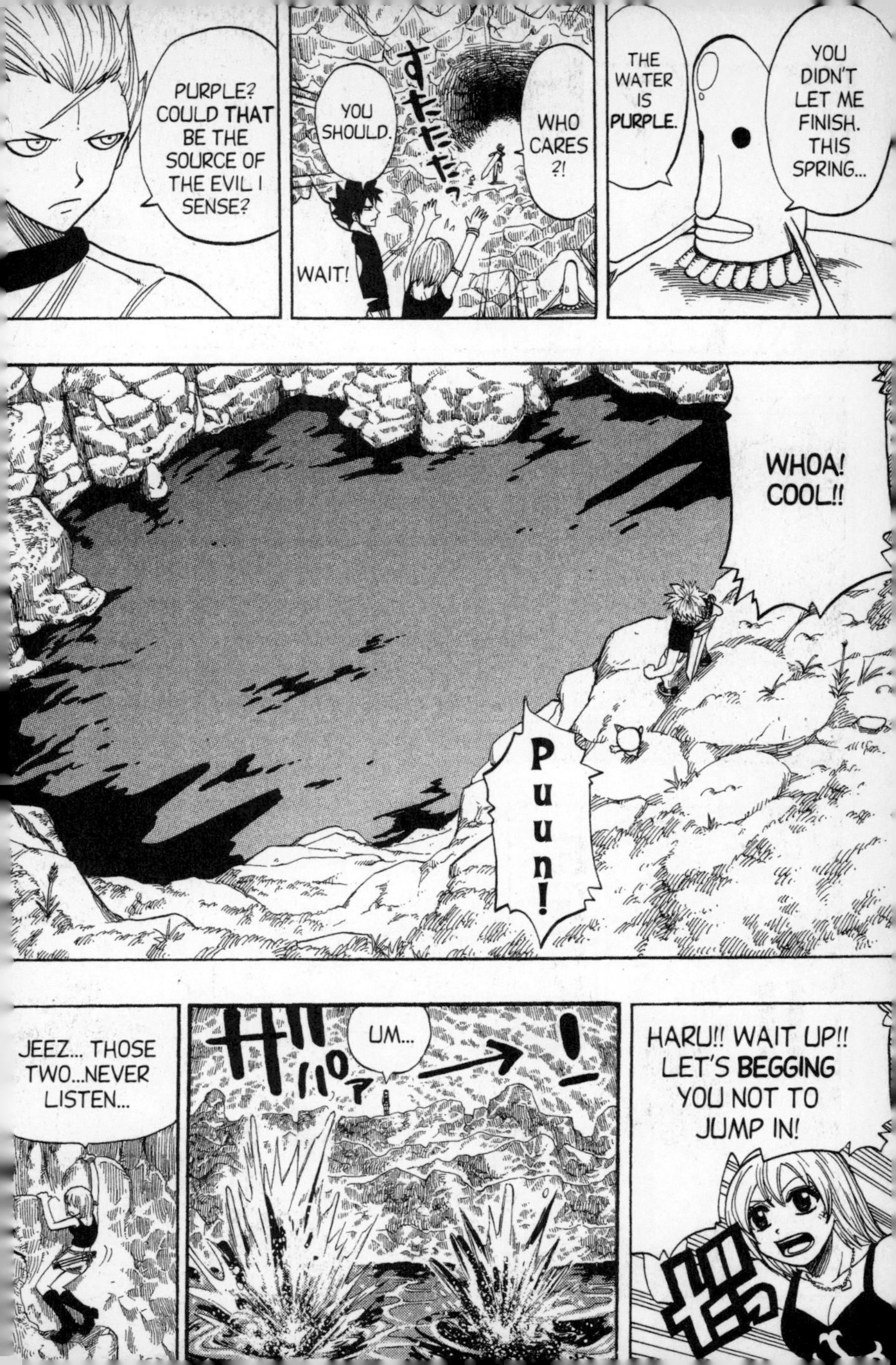

YOU DIDN'T LET ME FINISH. THIS SPRING...
THE WATER IS PURPLE.
WHO CARES?!
すたたたっ
YOU SHOULD.
WAIT!
PURPLE? COULD THAT BE THE SOURCE OF THE EVIL I SENSE?
WHOA! COOL!!
Puun!
HARU!! WAIT UP!! LET'S BEGGING YOU NOT TO JUMP IN!
!
UM...
JEEZ... THOSE TWO...NEVER LISTEN...

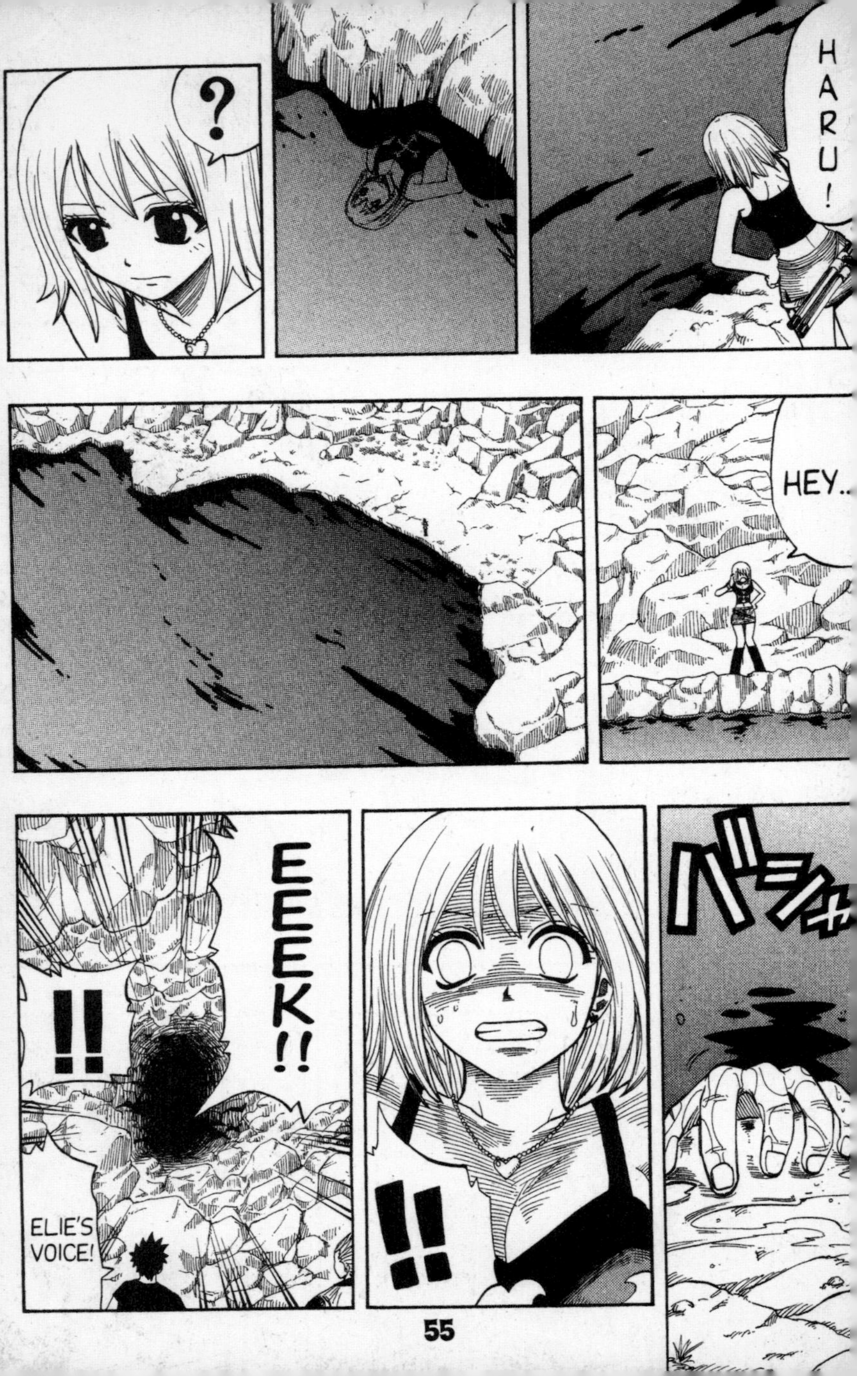
HARU!
?
HEY...
!!
EEEK!!
!!
ELIE'S VOICE!

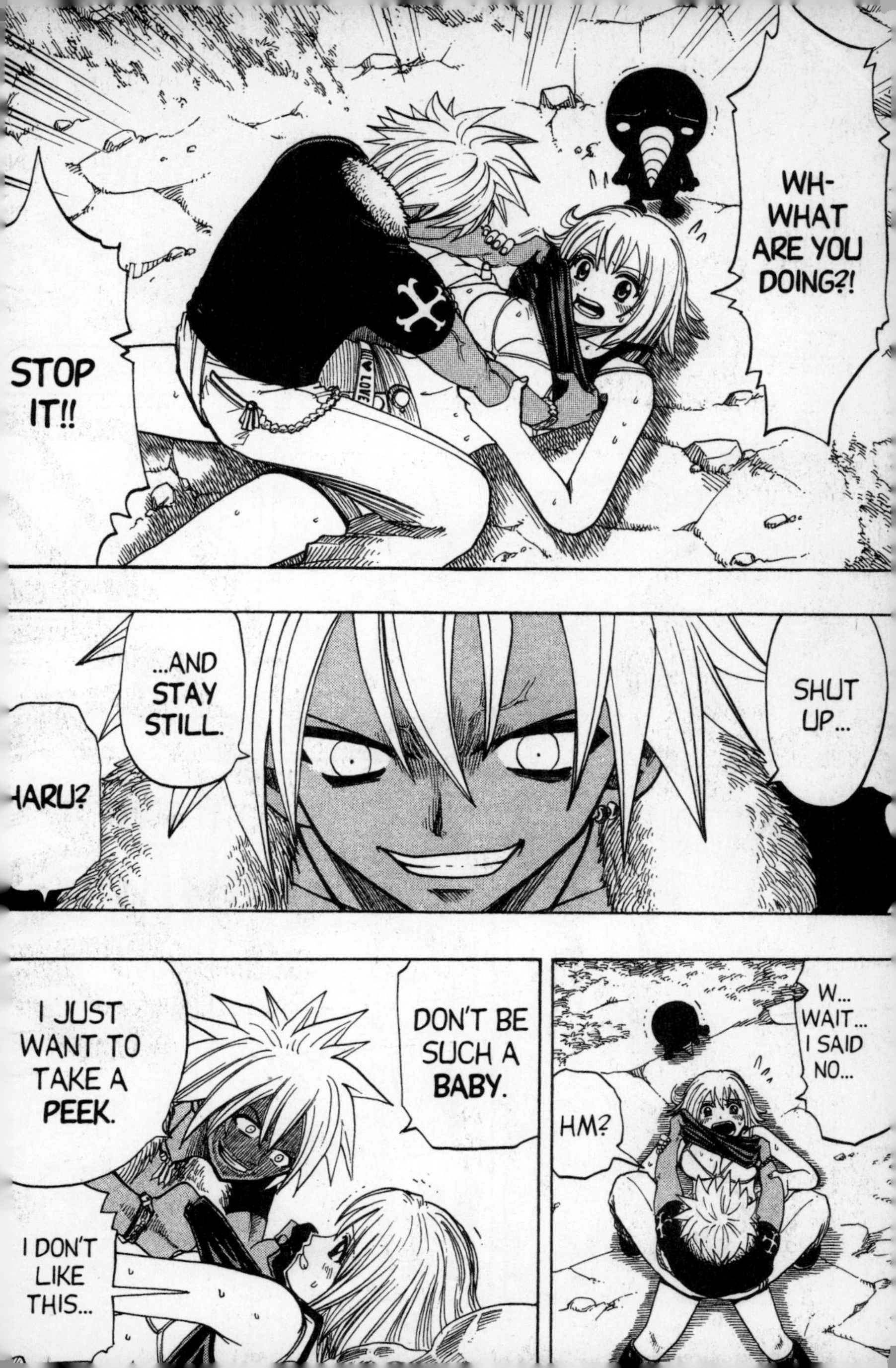
WH- WHAT ARE YOU DOING?!
STOP IT!!
SHUT UP...
...AND STAY STILL.
HARU?
W... WAIT... I SAID NO...
HM?
DON'T BE SUCH A BABY.
I JUST WANT TO TAKE A PEEK.
I DON'T LIKE THIS...

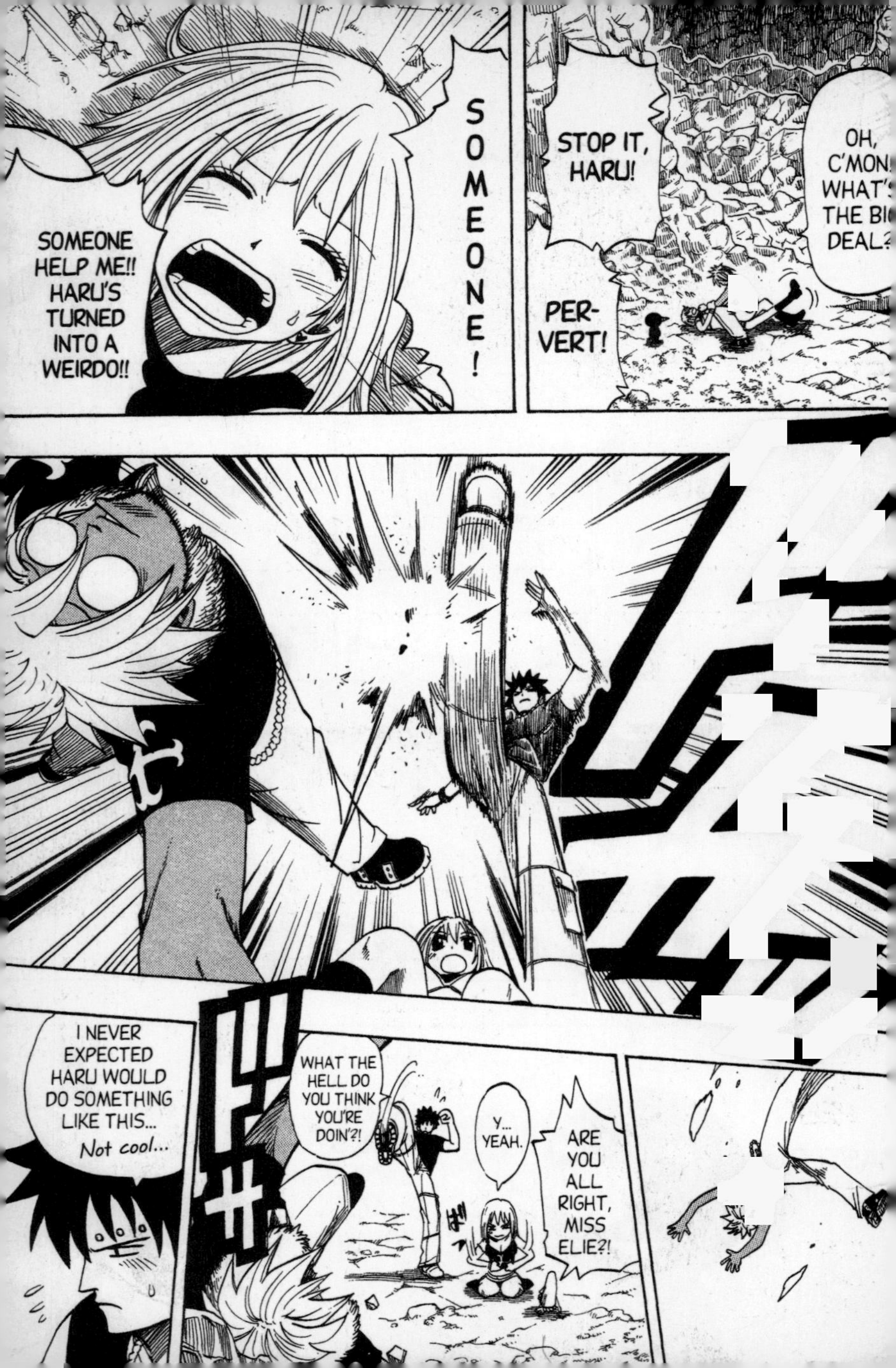
OH, C'MON! WHAT'S THE BIG DEAL?
STOP IT, HARU!
PER-VERT!
SOMEONE!
SOMEONE HELP ME!! HARU'S TURNED INTO A WEIRDO!!
ARE YOU ALL RIGHT, MISS ELIE?!
Y... YEAH.
WHAT THE HELL DO YOU THINK YOU'RE DOIN'?!
I NEVER EXPECTED HARU WOULD DO SOMETHING LIKE THIS...
Not cool...

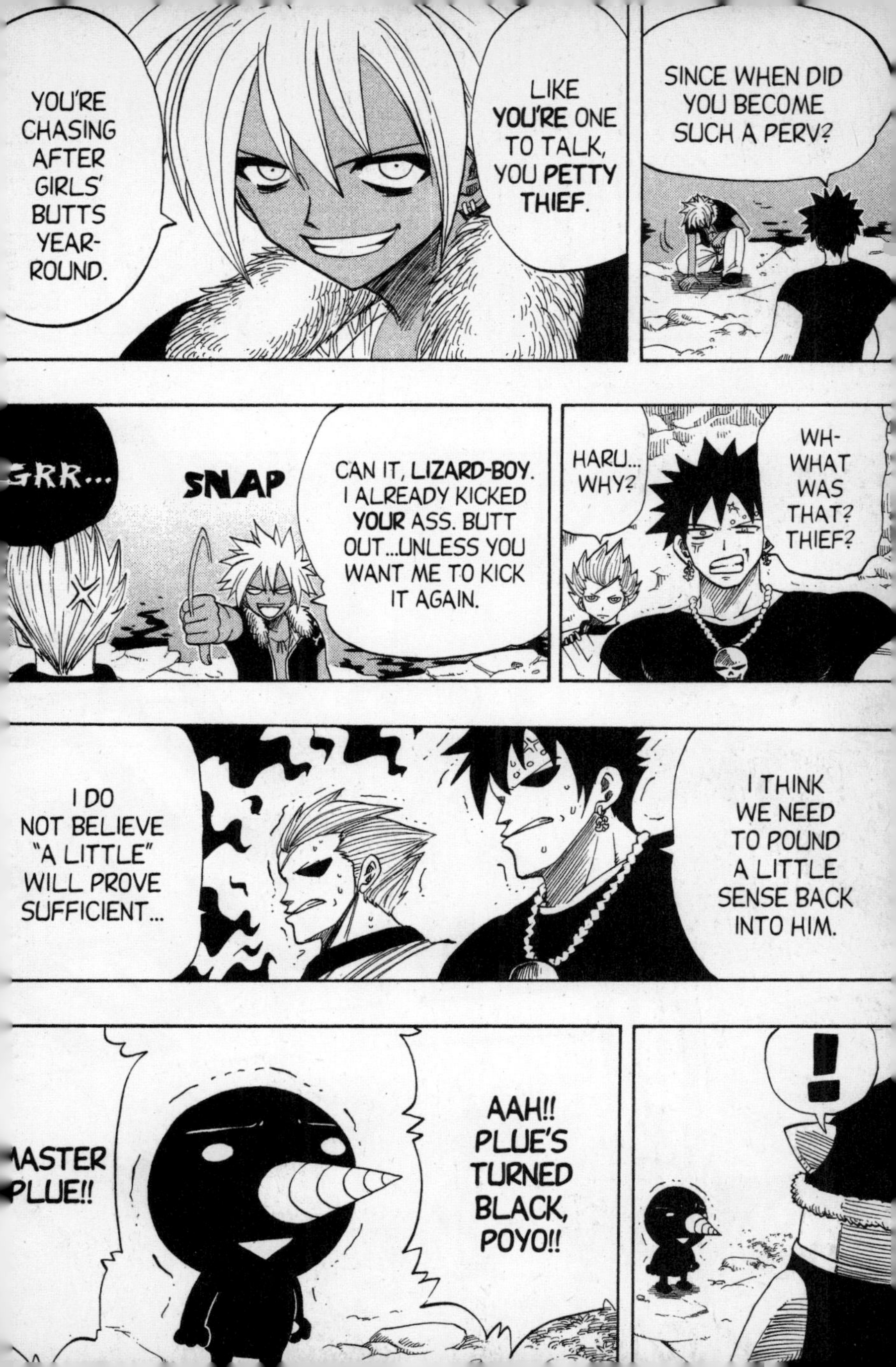
SINCE WHEN DID YOU BECOME SUCH A PERV?
LIKE YOU'RE ONE TO TALK, YOU PETTY THIEF.
YOU'RE CHASING AFTER GIRLS' BUTTS YEAR-ROUND.
WH- WHAT WAS THAT? THIEF?
HARU... WHY?
CAN IT, LIZARD-BOY. I ALREADY KICKED YOUR ASS. BUTT OUT...UNLESS YOU WANT ME TO KICK IT AGAIN.
SNAP
GRR...
I THINK WE NEED TO POUND A LITTLE SENSE BACK INTO HIM.
I DO NOT BELIEVE "A LITTLE" WILL PROVE SUFFICIENT...
!
AAH!! PLUE'S TURNED BLACK, POYO!!
MASTER PLUE!!

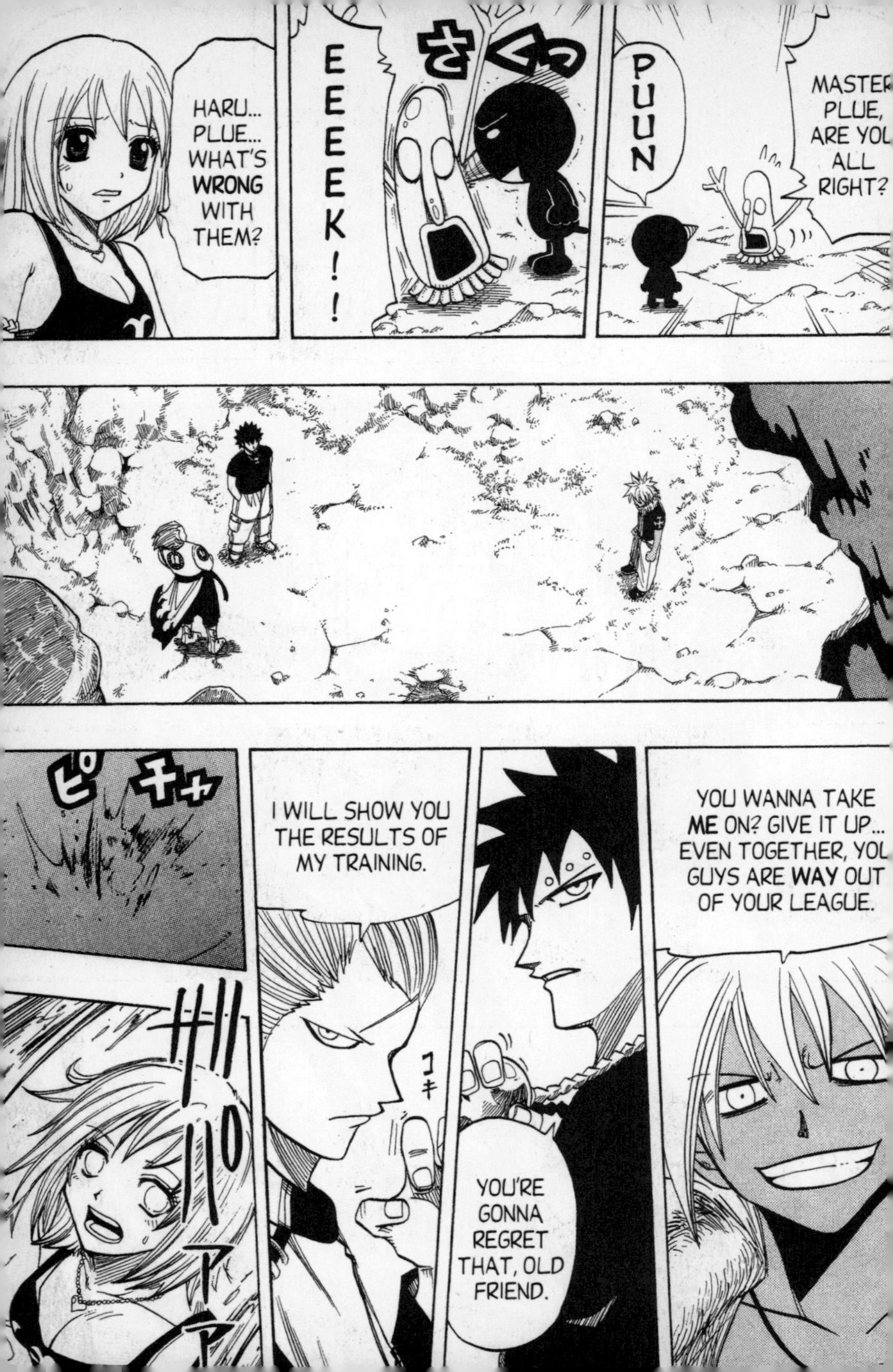
MASTER PLUE, ARE YOU ALL RIGHT?
PUUN
EEEEK!!
さくっ
HARU... PLUE... WHAT'S WRONG WITH THEM?
YOU WANNA TAKE ME ON? GIVE IT UP... EVEN TOGETHER, YOU GUYS ARE WAY OUT OF YOUR LEAGUE.
YOU'RE GONNA REGRET THAT, OLD FRIEND.
コキ
I WILL SHOW YOU THE RESULTS OF MY TRAINING.
ピチャ
ザ
ハア

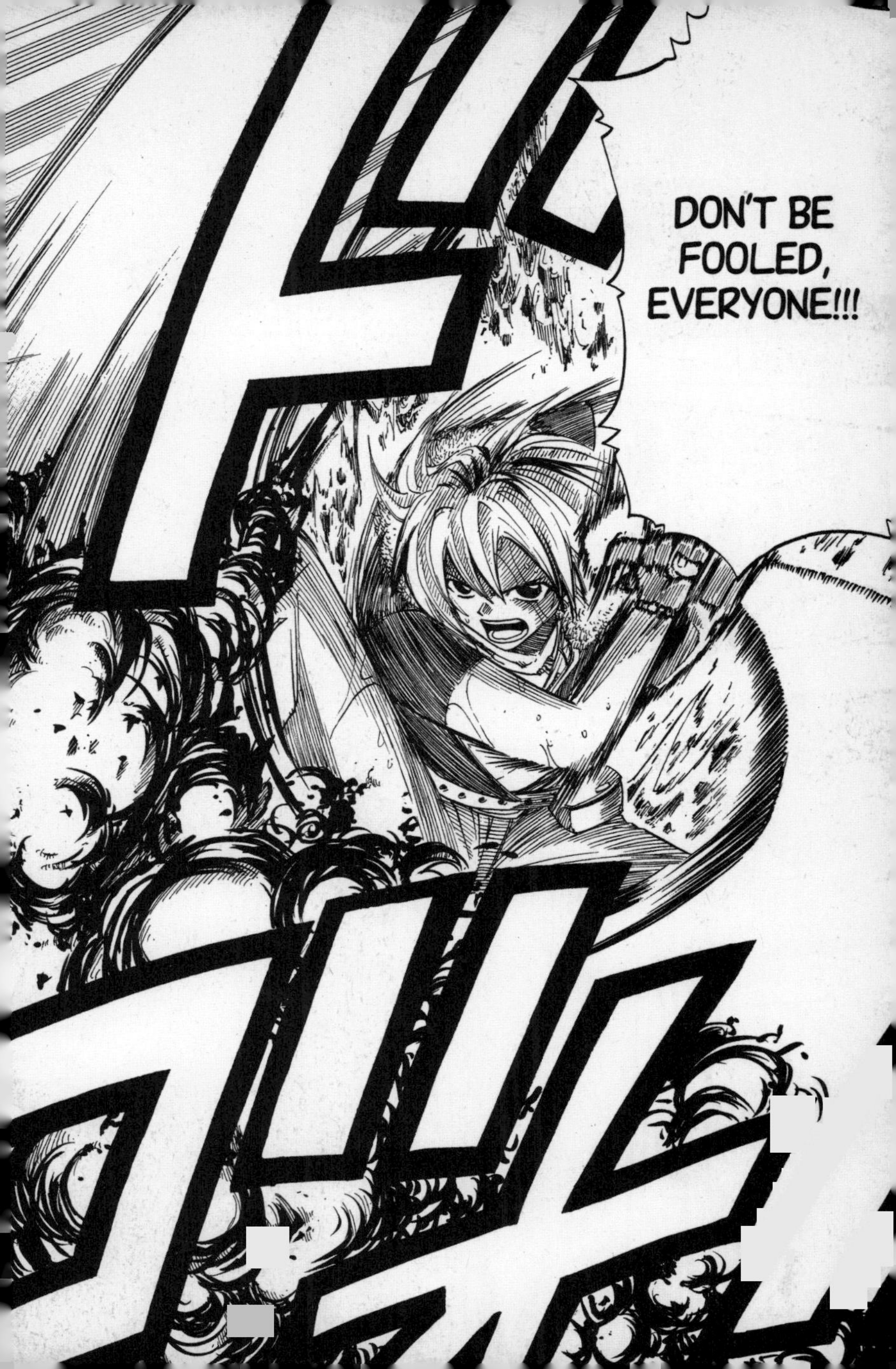
DON'T BE FOOLED, EVERYONE!!!

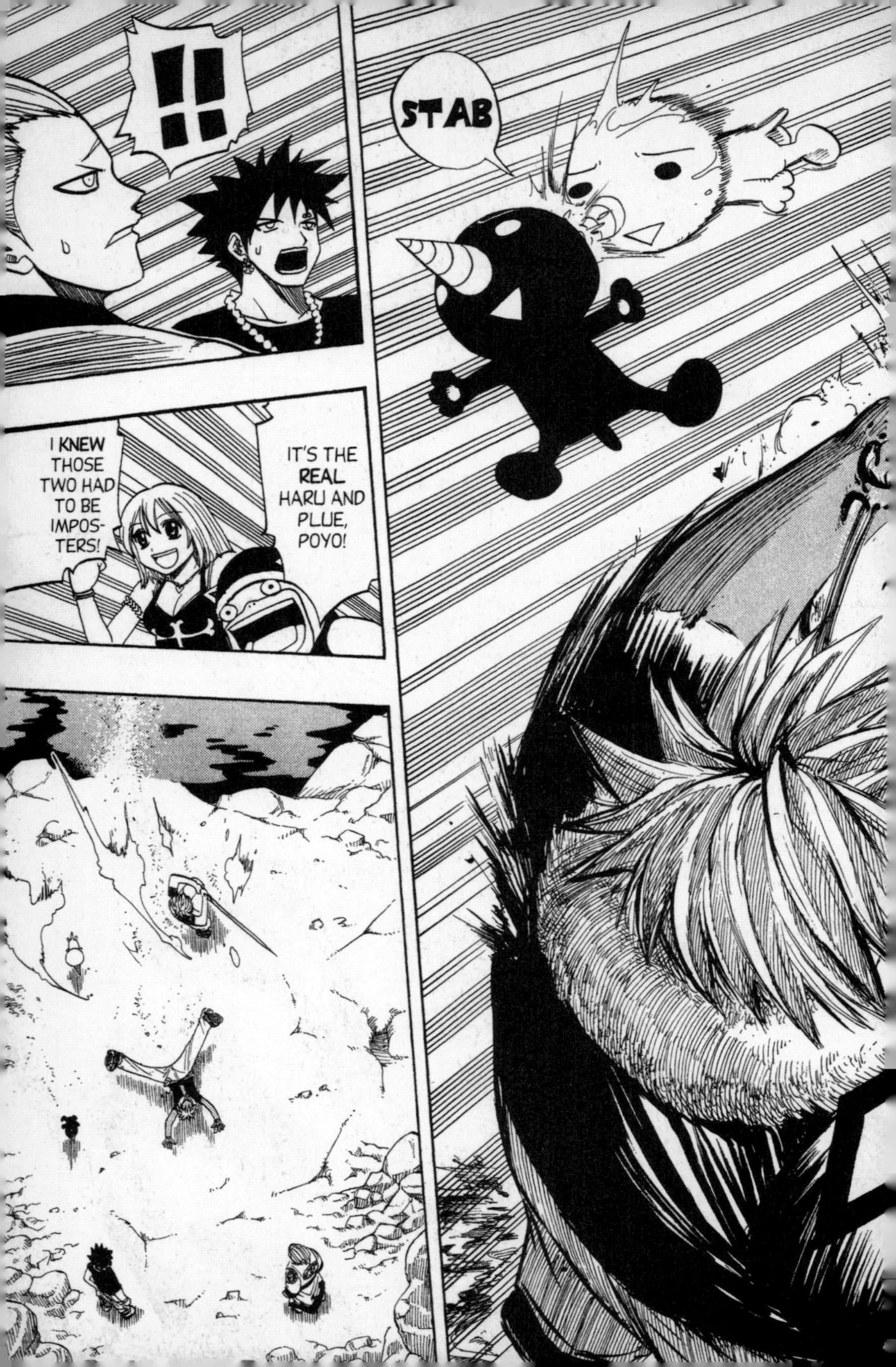
STAB
!!
IT'S THE REAL HARU AND PLUE, POYO!
I KNEW THOSE TWO HAD TO BE IMPOSTERS!

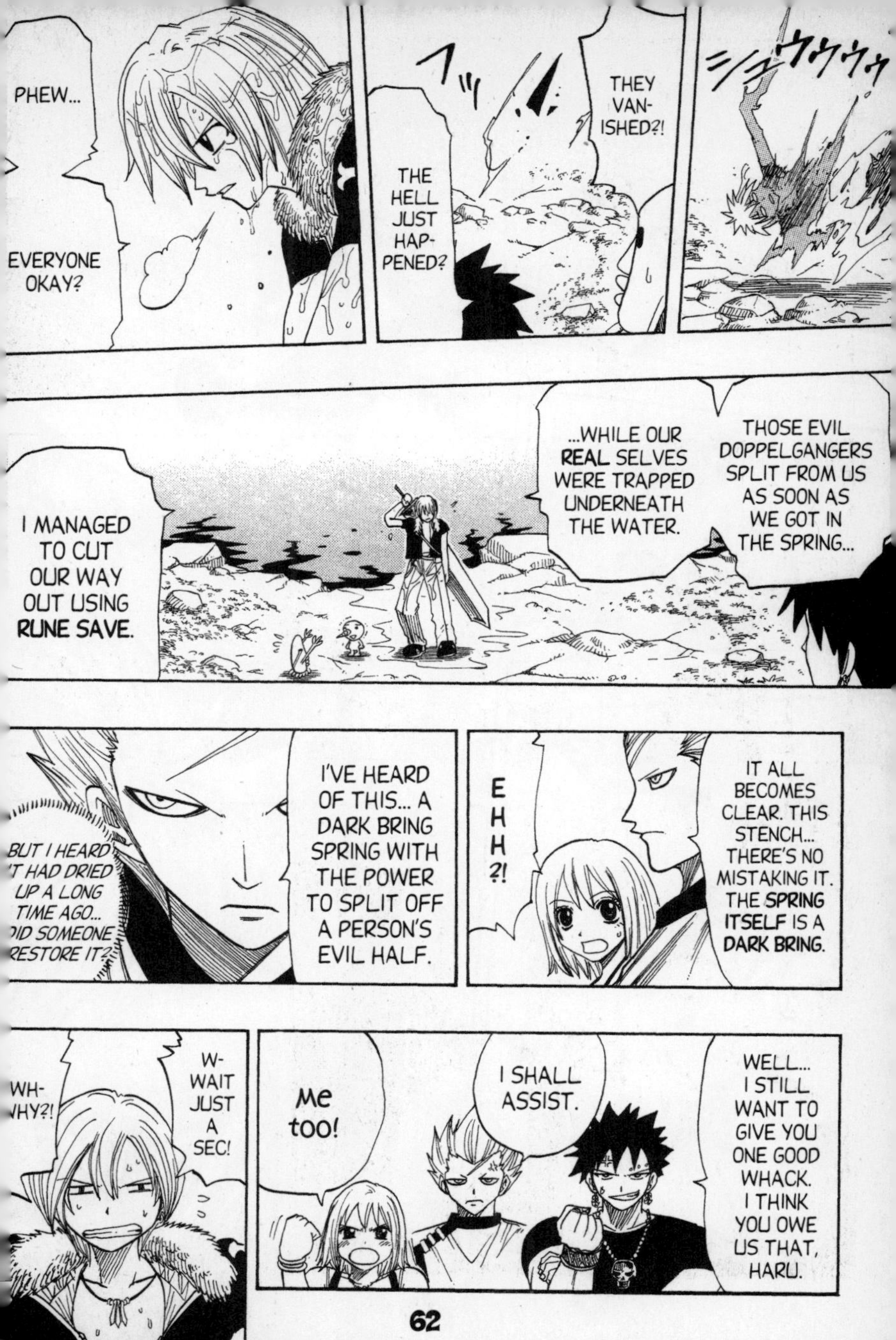
シュウウウゥ
THEY VANISHED?!
THE HELL JUST HAPPENED?
PHEW...
EVERYONE OKAY?
THOSE EVIL DOPPELGANGERS SPLIT FROM US AS SOON AS WE GOT IN THE SPRING...
...WHILE OUR REAL SELVES WERE TRAPPED UNDERNEATH THE WATER.
I MANAGED TO CUT OUR WAY OUT USING RUNE SAVE.
IT ALL BECOMES CLEAR. THIS STENCH... THERE'S NO MISTAKING IT. THE SPRING ITSELF IS A DARK BRING.
EHH?!
I'VE HEARD OF THIS... A DARK BRING SPRING WITH THE POWER TO SPLIT OFF A PERSON'S EVIL HALF.
BUT I HEARD 'T HAD DRIED UP A LONG TIME AGO... ID SOMEONE RESTORE IT?
WELL... I STILL WANT TO GIVE YOU ONE GOOD WHACK. I THINK YOU OWE US THAT, HARU.
I SHALL ASSIST.
Me too!
W-WAIT JUST A SEC!
WH- HY?!

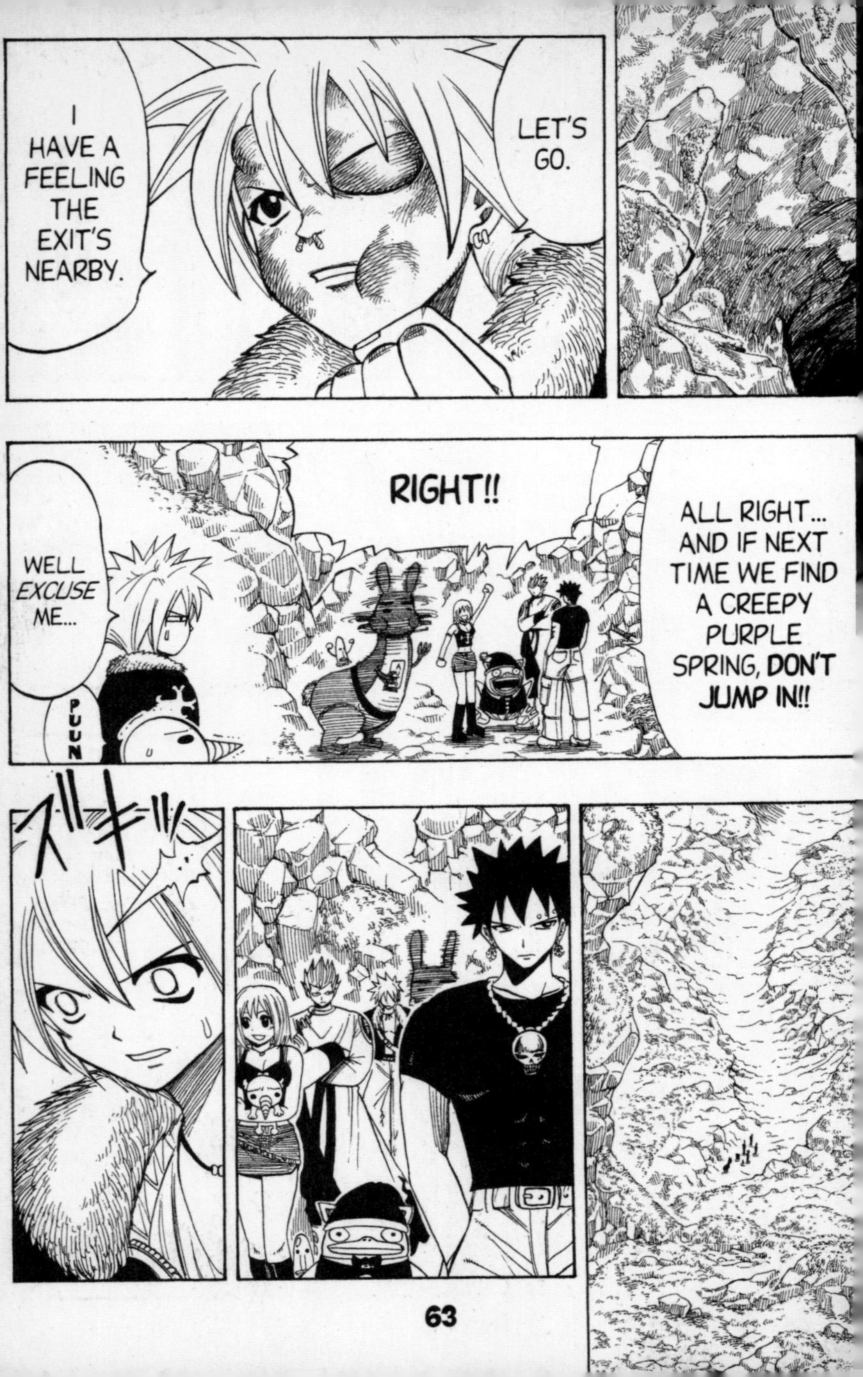
LET'S GO.
I HAVE A FEELING THE EXIT'S NEARBY.
ALL RIGHT... AND IF NEXT TIME WE FIND A CREEPY PURPLE SPRING, **DON'T JUMP IN!!**
RIGHT!!
WELL *EXCUSE* ME...
PUUN

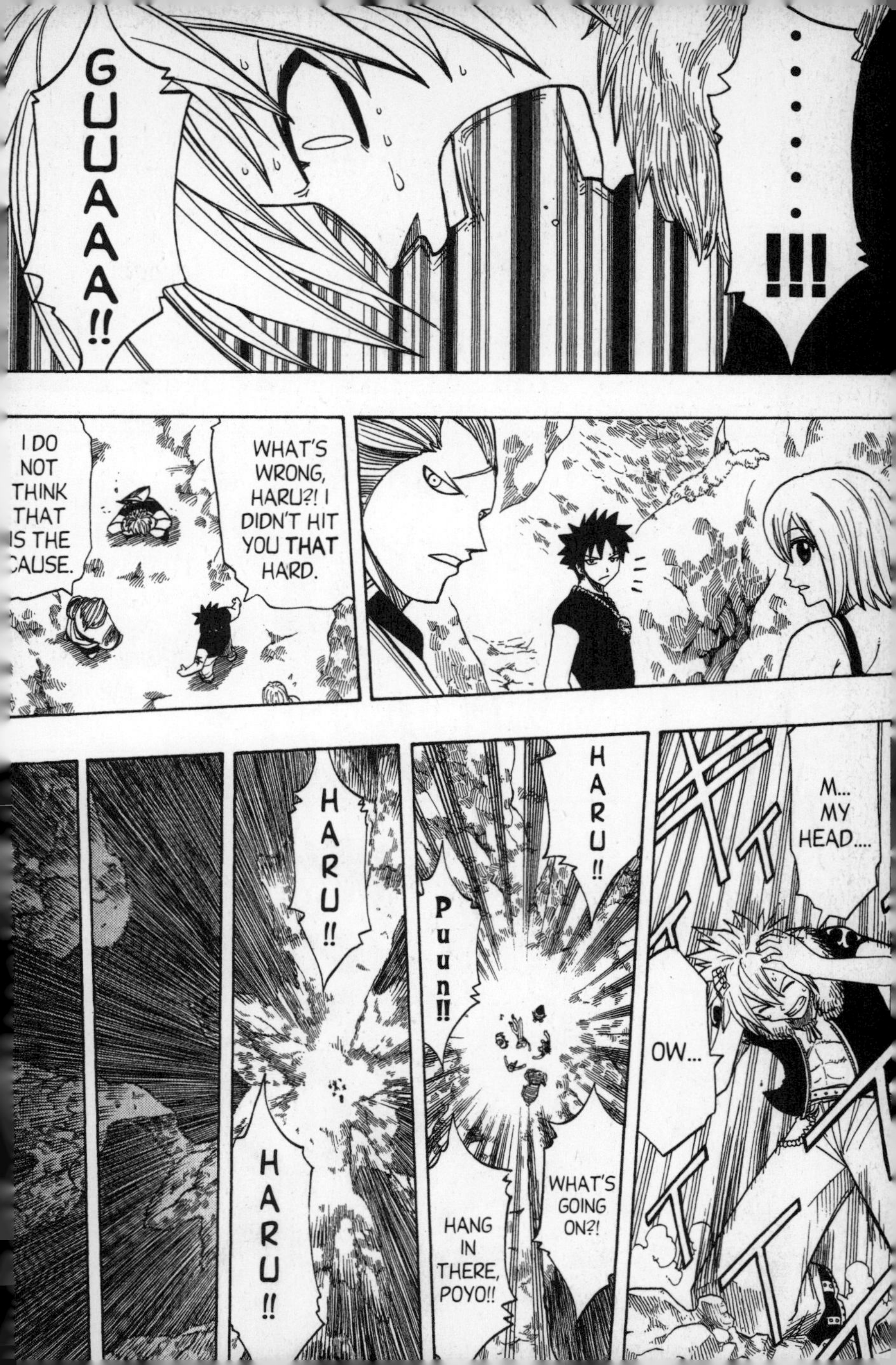
......!!!
GUUAAAA!!
WHAT'S WRONG, HARU?! I DIDN'T HIT YOU THAT HARD.
I DO NOT THINK THAT IS THE CAUSE.
M... MY HEAD...
OW...
HARU!!
Puun!!
WHAT'S GOING ON?!
HANG IN THERE, POYO!!
HARU!!
HARU!!

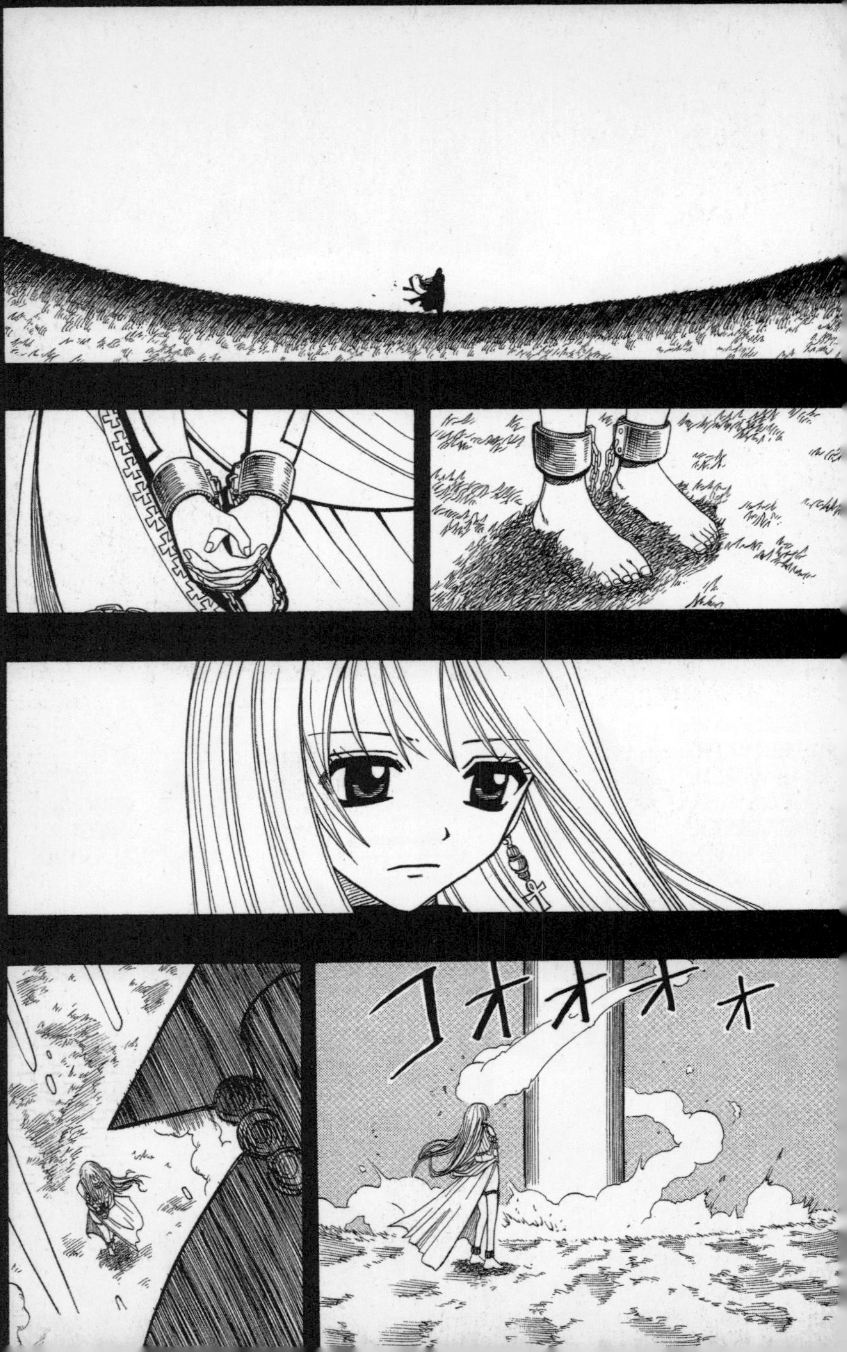
コオオオォ

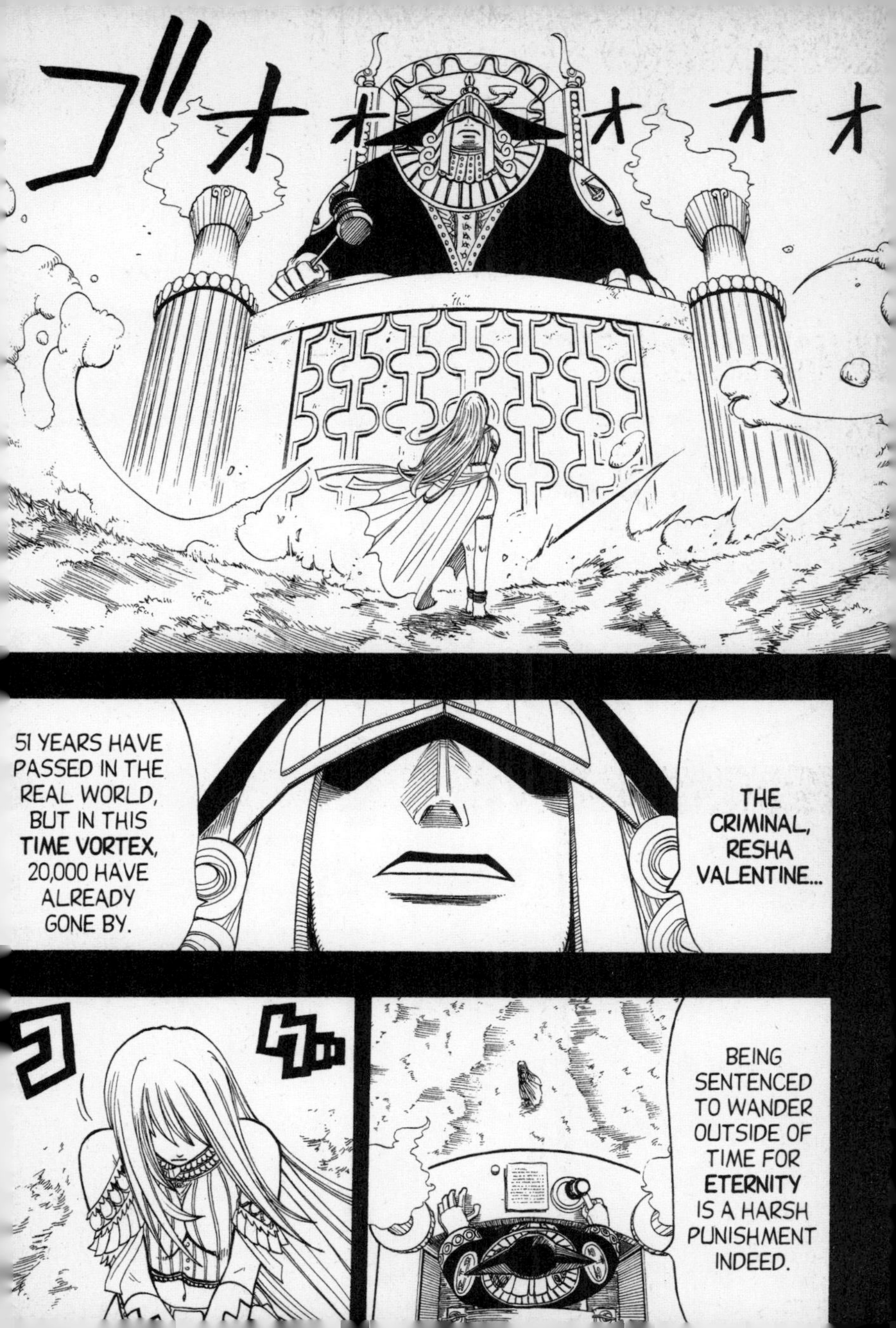
ゴオォオオオ
THE CRIMINAL, RESHA VALENTINE...
51 YEARS HAVE PASSED IN THE REAL WORLD, BUT IN THIS TIME VORTEX, 20,000 HAVE ALREADY GONE BY.
BEING SENTENCED TO WANDER OUTSIDE OF TIME FOR ETERNITY IS A HARSH PUNISHMENT INDEED.

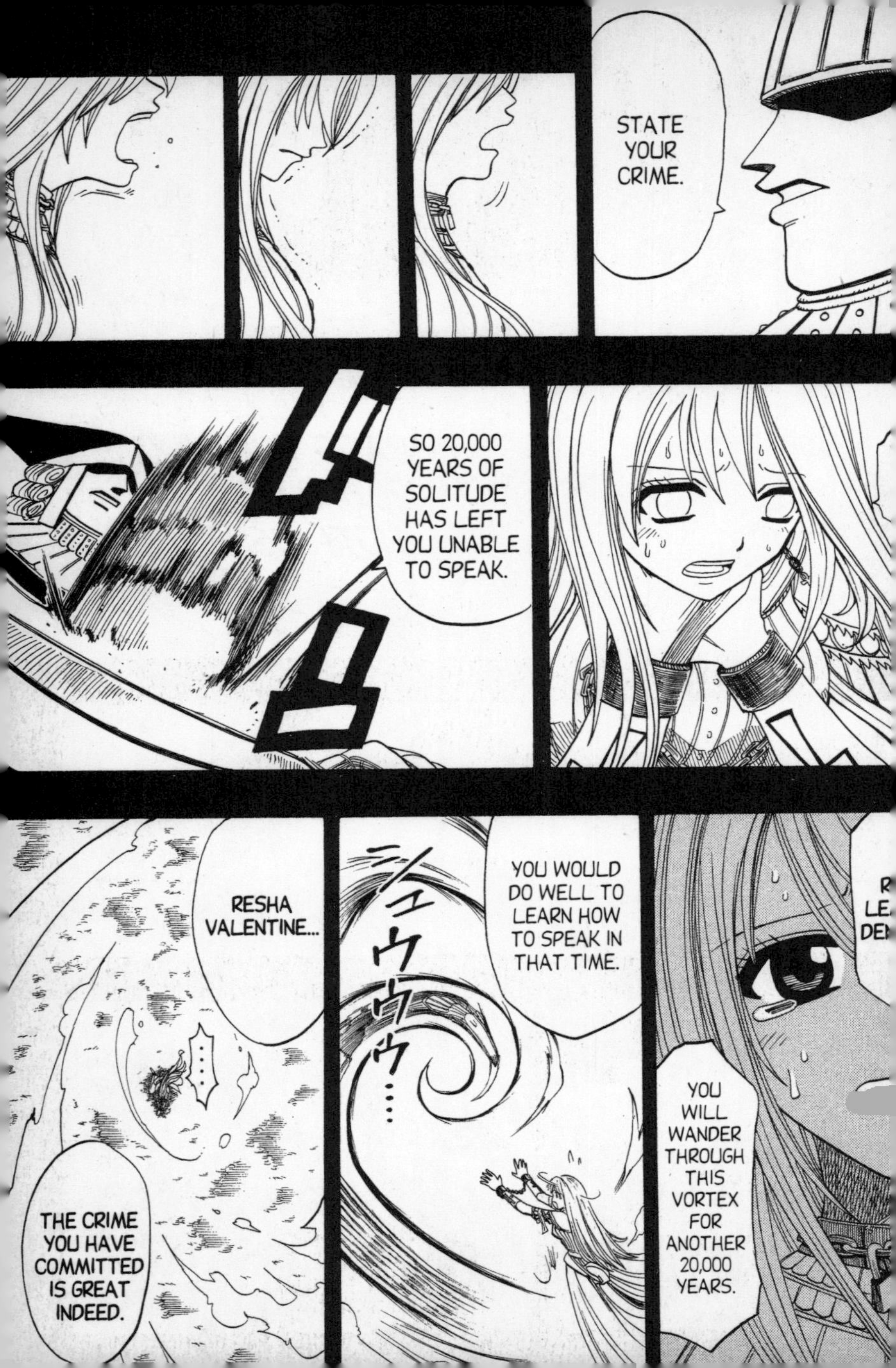
STATE YOUR CRIME.
SO 20,000 YEARS OF SOLITUDE HAS LEFT YOU UNABLE TO SPEAK.
YOU WILL WANDER THROUGH THIS VORTEX FOR ANOTHER 20,000 YEARS.
YOU WOULD DO WELL TO LEARN HOW TO SPEAK IN THAT TIME.
シュウウウ……
RESHA VALENTINE...
……
THE CRIME YOU HAVE COMMITTED IS GREAT INDEED.

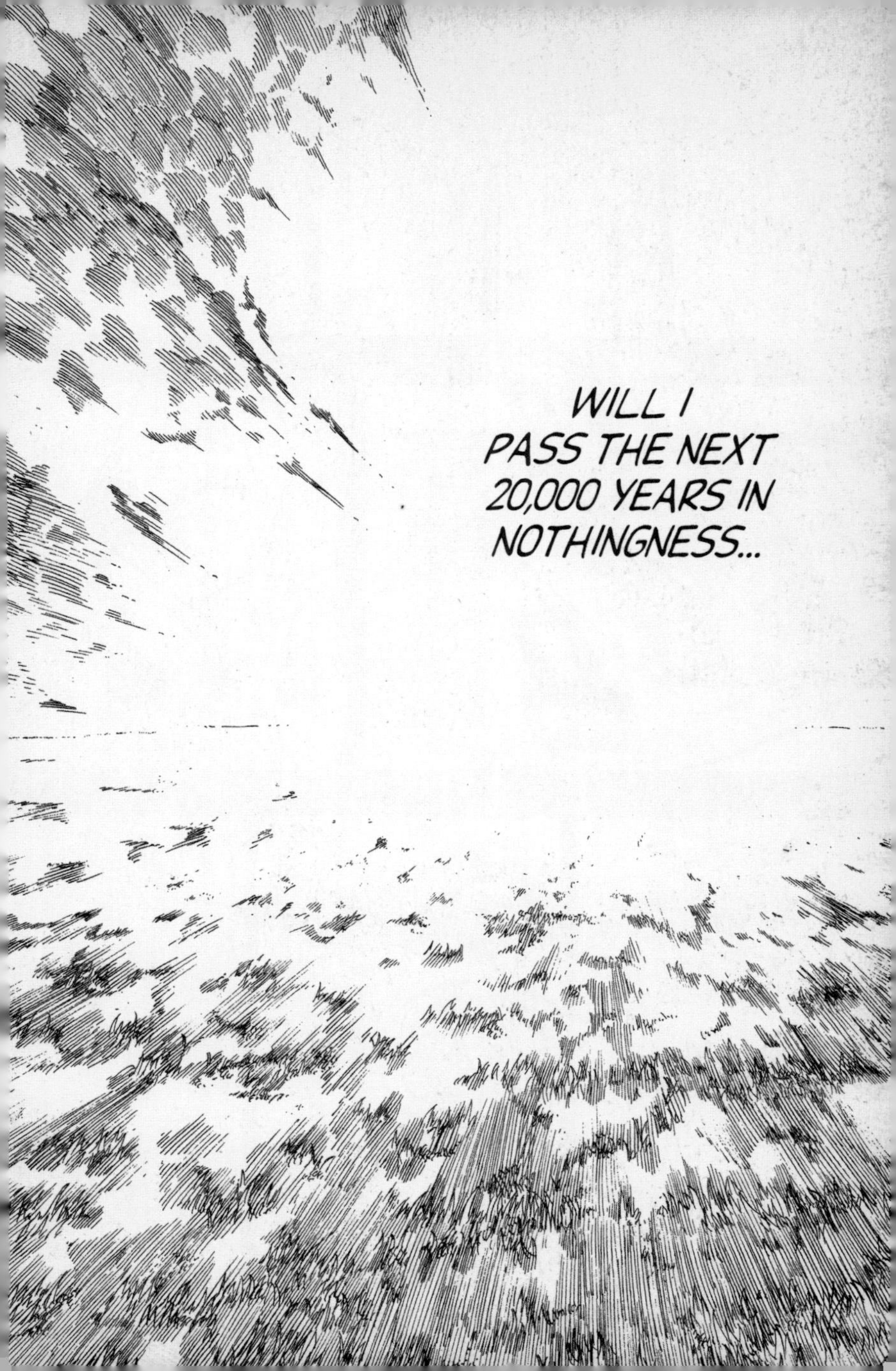
WILL I PASS THE NEXT 20,000 YEARS IN NOTHINGNESS...

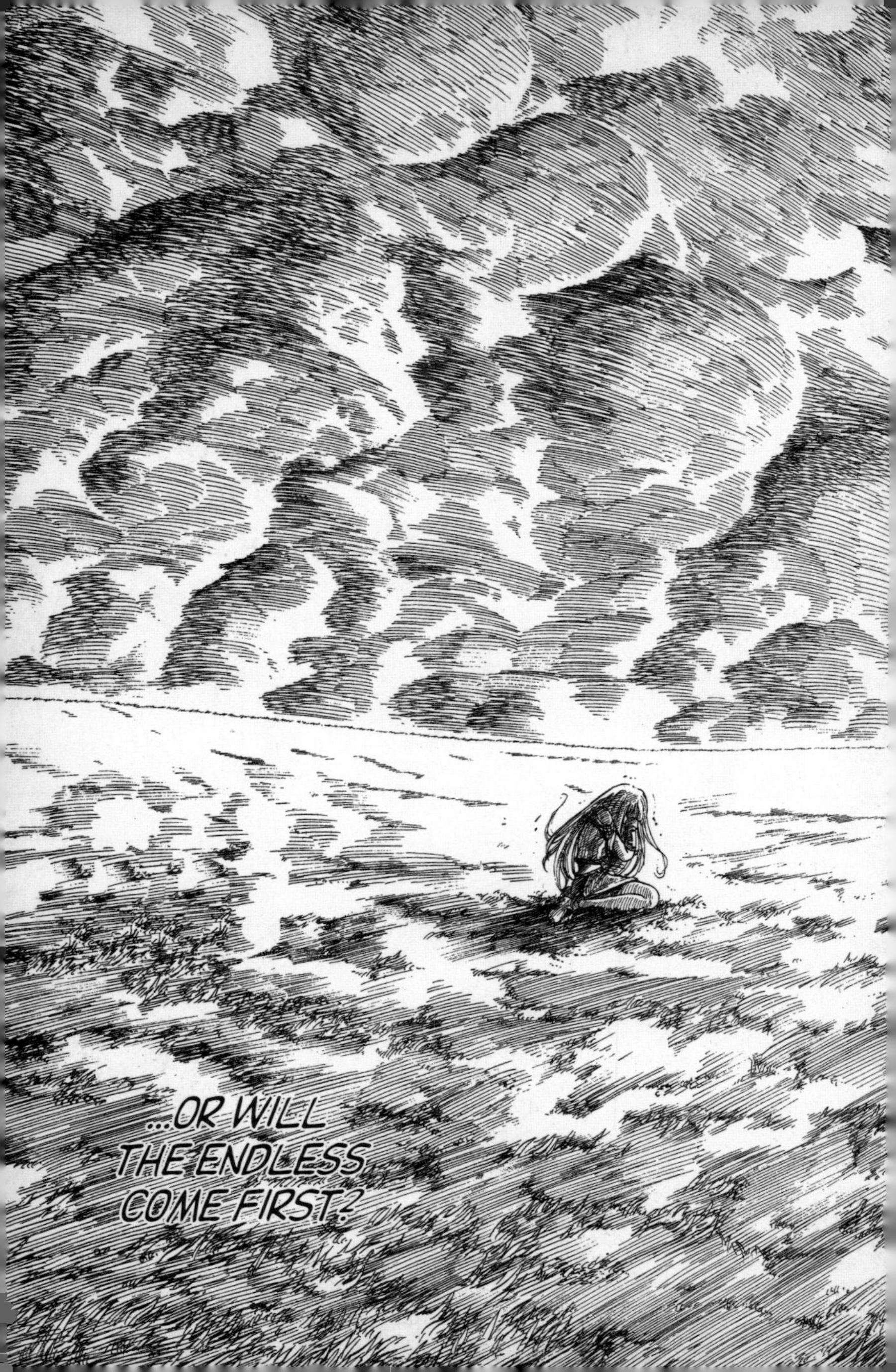
...OR WILL THE ENDLESS COME FIRST?

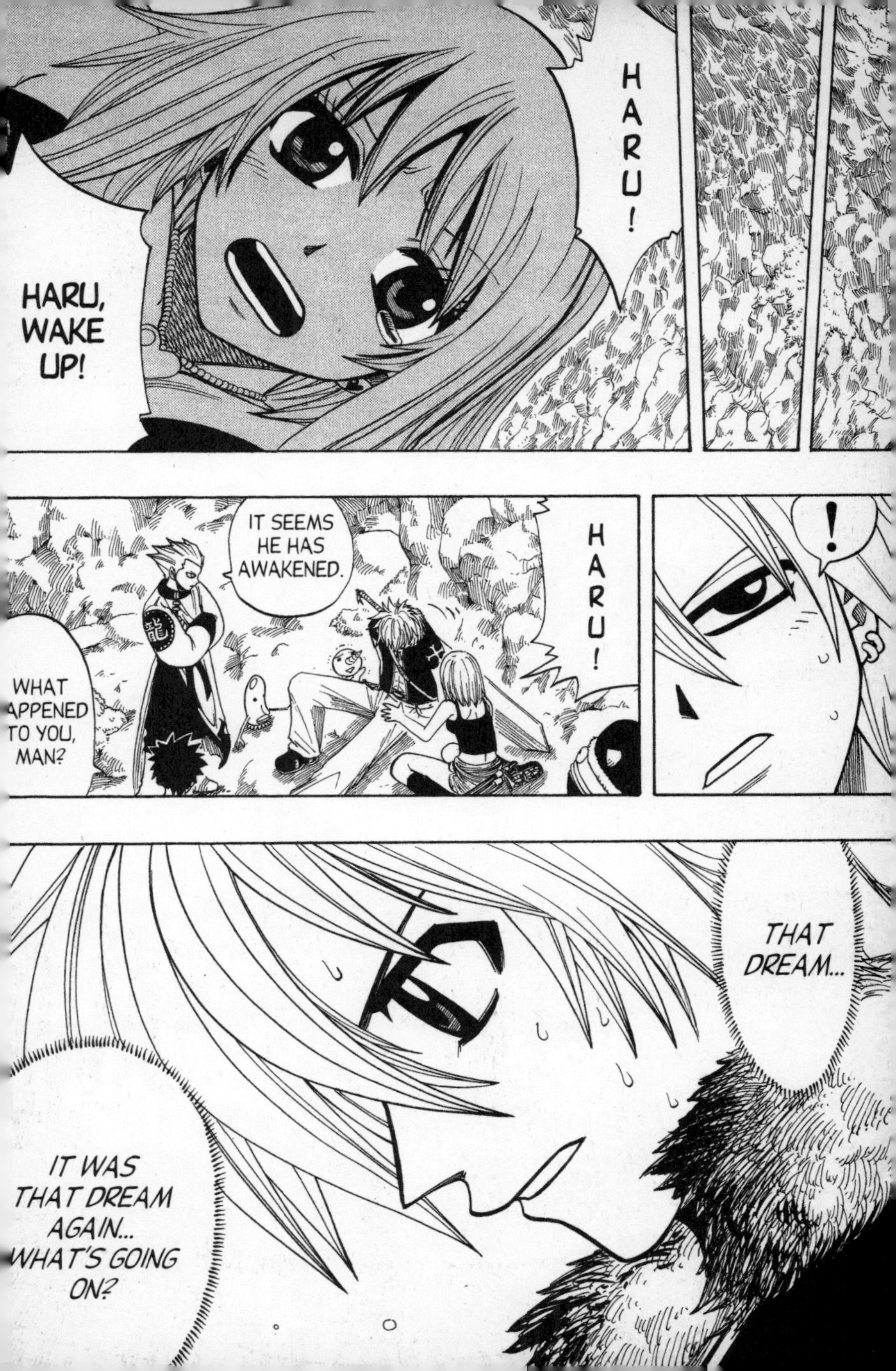
HARU!
HARU, WAKE UP!
!
HARU!
IT SEEMS HE HAS AWAKENED.
WHAT APPENED TO YOU, MAN?
THAT DREAM...
IT WAS THAT DREAM AGAIN... WHAT'S GOING ON?

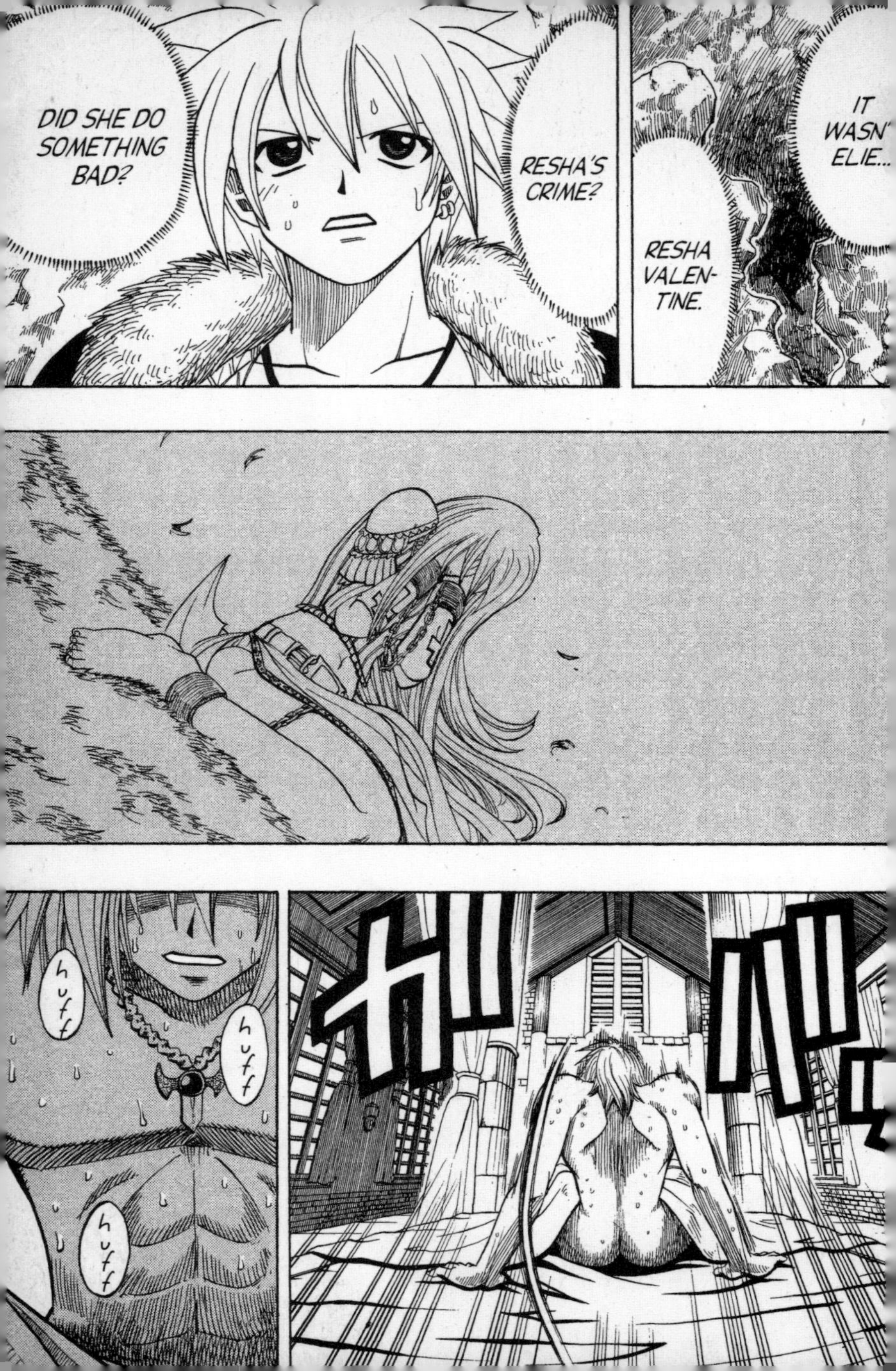

IT WASN' ELIE...
RESHA VALEN-TINE.
RESHA'S CRIME?
DID SHE DO SOMETHING BAD?
huff
huff
huff

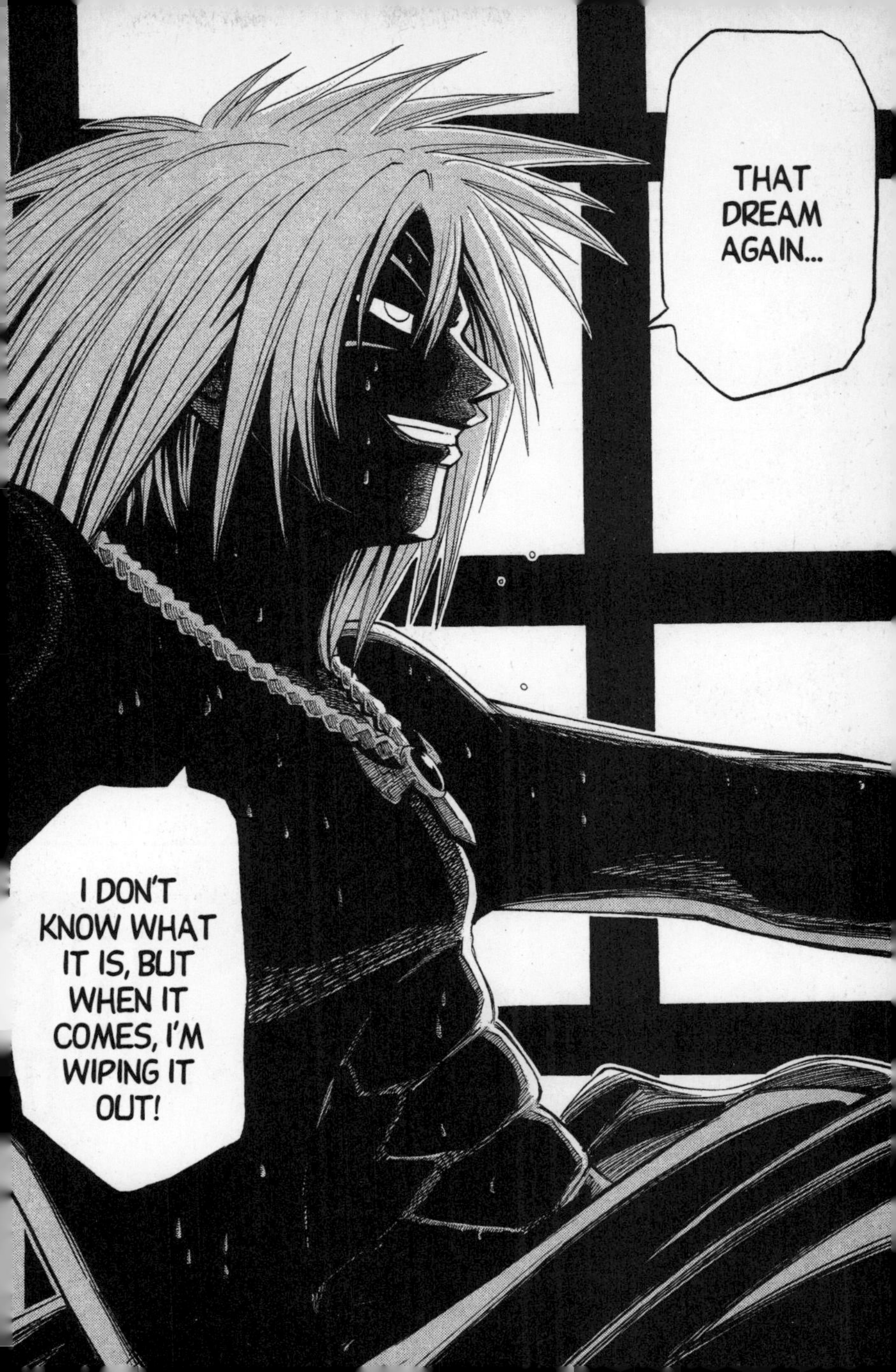
THAT DREAM AGAIN...
I DON'T KNOW WHAT IT IS, BUT WHEN IT COMES, I'M WIPING IT OUT!

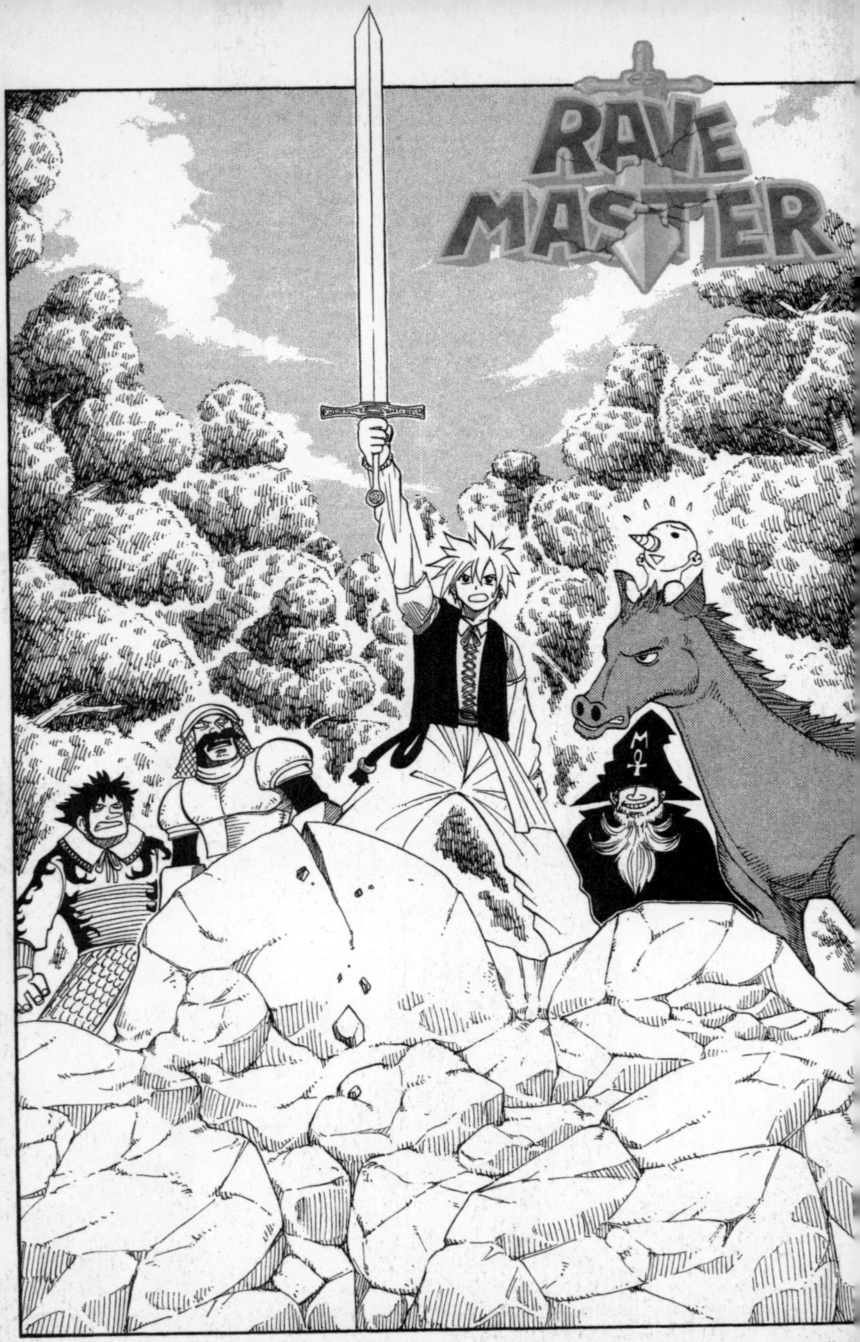
RAVE MASTER

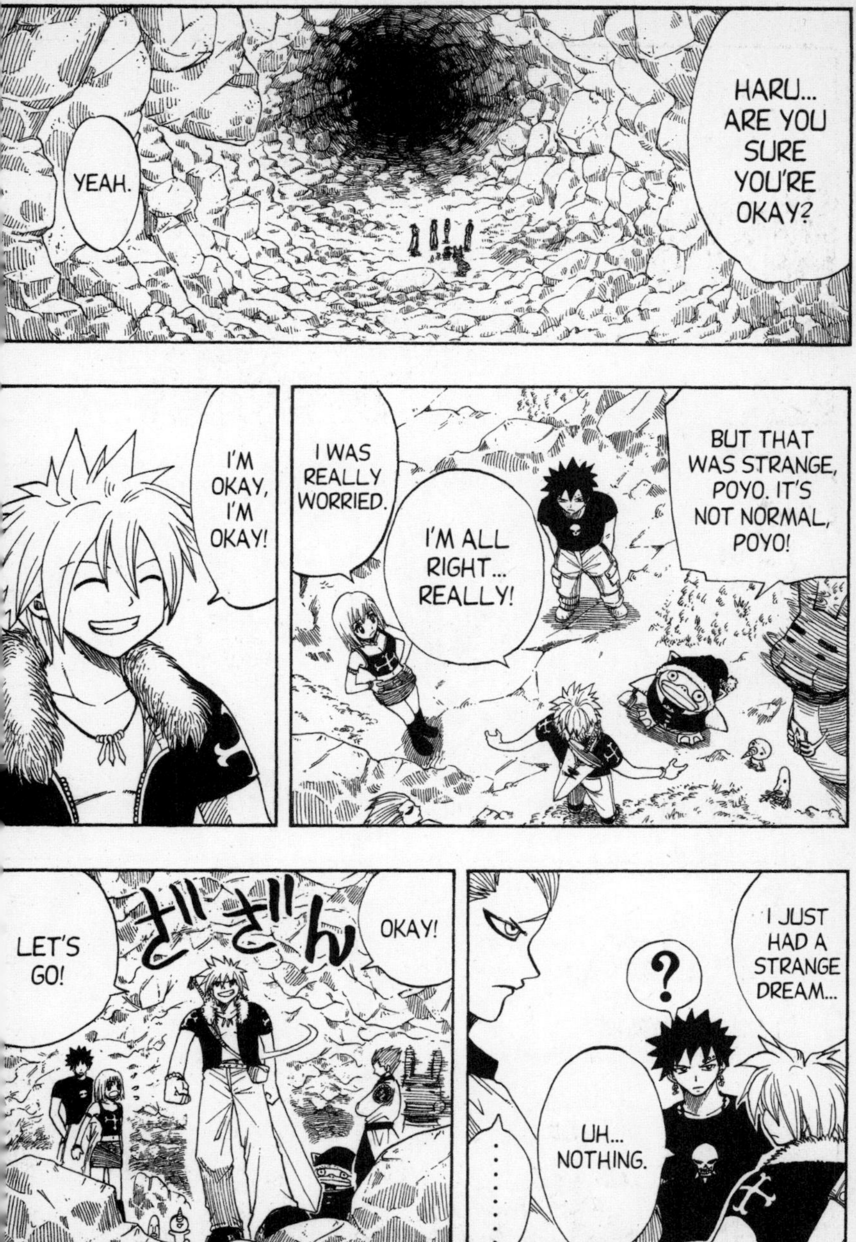
HARU... ARE YOU SURE YOU'RE OKAY?
YEAH.
BUT THAT WAS STRANGE, POYO. IT'S NOT NORMAL, POYO!
I WAS REALLY WORRIED.
I'M ALL RIGHT... REALLY!
I'M OKAY, I'M OKAY!
I JUST HAD A STRANGE DREAM...
?
UH... NOTHING.
......
OKAY!
LET'S GO!

RAVE:101 ✠ TO THE NEVER-ENDING FUTURE

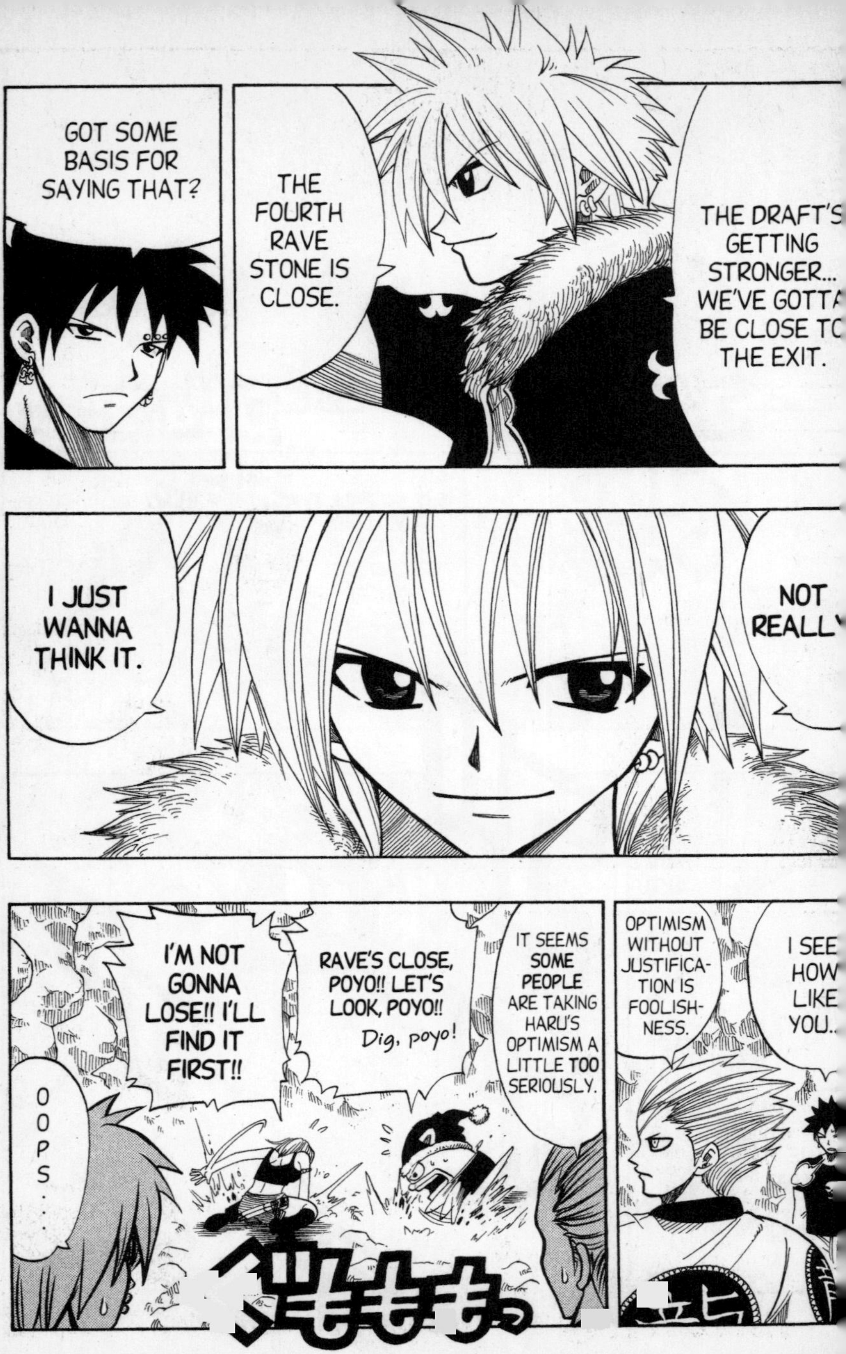
THE DRAFT'S GETTING STRONGER... WE'VE GOTTA BE CLOSE TO THE EXIT.
THE FOURTH RAVE STONE IS CLOSE.
GOT SOME BASIS FOR SAYING THAT?
NOT REALLY
I JUST WANNA THINK IT.
I SEE HOW LIKE YOU...
OPTIMISM WITHOUT JUSTIFICATION IS FOOLISHNESS.
IT SEEMS SOME PEOPLE ARE TAKING HARU'S OPTIMISM A LITTLE TOO SERIOUSLY.
RAVE'S CLOSE, POYO!! LET'S LOOK, POYO!!
Dig, poyo!
I'M NOT GONNA LOSE!! I'LL FIND IT FIRST!!
OOPS...

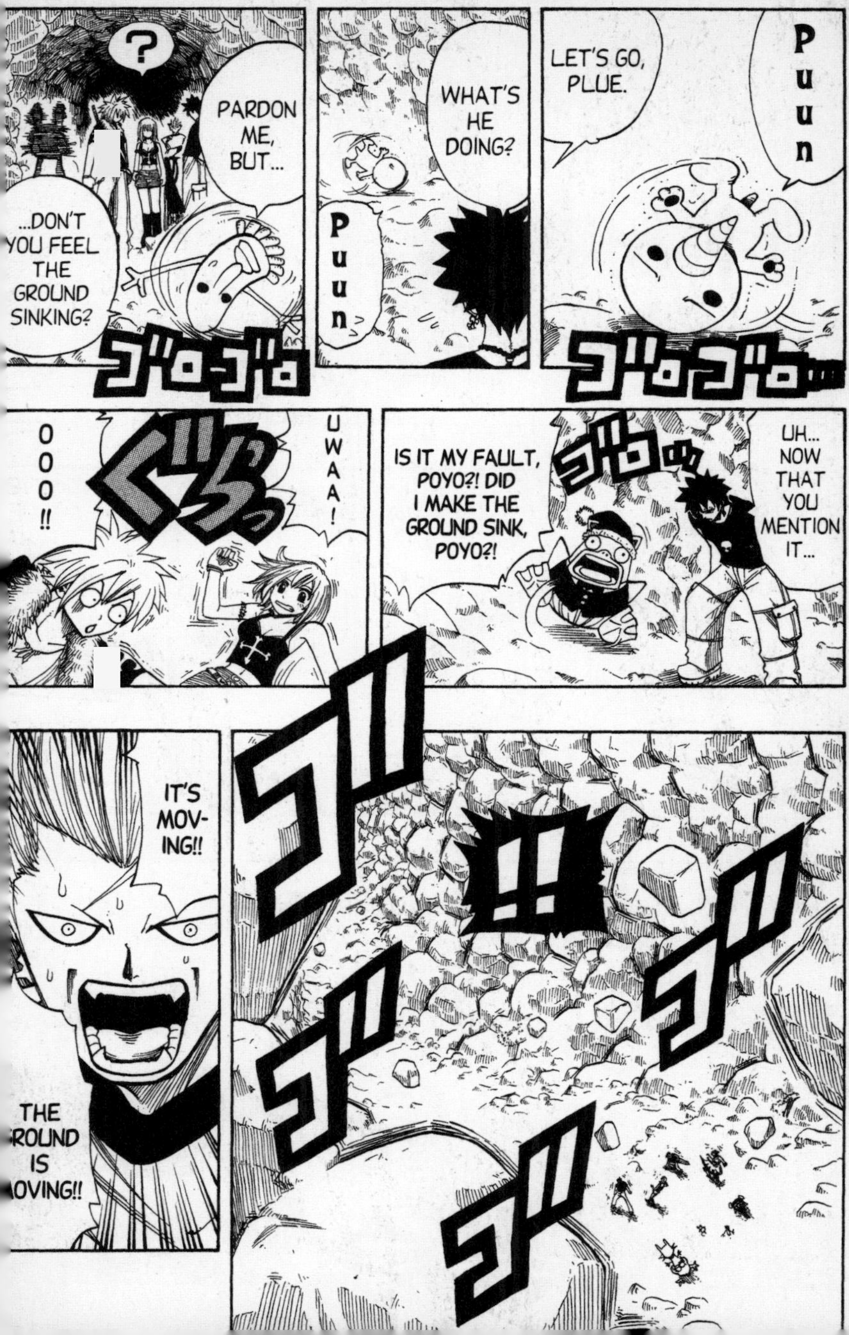
Puun
LET'S GO, PLUE.
WHAT'S HE DOING?
Puun
?
PARDON ME, BUT...
...DON'T YOU FEEL THE GROUND SINKING?
UH... NOW THAT YOU MENTION IT...
IS IT MY FAULT, POYO?! DID I MAKE THE GROUND SINK, POYO?!
UWAAA!
OOOO!!
!!
IT'S MOVING!!
THE ROUND IS OVING!!

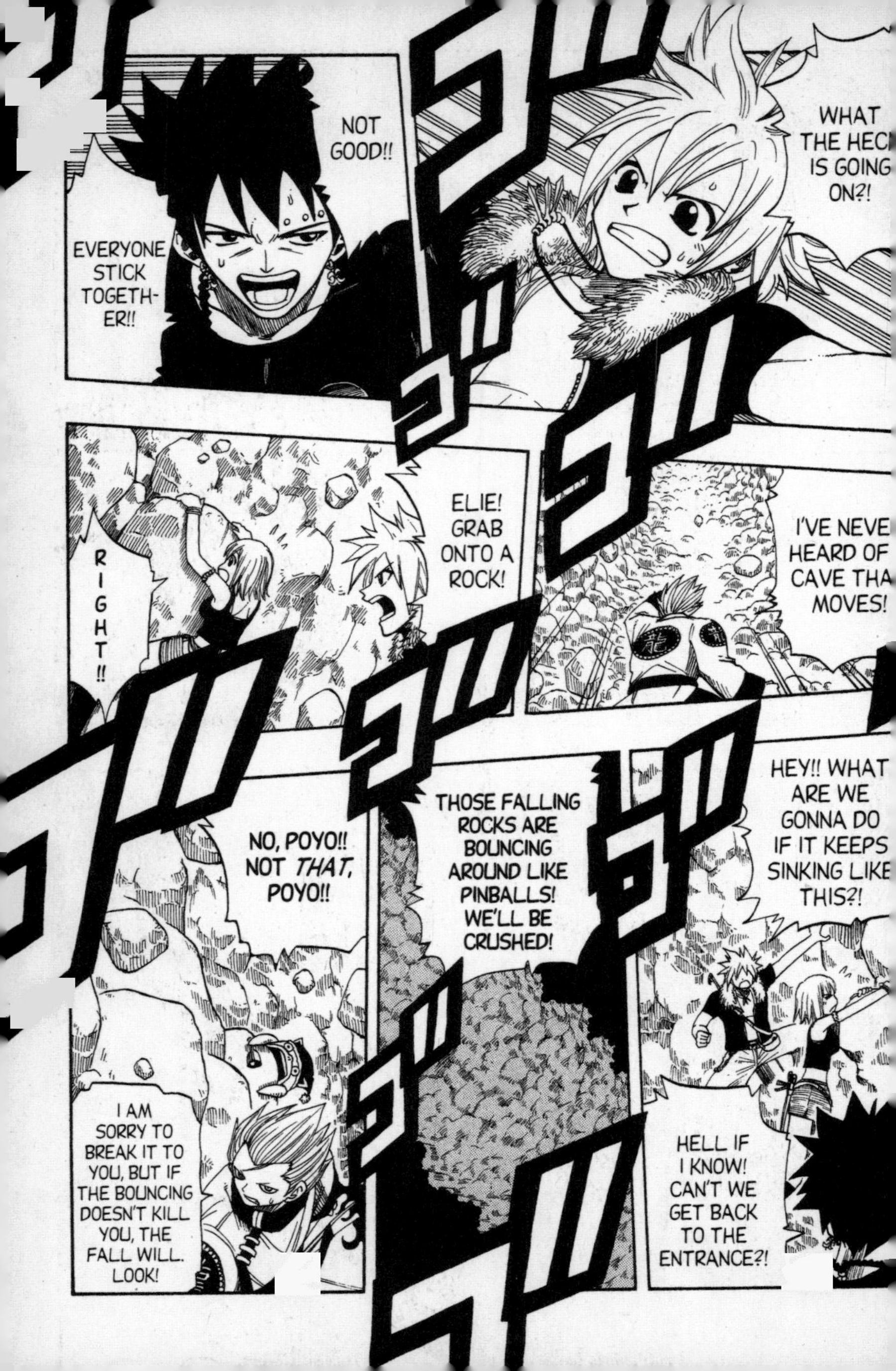
WHAT THE HEC IS GOING ON?!
NOT GOOD!!
EVERYONE STICK TOGETH-ER!!
I'VE NEVE HEARD OF CAVE THA MOVES!
ELIE! GRAB ONTO A ROCK!
RIGHT!!
HEY!! WHAT ARE WE GONNA DO IF IT KEEPS SINKING LIKE THIS?!
HELL IF I KNOW! CAN'T WE GET BACK TO THE ENTRANCE?!
THOSE FALLING ROCKS ARE BOUNCING AROUND LIKE PINBALLS! WE'LL BE CRUSHED!
NO, POYO!! NOT *THAT*, POYO!!
I AM SORRY TO BREAK IT TO YOU, BUT IF THE BOUNCING DOESN'T KILL YOU, THE FALL WILL. LOOK!

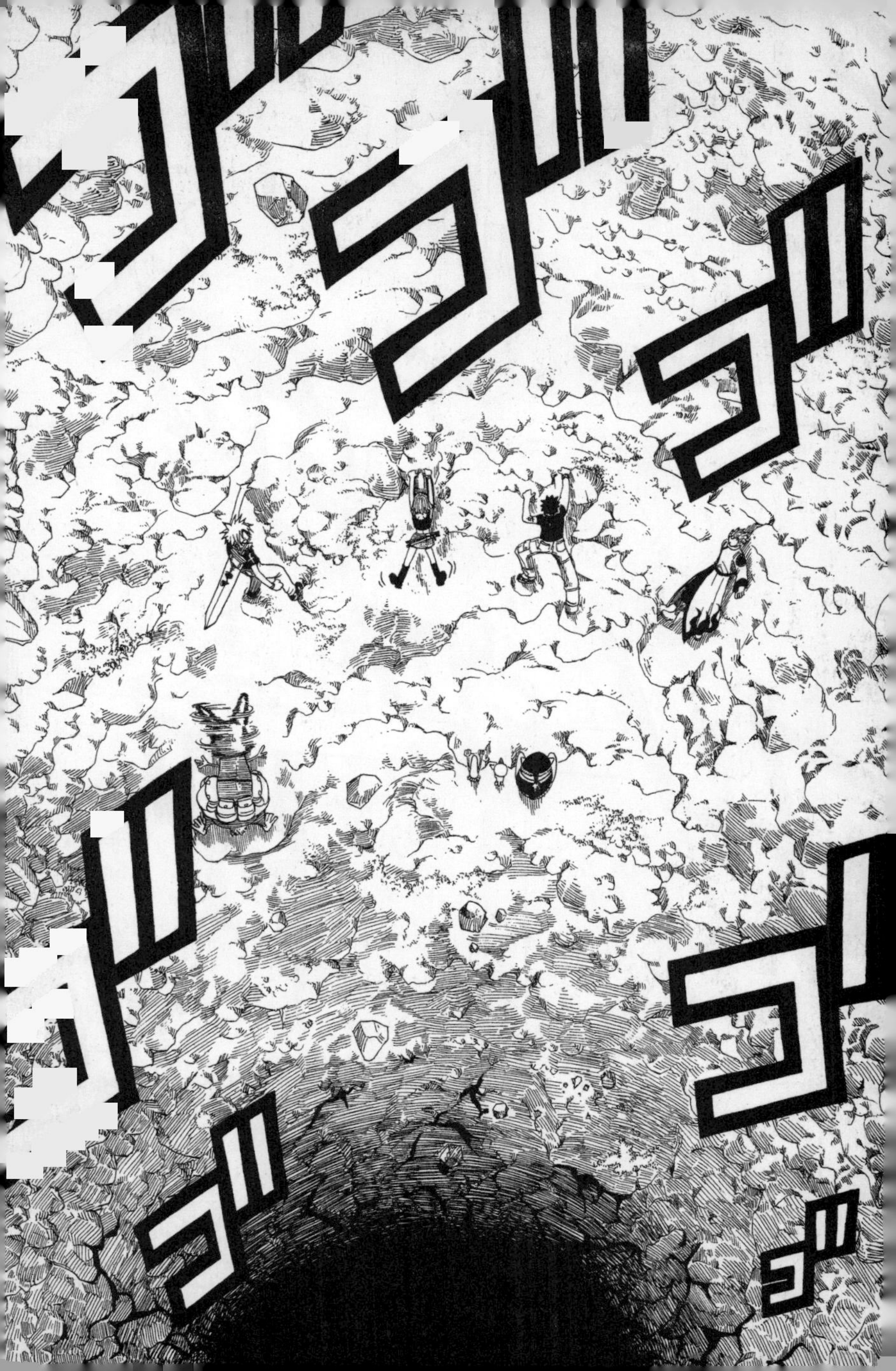
ゴゴゴ
ゴゴゴゴ

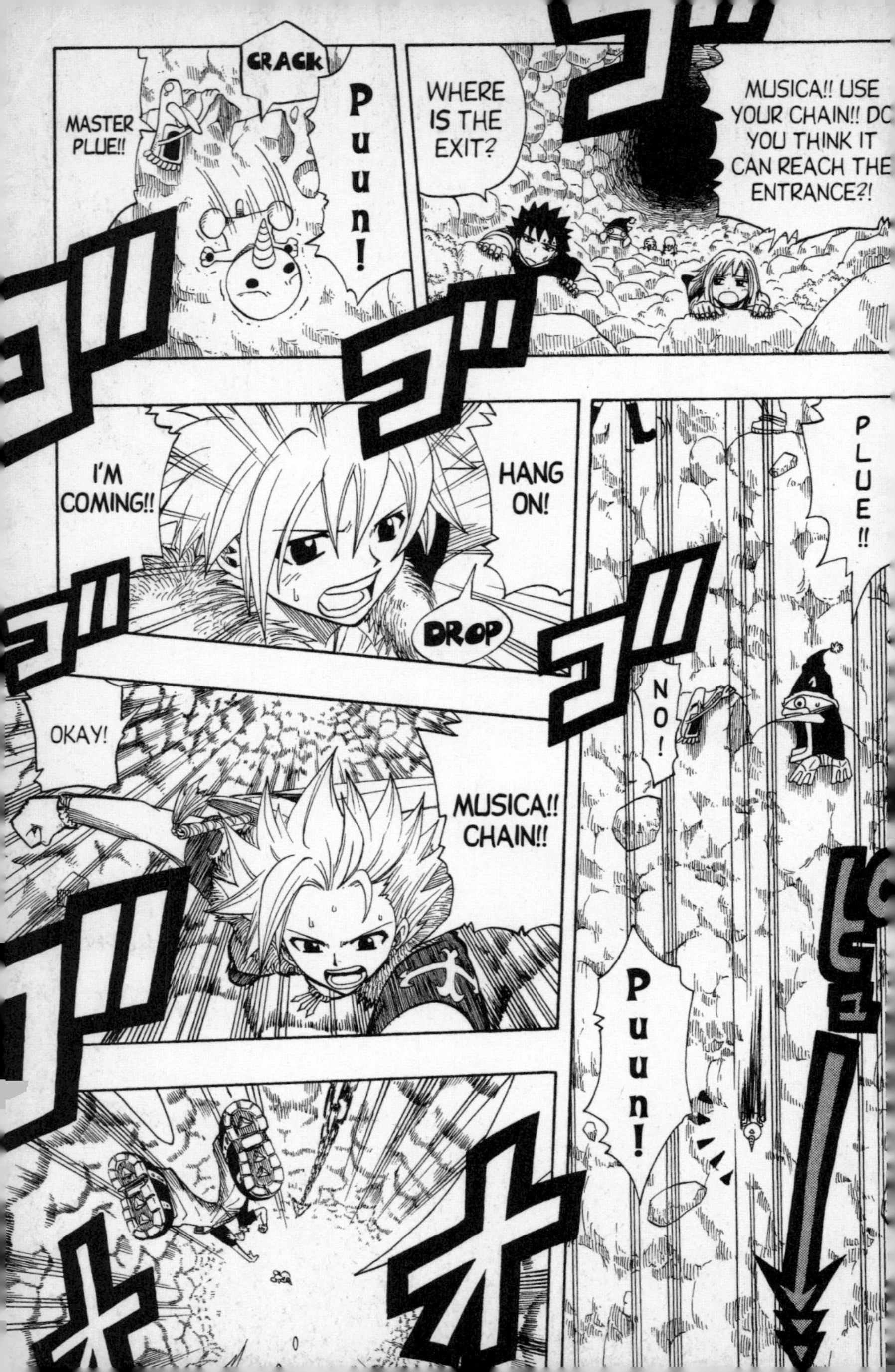
MUSICA!! USE YOUR CHAIN!! DO YOU THINK IT CAN REACH THE ENTRANCE?!
WHERE IS THE EXIT?
CRACK
Puun!
MASTER PLUE!!
PLUE!!
NO!
Puun!
HANG ON!
I'M COMING!!
DROP
MUSICA!! CHAIN!!
OKAY!

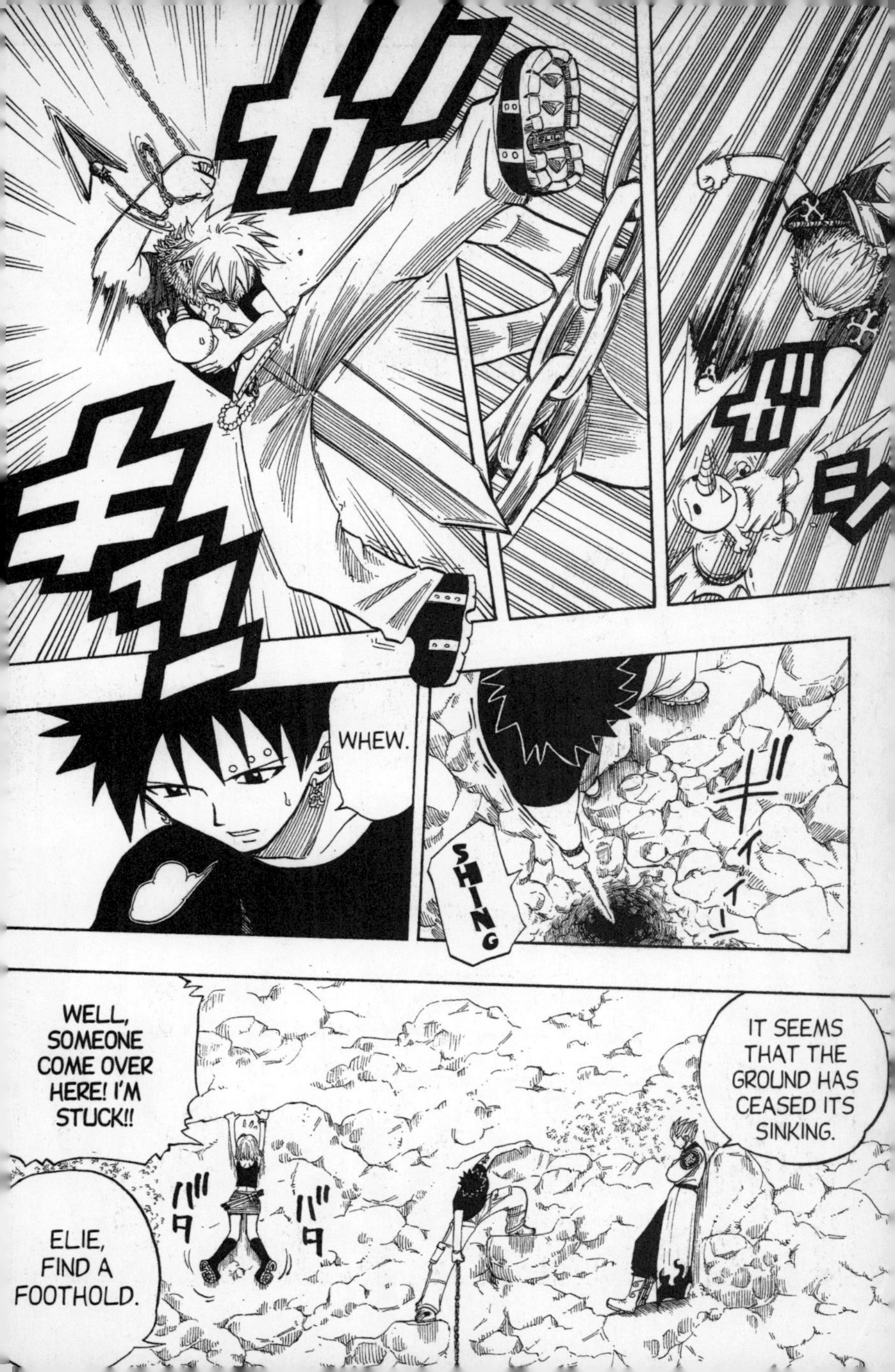
SHING
WHEW.
IT SEEMS THAT THE GROUND HAS CEASED ITS SINKING.
WELL, SOMEONE COME OVER HERE! I'M STUCK!!
ELIE, FIND A FOOTHOLD.

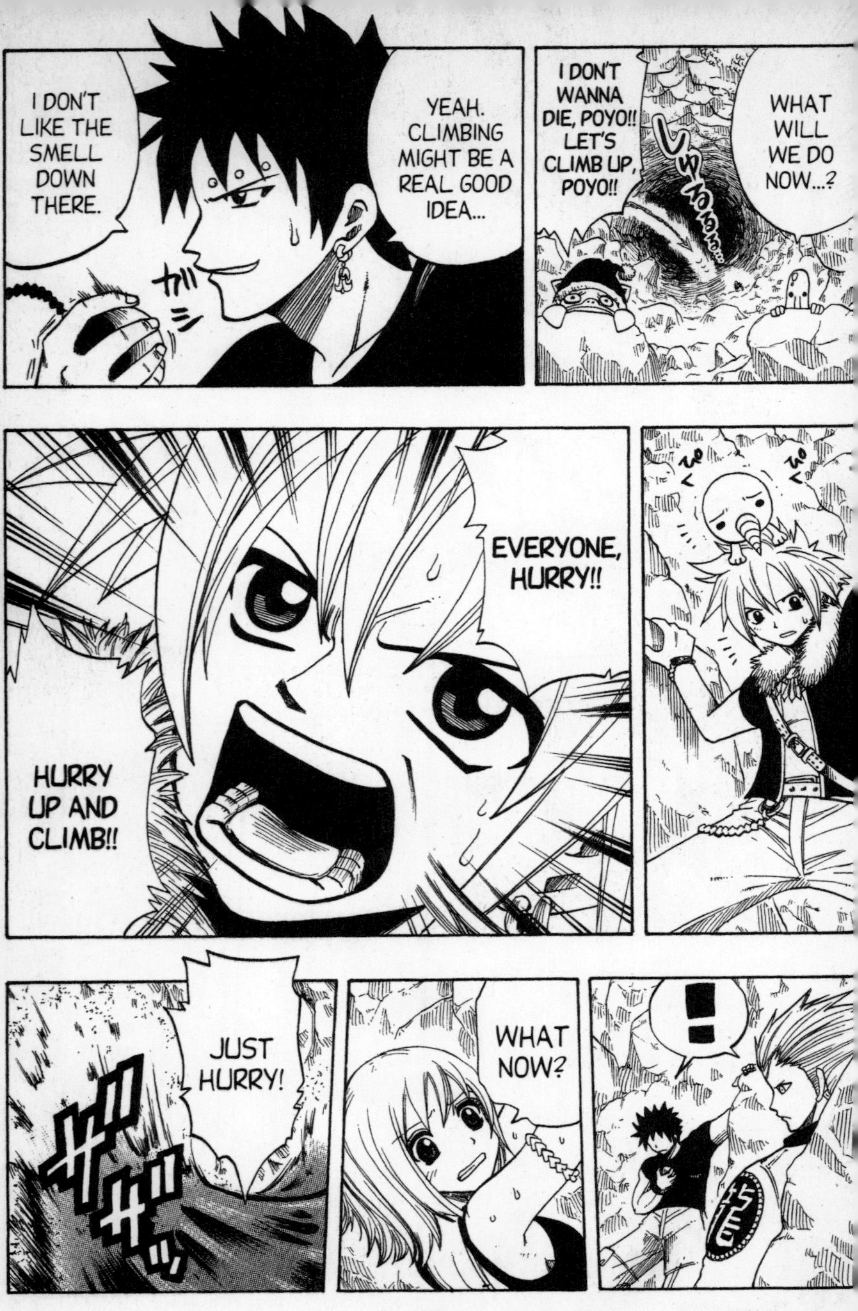
WHAT WILL WE DO NOW...?
I DON'T WANNA DIE, POYO!! LET'S CLIMB UP, POYO!!
YEAH. CLIMBING MIGHT BE A REAL GOOD IDEA...
I DON'T LIKE THE SMELL DOWN THERE.
EVERYONE, HURRY!!
HURRY UP AND CLIMB!!
!
WHAT NOW?
JUST HURRY!

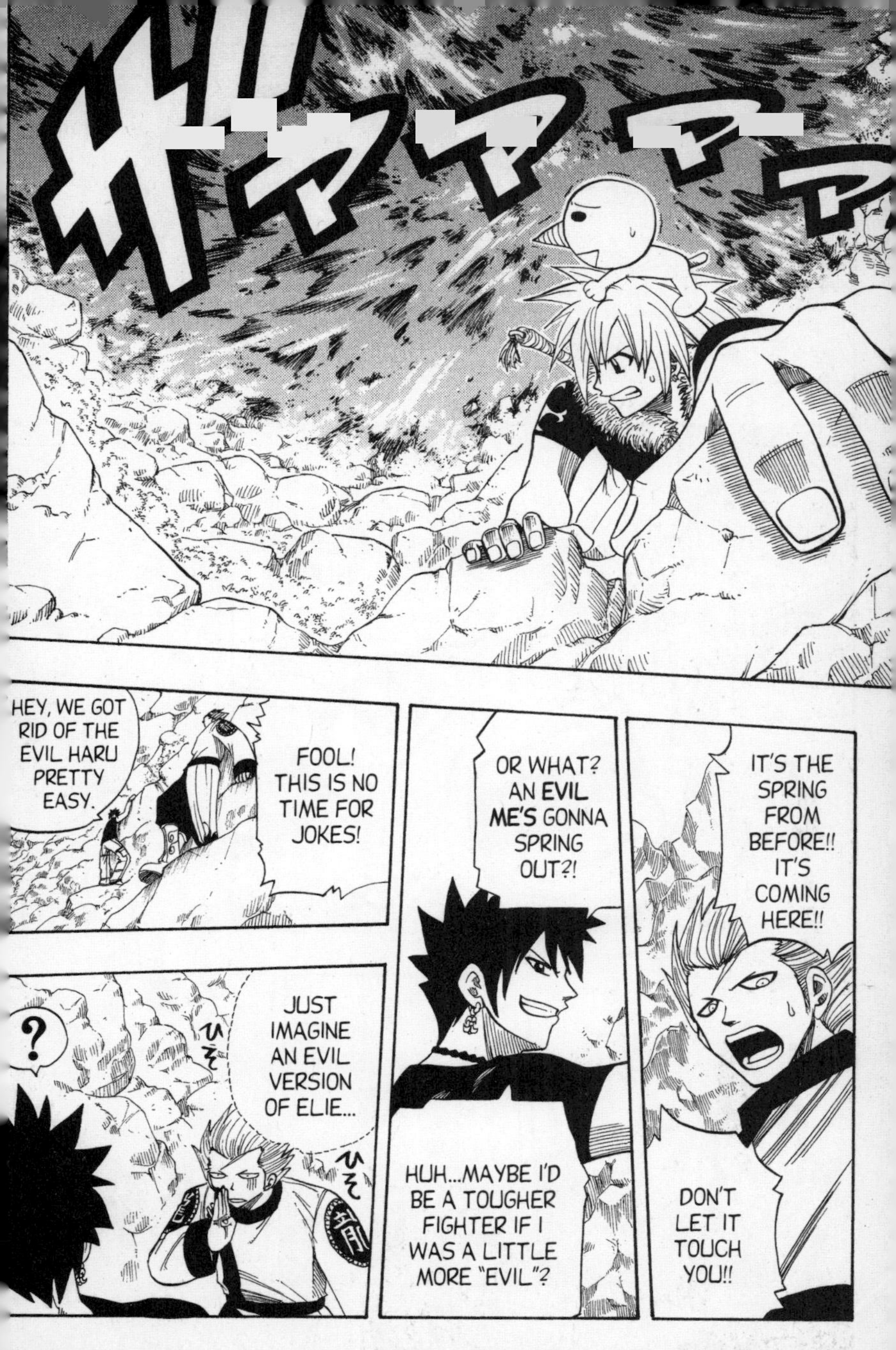
HEY, WE GOT RID OF THE EVIL HARU PRETTY EASY.
FOOL! THIS IS NO TIME FOR JOKES!
?
JUST IMAGINE AN EVIL VERSION OF ELIE...
ひそ
ひそ
OR WHAT? AN EVIL ME'S GONNA SPRING OUT?!
HUH...MAYBE I'D BE A TOUGHER FIGHTER IF I WAS A LITTLE MORE "EVIL"?
IT'S THE SPRING FROM BEFORE!! IT'S COMING HERE!!
DON'T LET IT TOUCH YOU!!

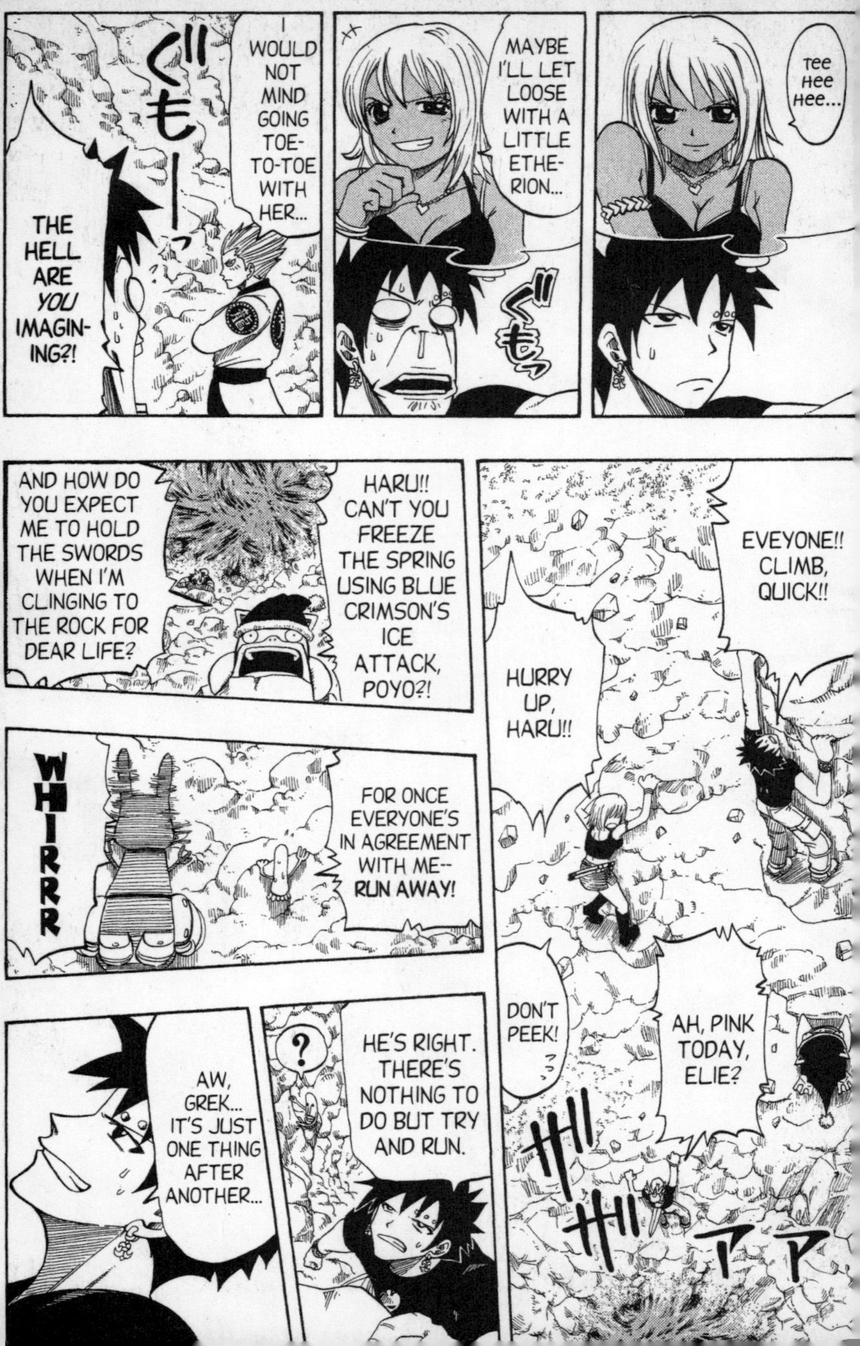
TEE HEE HEE...
MAYBE I'LL LET LOOSE WITH A LITTLE ETHERION...
I WOULD NOT MIND GOING TOE-TO-TOE WITH HER...
THE HELL ARE YOU IMAGINING?!
EVEYONE!! CLIMB, QUICK!!
HURRY UP, HARU!!
AH, PINK TODAY, ELIE?
DON'T PEEK!
HARU!! CAN'T YOU FREEZE THE SPRING USING BLUE CRIMSON'S ICE ATTACK, POYO?!
AND HOW DO YOU EXPECT ME TO HOLD THE SWORDS WHEN I'M CLINGING TO THE ROCK FOR DEAR LIFE?
FOR ONCE EVERYONE'S IN AGREEMENT WITH ME-- RUN AWAY!
WHIRRR
?
HE'S RIGHT. THERE'S NOTHING TO DO BUT TRY AND RUN.
AW, GREK... IT'S JUST ONE THING AFTER ANOTHER...

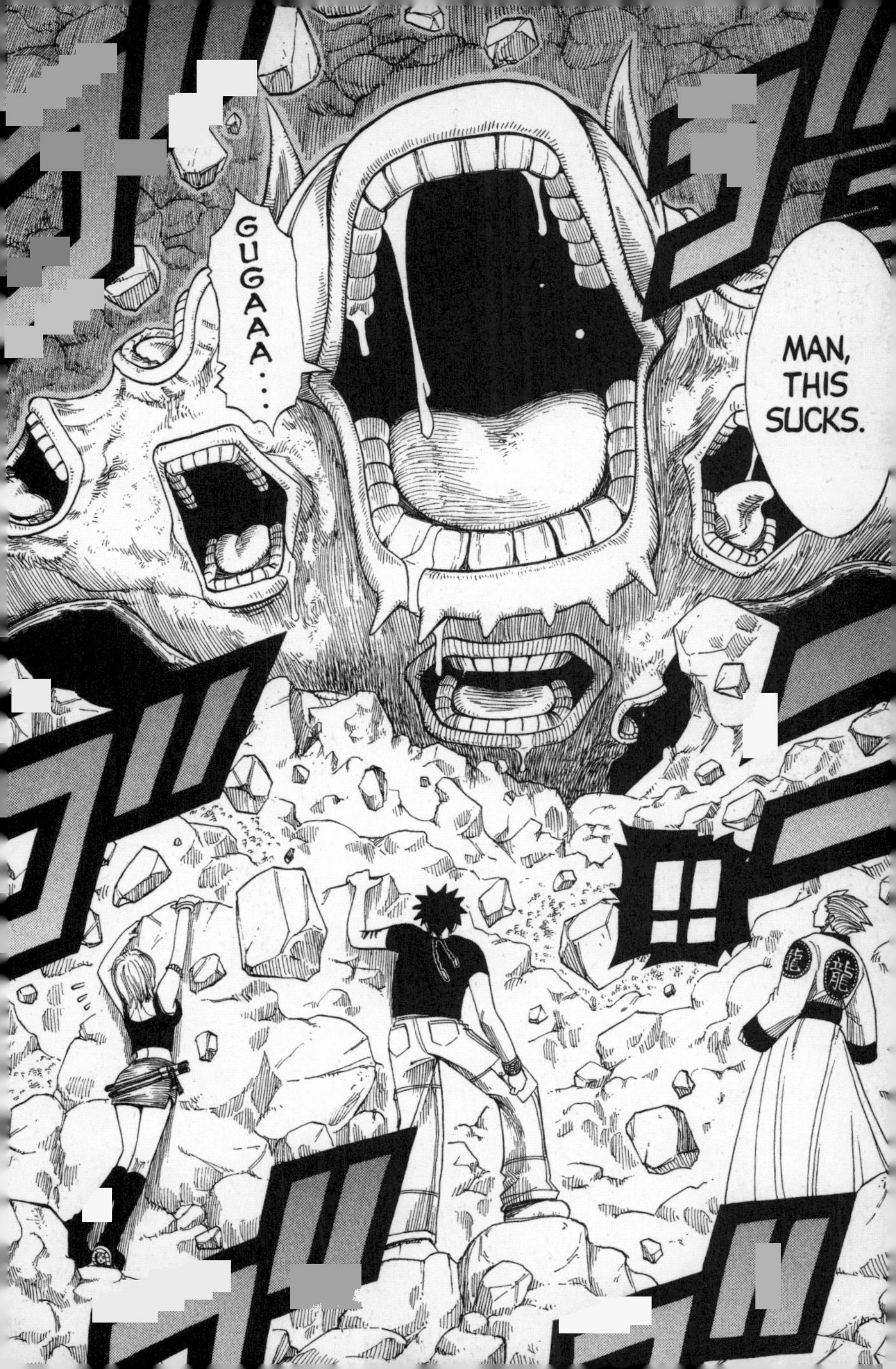
MAN, THIS SUCKS.
GUGAAA...
!!

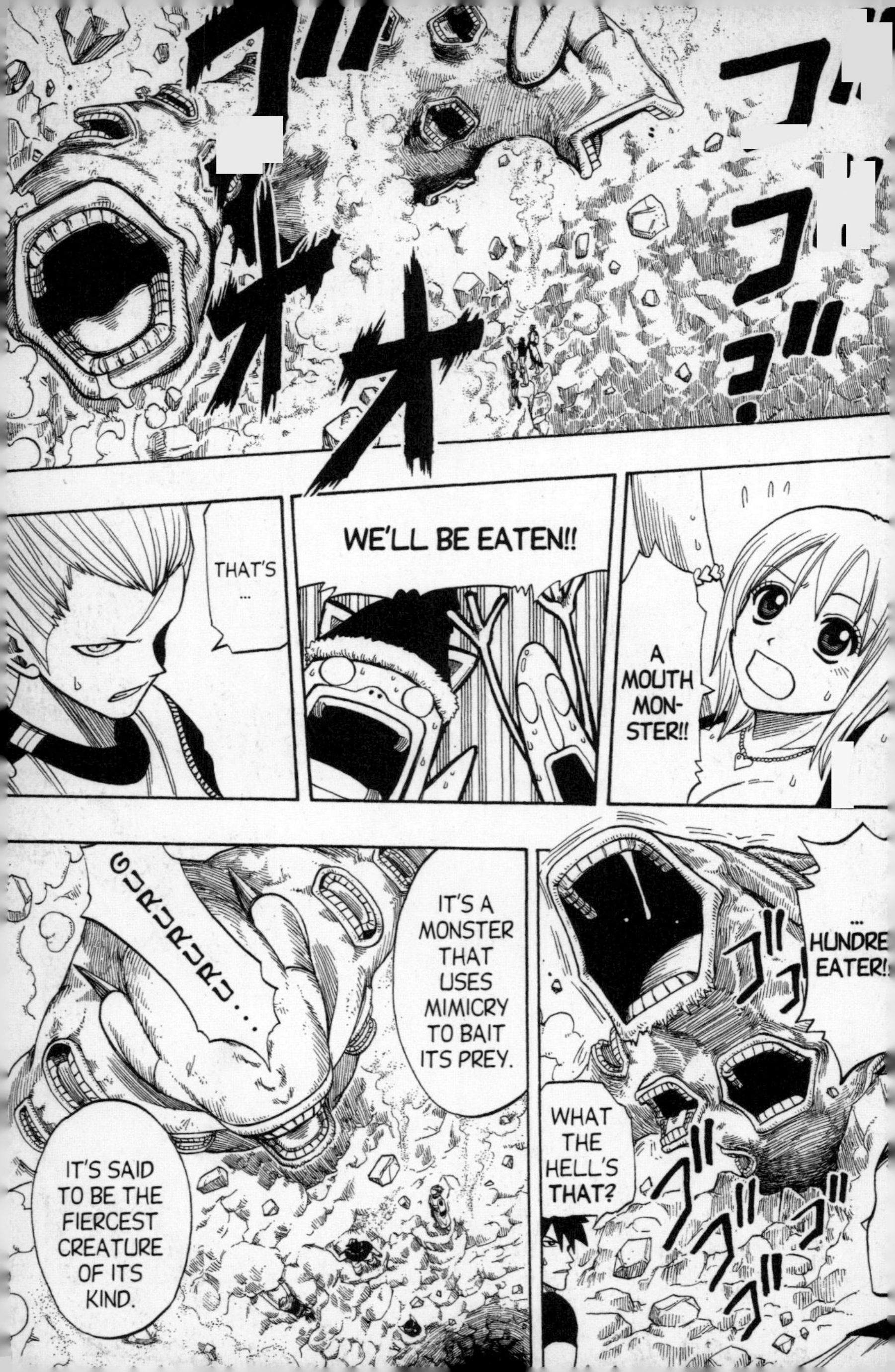
A MOUTH MONSTER!!
WE'LL BE EATEN!!
THAT'S ...
... HUNDRE EATER!!
WHAT THE HELL'S THAT?
IT'S A MONSTER THAT USES MIMICRY TO BAIT ITS PREY.
GURURURURU...
IT'S SAID TO BE THE FIERCEST CREATURE OF ITS KIND.

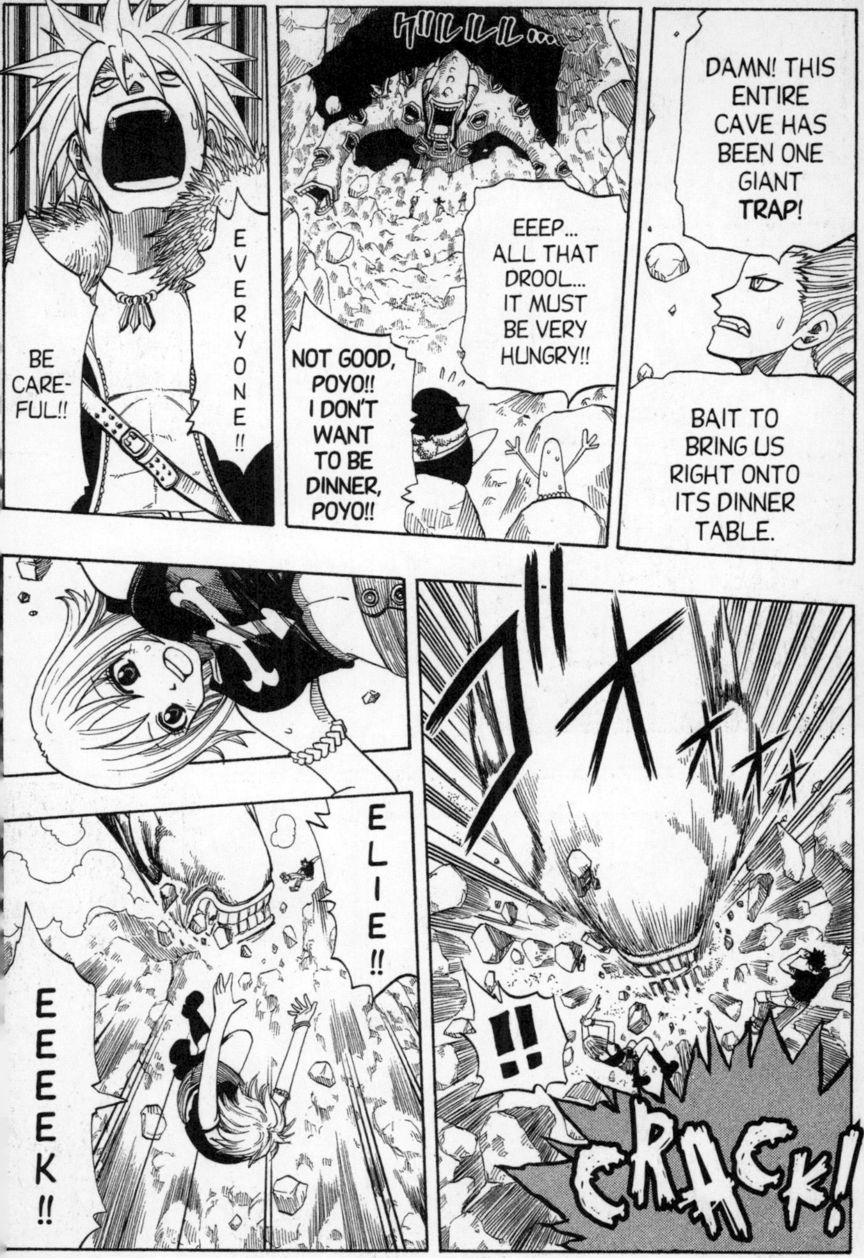
DAMN! THIS ENTIRE CAVE HAS BEEN ONE GIANT **TRAP!**
BAIT TO BRING US RIGHT ONTO ITS DINNER TABLE.
EEEP... ALL THAT DROOL... IT MUST BE VERY HUNGRY!!
NOT GOOD, POYO!! I DON'T WANT TO BE DINNER, POYO!!
EVERYONE!!
BE CAREFUL!!
!!
CRACK!
ELIE!!
EEEEEK!!

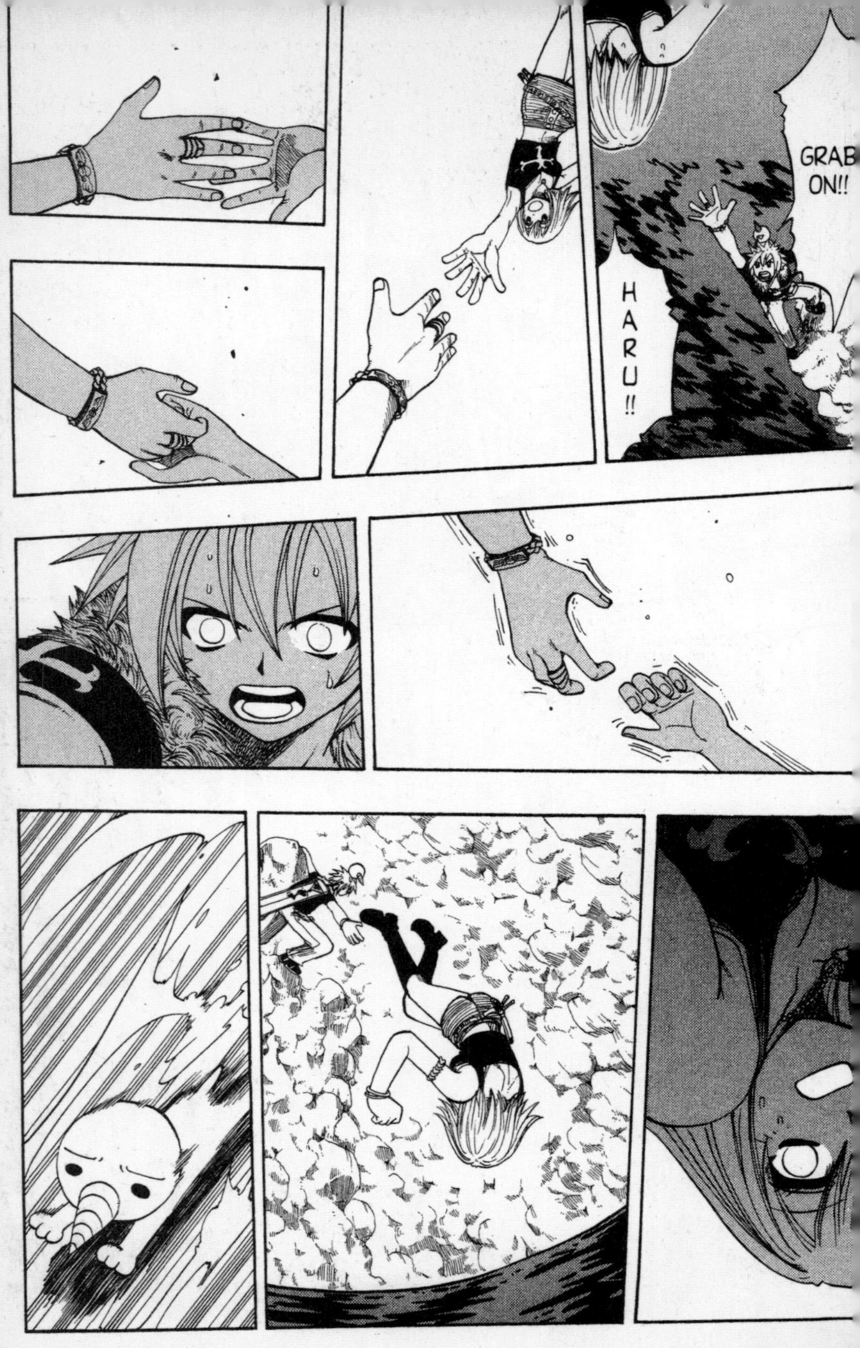
GRAB ON!!
HARU!!

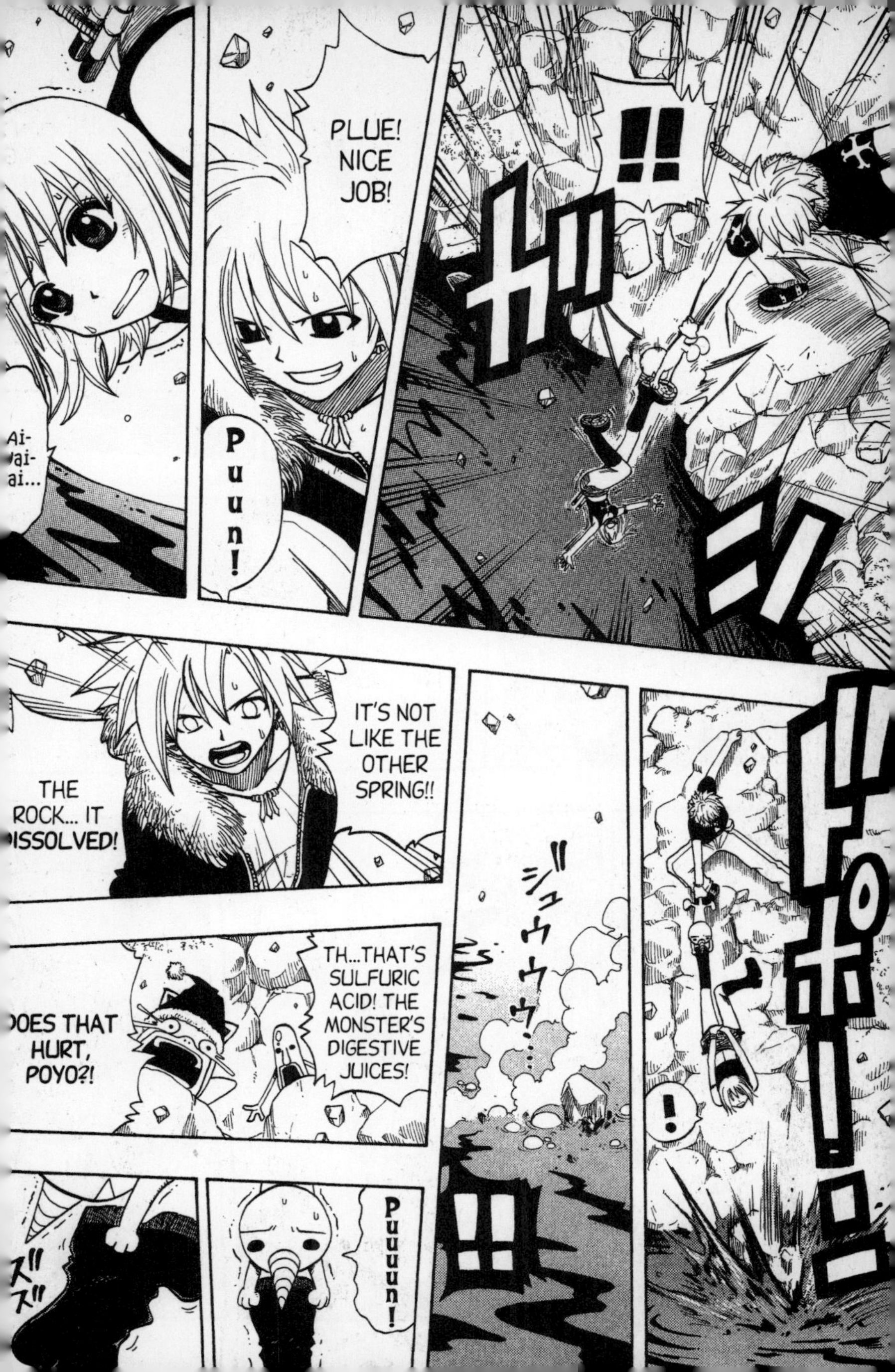
PLUE! NICE JOB!
Puun!
Ai-wai-ai...
ドッポーン!!
!
ジュウウウ...
!!
IT'S NOT LIKE THE OTHER SPRING!!
THE ROCK... IT DISSOLVED!
TH...THAT'S SULFURIC ACID! THE MONSTER'S DIGESTIVE JUICES!
DOES THAT HURT, POYO?!
Puuuun!
ズズ

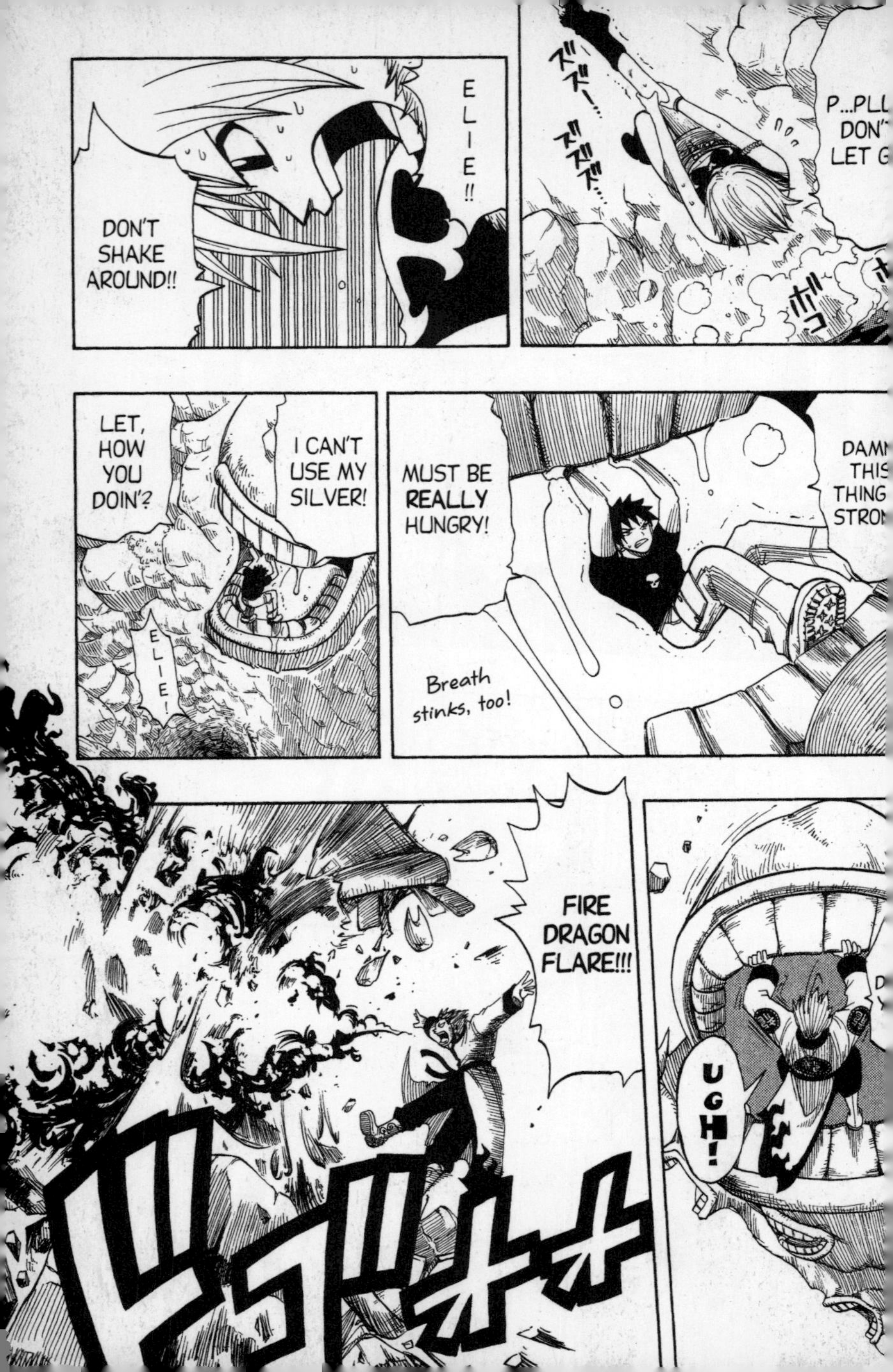
P...PLL
DON'T
LET G
ELIE!!
DON'T SHAKE AROUND!!
DAMN THIS THING STRON
MUST BE REALLY HUNGRY!
Breath stinks, too!
I CAN'T USE MY SILVER!
LET, HOW YOU DOIN'?
ELIE!
UGH!
FIRE DRAGON FLARE!!!

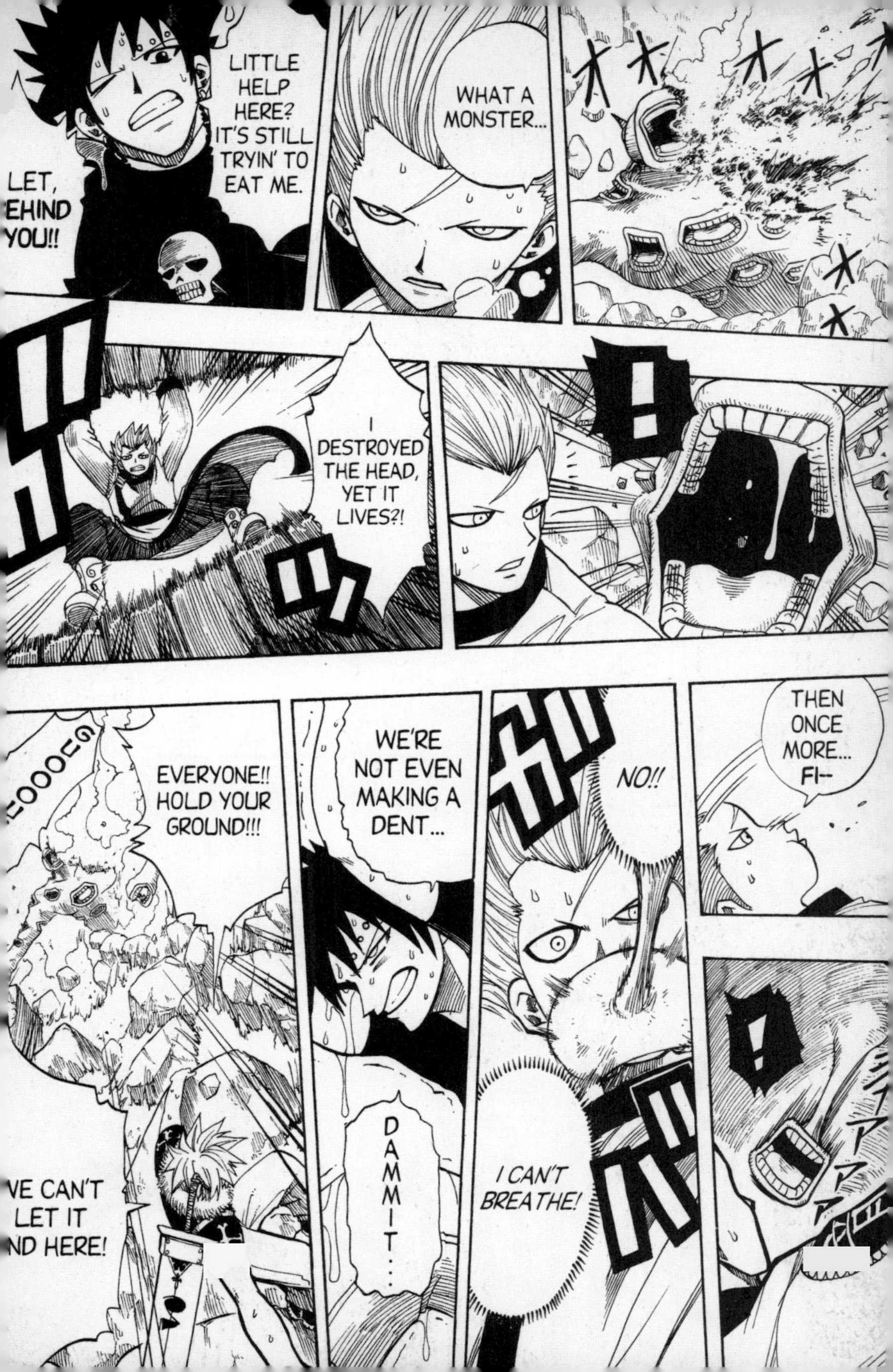
WHAT A MONSTER...
LITTLE HELP HERE? IT'S STILL TRYIN' TO EAT ME.
LET, EHIND YOU!!
!
I DESTROYED THE HEAD, YET IT LIVES?!
THEN ONCE MORE... FI--
!
NO!!
I CAN'T BREATHE!
WE'RE NOT EVEN MAKING A DENT...
DAMMIT...
EVERYONE!! HOLD YOUR GROUND!!!
VE CAN'T LET IT ND HERE!

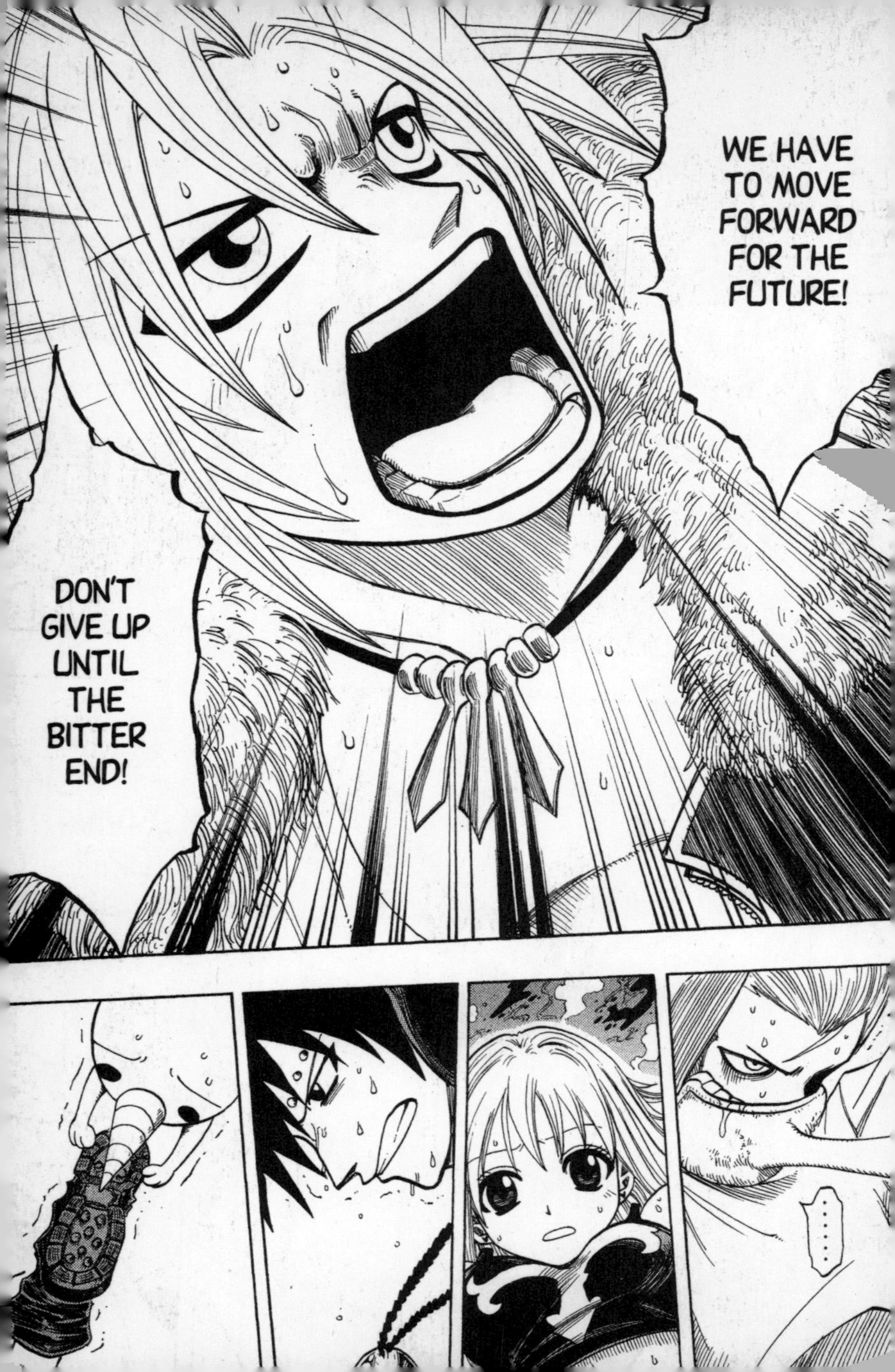
WE HAVE TO MOVE FORWARD FOR THE FUTURE!
DON'T GIVE UP UNTIL THE BITTER END!
......

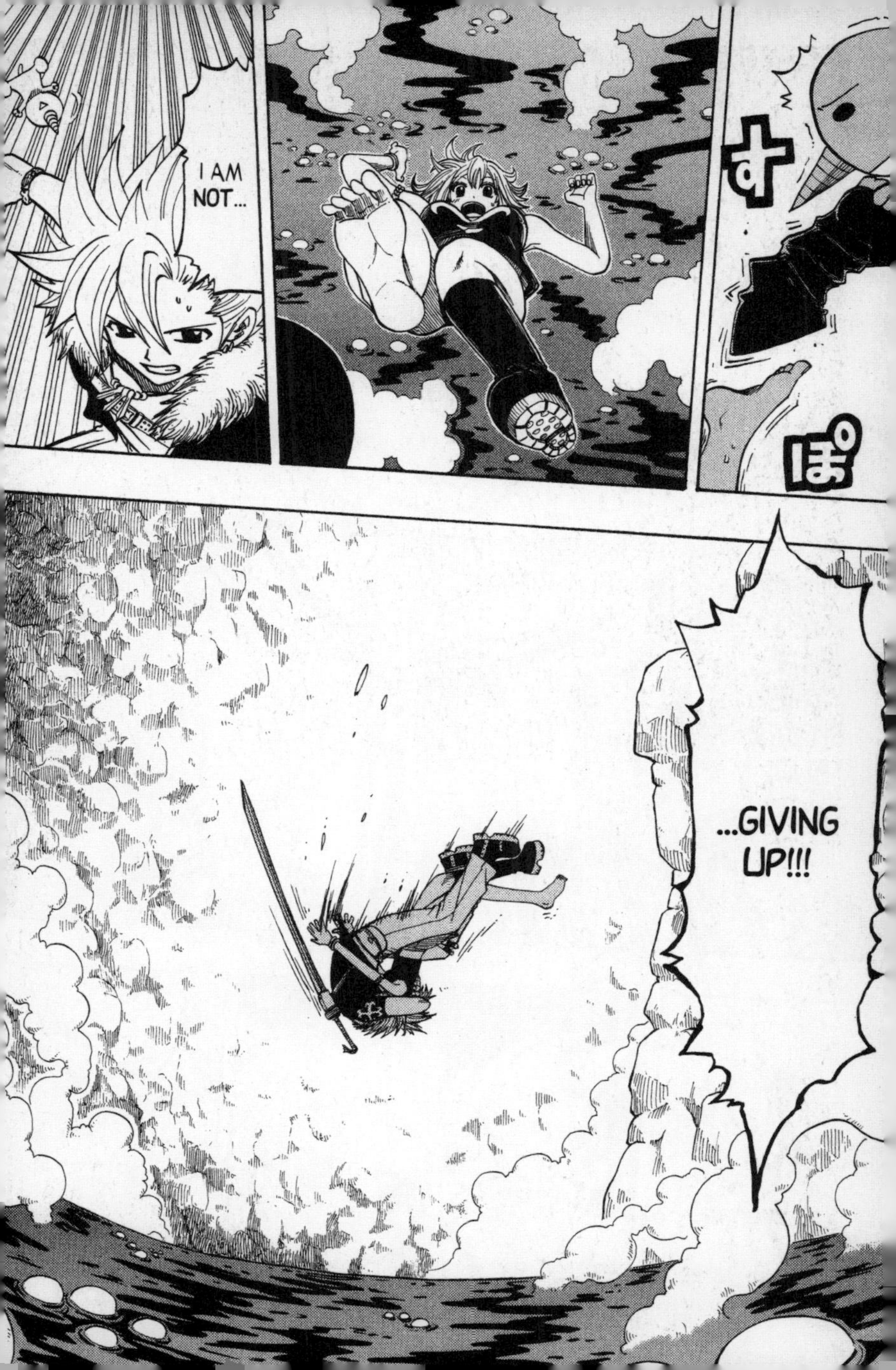
す
ぽ
I AM NOT...
...GIVING UP!!!

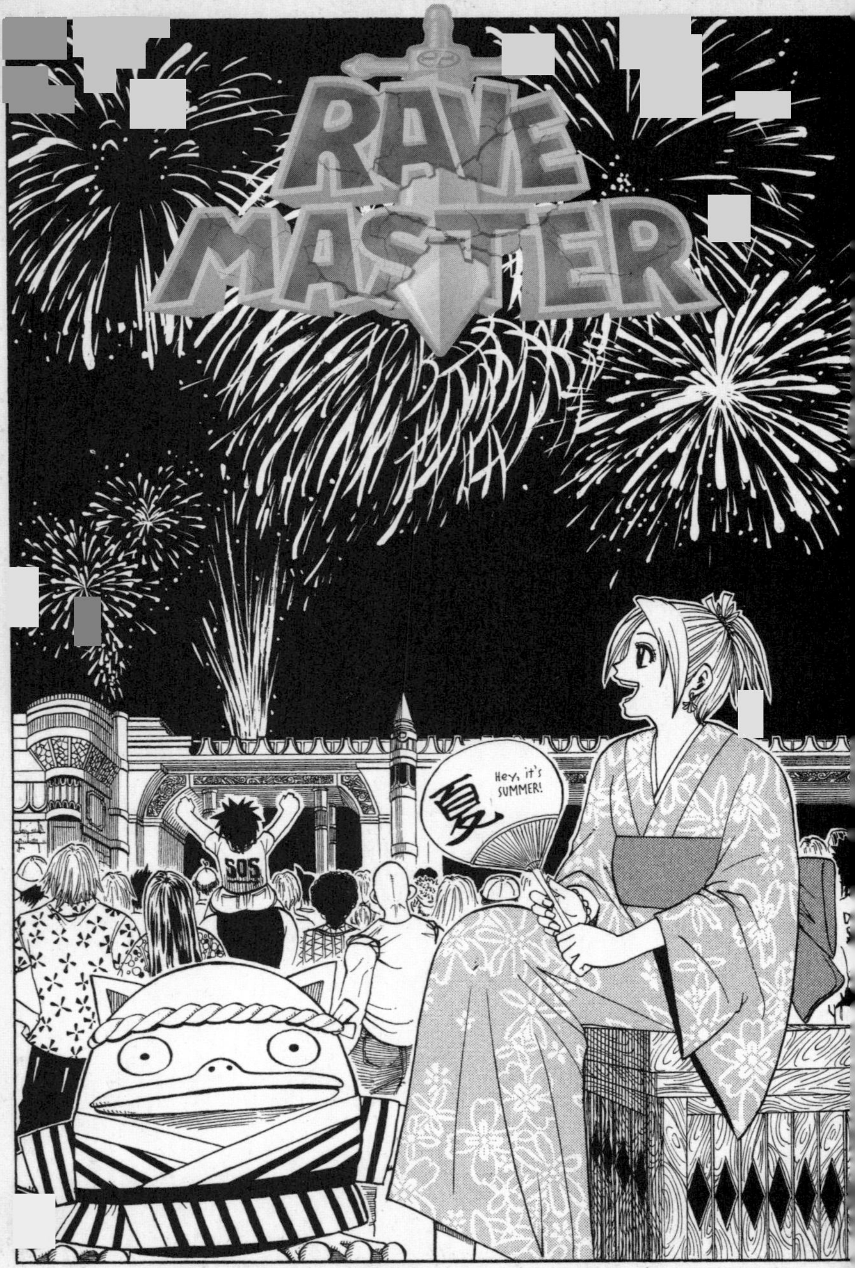
RAVE MASTER
夏
Hey, it's SUMMER!
SOS

RAVE:102 ✚ BELLY OF THE BEAST

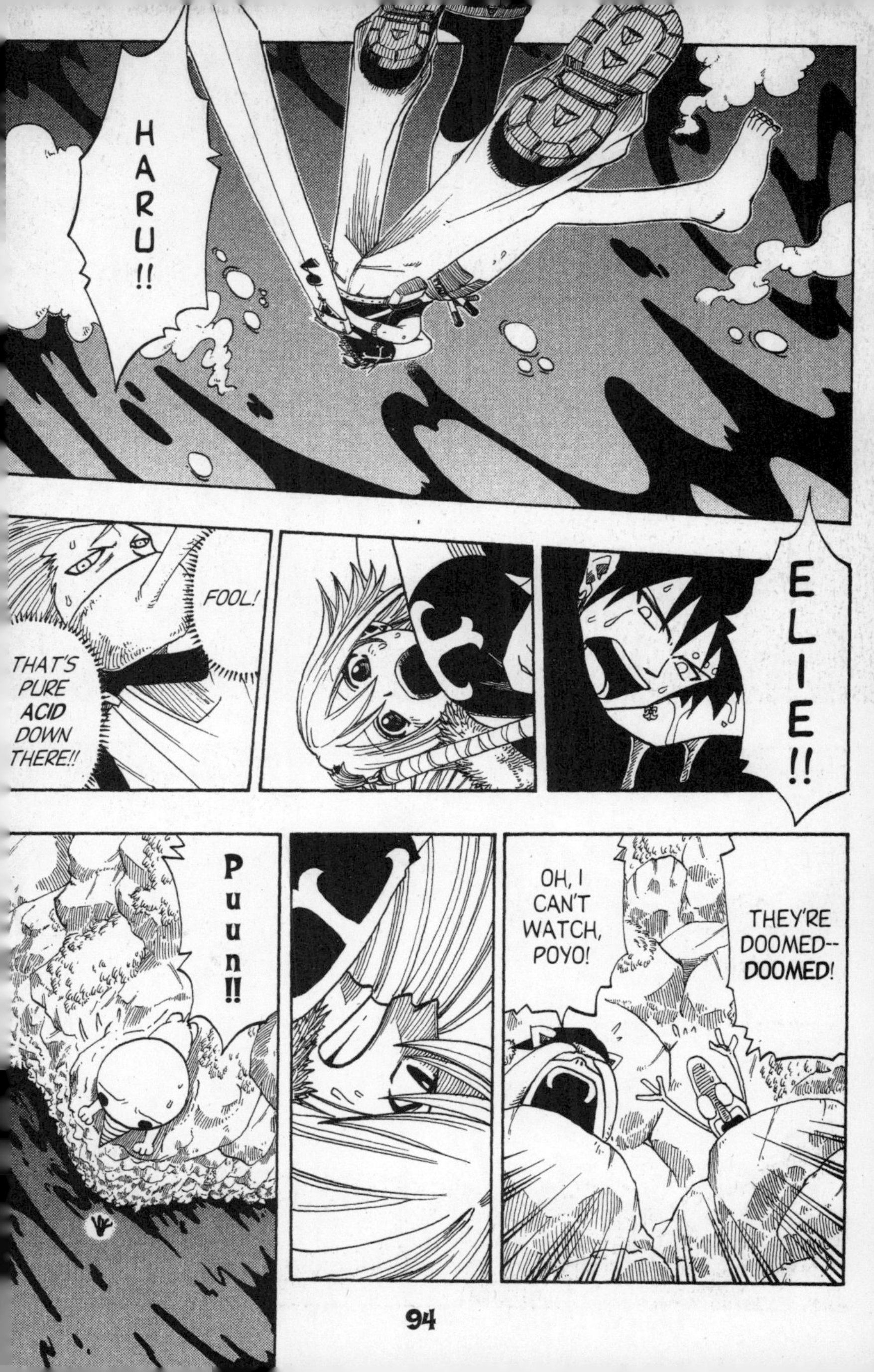
HARU!!
ELIE!!
FOOL!
THAT'S PURE ACID DOWN THERE!!
THEY'RE DOOMED-- DOOMED!
OH, I CAN'T WATCH, POYO!
Puuun!!

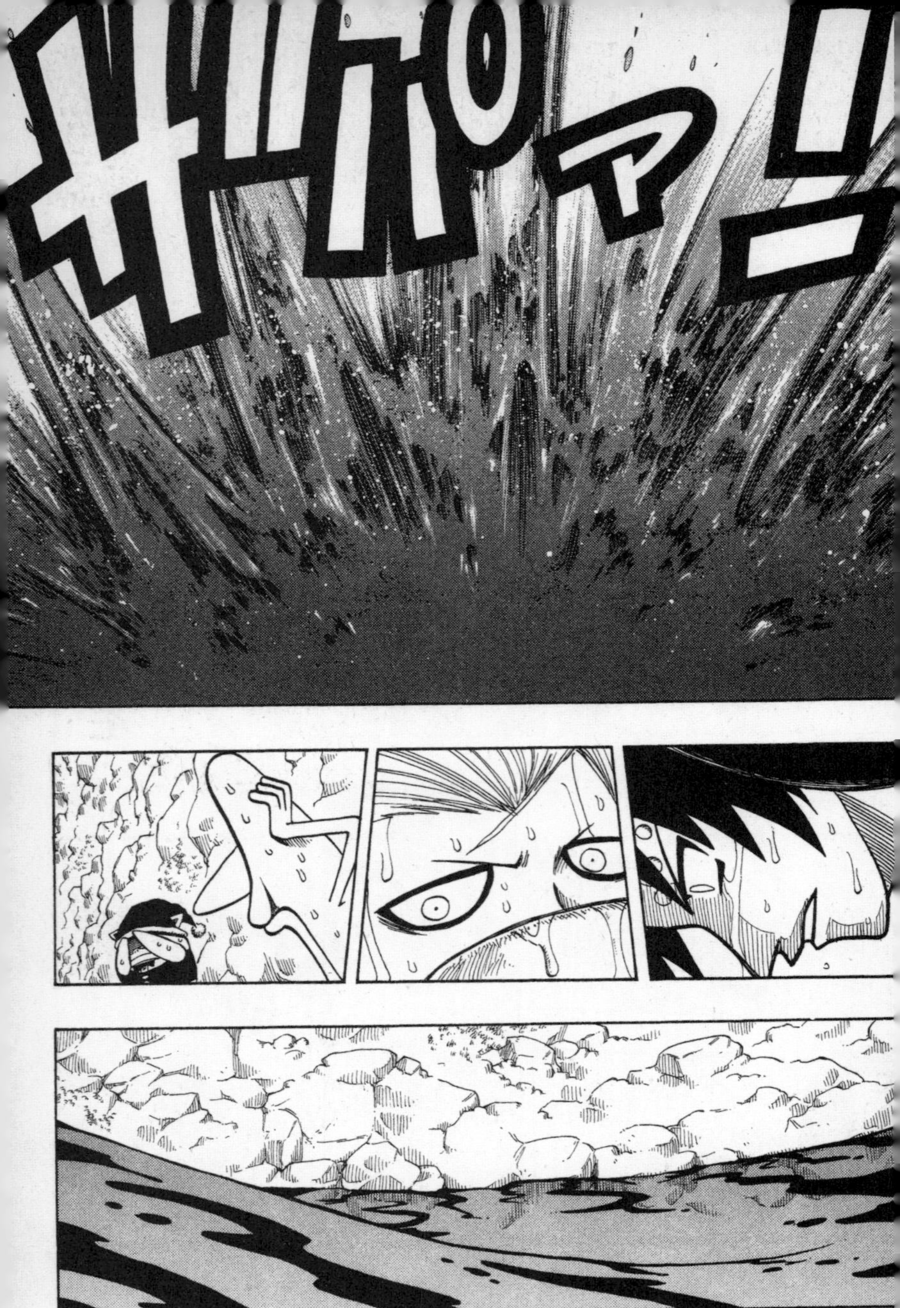

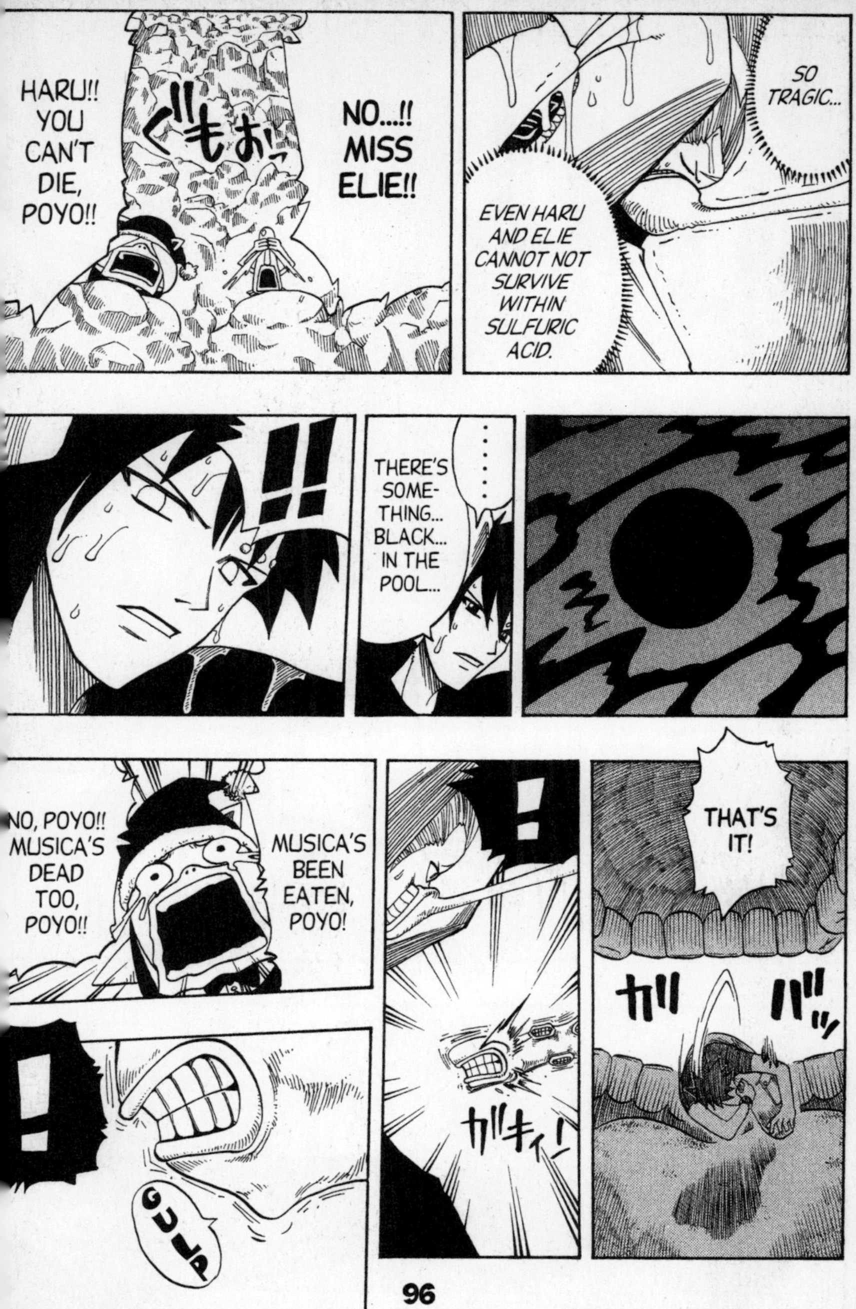
SO TRAGIC...
EVEN HARU AND ELIE CANNOT NOT SURVIVE WITHIN SULFURIC ACID.
NO...!! MISS ELIE!!
ぐもぉ!っ
HARU!! YOU CAN'T DIE, POYO!!
......
THERE'S SOME-THING... BLACK... IN THE POOL...
!!
THAT'S IT!
カリ
バッ
!
ガキィ!
MUSICA'S BEEN EATEN, POYO!
NO, POYO!! MUSICA'S DEAD TOO, POYO!!
!
GULP

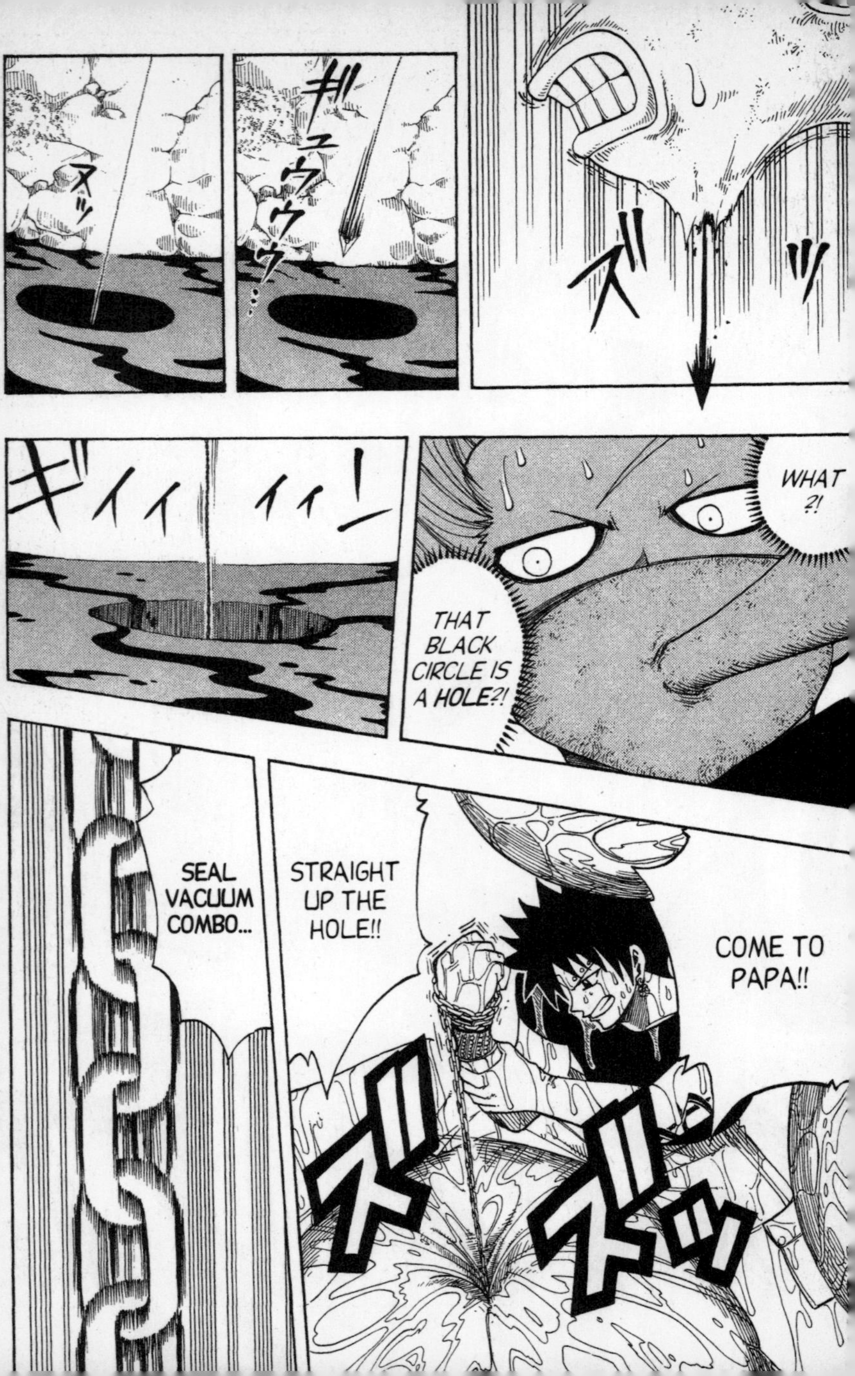

ズッ
ギュウウウ…
ズッ
WHAT ?!
THAT BLACK CIRCLE IS A HOLE?!
ギイイイイィー
STRAIGHT UP THE HOLE!!
COME TO PAPA!!
ズズッ
SEAL VACUUM COMBO...

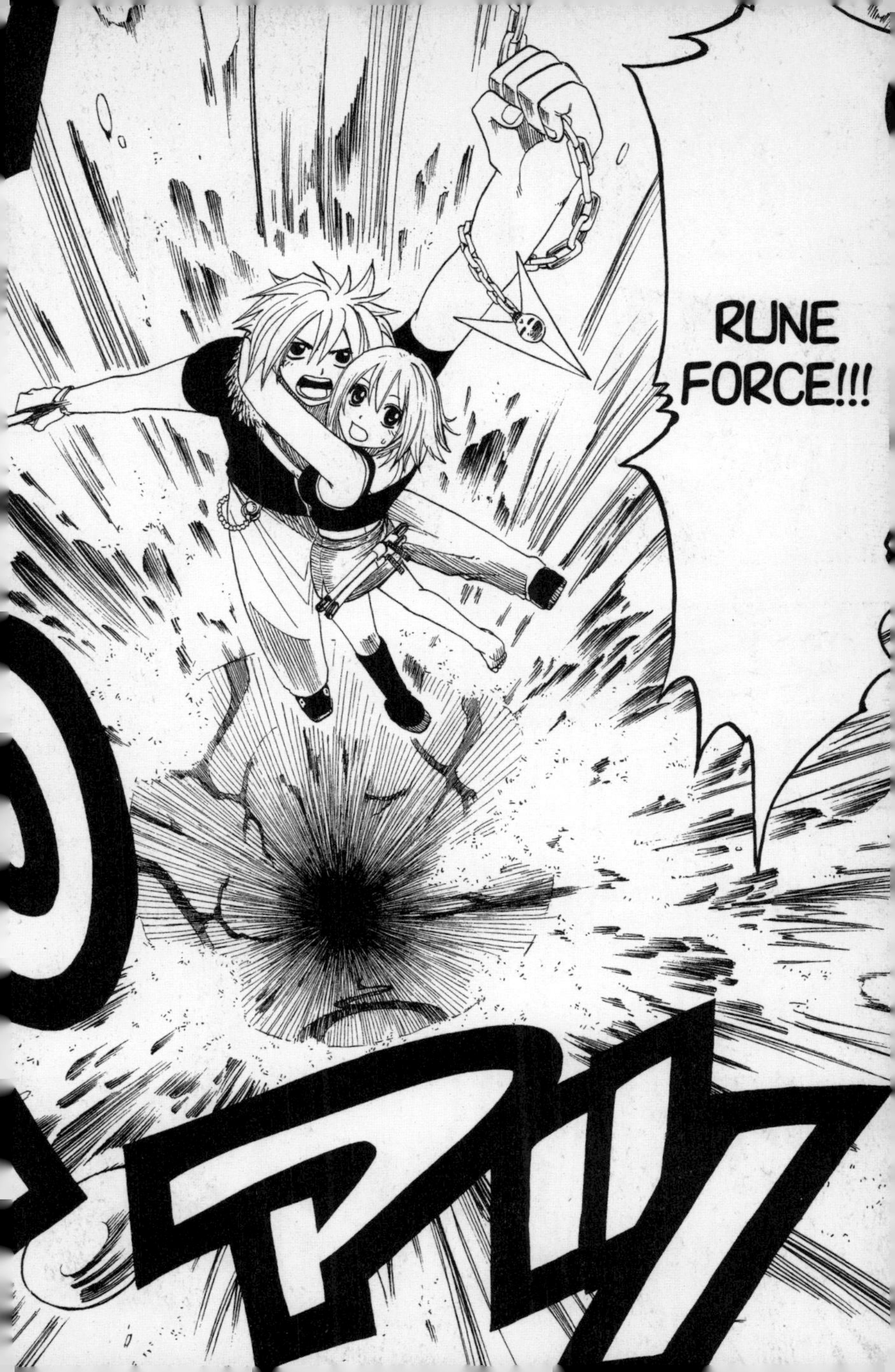
RUNE FORCE!!!

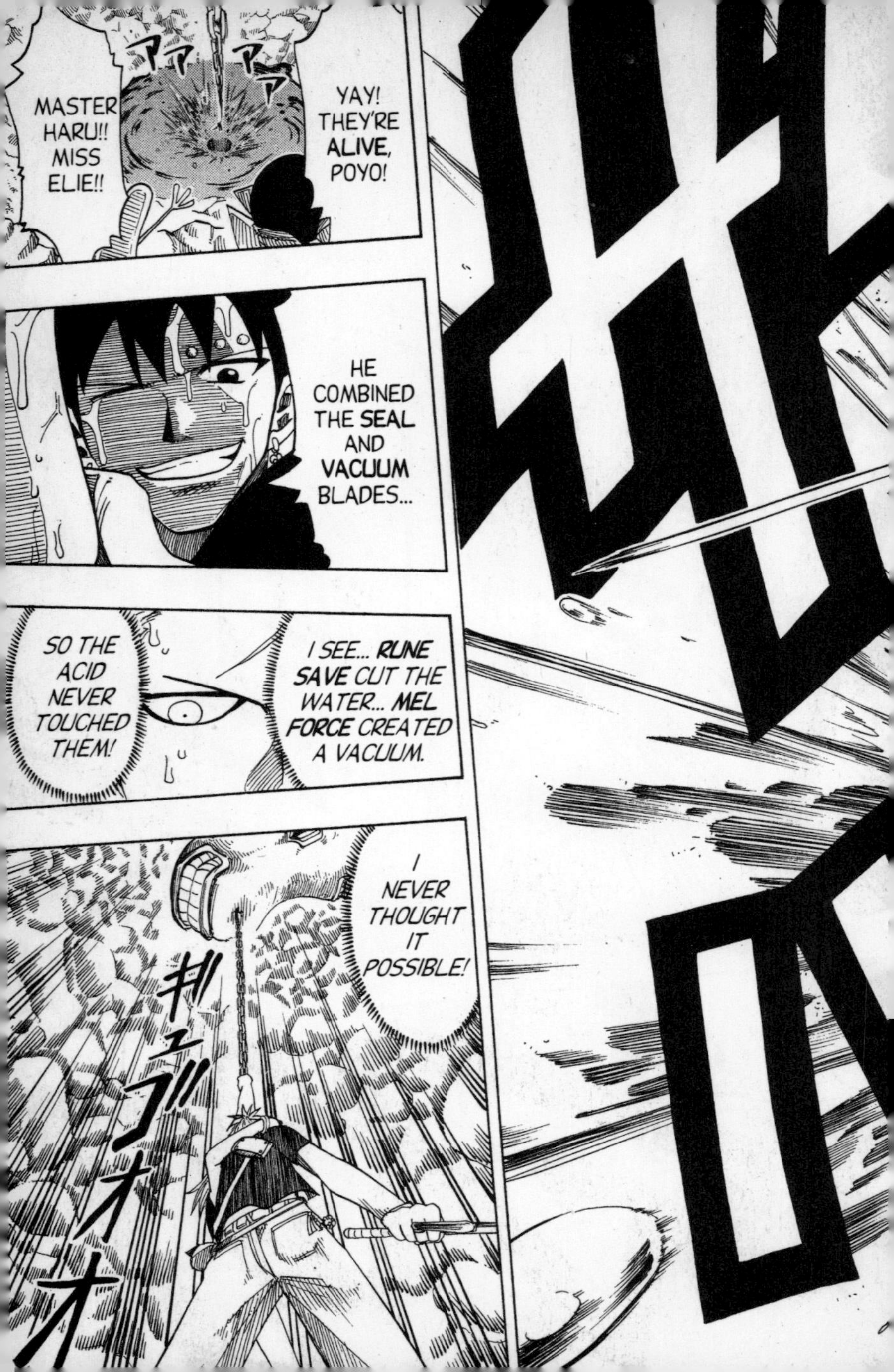
YAY! THEY'RE ALIVE, POYO!
MASTER HARU!! MISS ELIE!!
HE COMBINED THE SEAL AND VACUUM BLADES...
I SEE... RUNE SAVE CUT THE WATER... MEL FORCE CREATED A VACUUM.
SO THE ACID NEVER TOUCHED THEM!
I NEVER THOUGHT IT POSSIBLE!

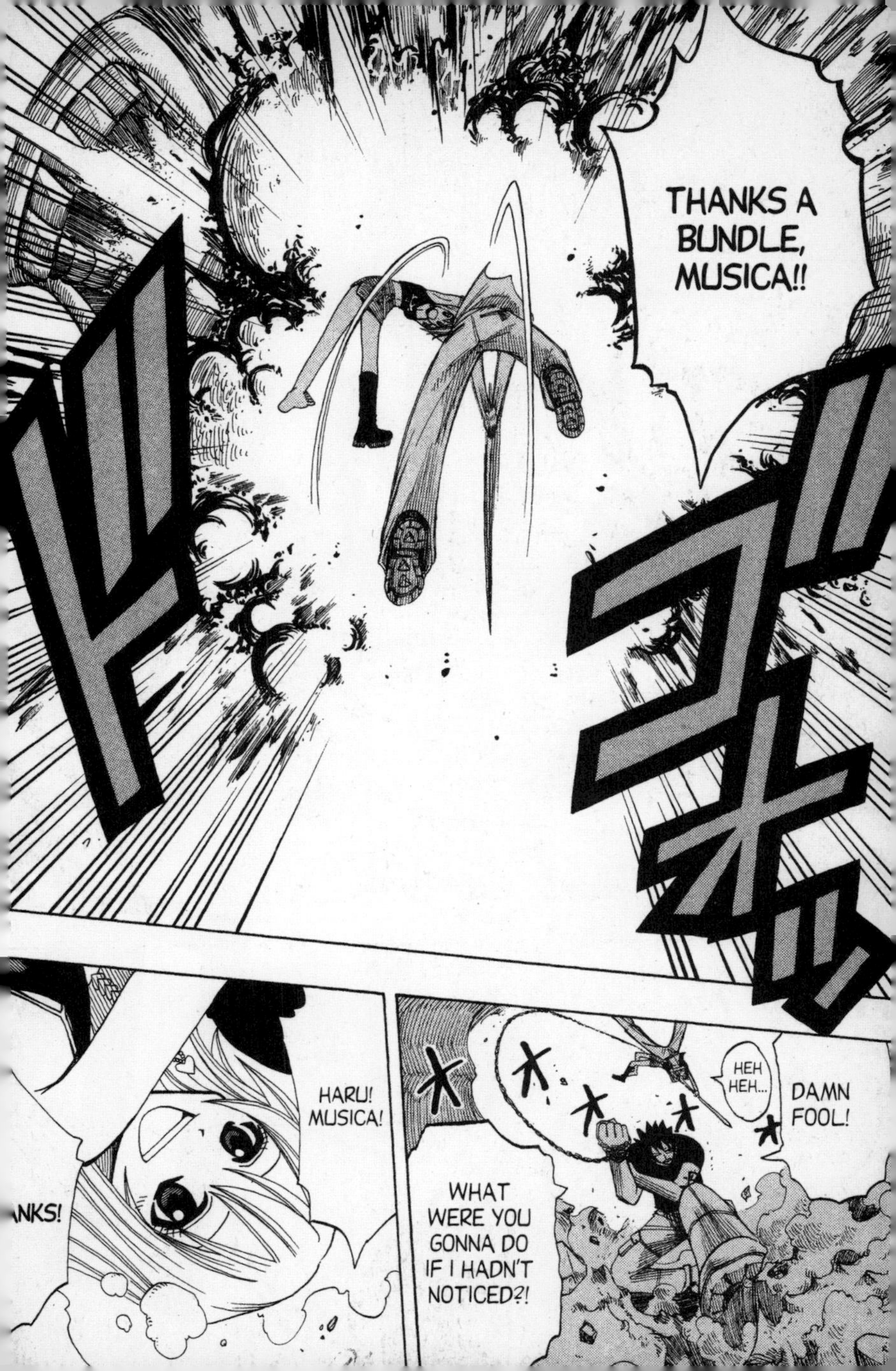
THANKS A BUNDLE, MUSICA!!
HEH HEH...
DAMN FOOL!
WHAT WERE YOU GONNA DO IF I HADN'T NOTICED?!
HARU! MUSICA!
ANKS!

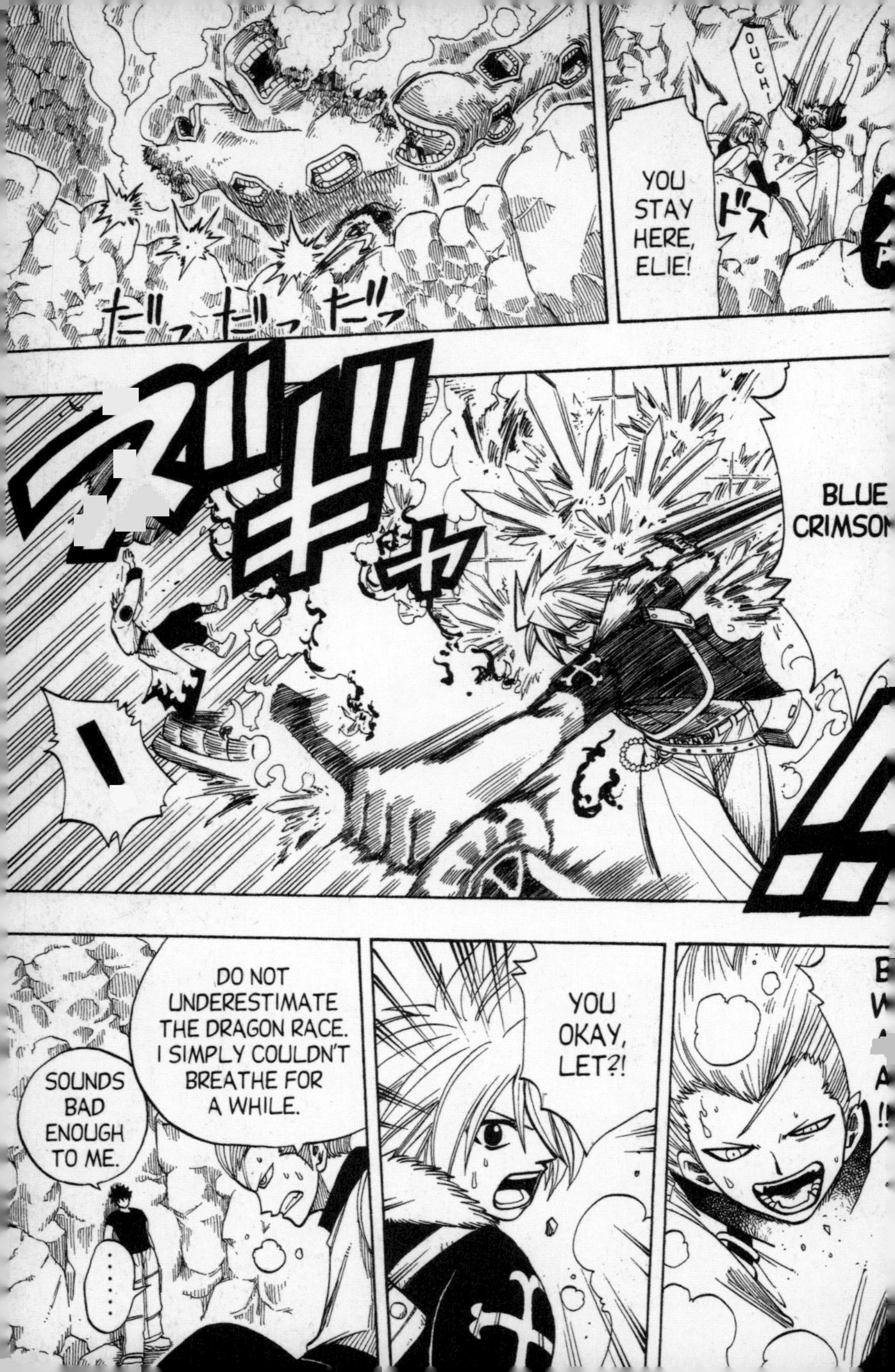

OUCH!
YOU STAY HERE, ELIE!
ドス
だっ だっ だっ
BLUE CRIMSON
BWAA!!
YOU OKAY, LET?!
DO NOT UNDERESTIMATE THE DRAGON RACE. I SIMPLY COULDN'T BREATHE FOR A WHILE.
SOUNDS BAD ENOUGH TO ME.
......

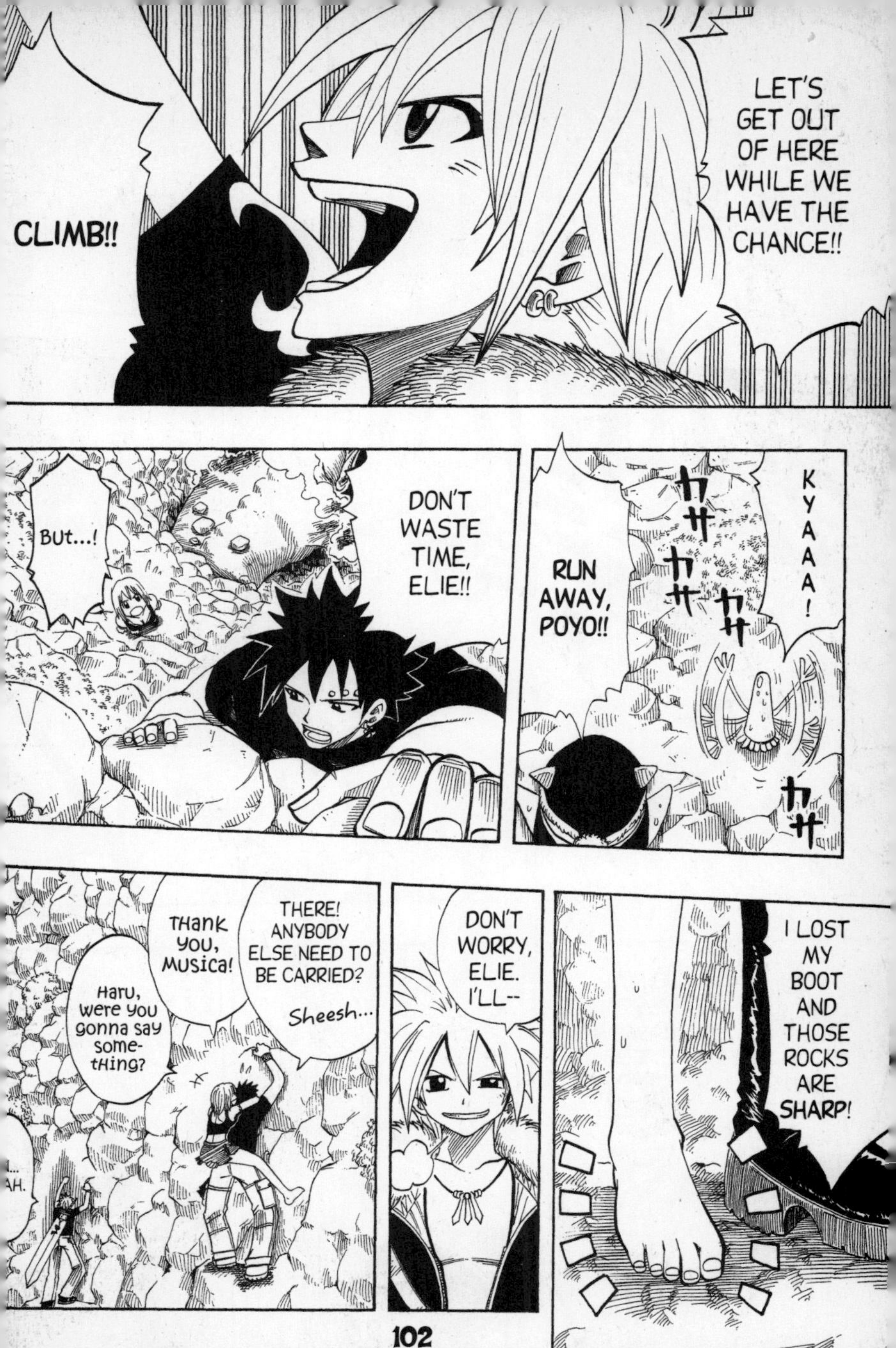
LET'S GET OUT OF HERE WHILE WE HAVE THE CHANCE!!
CLIMB!!
KYAAAA!
カサ カサ カサ
RUN AWAY, POYO!!
カサ
DON'T WASTE TIME, ELIE!!
But...!
I LOST MY BOOT AND THOSE ROCKS ARE SHARP!
DON'T WORRY, ELIE. I'LL--
THERE! ANYBODY ELSE NEED TO BE CARRIED?
Sheesh...
Thank you, Musica!
Haru, were you gonna say something?

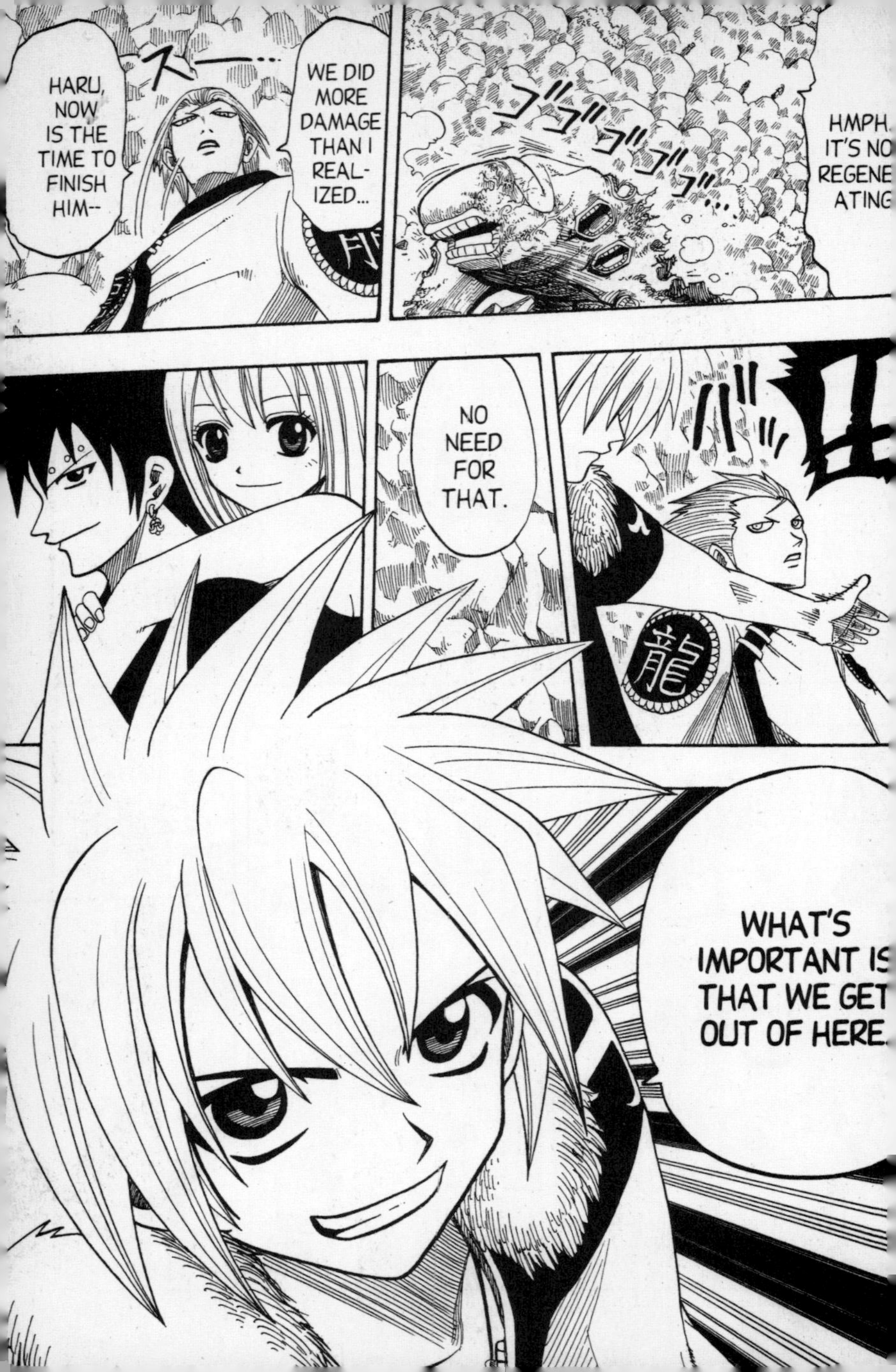
HMPH. IT'S NO REGENE ATING
WE DID MORE DAMAGE THAN I REAL- IZED...
HARU, NOW IS THE TIME TO FINISH HIM--
NO NEED FOR THAT.
WHAT'S IMPORTANT IS THAT WE GET OUT OF HERE.

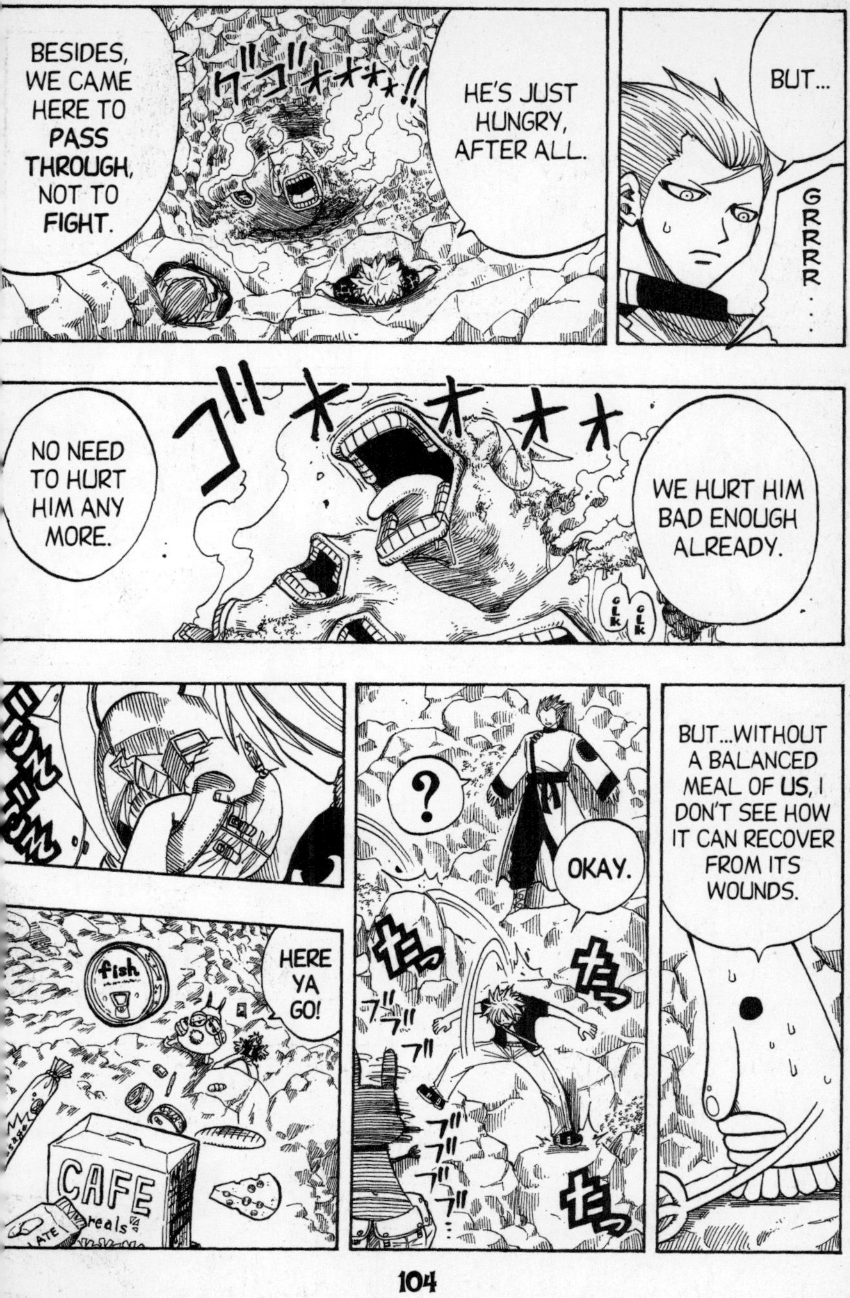
BUT...
GRRRR...
HE'S JUST HUNGRY, AFTER ALL.
BESIDES, WE CAME HERE TO PASS THROUGH, NOT TO FIGHT.
WE HURT HIM BAD ENOUGH ALREADY.
GLK GLK
NO NEED TO HURT HIM ANY MORE.
BUT...WITHOUT A BALANCED MEAL OF US, I DON'T SEE HOW IT CAN RECOVER FROM ITS WOUNDS.
OKAY.
?
HERE YA GO!
fish
CAFE

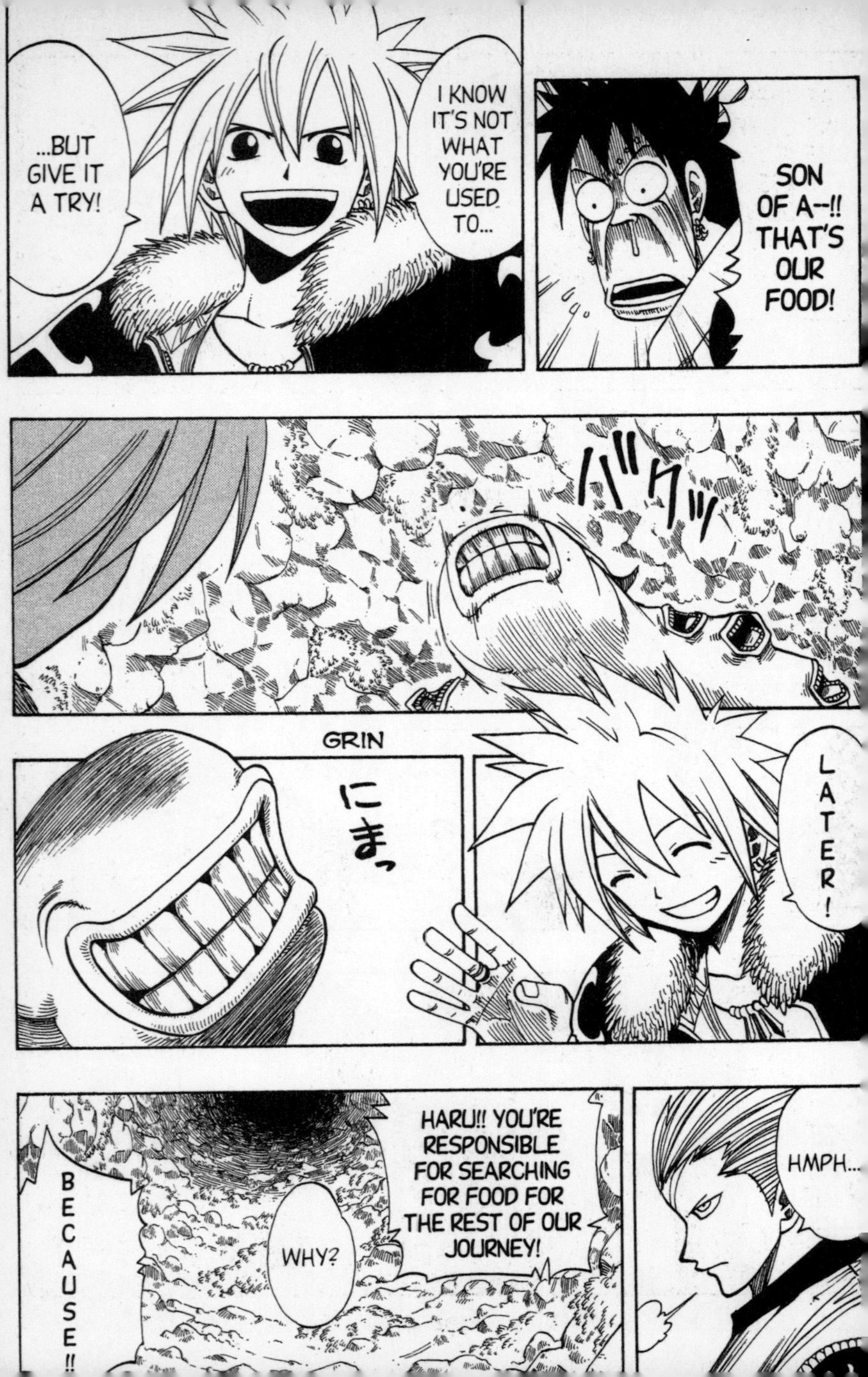

SON OF A--!! THAT'S OUR FOOD!
I KNOW IT'S NOT WHAT YOU'RE USED TO...
...BUT GIVE IT A TRY!
バクッ
LATER!
GRIN
にまっ
HMPH...
HARU!! YOU'RE RESPONSIBLE FOR SEARCHING FOR FOOD FOR THE REST OF OUR JOURNEY!
WHY?
BECAUSE!!

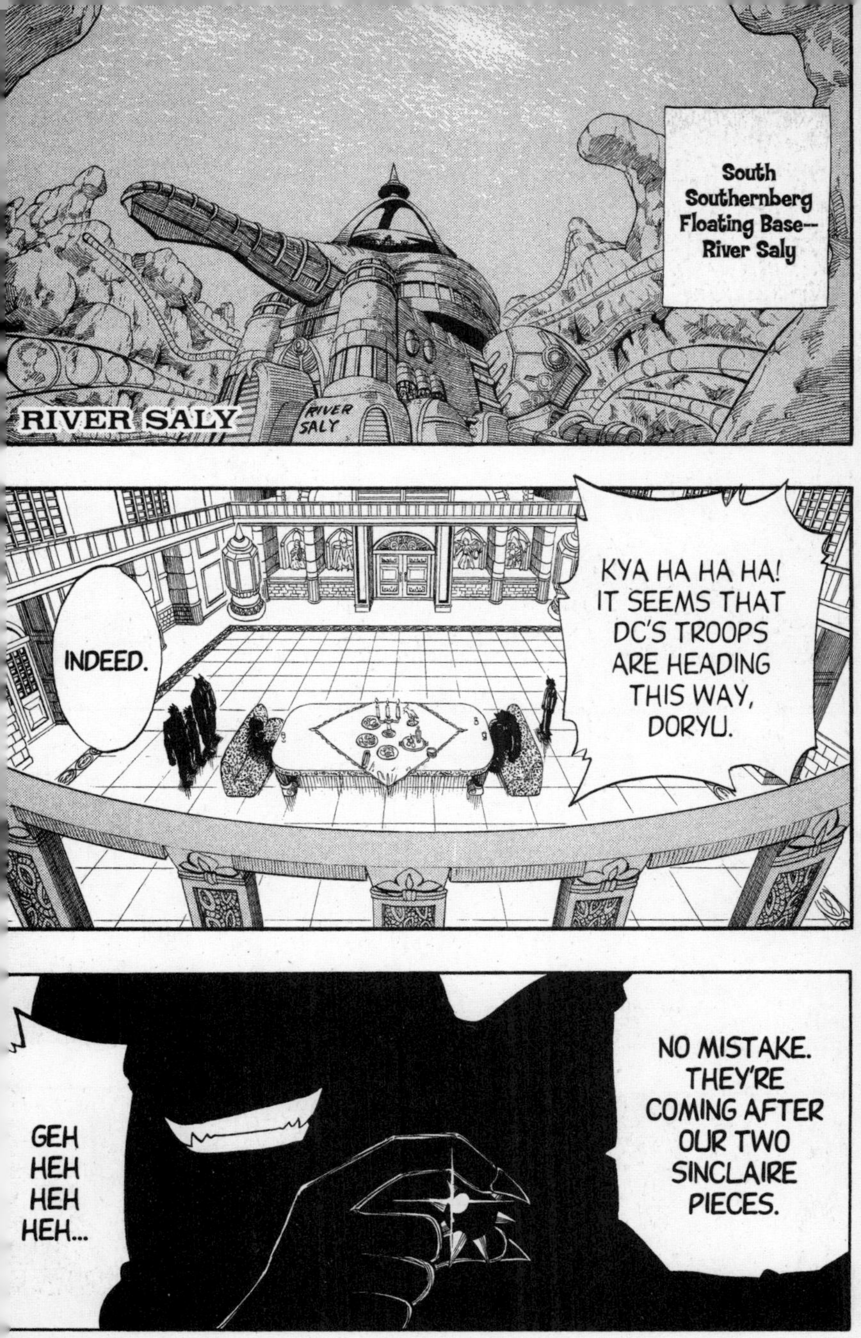
South Southernberg Floating Base-- River Saly
RIVER SALY
RIVER SALY
KYA HA HA HA! IT SEEMS THAT DC'S TROOPS ARE HEADING THIS WAY, DORYU.
INDEED.
NO MISTAKE. THEY'RE COMING AFTER OUR TWO SINCLAIRE PIECES.
GEH HEH HEH HEH...

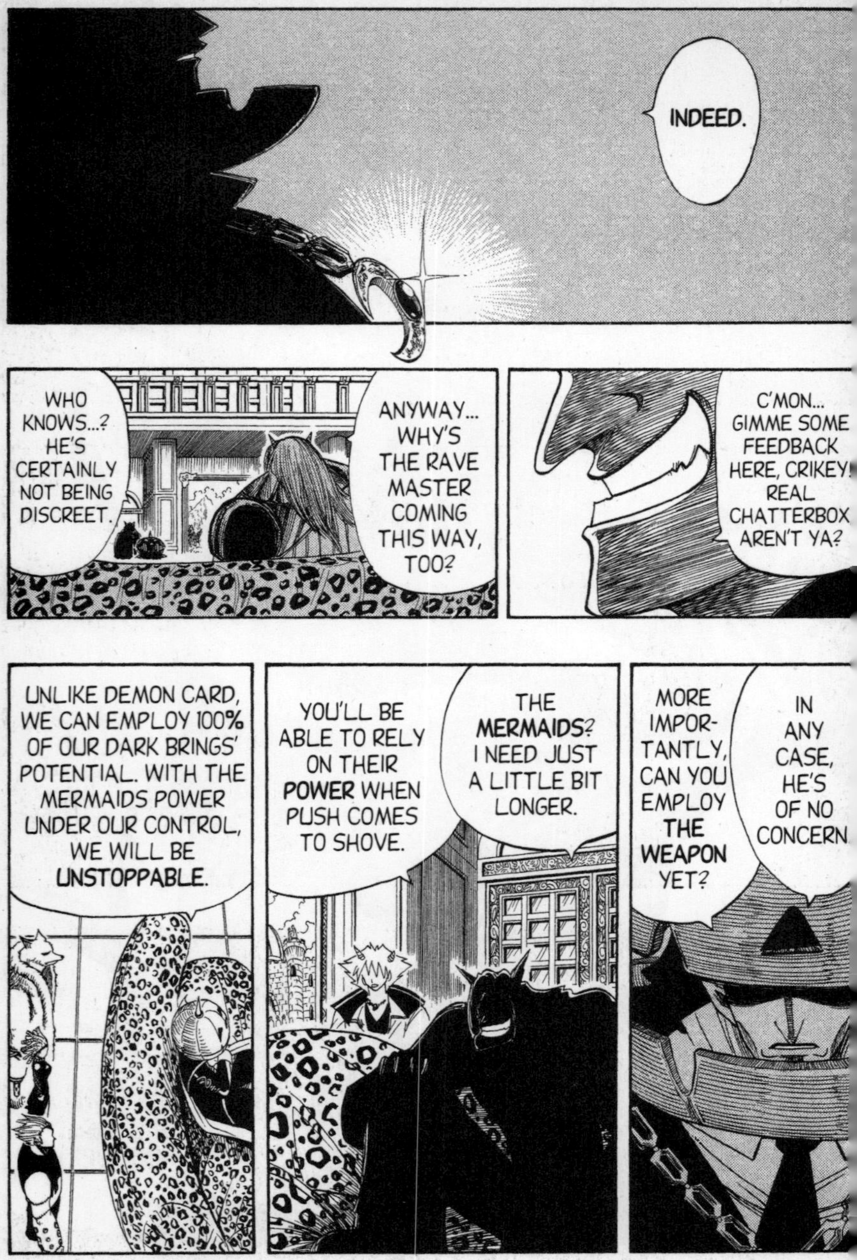
INDEED.
C'MON... GIMME SOME FEEDBACK HERE, CRIKEY! REAL CHATTERBOX AREN'T YA?
ANYWAY... WHY'S THE RAVE MASTER COMING THIS WAY, TOO?
WHO KNOWS...? HE'S CERTAINLY NOT BEING DISCREET.
IN ANY CASE, HE'S OF NO CONCERN.
MORE IMPORTANTLY, CAN YOU EMPLOY THE WEAPON YET?
THE MERMAIDS? I NEED JUST A LITTLE BIT LONGER.
YOU'LL BE ABLE TO RELY ON THEIR POWER WHEN PUSH COMES TO SHOVE.
UNLIKE DEMON CARD, WE CAN EMPLOY 100% OF OUR DARK BRINGS' POTENTIAL. WITH THE MERMAIDS POWER UNDER OUR CONTROL, WE WILL BE UNSTOPPABLE.

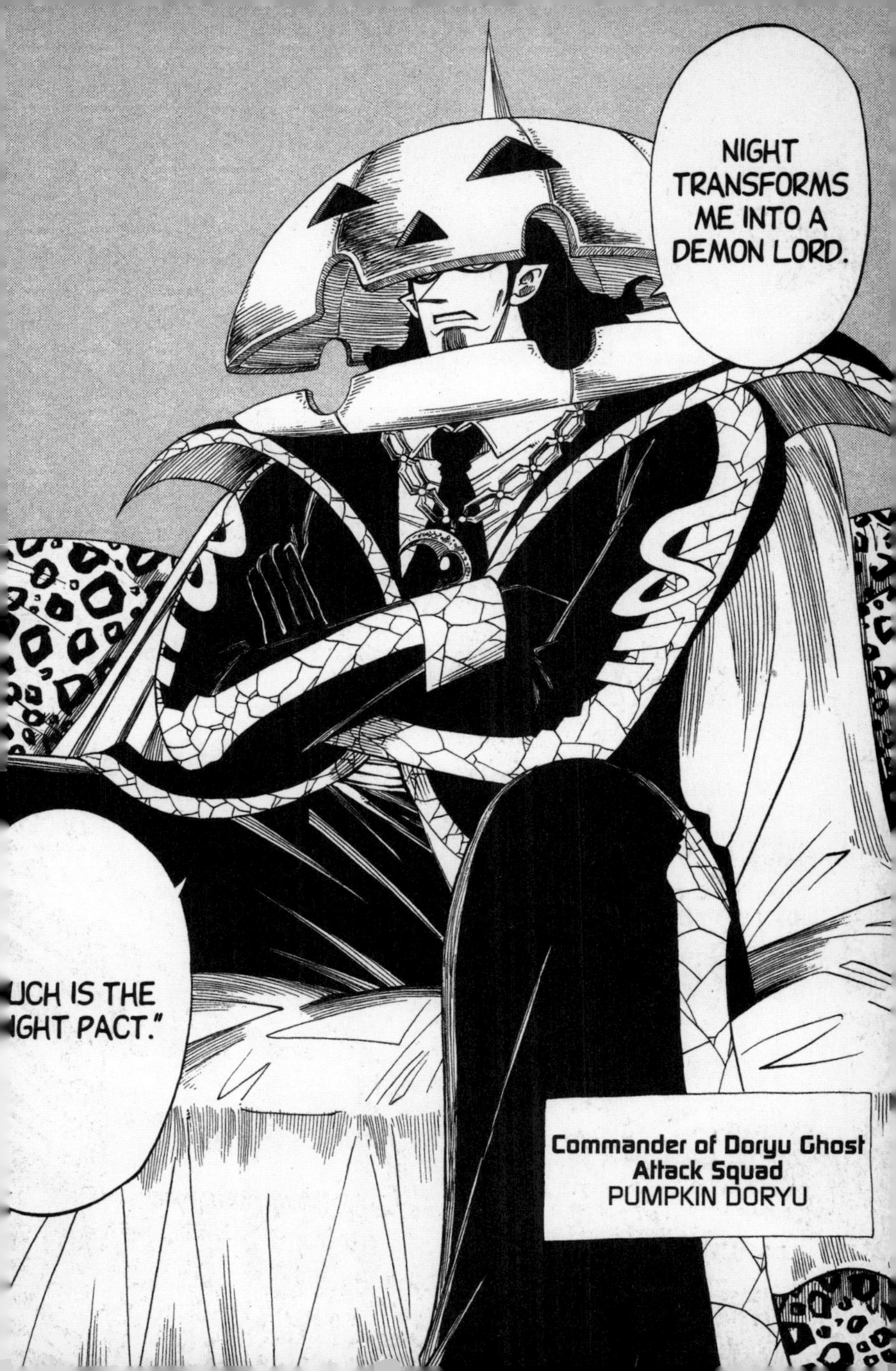
NIGHT TRANSFORMS ME INTO A DEMON LORD.
UCH IS THE IGHT PACT."
Commander of Doryu Ghost Attack Squad PUMPKIN DORYU

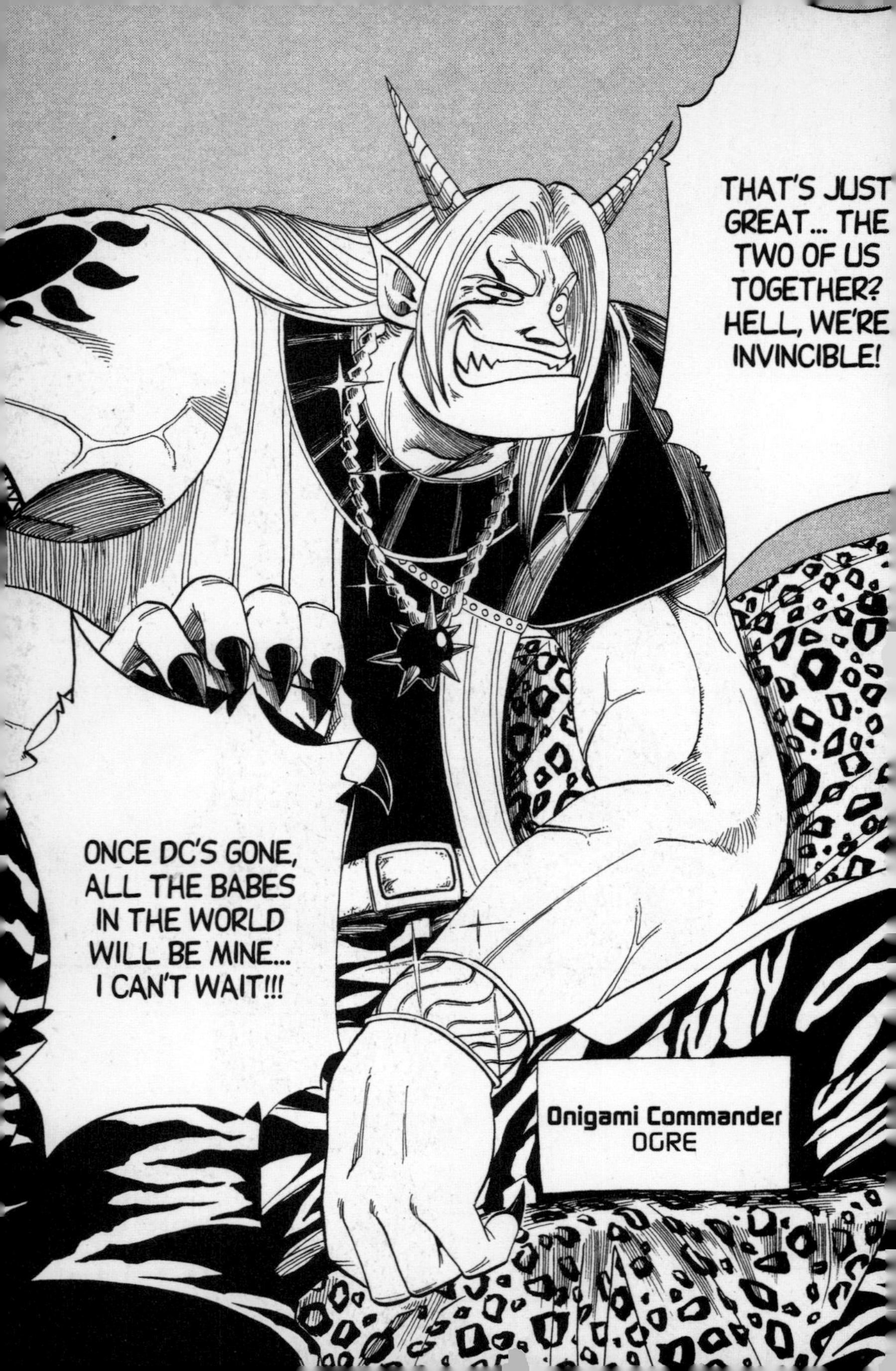
THAT'S JUST GREAT... THE TWO OF US TOGETHER? HELL, WE'RE INVINCIBLE!
Onigami Commander OGRE
ONCE DC'S GONE, ALL THE BABES IN THE WORLD WILL BE MINE... I CAN'T WAIT!!!

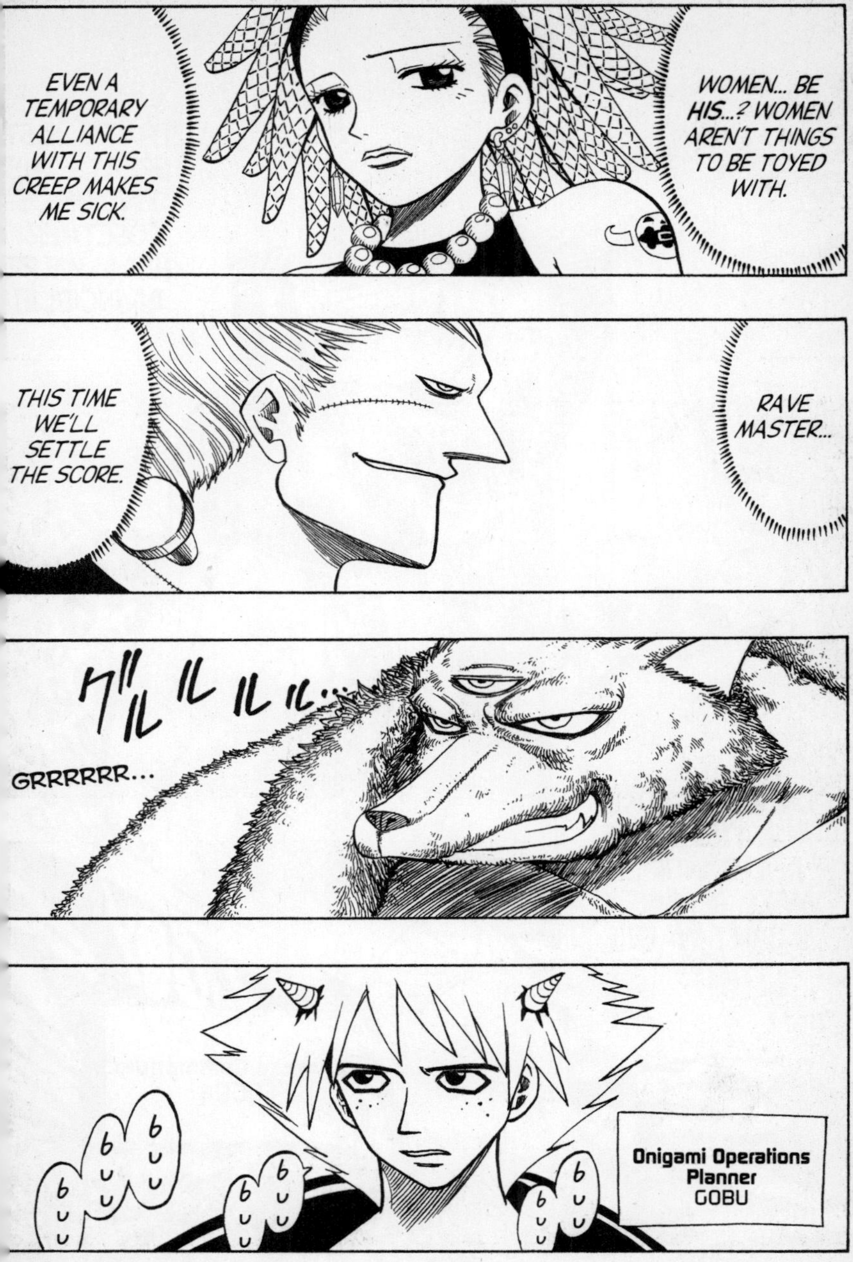
WOMEN... BE HIS...? WOMEN AREN'T THINGS TO BE TOYED WITH.
EVEN A TEMPORARY ALLIANCE WITH THIS CREEP MAKES ME SICK.
RAVE MASTER...
THIS TIME WE'LL SETTLE THE SCORE.
グルルルル...
GRRRRRR...
Onigami Operations Planner
GOBU
buu
buu
buu
buu
buu
buu
buu

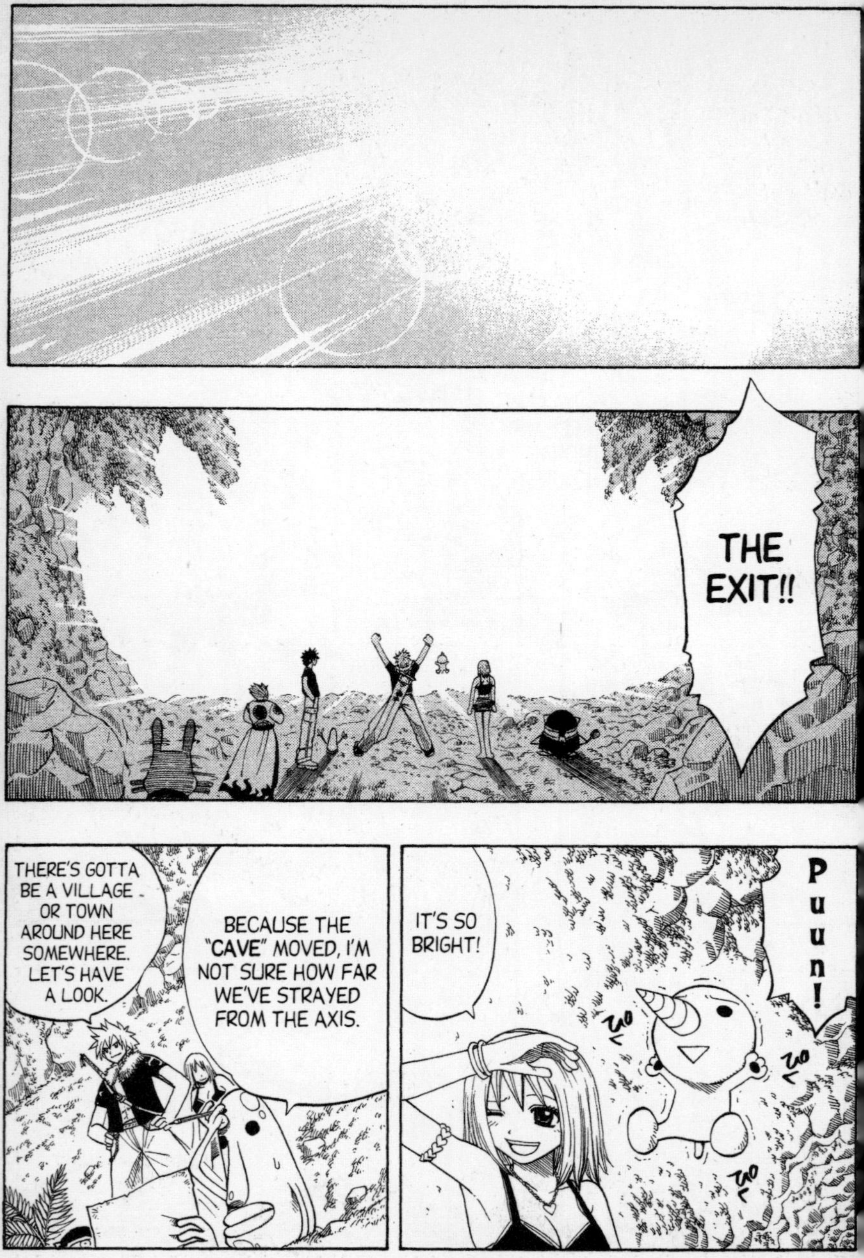
THE EXIT!!
Puun!
IT'S SO BRIGHT!
BECAUSE THE "CAVE" MOVED, I'M NOT SURE HOW FAR WE'VE STRAYED FROM THE AXIS.
THERE'S GOTTA BE A VILLAGE OR TOWN AROUND HERE SOMEWHERE. LET'S HAVE A LOOK.

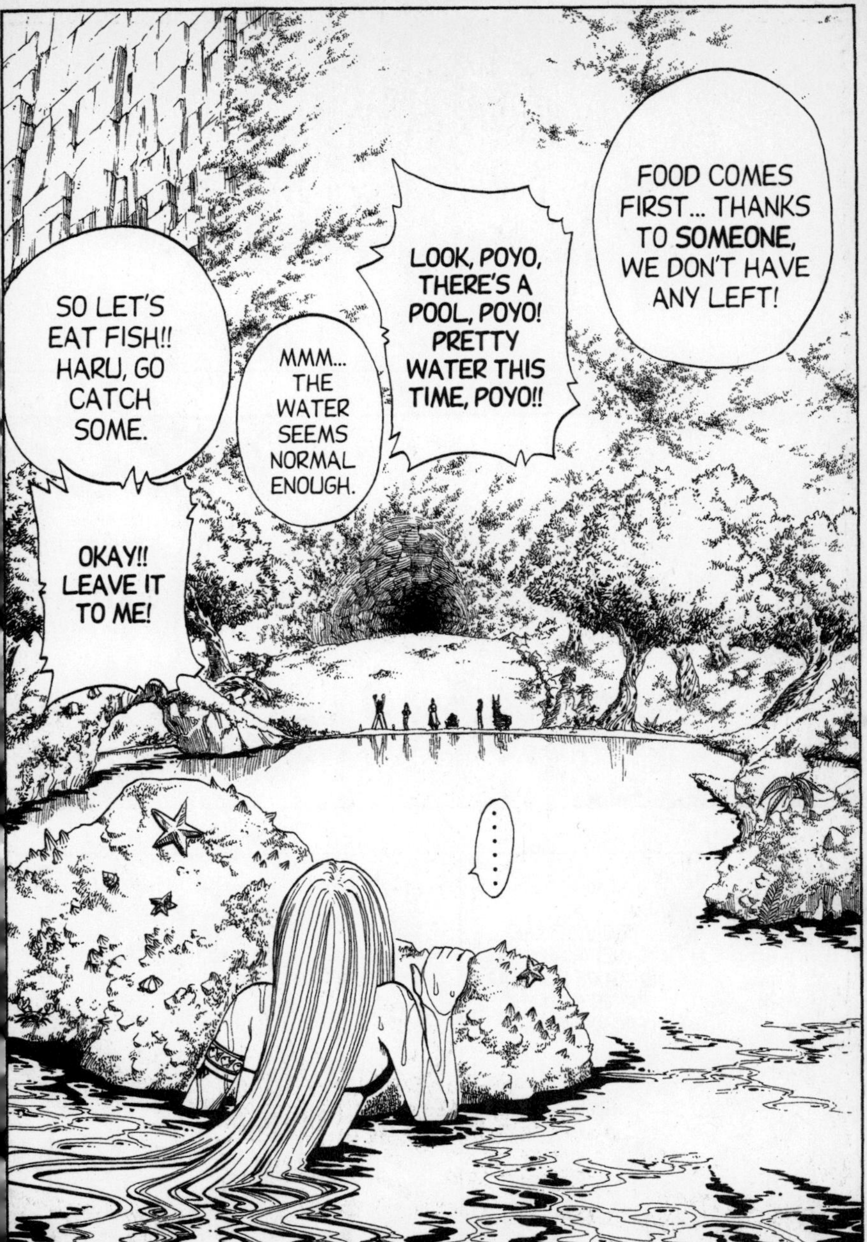
FOOD COMES FIRST... THANKS TO SOMEONE, WE DON'T HAVE ANY LEFT!
LOOK, POYO, THERE'S A POOL, POYO! PRETTY WATER THIS TIME, POYO!!
MMM... THE WATER SEEMS NORMAL ENOUGH.
SO LET'S EAT FISH!! HARU, GO CATCH SOME.
OKAY!! LEAVE IT TO ME!
......

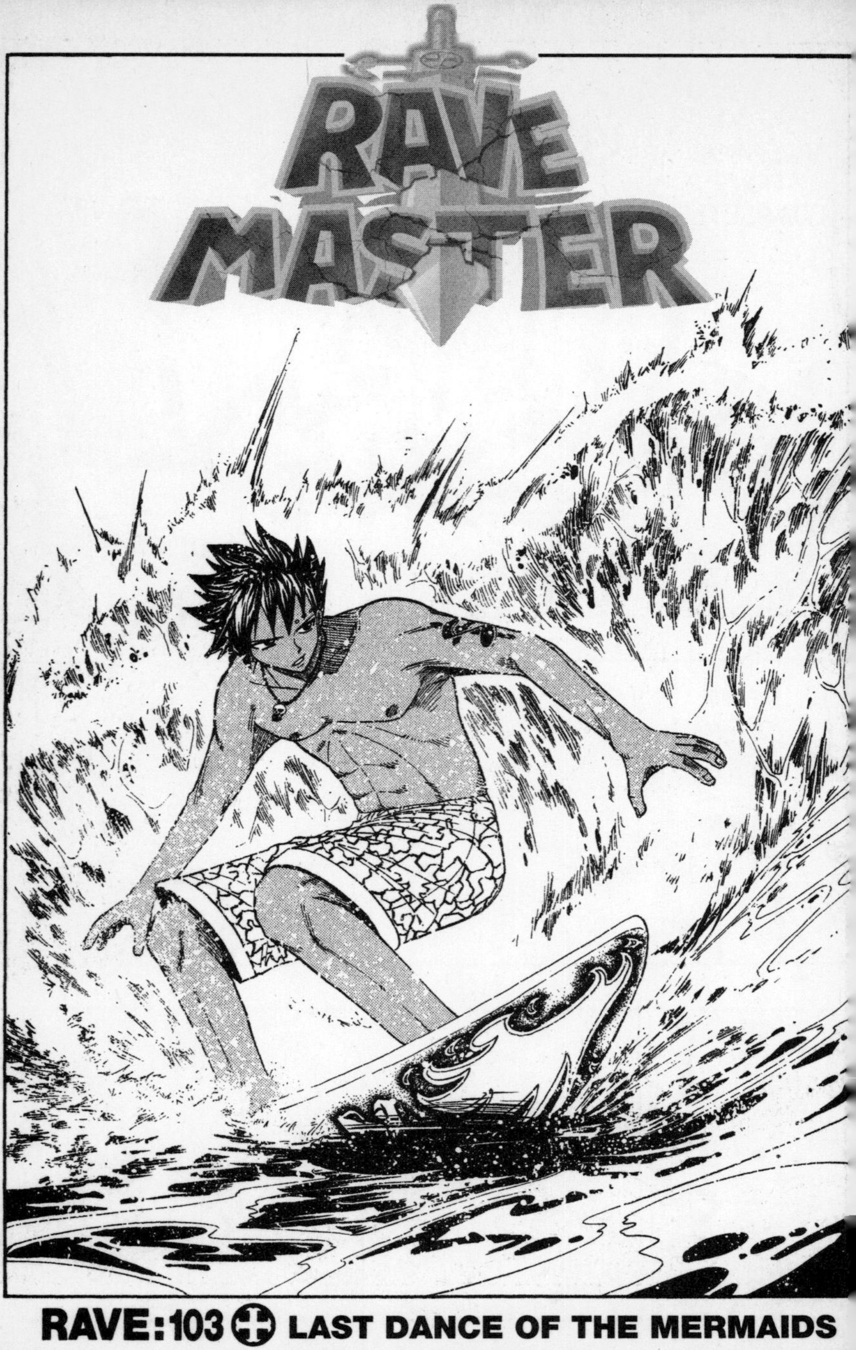
RAVE MASTER

RAVE:103 ✚ LAST DANCE OF THE MERMAIDS

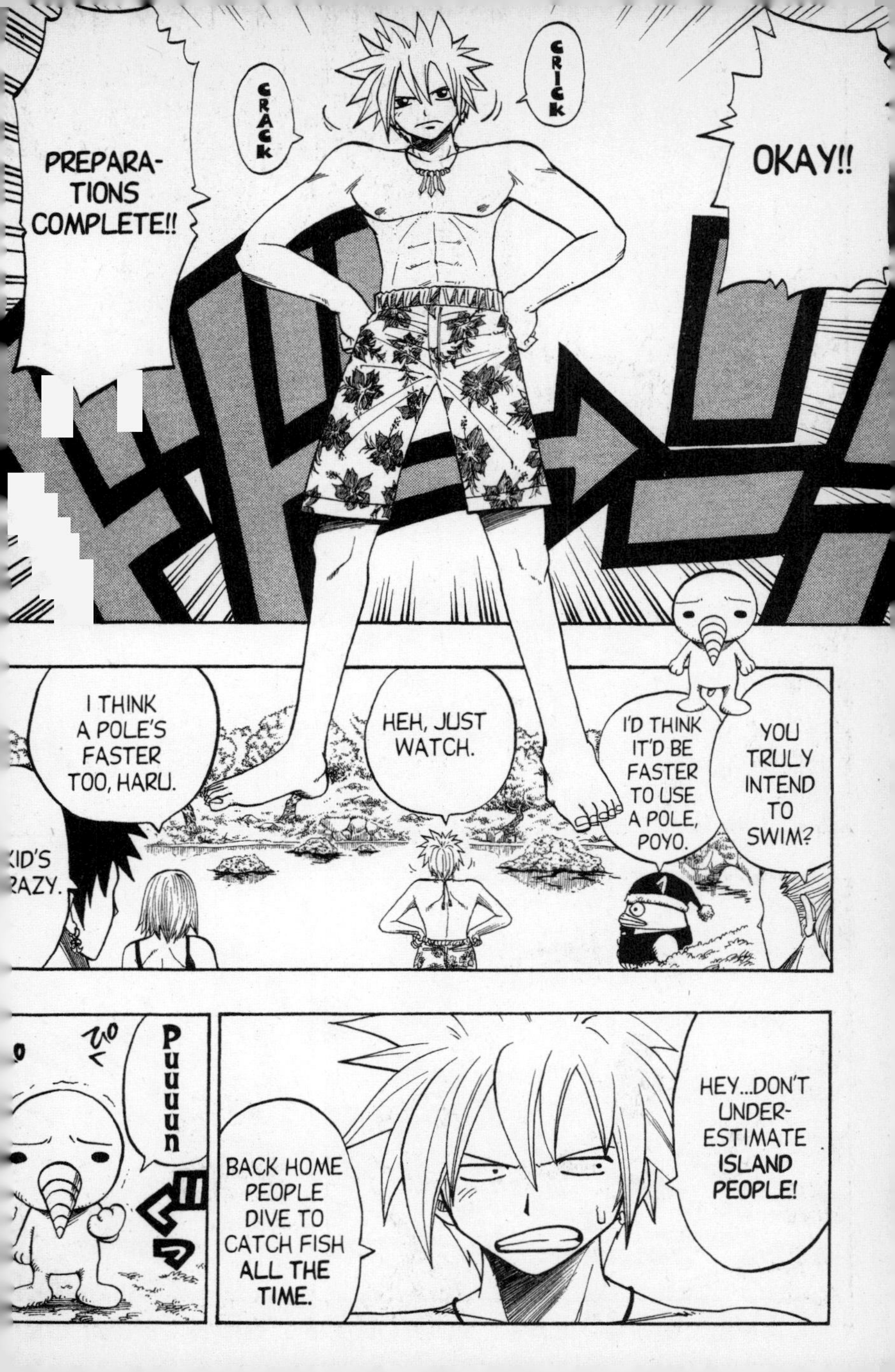
OKAY!!
CRICK
CRACK
PREPARATIONS COMPLETE!!
YOU TRULY INTEND TO SWIM?
I'D THINK IT'D BE FASTER TO USE A POLE, POYO.
HEH, JUST WATCH.
I THINK A POLE'S FASTER TOO, HARU.
HEY...DON'T UNDER-ESTIMATE ISLAND PEOPLE!
BACK HOME PEOPLE DIVE TO CATCH FISH ALL THE TIME.
Puuuun

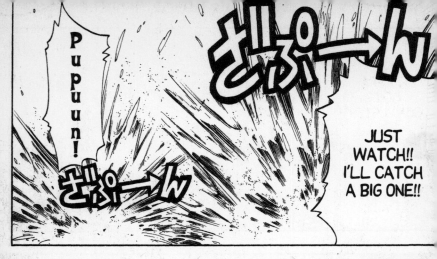

どぷーん
JUST WATCH!! I'LL CATCH A BIG ONE!!
Pupuun!
どぷーん
ボコ
ボコ
Puun
ばしゃ ばしゃ
Puun
ばしゃ ばしゃ
ボコ
ボコ
ボコ
MASTER PLUE, WHY DID YOU JUMP IN IF YOU COULDN'T SWIM?
HEY...I WANNA GO OVER THERE AND WASH UP.
SURE... HAVE FUN.
DON'T PEEK, NOW.
DON'T WORRY, I'LL STAND GUARD!!

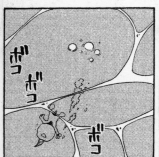

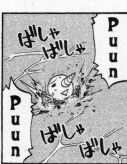

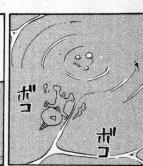

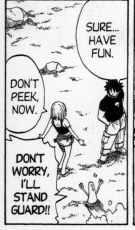

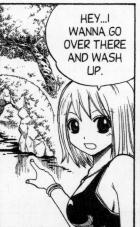

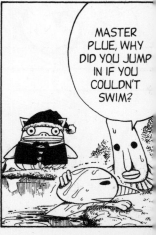

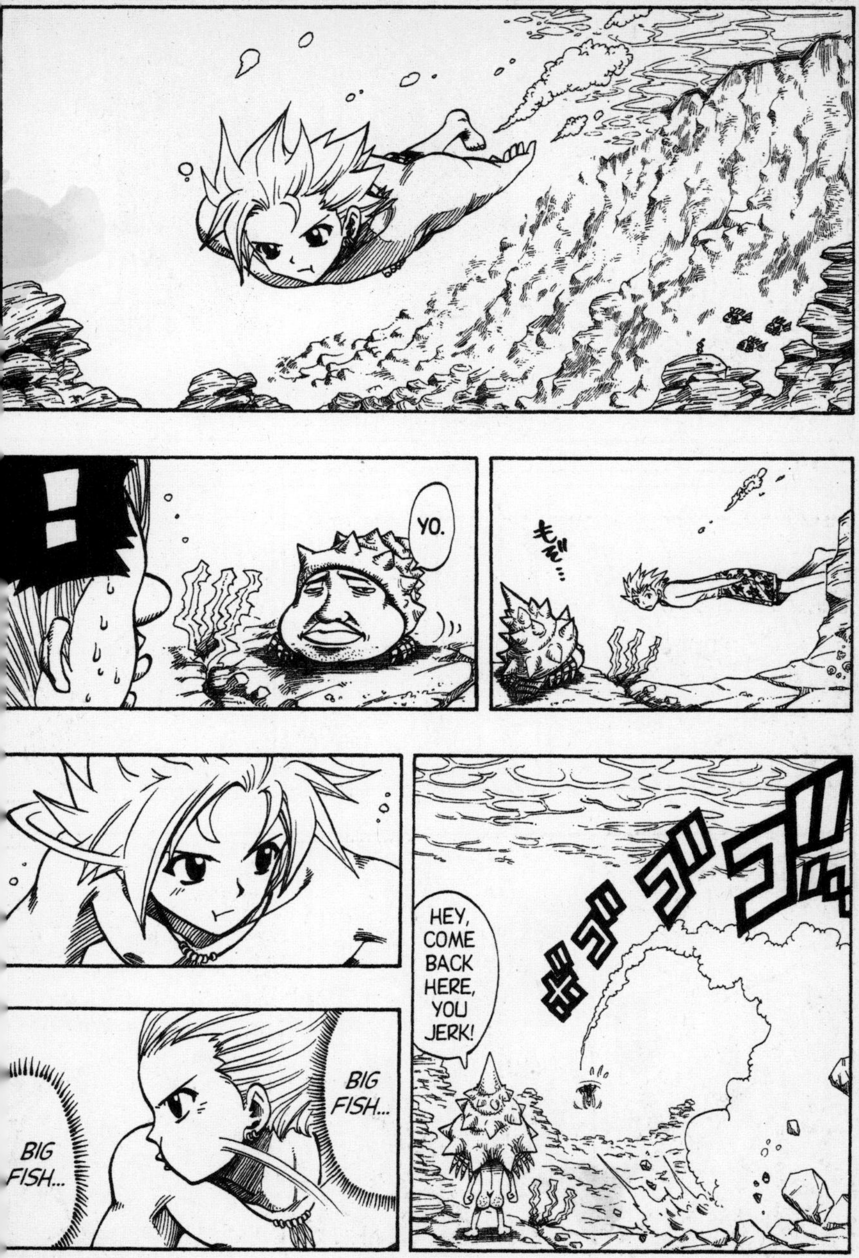
もぞ…
YO.
HEY, COME BACK HERE, YOU JERK!
BIG FISH...
BIG FISH...

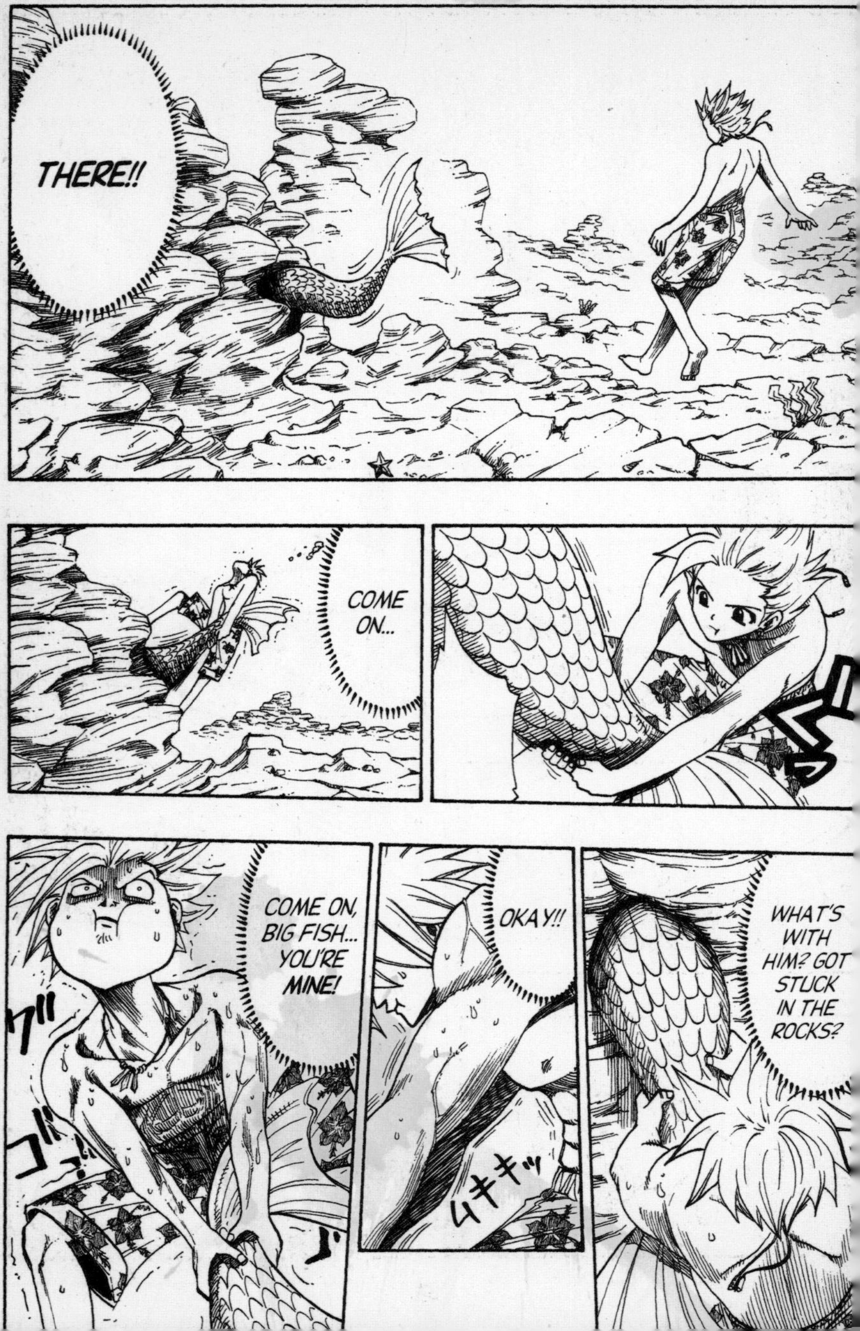
THERE!!
COME ON...
WHAT'S WITH HIM? GOT STUCK IN THE ROCKS?
OKAY!!
ムキキッ
COME ON, BIG FISH... YOU'RE MINE!

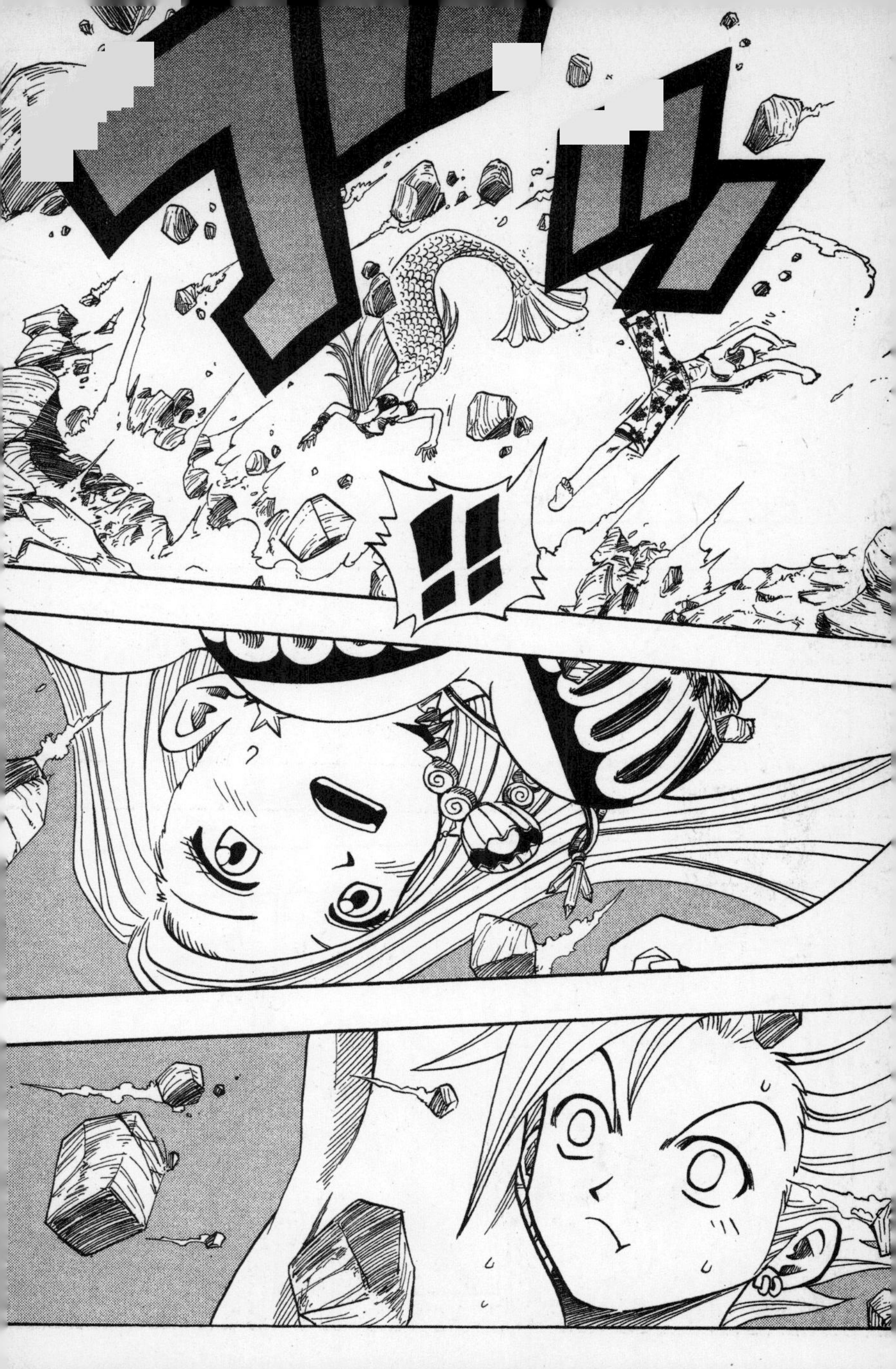
!!

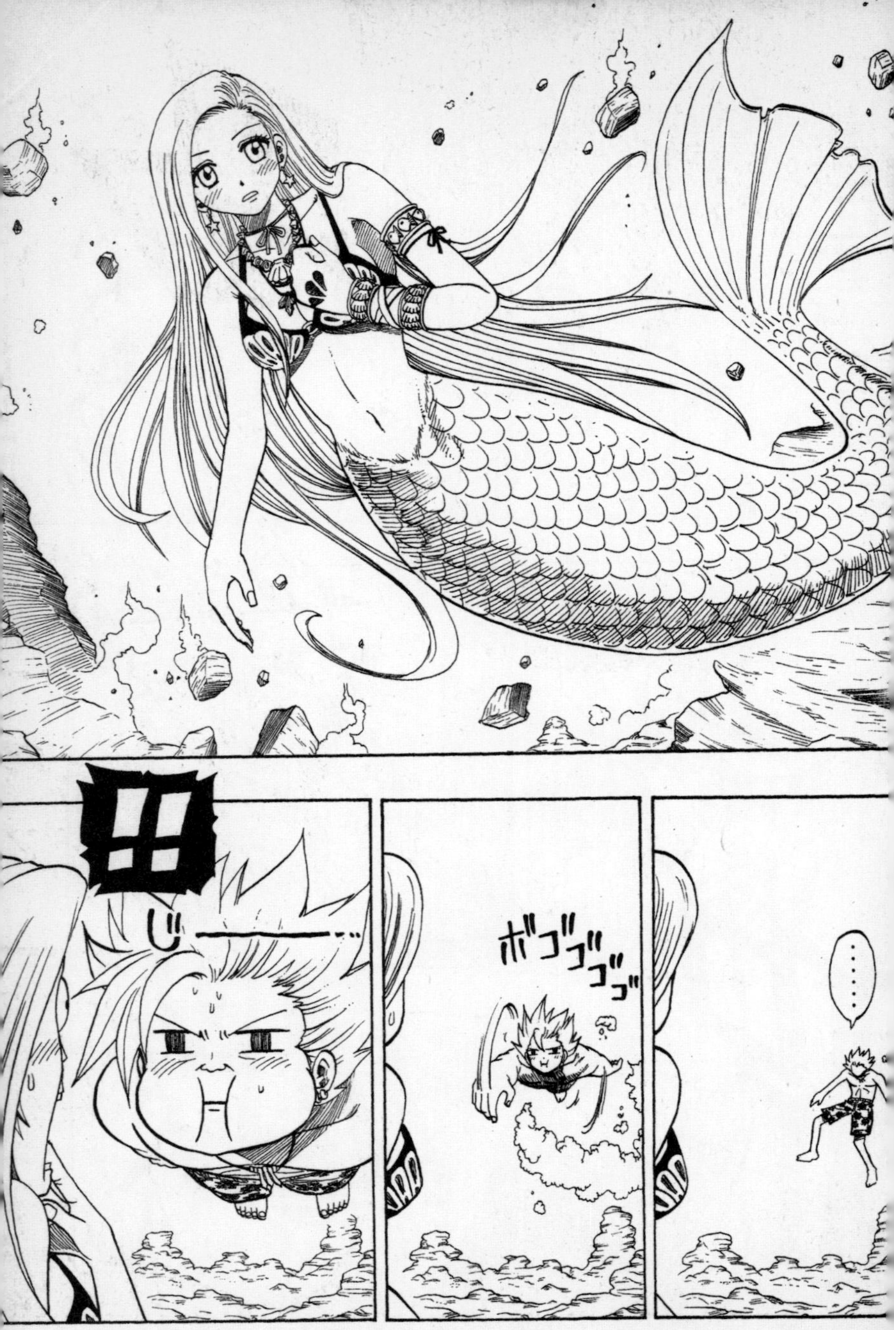
……
ボゴゴゴ
!!
じーーー…

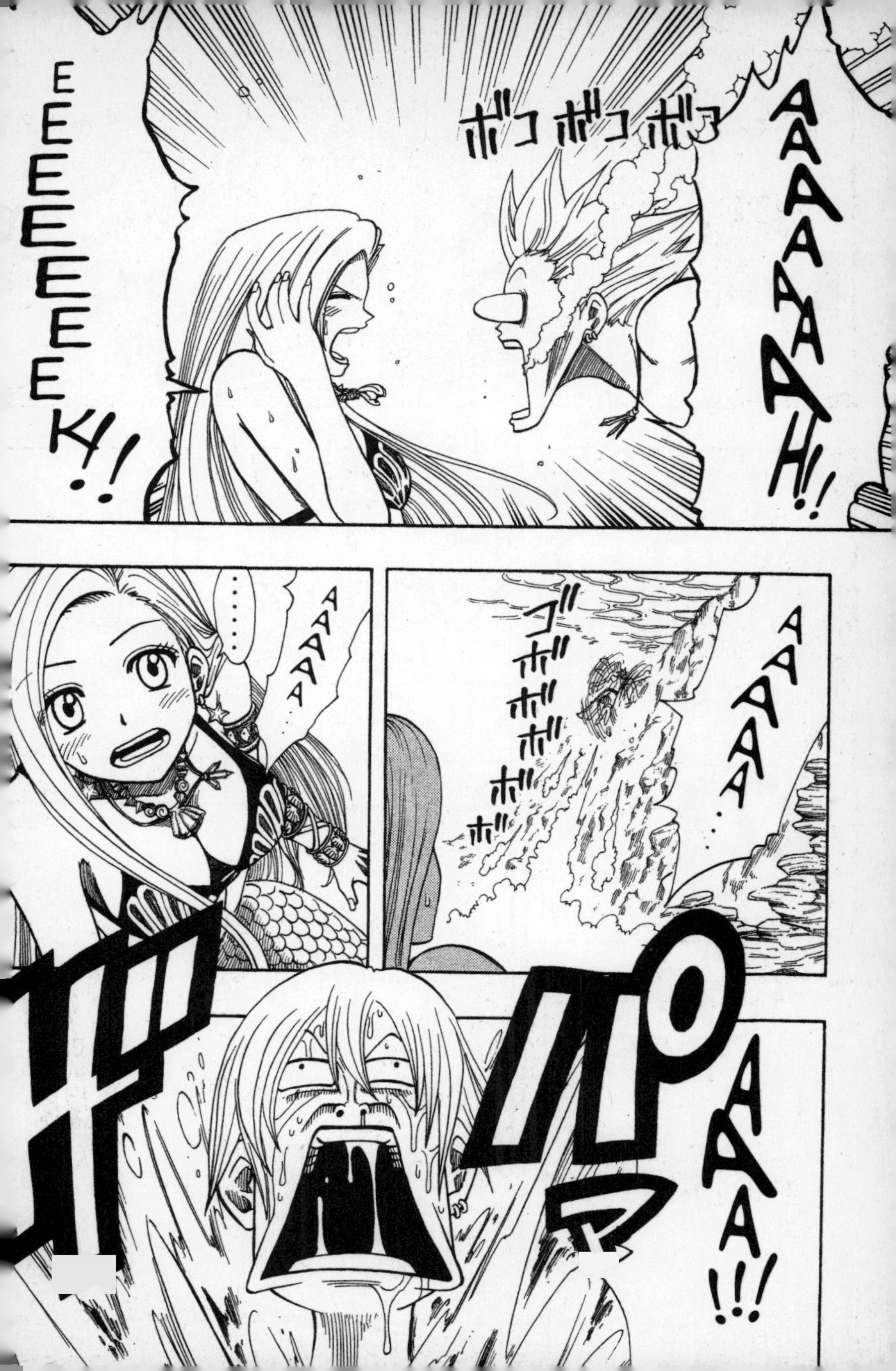
AAAAAAAH!!
ボコボコボコ
EEEEEEEK!!
ゴボボボボボ
AAAAA...
......
AAAAA...
AAA!!!

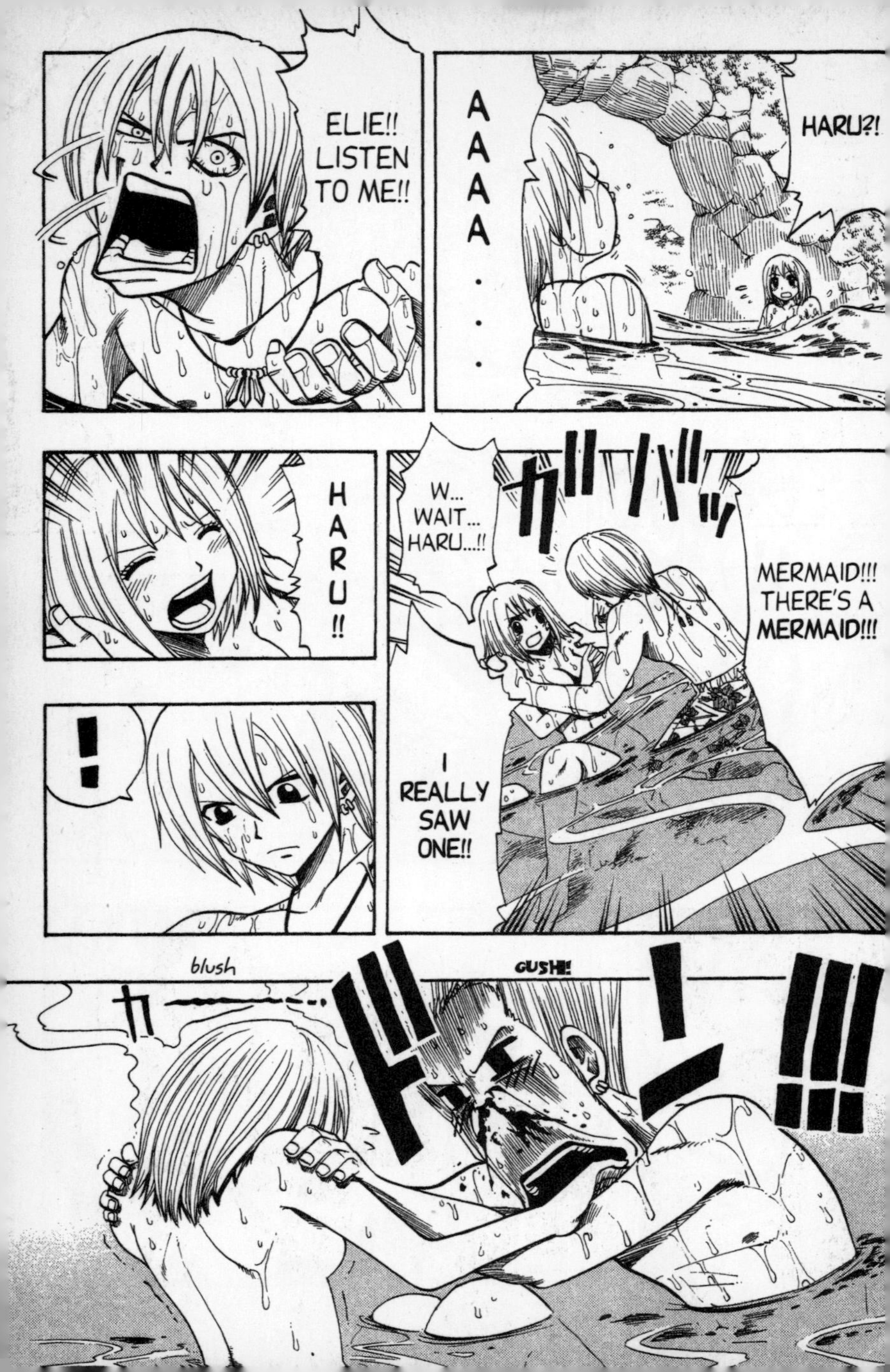
HARU?!
AAAA....
ELIE!! LISTEN TO ME!!
ガバッ
MERMAID!!! THERE'S A MERMAID!!!
W... WAIT... HARU...!!
I REALLY SAW ONE!!
HARU!!
!
GUSH!
ドーン!!!
blush
カー

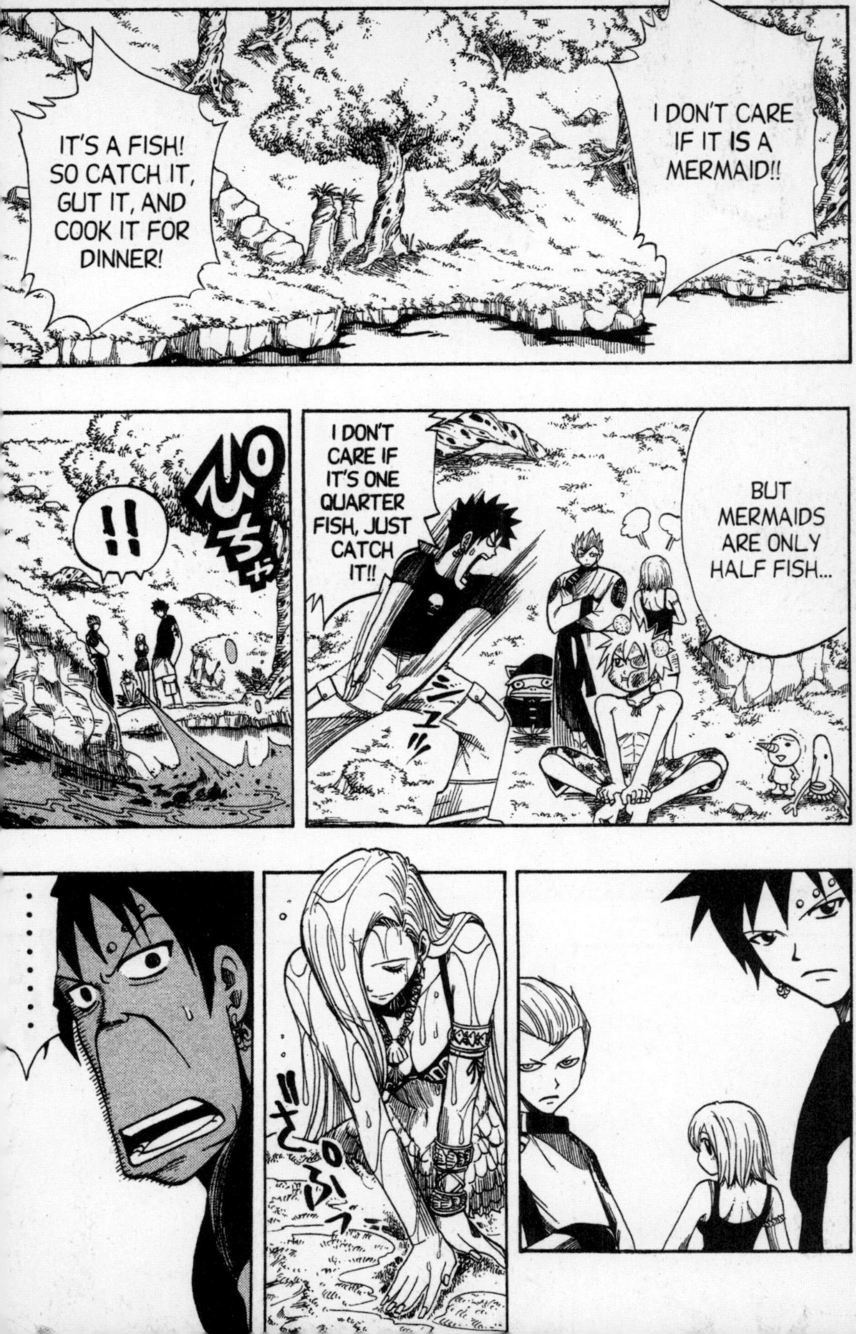

I DON'T CARE IF IT IS A MERMAID!!
IT'S A FISH! SO CATCH IT, GUT IT, AND COOK IT FOR DINNER!
BUT MERMAIDS ARE ONLY HALF FISH...
I DON'T CARE IF IT'S ONE QUARTER FISH, JUST CATCH IT!!
!!
ぴちゃ
......

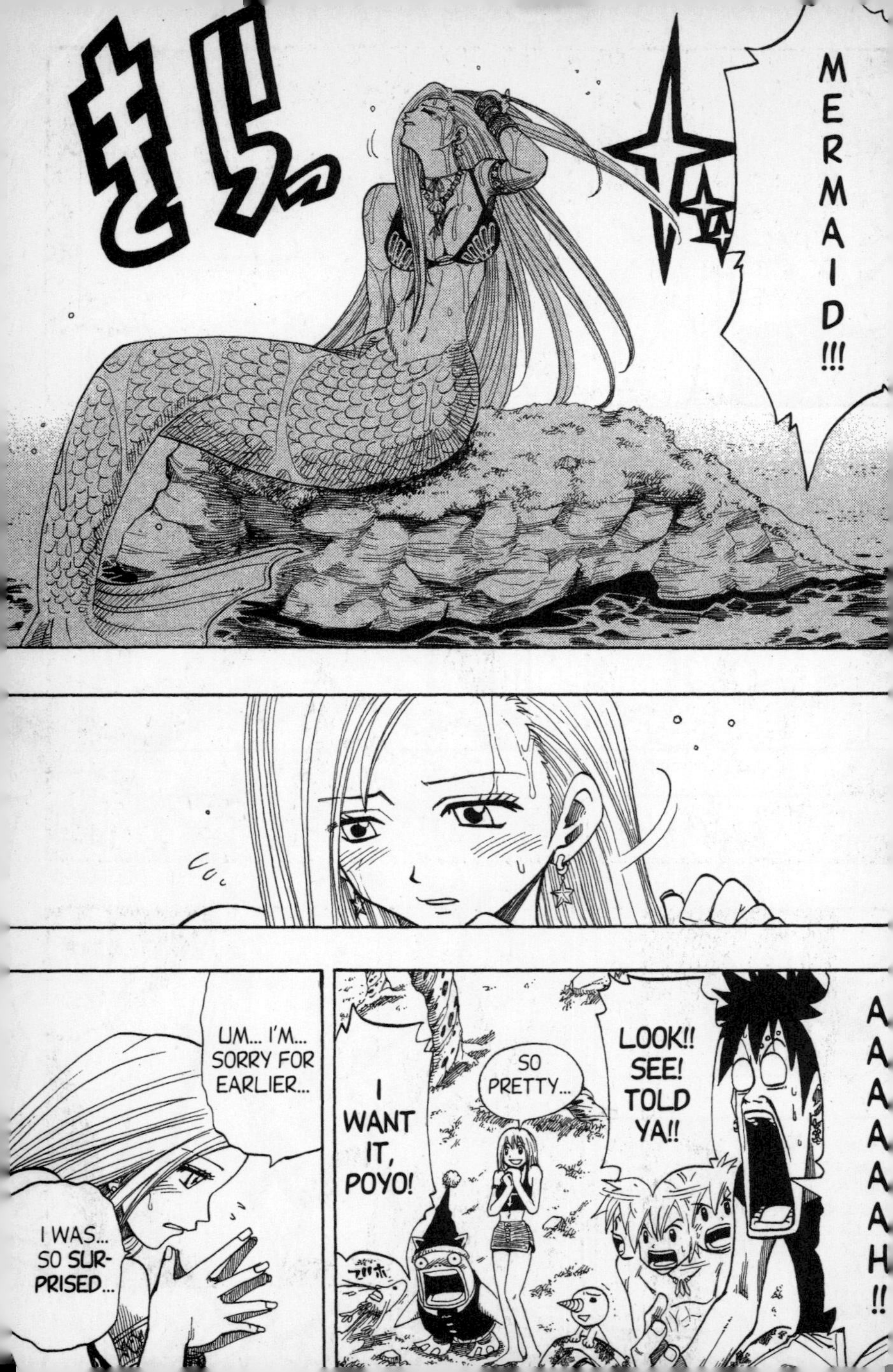
MERMAID!!!
きらっ
AAAAAAAH!!
LOOK!! SEE! TOLD YA!!
SO PRETTY...
I WANT IT, POYO!
UM... I'M... SORRY FOR EARLIER...
I WAS... SO SURPRISED...

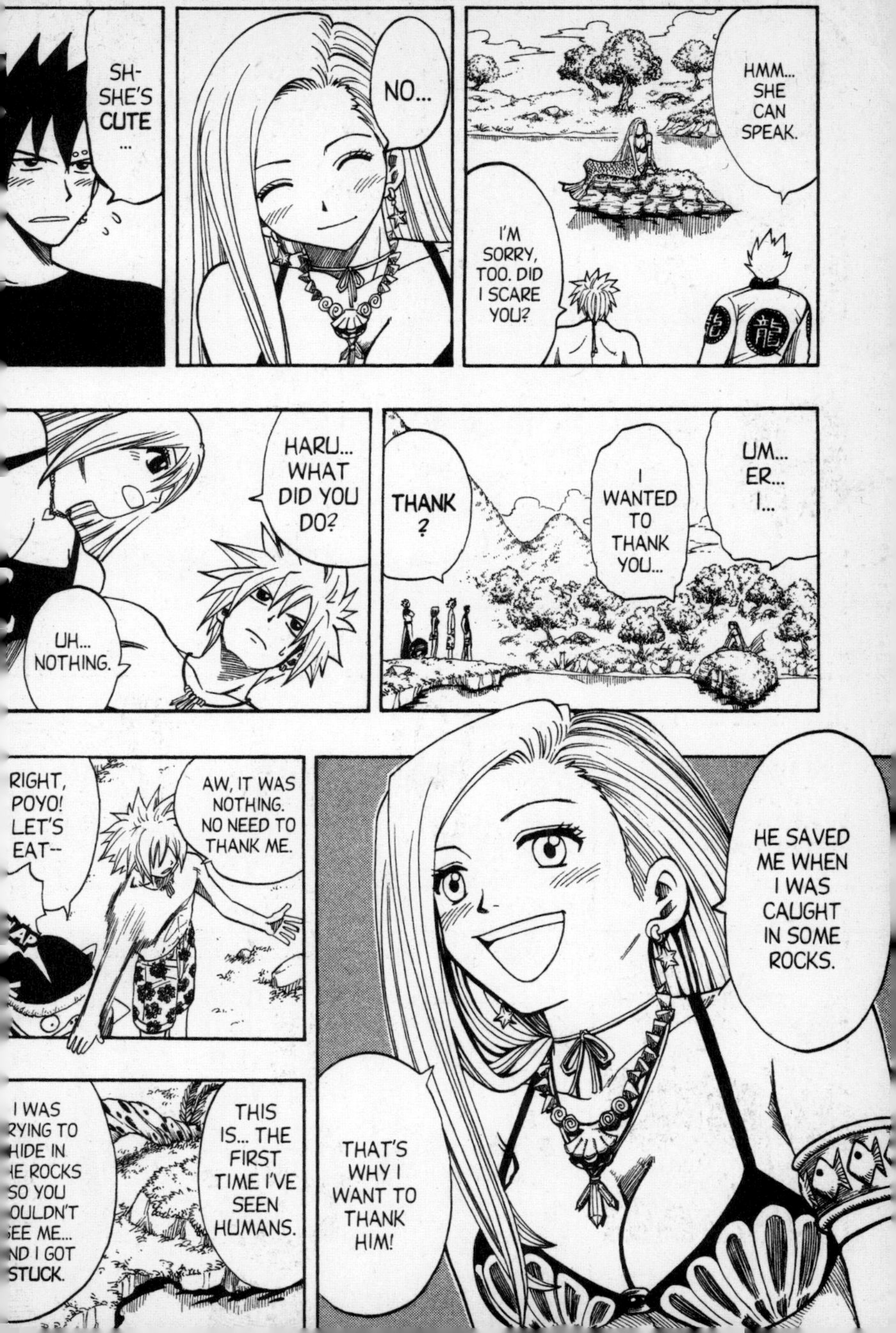
HMM... SHE CAN SPEAK.
I'M SORRY, TOO. DID I SCARE YOU?
NO...
SH-SHE'S CUTE...
UM... ER... I...
I WANTED TO THANK YOU...
THANK?
HARU... WHAT DID YOU DO?
UH... NOTHING.
HE SAVED ME WHEN I WAS CAUGHT IN SOME ROCKS.
THAT'S WHY I WANT TO THANK HIM!
AW, IT WAS NOTHING. NO NEED TO THANK ME.
RIGHT, POYO! LET'S EAT--
THIS IS... THE FIRST TIME I'VE SEEN HUMANS.
I WAS RYING TO HIDE IN HE ROCKS SO YOU OULDN'T SEE ME... ND I GOT STUCK.

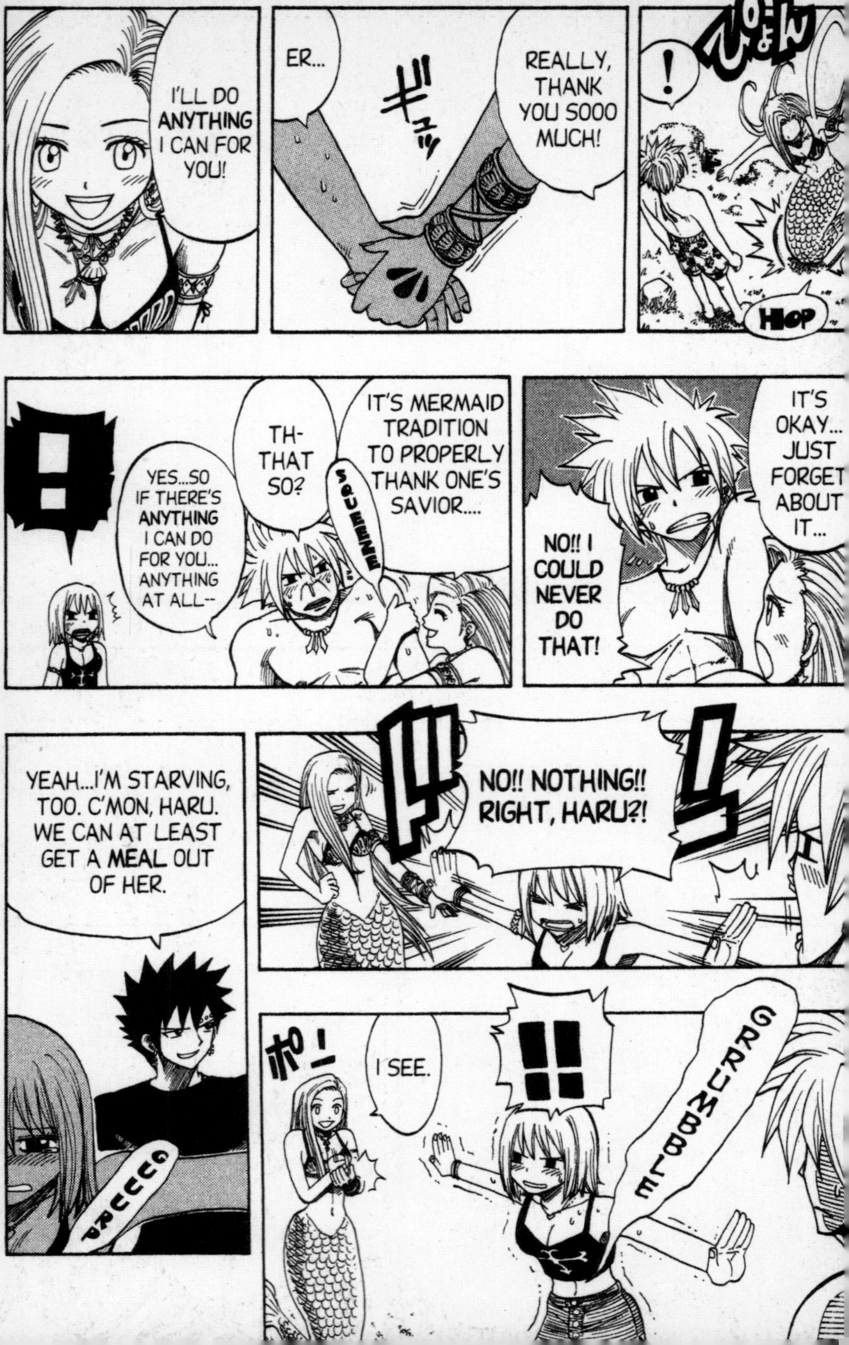
!
ぴょん
HOP
REALLY, THANK YOU SOOO MUCH!
ギュッ
ER...
I'LL DO ANYTHING I CAN FOR YOU!
IT'S OKAY... JUST FORGET ABOUT IT...
NO!! I COULD NEVER DO THAT!
IT'S MERMAID TRADITION TO PROPERLY THANK ONE'S SAVIOR....
TH- THAT SO?
SQUEEEE
YES...SO IF THERE'S ANYTHING I CAN DO FOR YOU... ANYTHING AT ALL--
!
NO!! NOTHING!! RIGHT, HARU?!
!!
GRRUMBBLE
I SEE.
YEAH...I'M STARVING, TOO. C'MON, HARU. WE CAN AT LEAST GET A MEAL OUT OF HER.

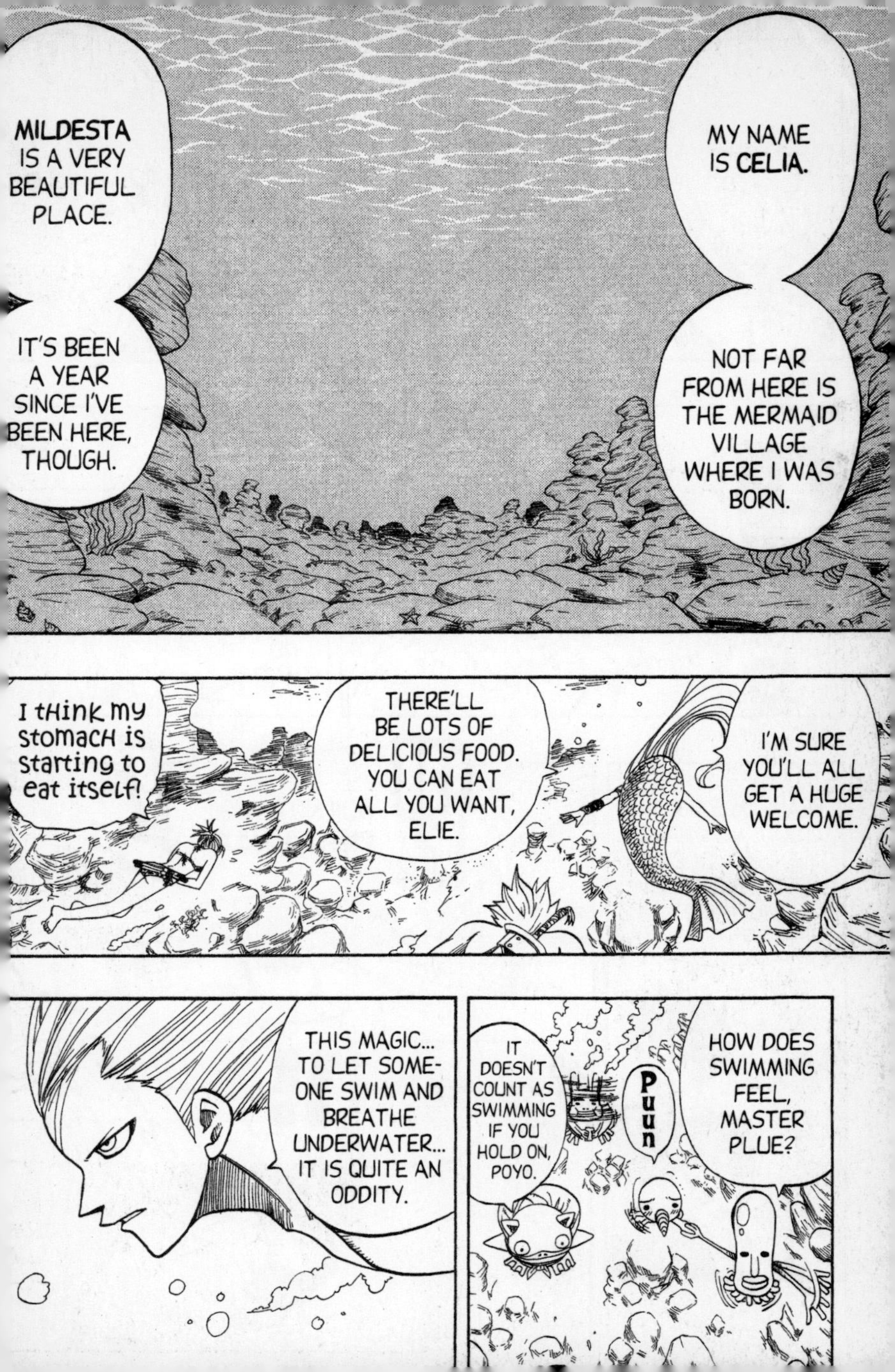
MY NAME IS CELIA.
NOT FAR FROM HERE IS THE MERMAID VILLAGE WHERE I WAS BORN.
MILDESTA IS A VERY BEAUTIFUL PLACE.
IT'S BEEN A YEAR SINCE I'VE BEEN HERE, THOUGH.
I'M SURE YOU'LL ALL GET A HUGE WELCOME.
THERE'LL BE LOTS OF DELICIOUS FOOD. YOU CAN EAT ALL YOU WANT, ELIE.
I think my stomach is starting to eat itself!
HOW DOES SWIMMING FEEL, MASTER PLUE?
Puun
IT DOESN'T COUNT AS SWIMMING IF YOU HOLD ON, POYO.
THIS MAGIC... TO LET SOME-ONE SWIM AND BREATHE UNDERWATER... IT IS QUITE AN ODDITY.

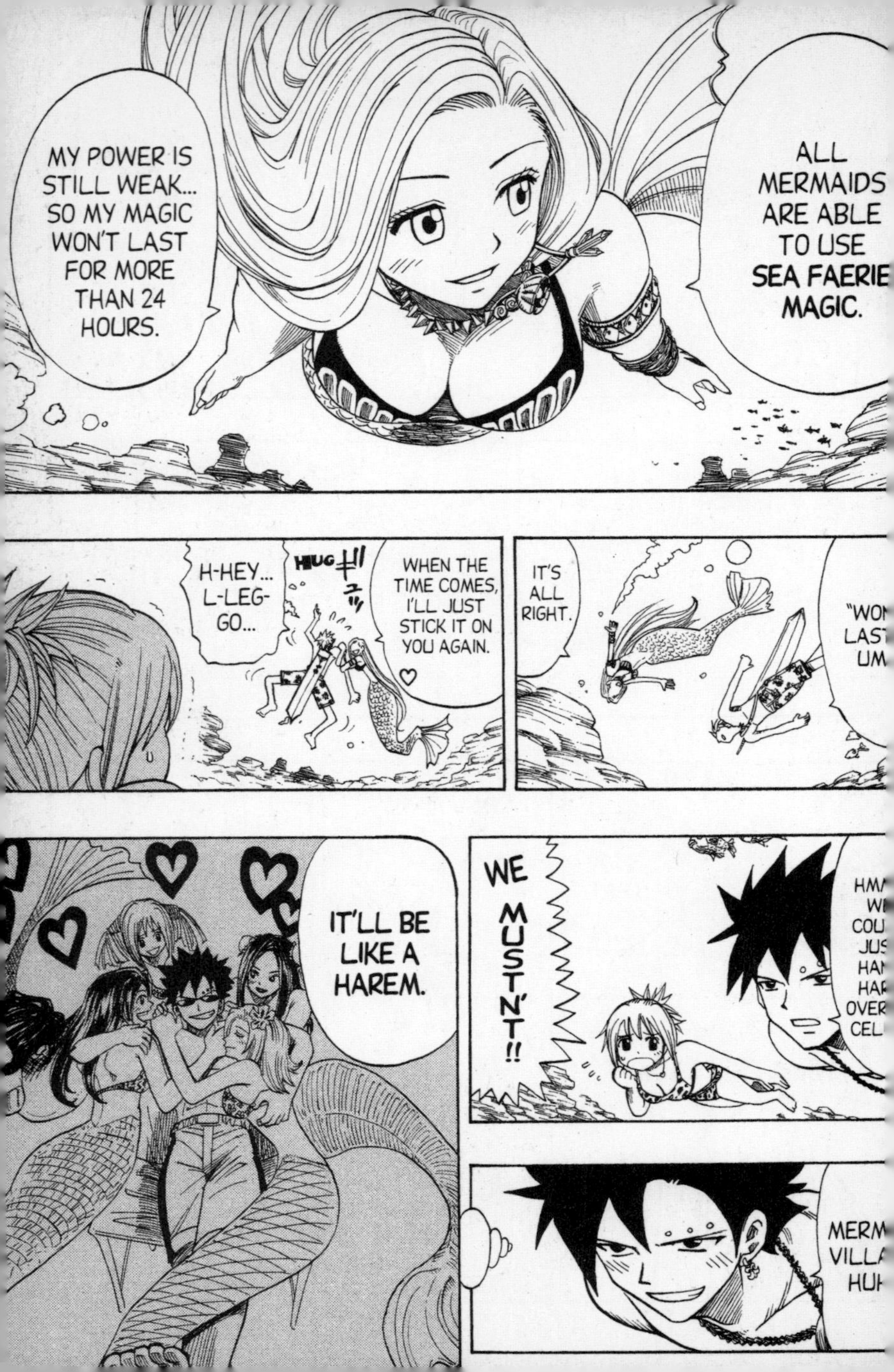
ALL MERMAIDS ARE ABLE TO USE SEA FAERIE MAGIC.
MY POWER IS STILL WEAK... SO MY MAGIC WON'T LAST FOR MORE THAN 24 HOURS.
"WON LAST UM
IT'S ALL RIGHT.
WHEN THE TIME COMES, I'LL JUST STICK IT ON YOU AGAIN.
HUG
H-HEY... L-LEG-GO...
HMA WE COU JUS HAN HAR OVER CEL
WE MUSTN'T!!
MERM VILLA HUH
IT'LL BE LIKE A HAREM.

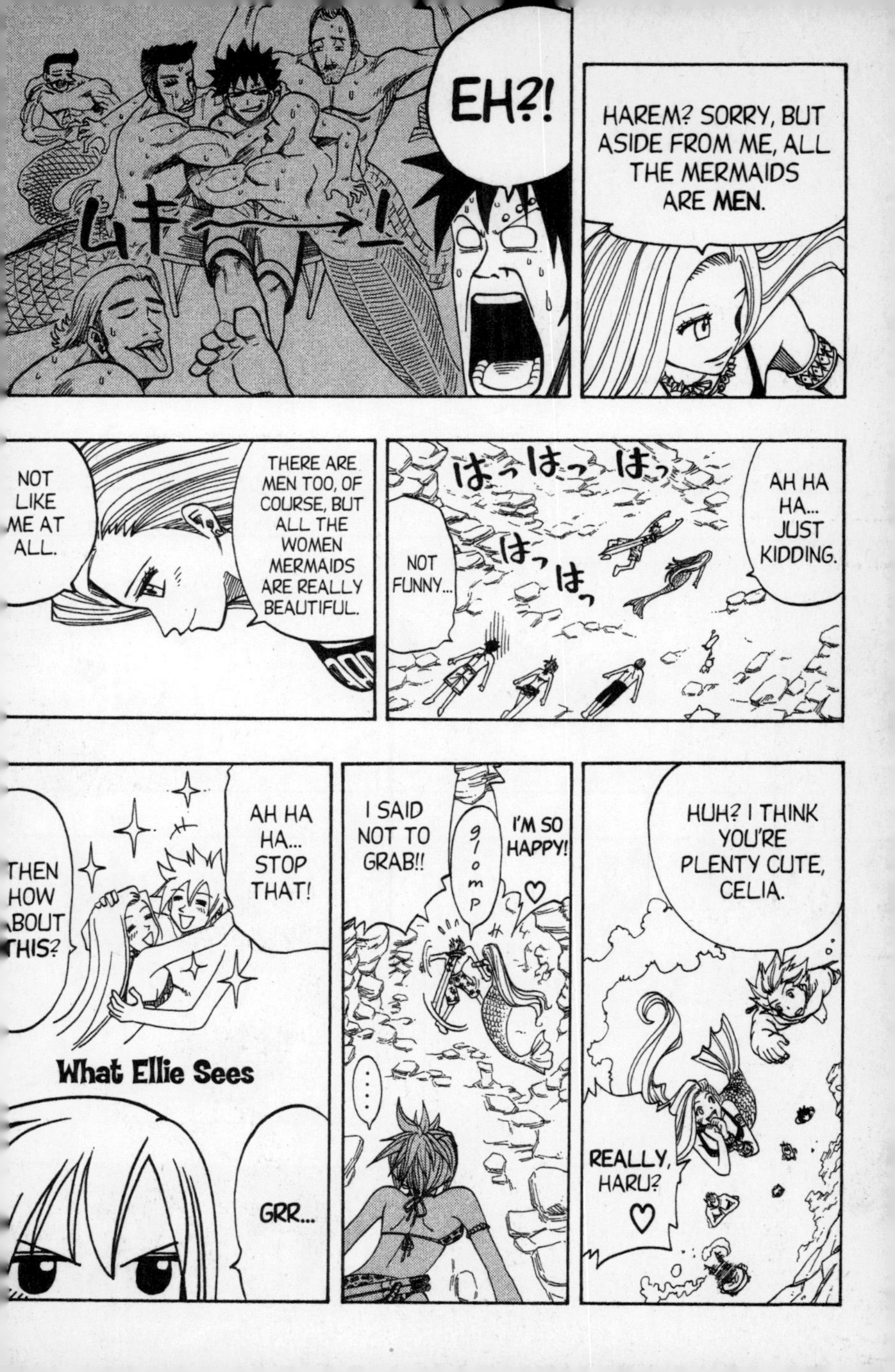
HAREM? SORRY, BUT ASIDE FROM ME, ALL THE MERMAIDS ARE MEN.
EH?!
ムキ〜〜ー
AH HA HA... JUST KIDDING.
NOT FUNNY...
はっはっはっはっはっ
THERE ARE MEN TOO, OF COURSE, BUT ALL THE WOMEN MERMAIDS ARE REALLY BEAUTIFUL.
NOT LIKE ME AT ALL.
HUH? I THINK YOU'RE PLENTY CUTE, CELIA.
REALLY, HARU? ♥
I'M SO HAPPY! ♥
GLOMP
I SAID NOT TO GRAB!!
......
AH HA HA... STOP THAT!
THEN HOW ABOUT THIS?
What Ellie Sees
GRR...

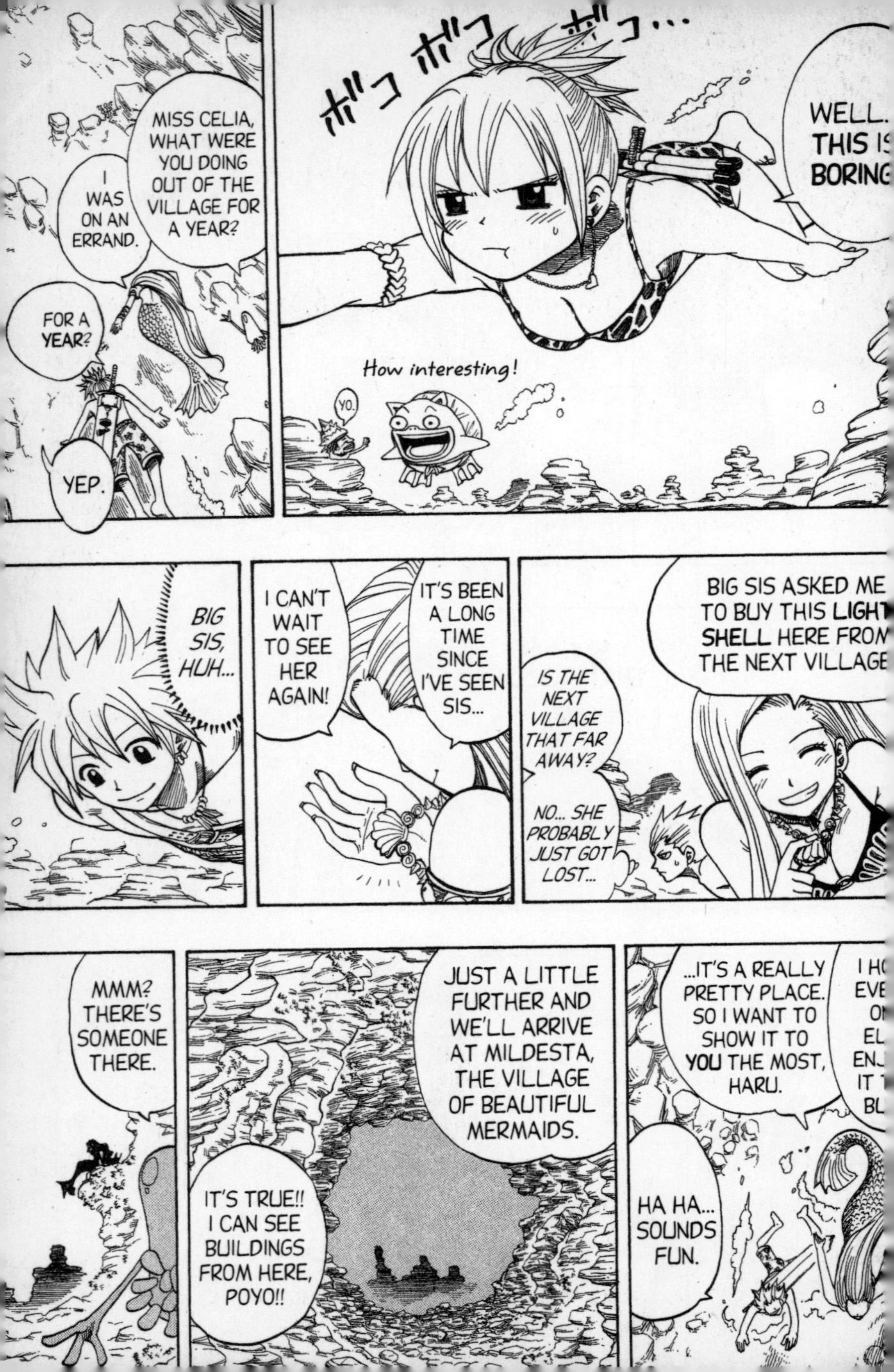
WELL.. THIS IS BORING
ボコ ボコ ボコ…
How interesting!
YO.
MISS CELIA, WHAT WERE YOU DOING OUT OF THE VILLAGE FOR A YEAR?
I WAS ON AN ERRAND.
FOR A YEAR?
YEP.
BIG SIS ASKED ME TO BUY THIS LIGHT SHELL HERE FROM THE NEXT VILLAGE
IS THE NEXT VILLAGE THAT FAR AWAY?
NO... SHE PROBABLY JUST GOT LOST...
IT'S BEEN A LONG TIME SINCE I'VE SEEN SIS...
I CAN'T WAIT TO SEE HER AGAIN!
BIG SIS, HUH...
...IT'S A REALLY PRETTY PLACE. SO I WANT TO SHOW IT TO YOU THE MOST, HARU.
HA HA... SOUNDS FUN.
JUST A LITTLE FURTHER AND WE'LL ARRIVE AT MILDESTA, THE VILLAGE OF BEAUTIFUL MERMAIDS.
IT'S TRUE!! I CAN SEE BUILDINGS FROM HERE, POYO!!
MMM? THERE'S SOMEONE THERE.

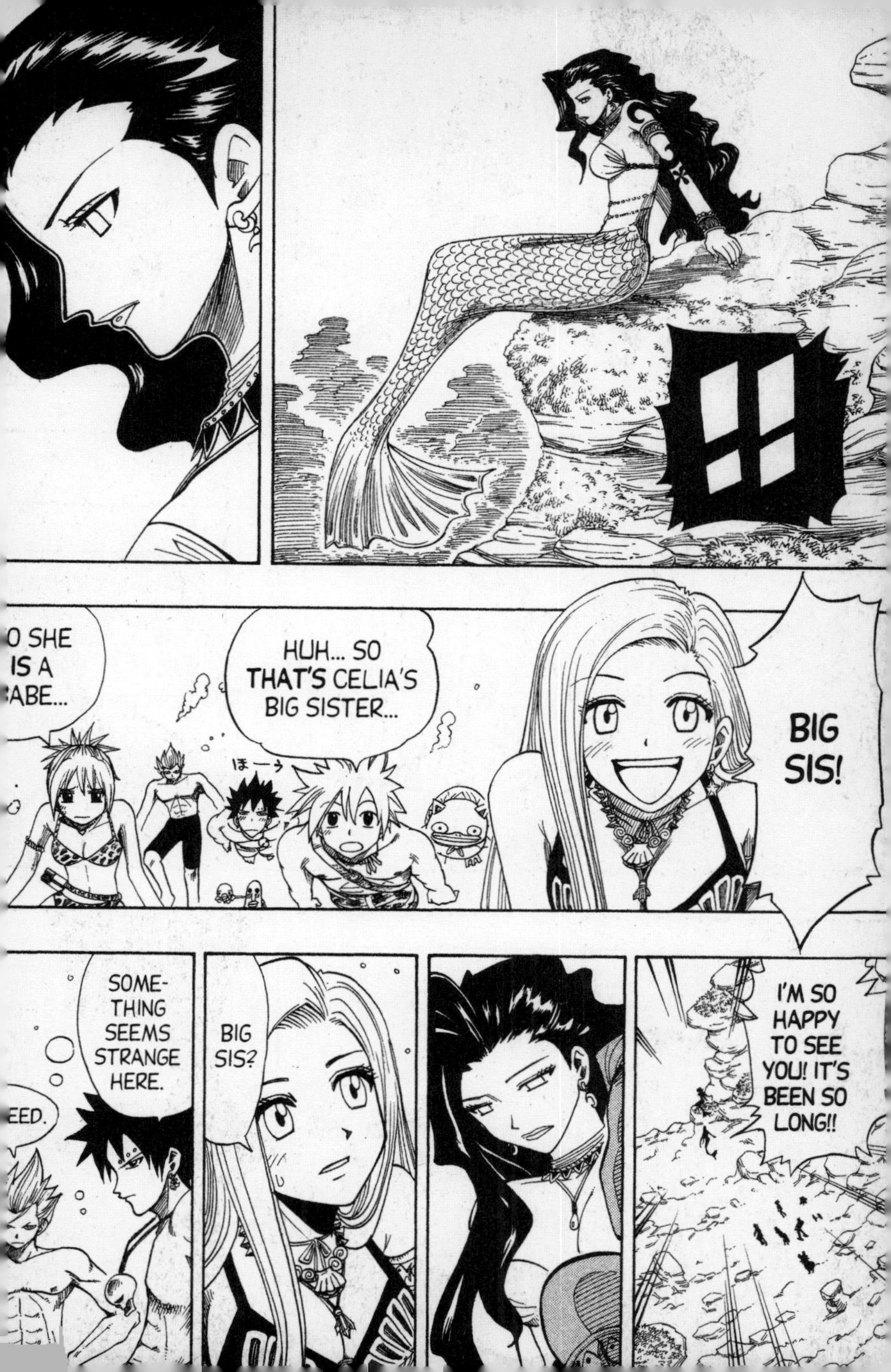
!!
BIG SIS!
HUH... SO THAT'S CELIA'S BIG SISTER...
O SHE IS A ABE...
I'M SO HAPPY TO SEE YOU! IT'S BEEN SO LONG!!
BIG SIS?
SOME-THING SEEMS STRANGE HERE.
EED.

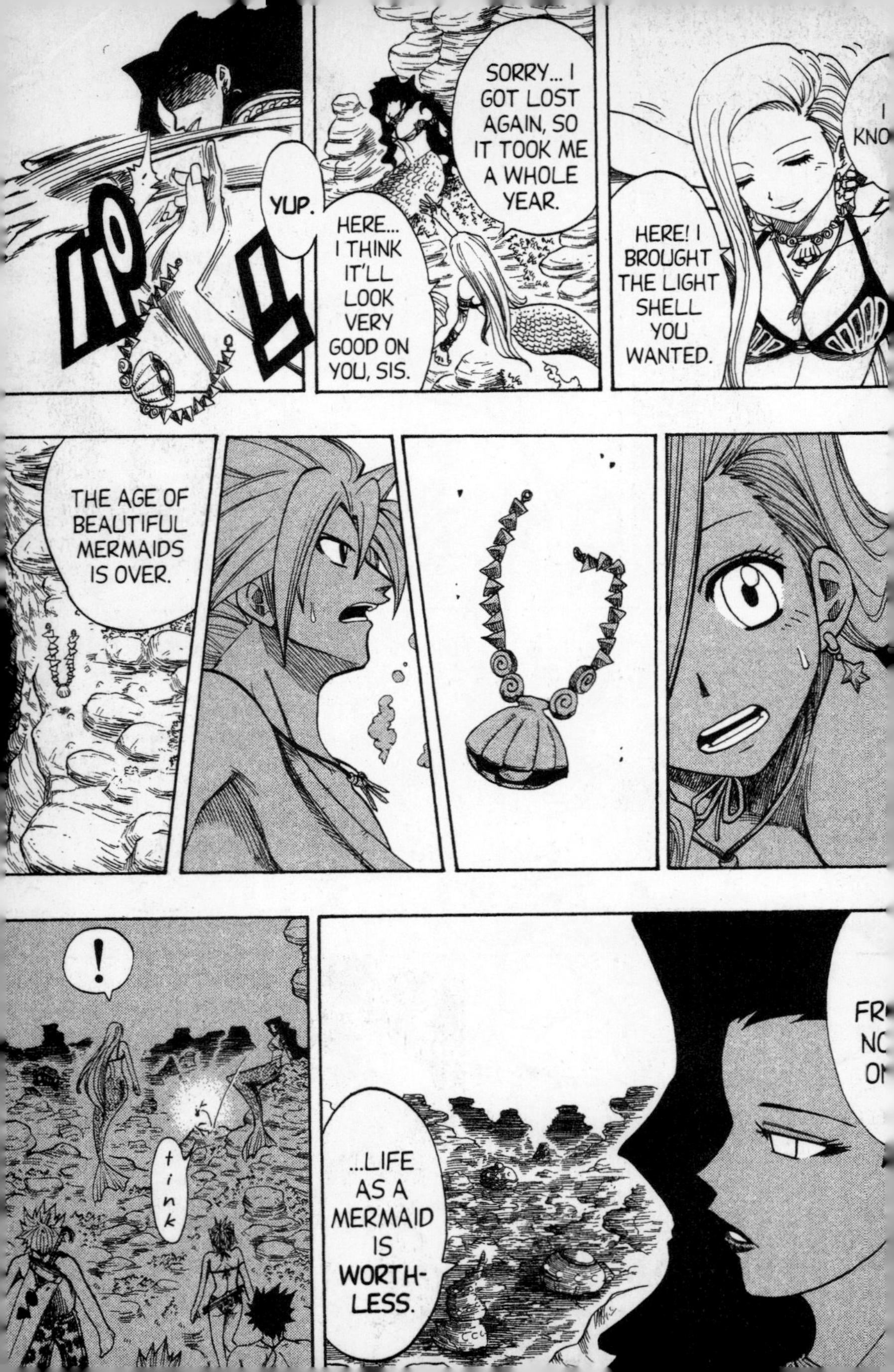
I KNO
HERE! I BROUGHT THE LIGHT SHELL YOU WANTED.
SORRY... I GOT LOST AGAIN, SO IT TOOK ME A WHOLE YEAR.
HERE... I THINK IT'LL LOOK VERY GOOD ON YOU, SIS.
YUP.
!?
THE AGE OF BEAUTIFUL MERMAIDS IS OVER.
...LIFE AS A MERMAID IS WORTHLESS.
!
tink

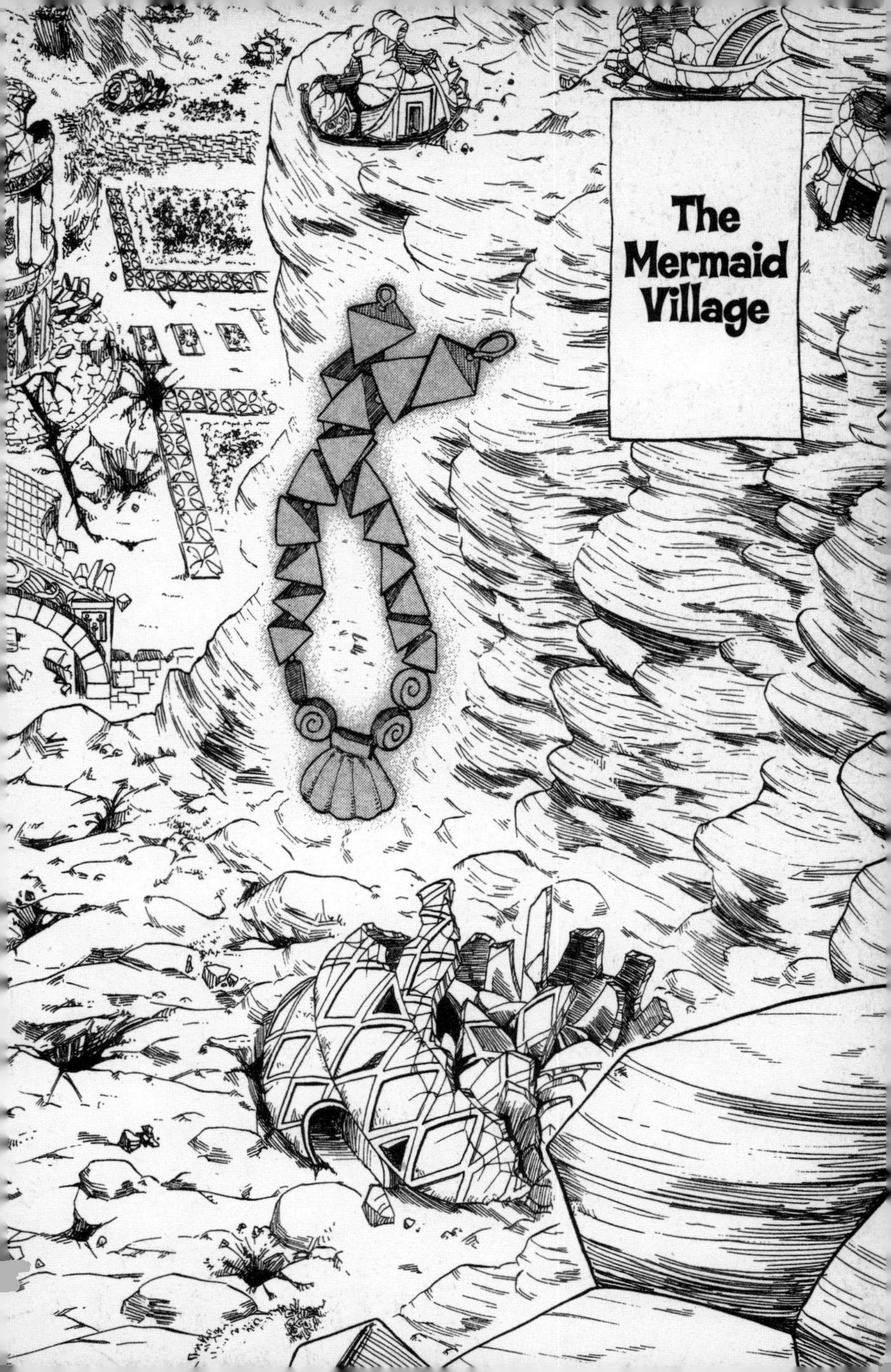
The Mermaid Village

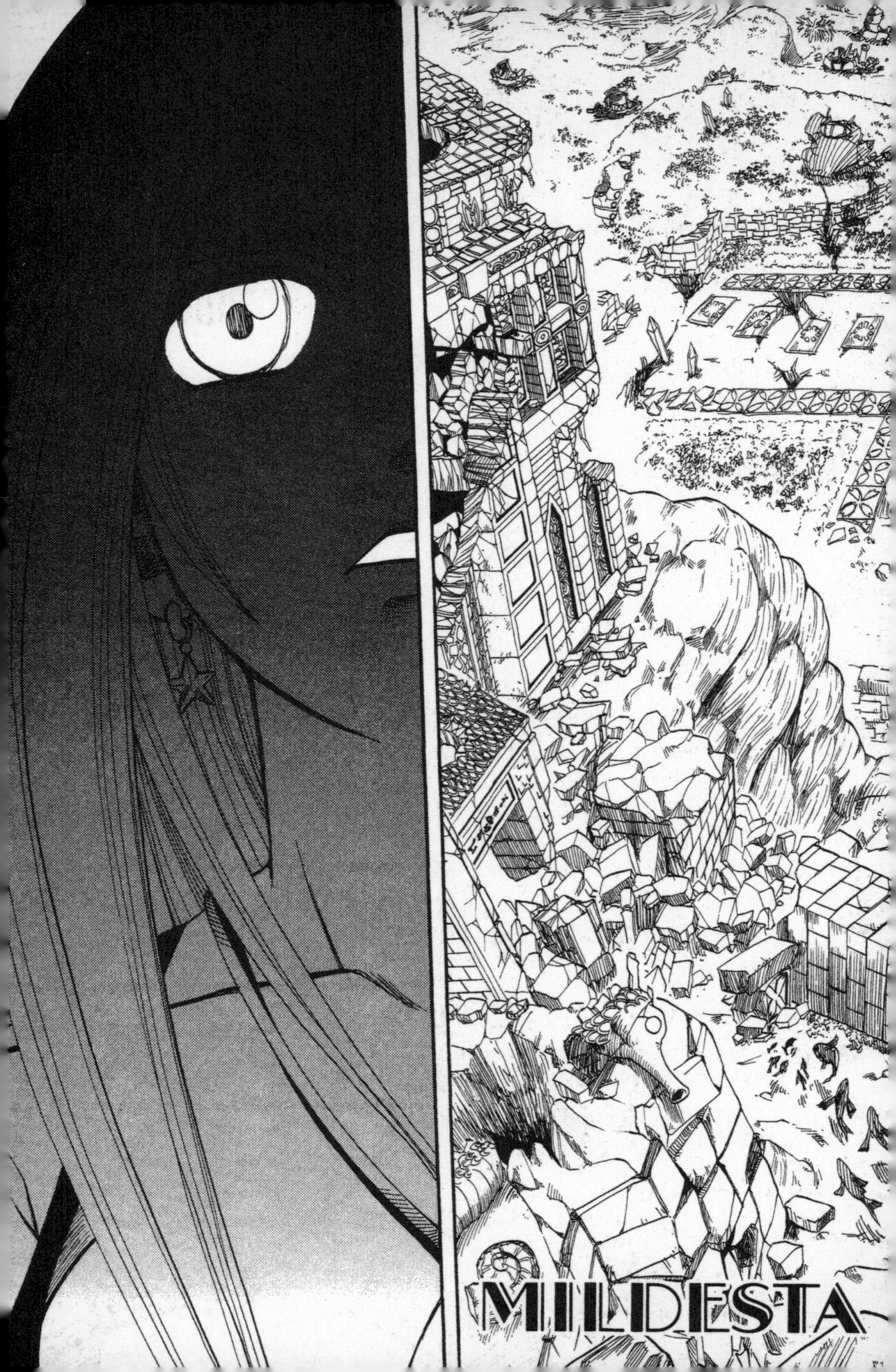
MILDESTA

Q&A CORNER!!

WELCOME BACK TO THE QUESTION CORNER! SORRY TO INTERRUPT THE STORY, BUT WE HAD TO PUT THE MAGAZINE "TEACH ME, HIRO-KUN!" QUESTION CORNER IN HERE SOMEWHERE.

THE NAME'S A LITTLE EMBARRASSING, ACTUALLY.

ANYWAY, LET'S BEGIN!

Q. Is Shuda's DB a Six Star DB? (like the other Oracion Six use?)

A. SORRY, I DIDN'T EXPLAIN IT. OOPS! BALLETTÄNZER ZEFFREA IS A SIX STAR DB.

Q. Elie's Tonfa Blasters in Vol. 11 were colored pink. Did she buy new ones?

A. THE TONFA BLASTERS COME IN MANY COLORS. THERE'S BLUE AND GOLD AND GREEN TOO. FIND ALL FIVE IF YOU HAVE SOME FREE TIME!

Q. Can you really beat the RAVE word search?!

A. WELL, SOME PEOPLE CAN!! AND THERE'S EVEN THE NAMES OF THE FOUR HOBBITS FROM *THE LORD OF THE RINGS* IN THERE!

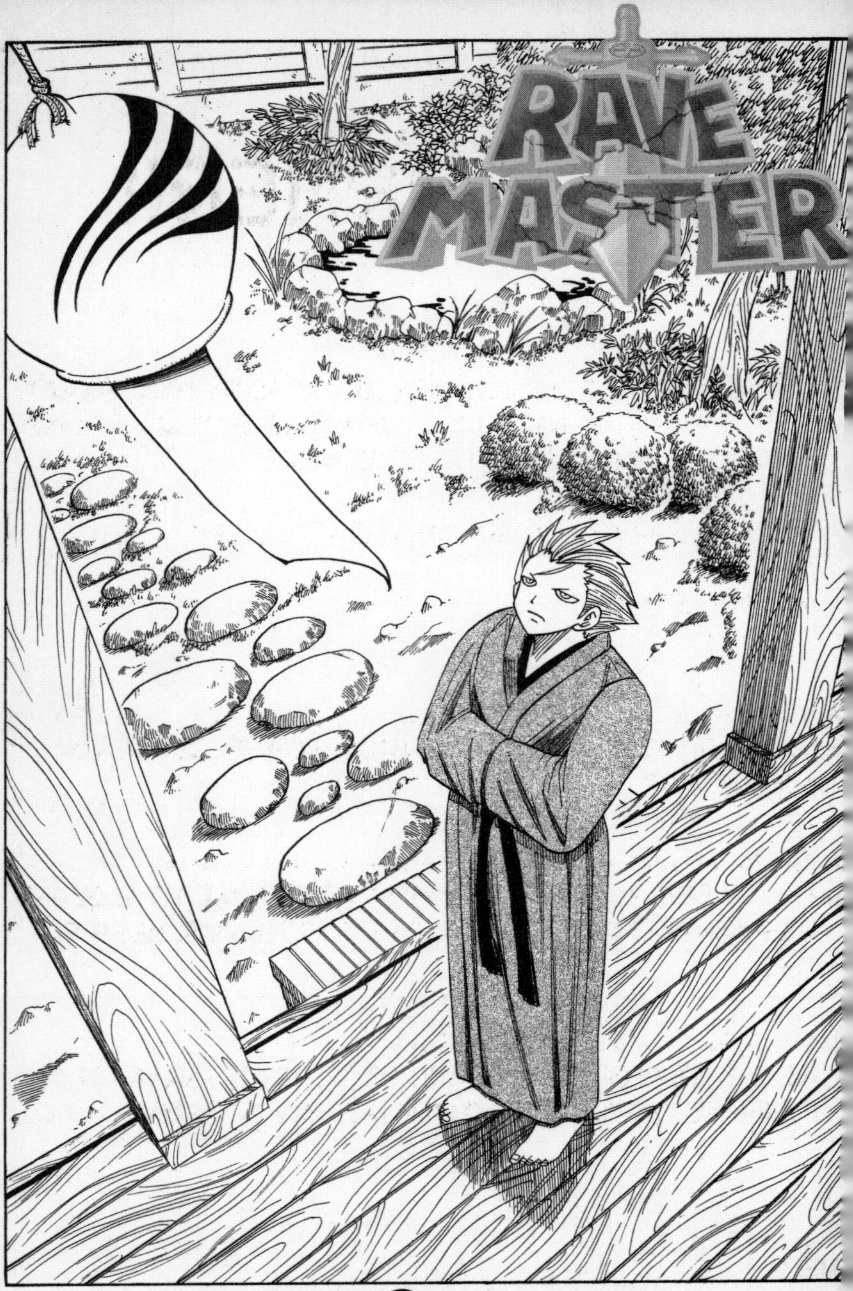
RAVE MASTER

RAVE:104 ✠ 1 GRAM PEACE

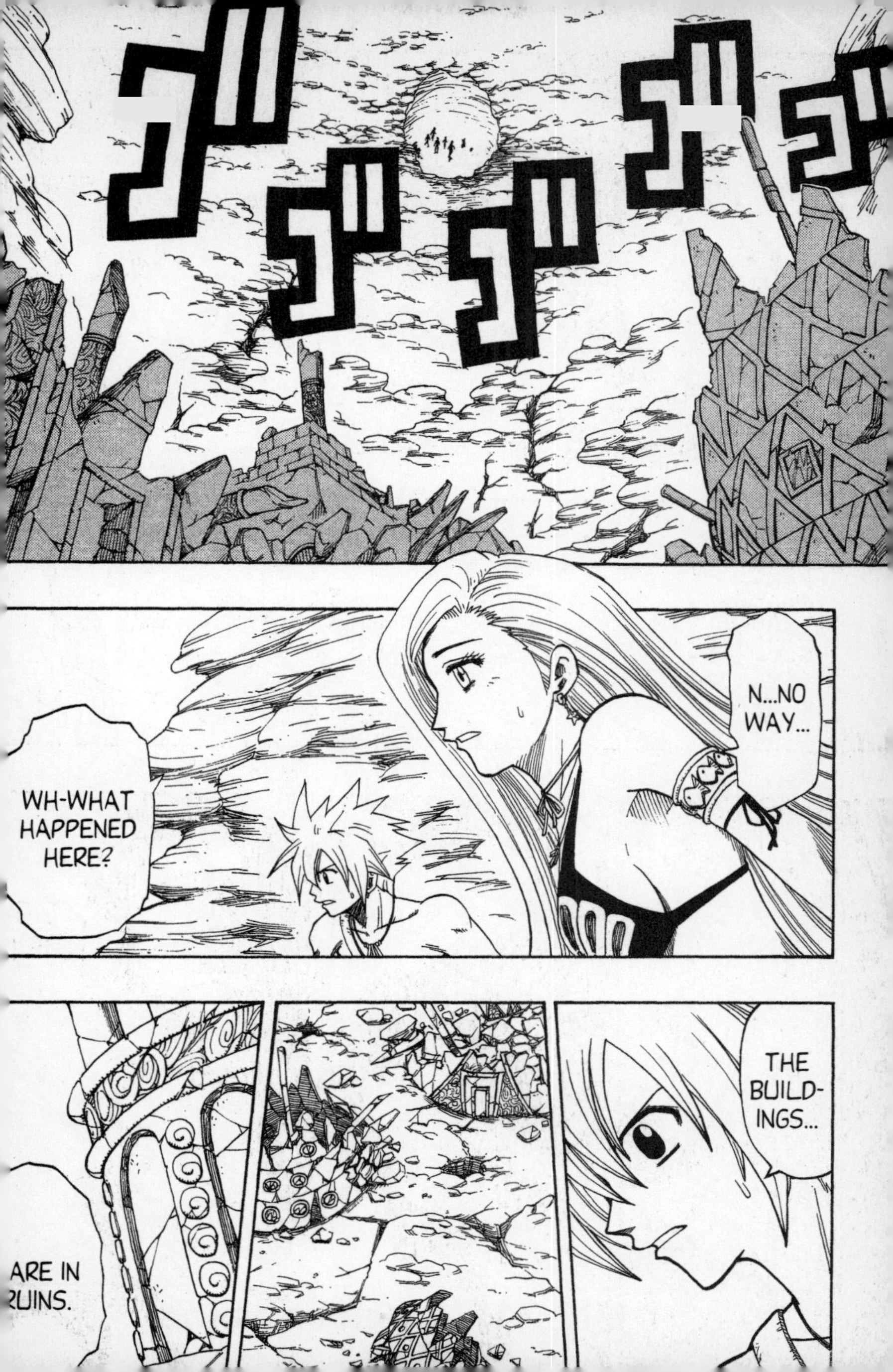
ゴゴゴゴゴ
N...NO WAY...
WH-WHAT HAPPENED HERE?
THE BUILD- INGS...
ARE IN RUINS.

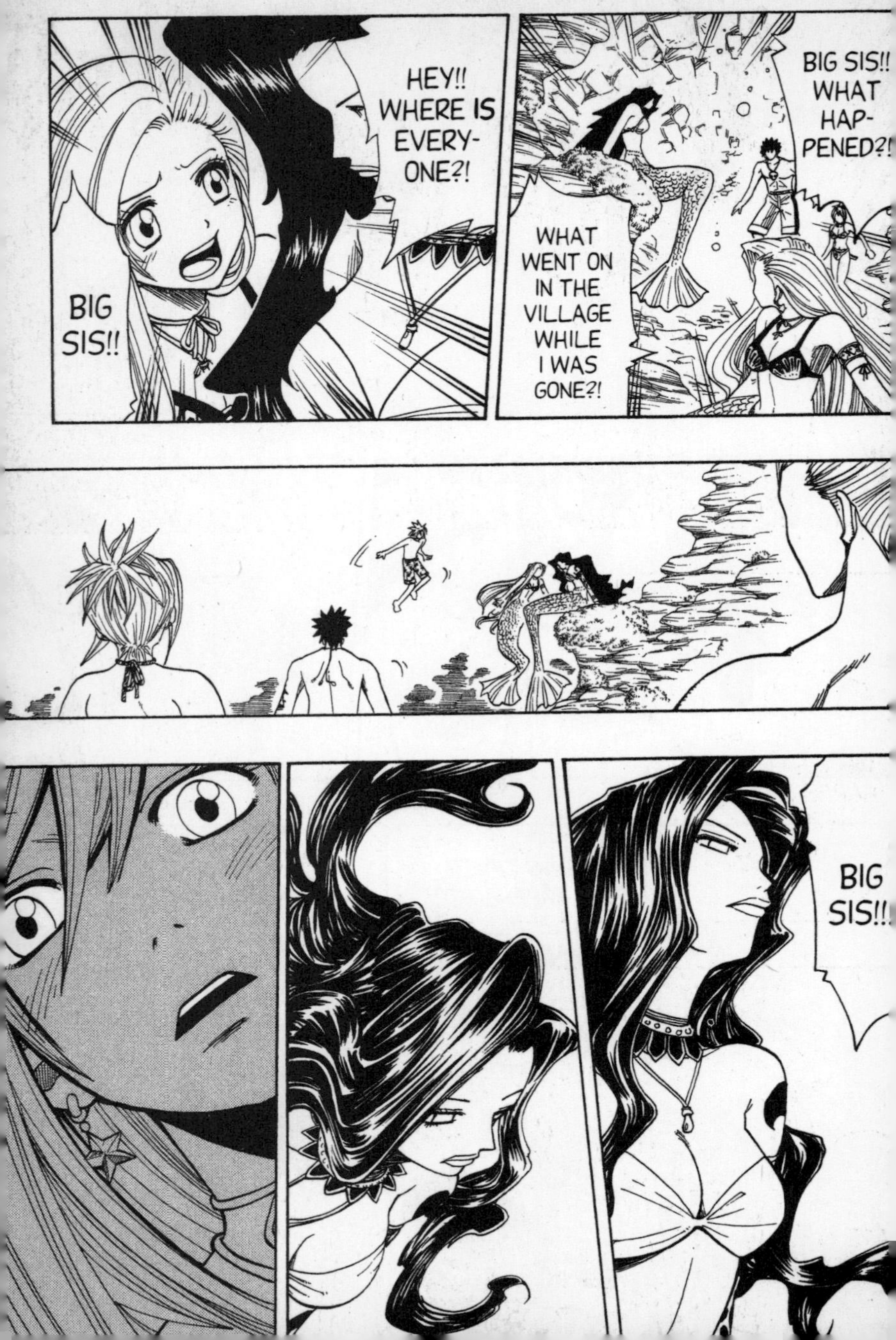
BIG SIS!! WHAT HAP-PENED?!
WHAT WENT ON IN THE VILLAGE WHILE I WAS GONE?!
HEY!! WHERE IS EVERY-ONE?!
BIG SIS!!
BIG SIS!!

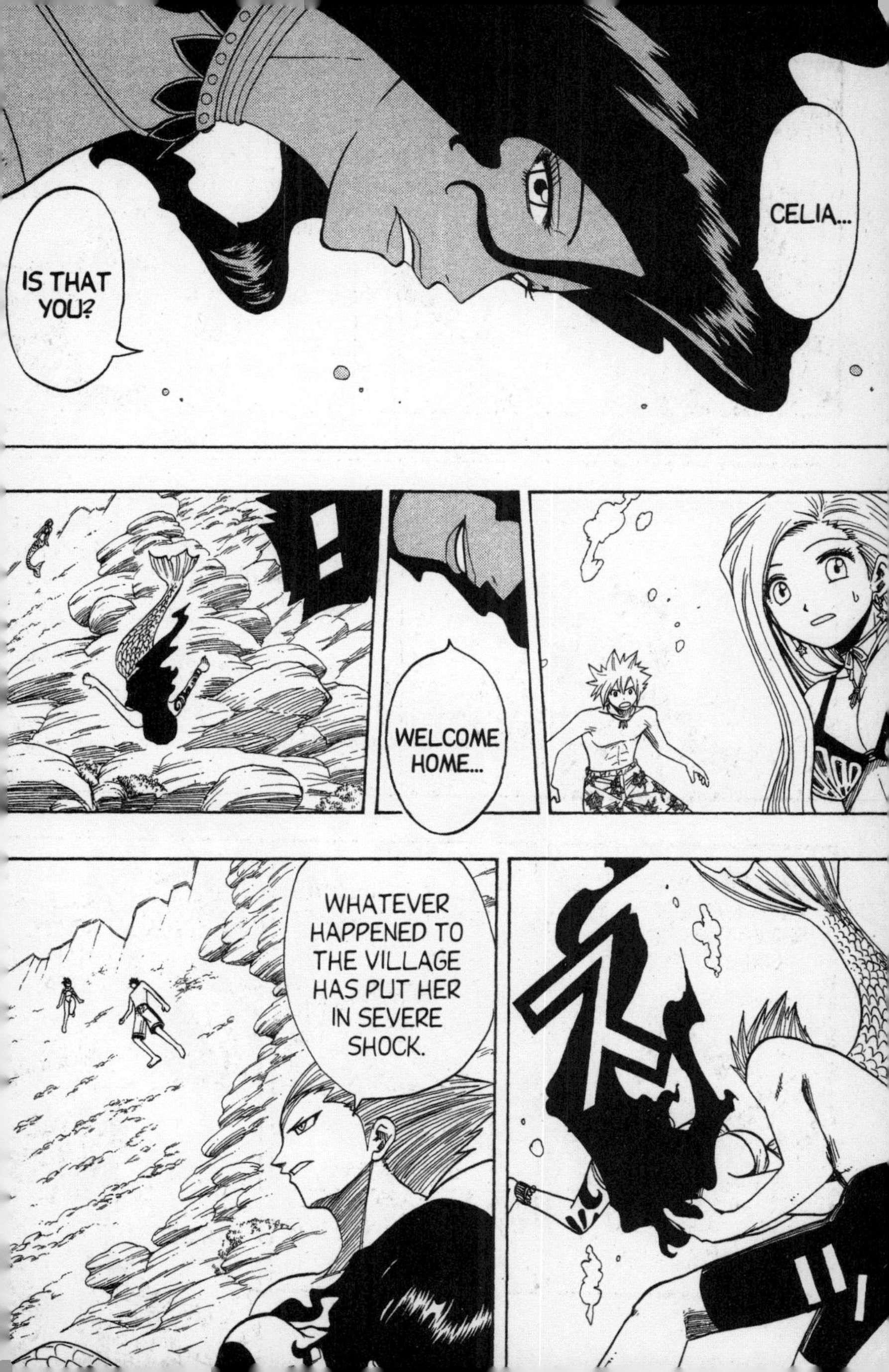
CELIA...
IS THAT YOU?
WELCOME HOME...
WHATEVER HAPPENED TO THE VILLAGE HAS PUT HER IN SEVERE SHOCK.

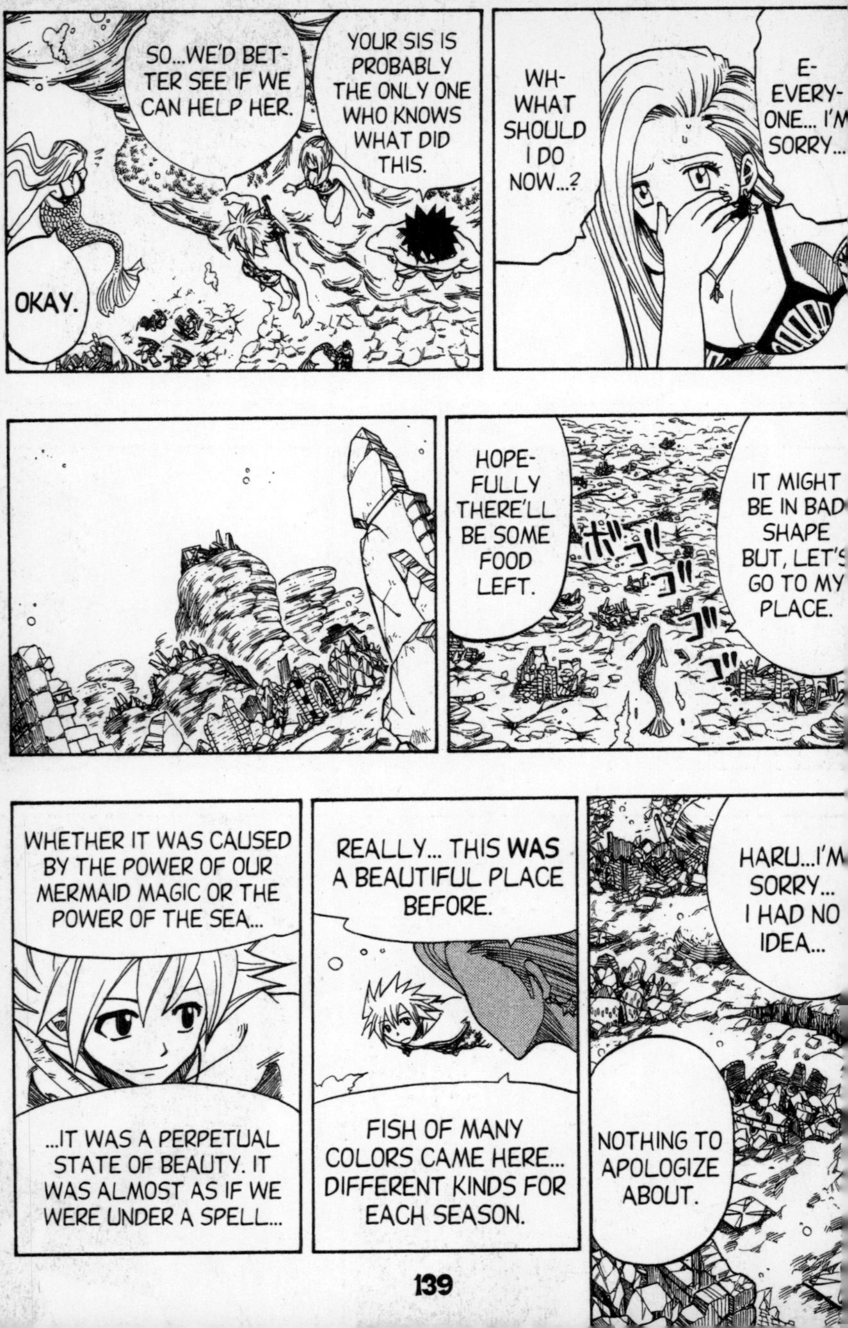
E- EVERY-ONE... I'M SORRY...
WH- WHAT SHOULD I DO NOW...?
YOUR SIS IS PROBABLY THE ONLY ONE WHO KNOWS WHAT DID THIS.
SO...WE'D BET-TER SEE IF WE CAN HELP HER.
OKAY.
IT MIGHT BE IN BAD SHAPE BUT, LET'S GO TO MY PLACE.
ボゴゴゴゴ
HOPE-FULLY THERE'LL BE SOME FOOD LEFT.
HARU...I'M SORRY... I HAD NO IDEA...
NOTHING TO APOLOGIZE ABOUT.
REALLY... THIS WAS A BEAUTIFUL PLACE BEFORE.
FISH OF MANY COLORS CAME HERE... DIFFERENT KINDS FOR EACH SEASON.
WHETHER IT WAS CAUSED BY THE POWER OF OUR MERMAID MAGIC OR THE POWER OF THE SEA...
...IT WAS A PERPETUAL STATE OF BEAUTY. IT WAS ALMOST AS IF WE WERE UNDER A SPELL...

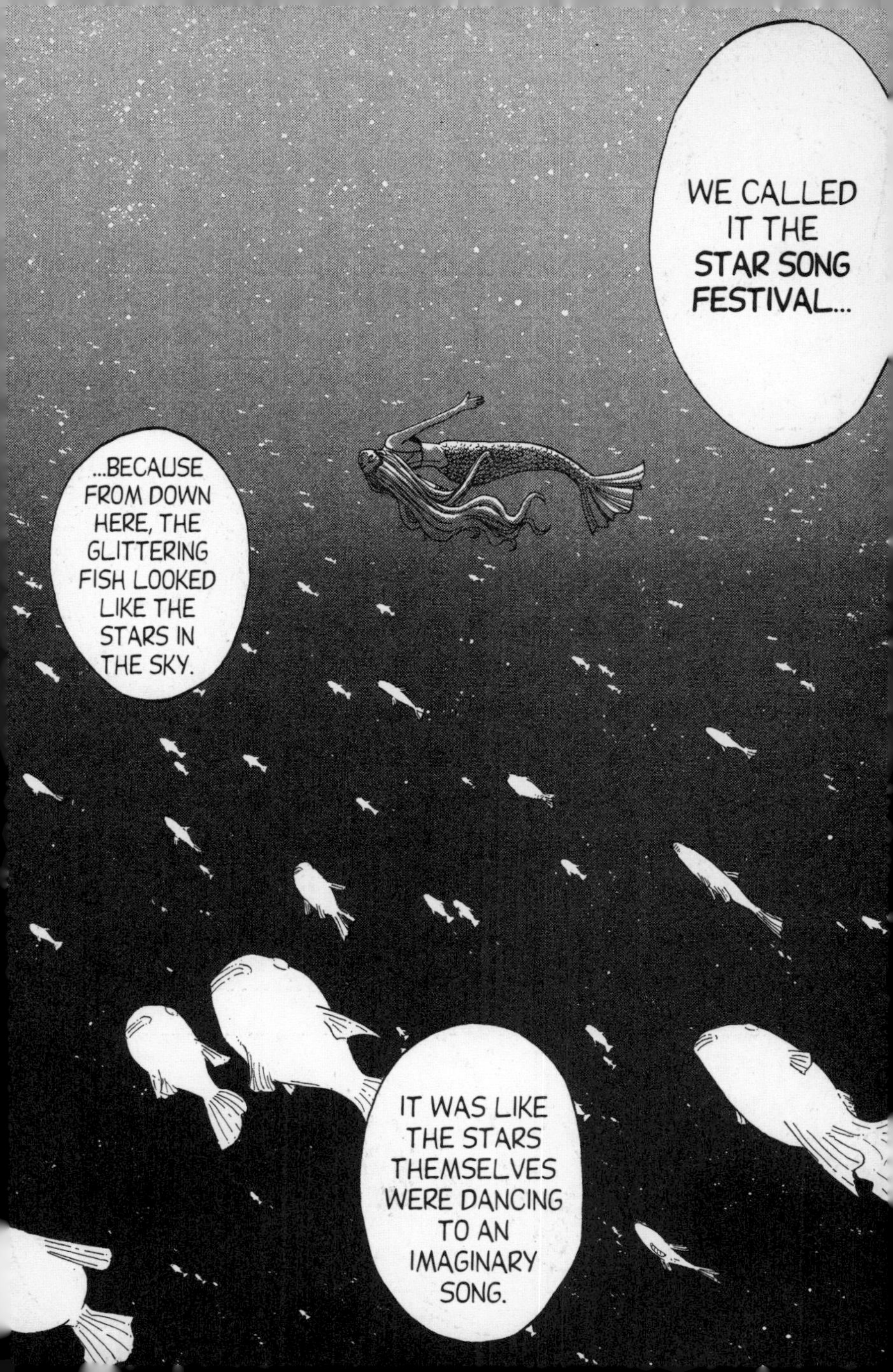
WE CALLED IT THE STAR SONG FESTIVAL...
...BECAUSE FROM DOWN HERE, THE GLITTERING FISH LOOKED LIKE THE STARS IN THE SKY.
IT WAS LIKE THE STARS THEMSELVES WERE DANCING TO AN IMAGINARY SONG.

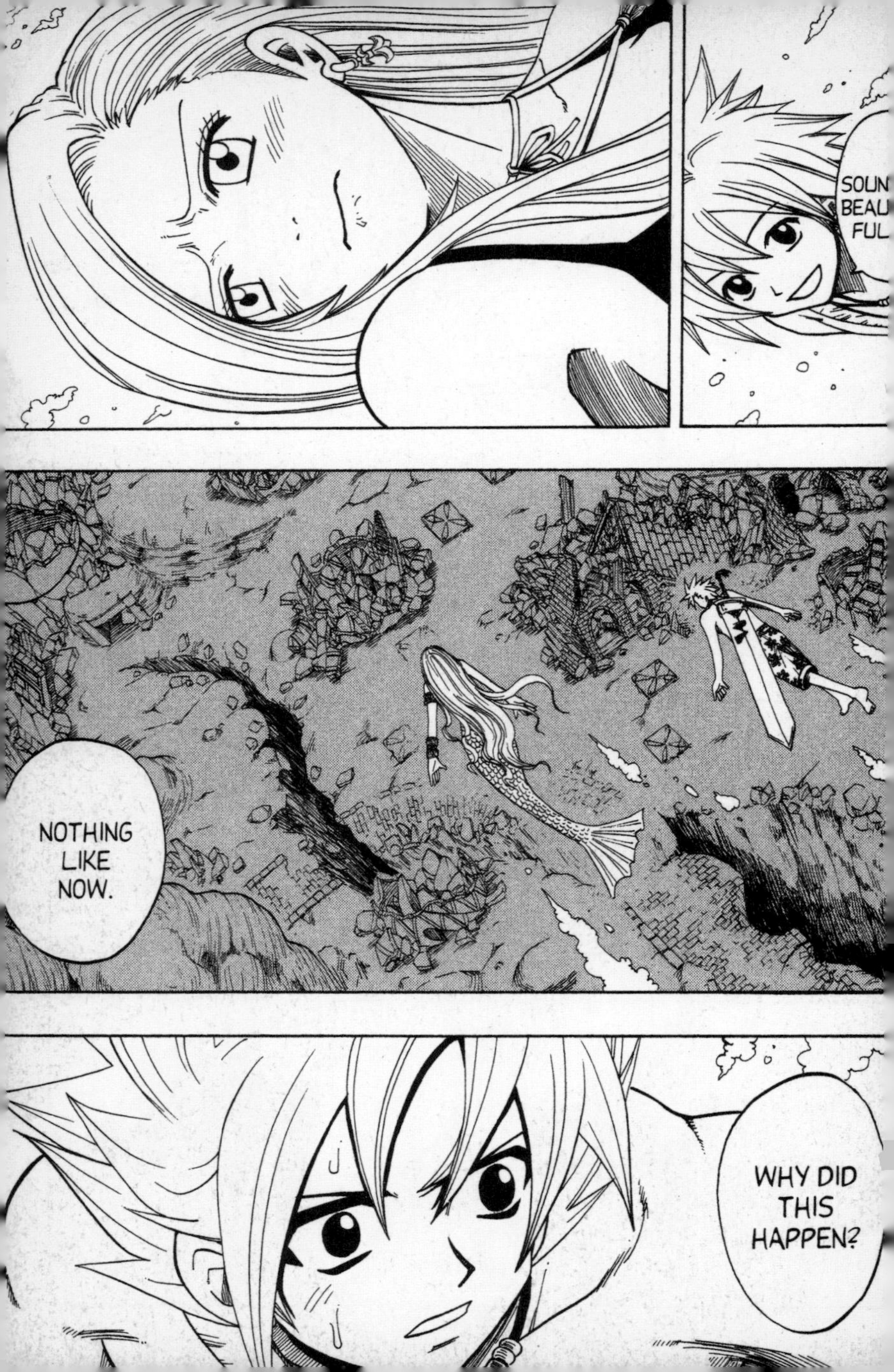
SOUN BEAU FUL
NOTHING LIKE NOW.
WHY DID THIS HAPPEN?

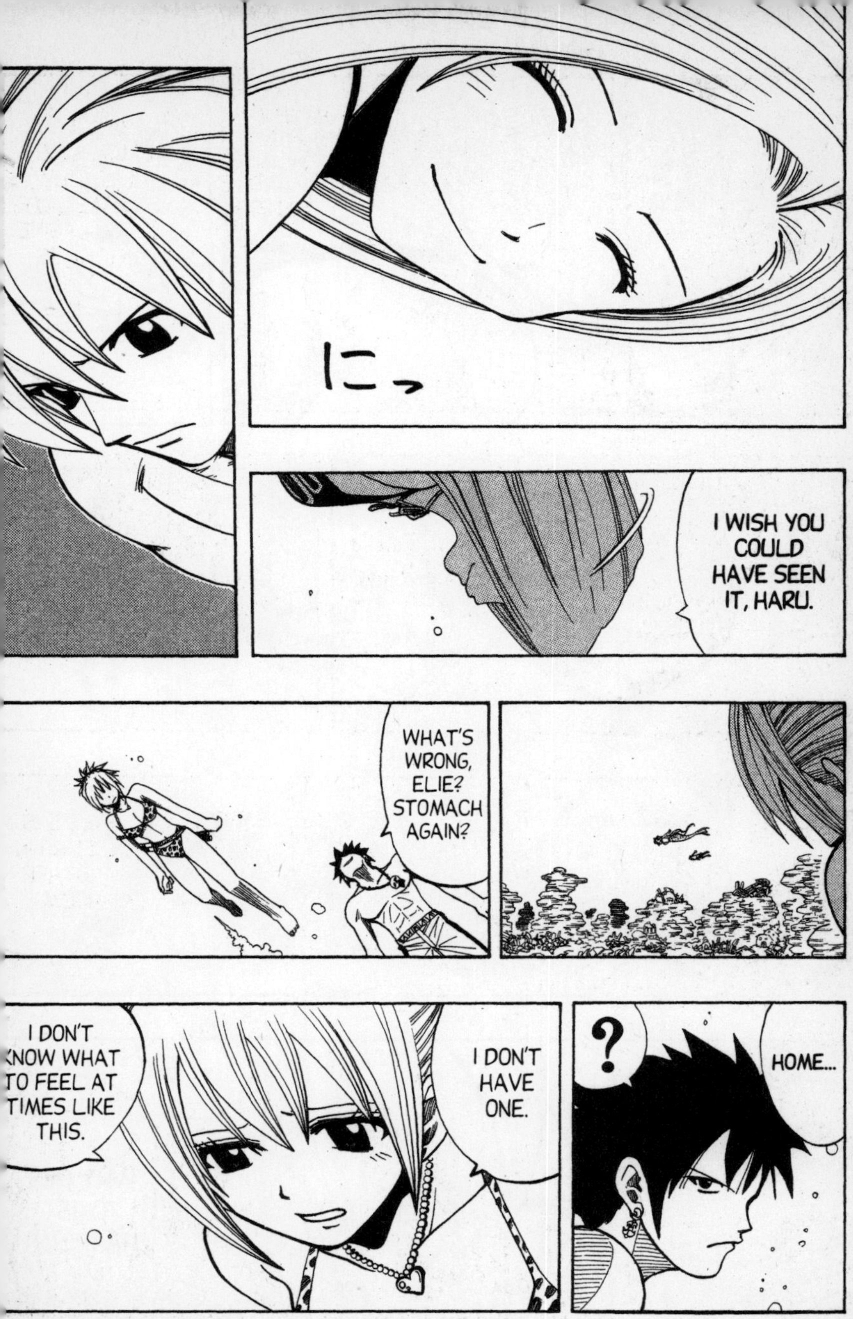
にっ
I WISH YOU COULD HAVE SEEN IT, HARU.
WHAT'S WRONG, ELIE? STOMACH AGAIN?
HOME...
?
I DON'T HAVE ONE.
I DON'T KNOW WHAT TO FEEL AT TIMES LIKE THIS.

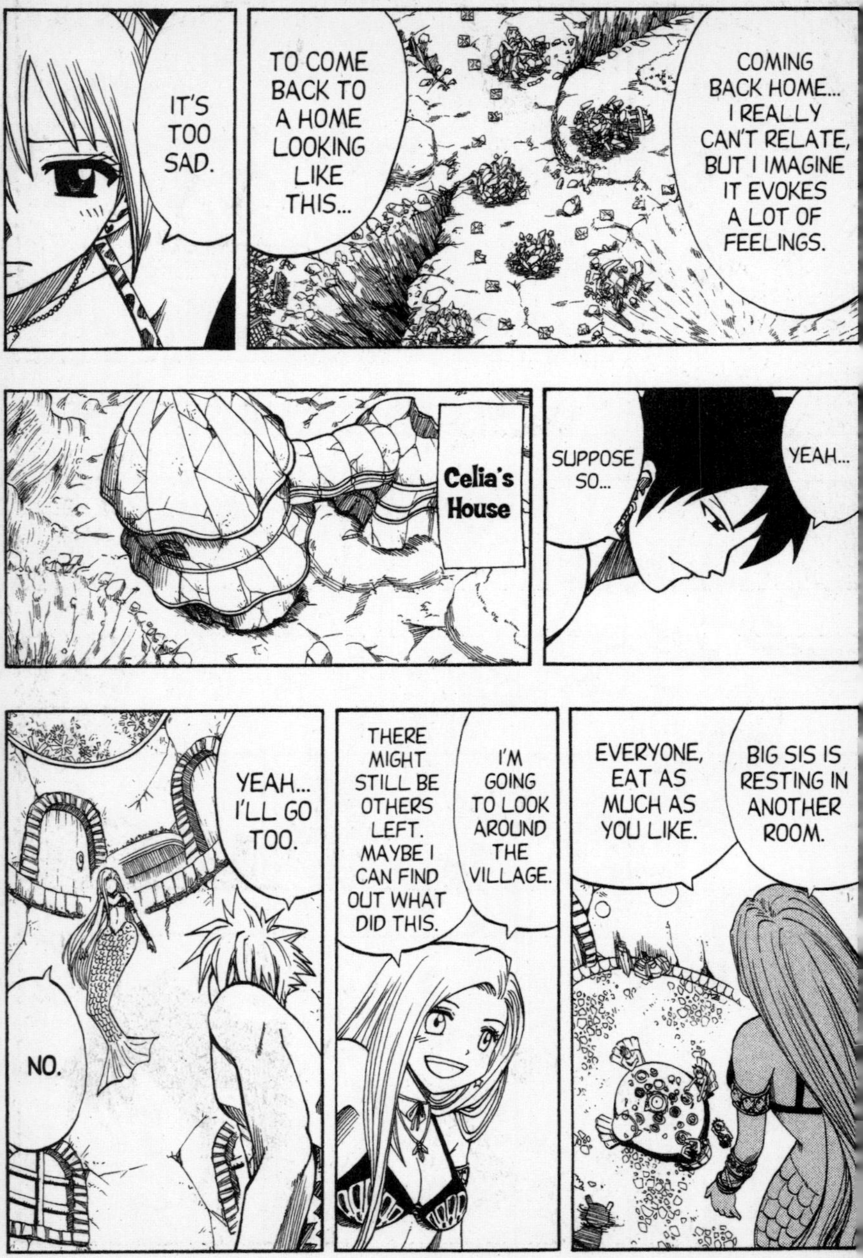
COMING BACK HOME... I REALLY CAN'T RELATE, BUT I IMAGINE IT EVOKES A LOT OF FEELINGS.
TO COME BACK TO A HOME LOOKING LIKE THIS...
IT'S TOO SAD.
YEAH...
SUPPOSE SO...
Celia's House
BIG SIS IS RESTING IN ANOTHER ROOM.
EVERYONE, EAT AS MUCH AS YOU LIKE.
I'M GOING TO LOOK AROUND THE VILLAGE.
THERE MIGHT STILL BE OTHERS LEFT. MAYBE I CAN FIND OUT WHAT DID THIS.
YEAH... I'LL GO TOO.
NO.

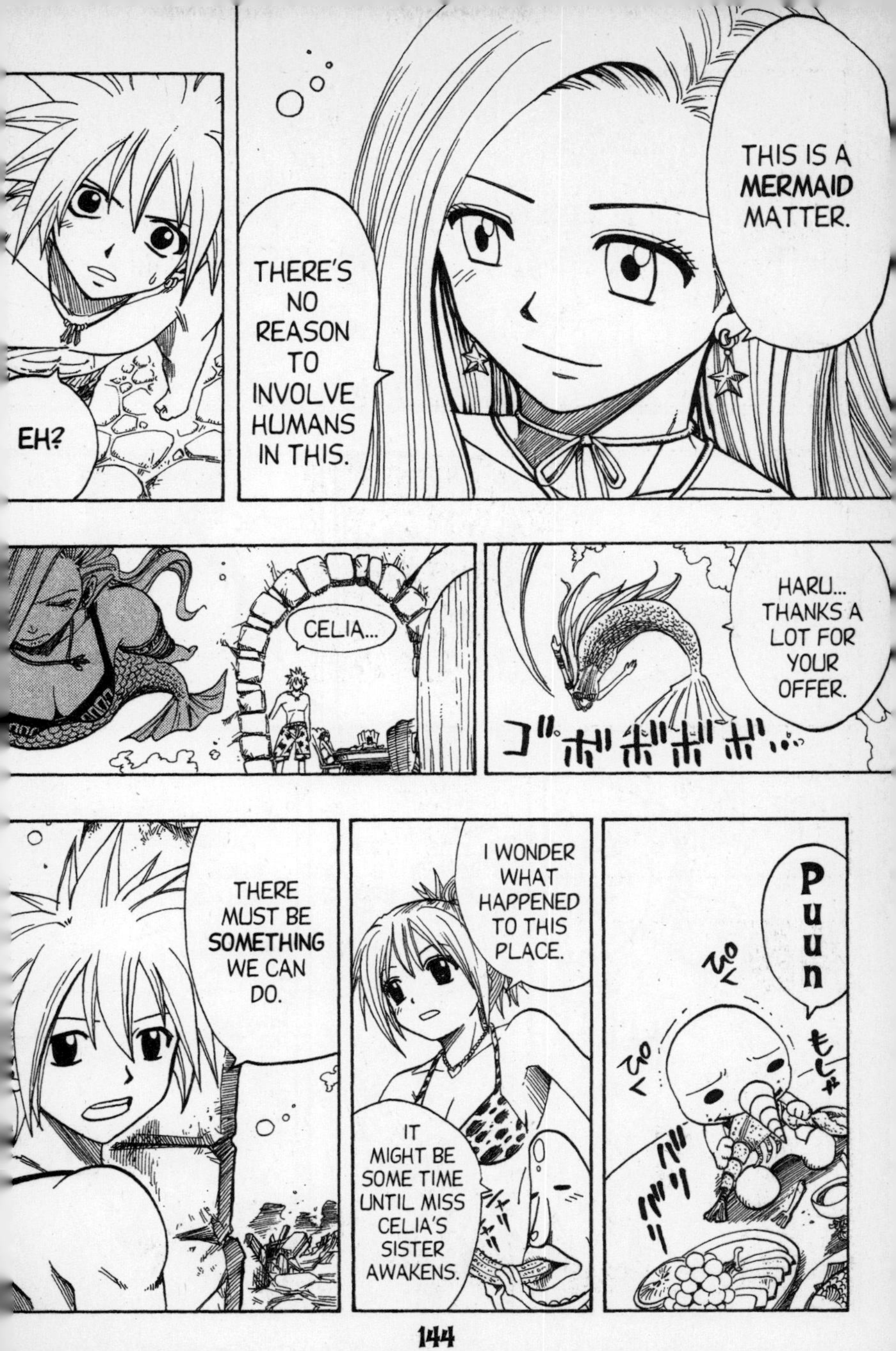
THIS IS A MERMAID MATTER.
THERE'S NO REASON TO INVOLVE HUMANS IN THIS.
EH?
HARU... THANKS A LOT FOR YOUR OFFER.
ゴボボボボ
CELIA...
Puun
ぴく
もしゃ
I WONDER WHAT HAPPENED TO THIS PLACE.
IT MIGHT BE SOME TIME UNTIL MISS CELIA'S SISTER AWAKENS.
THERE MUST BE SOMETHING WE CAN DO.

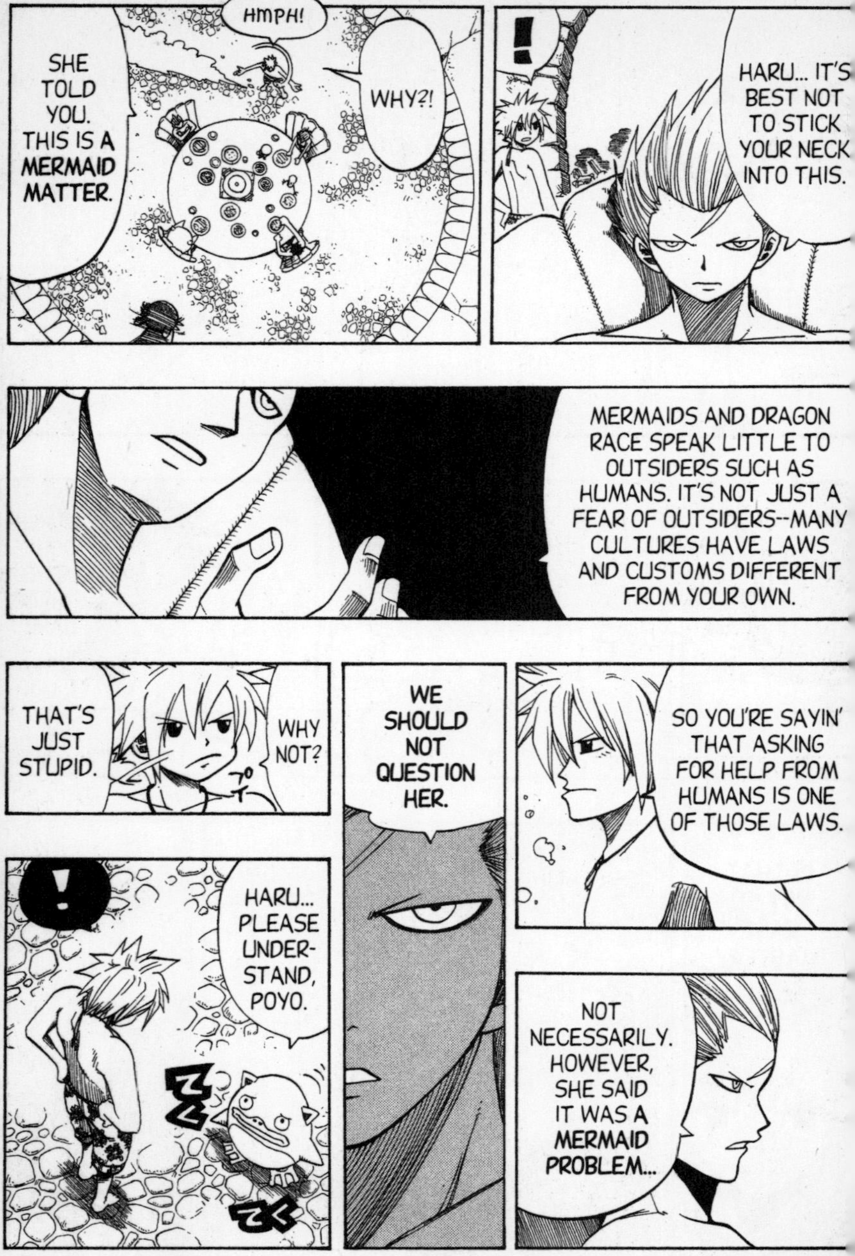
!
HARU... IT'S BEST NOT TO STICK YOUR NECK INTO THIS.
HMPH!
WHY?!
SHE TOLD YOU. THIS IS A MERMAID MATTER.
MERMAIDS AND DRAGON RACE SPEAK LITTLE TO OUTSIDERS SUCH AS HUMANS. IT'S NOT JUST A FEAR OF OUTSIDERS--MANY CULTURES HAVE LAWS AND CUSTOMS DIFFERENT FROM YOUR OWN.
SO YOU'RE SAYIN' THAT ASKING FOR HELP FROM HUMANS IS ONE OF THOSE LAWS.
NOT NECESSARILY. HOWEVER, SHE SAID IT WAS A MERMAID PROBLEM...
WE SHOULD NOT QUESTION HER.
WHY NOT?
THAT'S JUST STUPID.
!
HARU... PLEASE UNDER-STAND, POYO.

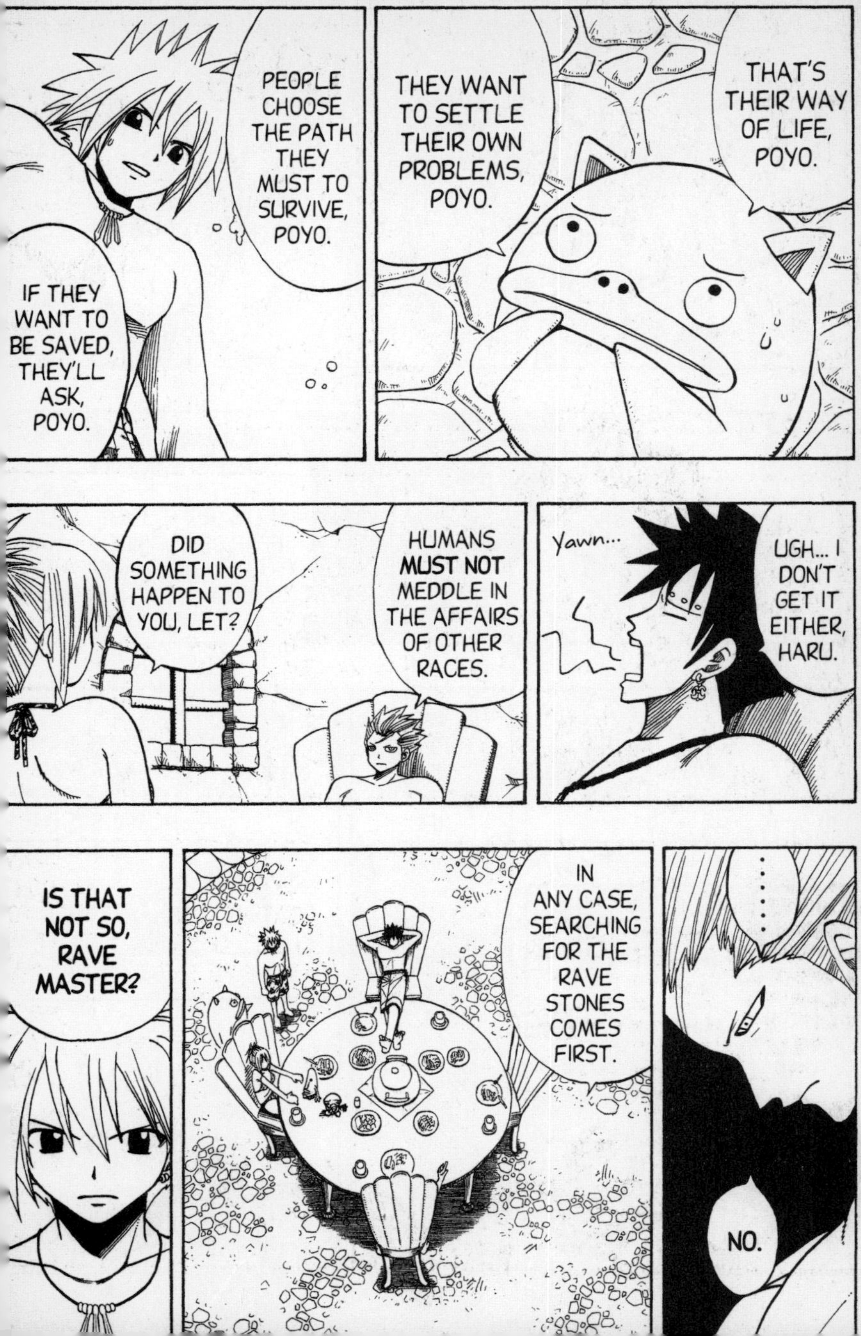
THAT'S THEIR WAY OF LIFE, POYO.
THEY WANT TO SETTLE THEIR OWN PROBLEMS, POYO.
PEOPLE CHOOSE THE PATH THEY MUST TO SURVIVE, POYO.
IF THEY WANT TO BE SAVED, THEY'LL ASK, POYO.
UGH... I DON'T GET IT EITHER, HARU.
Yawn...
HUMANS MUST NOT MEDDLE IN THE AFFAIRS OF OTHER RACES.
DID SOMETHING HAPPEN TO YOU, LET?
......
NO.
IN ANY CASE, SEARCHING FOR THE RAVE STONES COMES FIRST.
IS THAT NOT SO, RAVE MASTER?

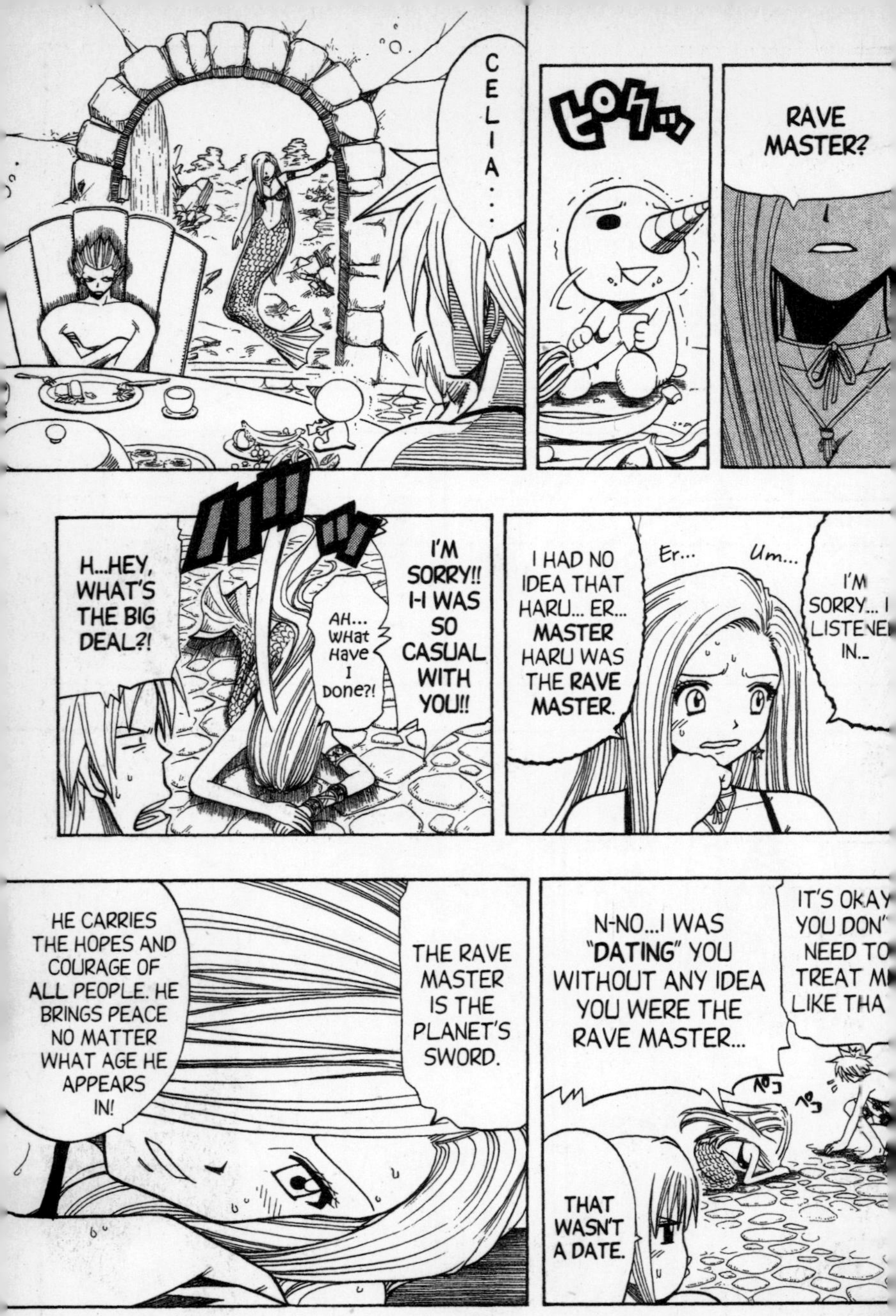
RAVE MASTER?
CELIA...
I'M SORRY... I LISTENE IN..
Um...
Er...
I HAD NO IDEA THAT HARU... ER... MASTER HARU WAS THE RAVE MASTER.
I'M SORRY!! I-I WAS SO CASUAL WITH YOU!!
AH... What Have I Done?!
H...HEY, WHAT'S THE BIG DEAL?!
IT'S OKAY YOU DON' NEED TO TREAT M LIKE THA
N-NO...I WAS "DATING" YOU WITHOUT ANY IDEA YOU WERE THE RAVE MASTER...
THAT WASN'T A DATE.
THE RAVE MASTER IS THE PLANET'S SWORD.
HE CARRIES THE HOPES AND COURAGE OF ALL PEOPLE. HE BRINGS PEACE NO MATTER WHAT AGE HE APPEARS IN!

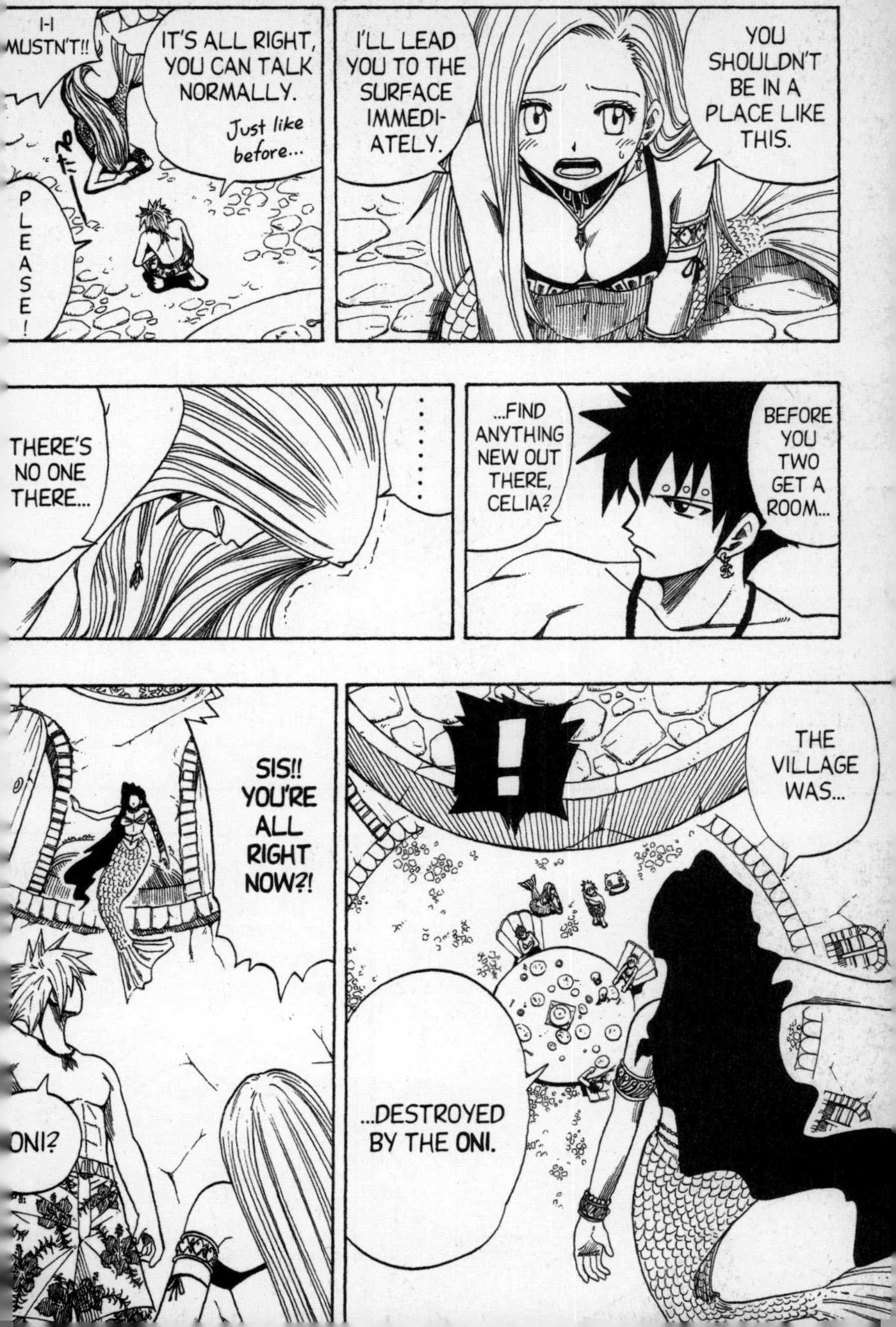
YOU SHOULDN'T BE IN A PLACE LIKE THIS.
I'LL LEAD YOU TO THE SURFACE IMMEDI-ATELY.
IT'S ALL RIGHT, YOU CAN TALK NORMALLY.
Just like before...
I-I MUSTN'T!!
PLEASE!
BEFORE YOU TWO GET A ROOM...
...FIND ANYTHING NEW OUT THERE, CELIA?
......
THERE'S NO ONE THERE...
!
THE VILLAGE WAS...
...DESTROYED BY THE ONI.
SIS!! YOU'RE ALL RIGHT NOW?!
ONI?

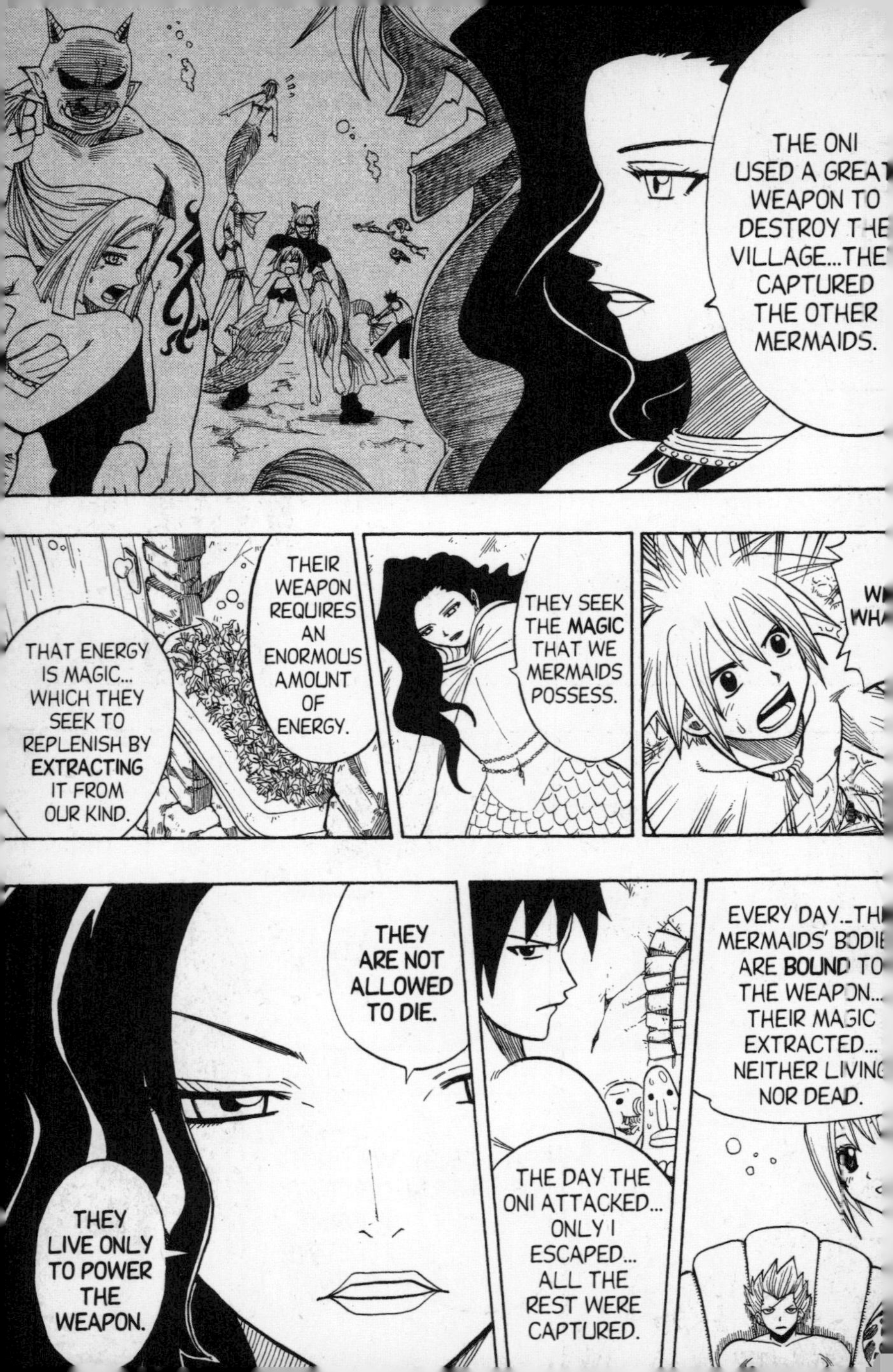
THE ONI USED A GREAT WEAPON TO DESTROY THE VILLAGE...THE CAPTURED THE OTHER MERMAIDS.
WH- WHA
THEY SEEK THE **MAGIC** THAT WE MERMAIDS POSSESS.
THEIR WEAPON REQUIRES AN ENORMOUS AMOUNT OF ENERGY.
THAT ENERGY IS MAGIC... WHICH THEY SEEK TO REPLENISH BY **EXTRACTING** IT FROM OUR KIND.
EVERY DAY...THE MERMAIDS' BODIE ARE **BOUND** TO THE WEAPON... THEIR MAGIC EXTRACTED... NEITHER LIVIN NOR DEAD.
THE DAY THE ONI ATTACKED... ONLY I ESCAPED... ALL THE REST WERE CAPTURED.
THEY ARE NOT ALLOWED TO DIE.
THEY LIVE ONLY TO POWER THE WEAPON.

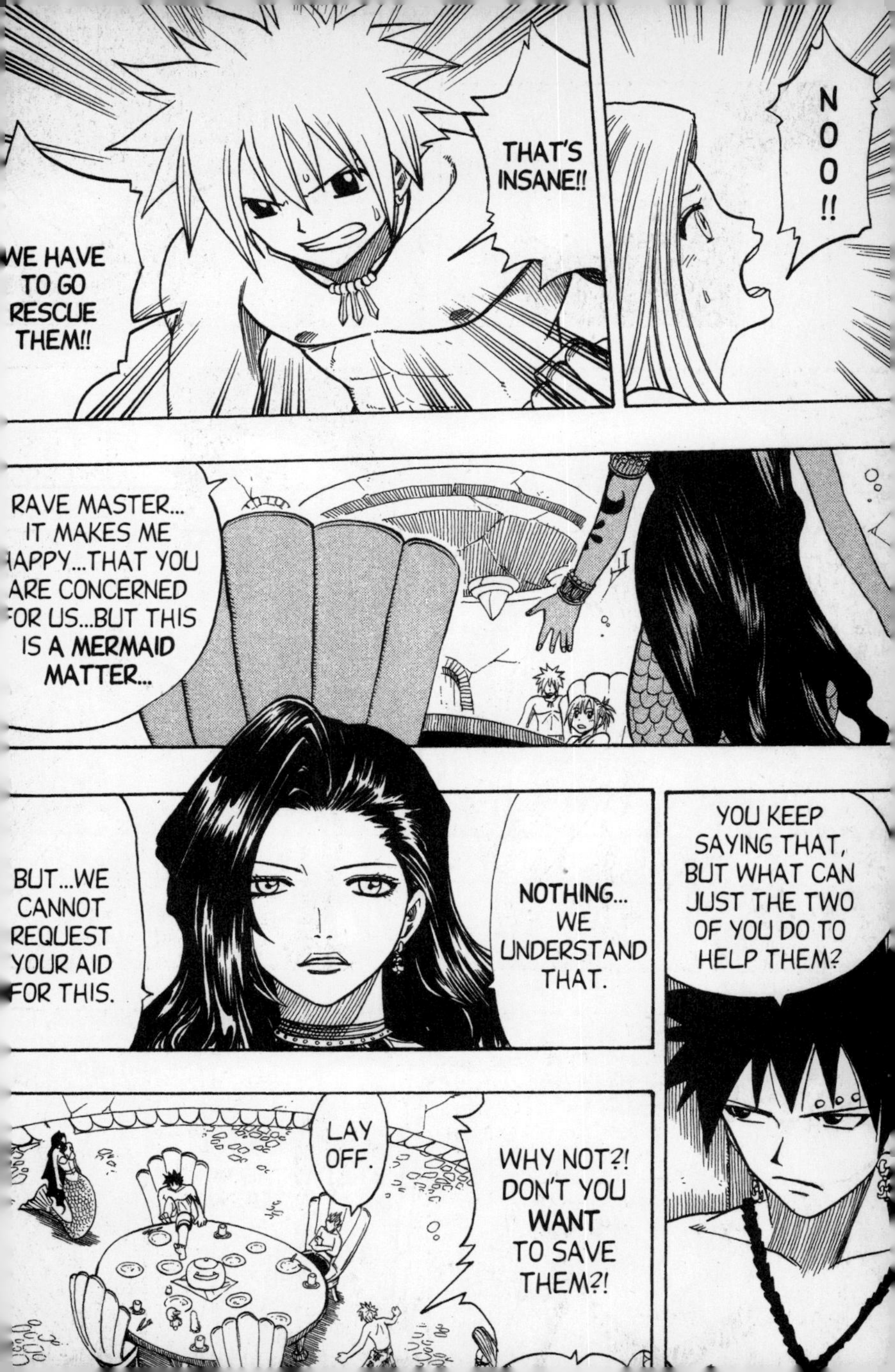
NOO!!
THAT'S INSANE!!
WE HAVE TO GO RESCUE THEM!!
RAVE MASTER... IT MAKES ME HAPPY...THAT YOU ARE CONCERNED FOR US...BUT THIS IS A MERMAID MATTER...
YOU KEEP SAYING THAT, BUT WHAT CAN JUST THE TWO OF YOU DO TO HELP THEM?
NOTHING... WE UNDERSTAND THAT.
BUT...WE CANNOT REQUEST YOUR AID FOR THIS.
WHY NOT?! DON'T YOU WANT TO SAVE THEM?!
LAY OFF.

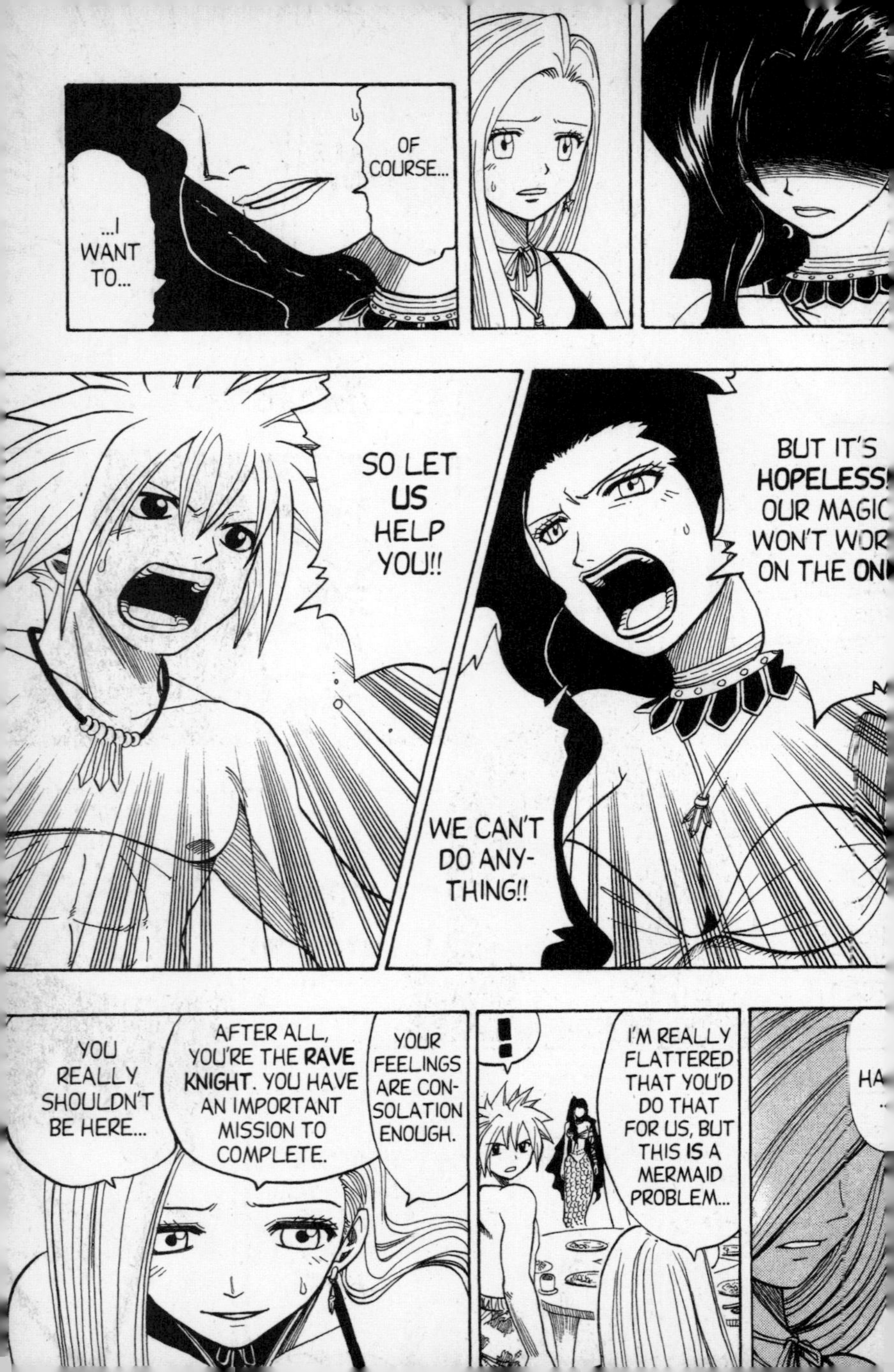
OF COURSE...
...I WANT TO...
BUT IT'S HOPELESS! OUR MAGIC WON'T WOR ON THE ON
WE CAN'T DO ANY-THING!!
SO LET US HELP YOU!!
HA ...
I'M REALLY FLATTERED THAT YOU'D DO THAT FOR US, BUT THIS IS A MERMAID PROBLEM...
!
YOUR FEELINGS ARE CON-SOLATION ENOUGH.
AFTER ALL, YOU'RE THE RAVE KNIGHT. YOU HAVE AN IMPORTANT MISSION TO COMPLETE.
YOU REALLY SHOULDN'T BE HERE...

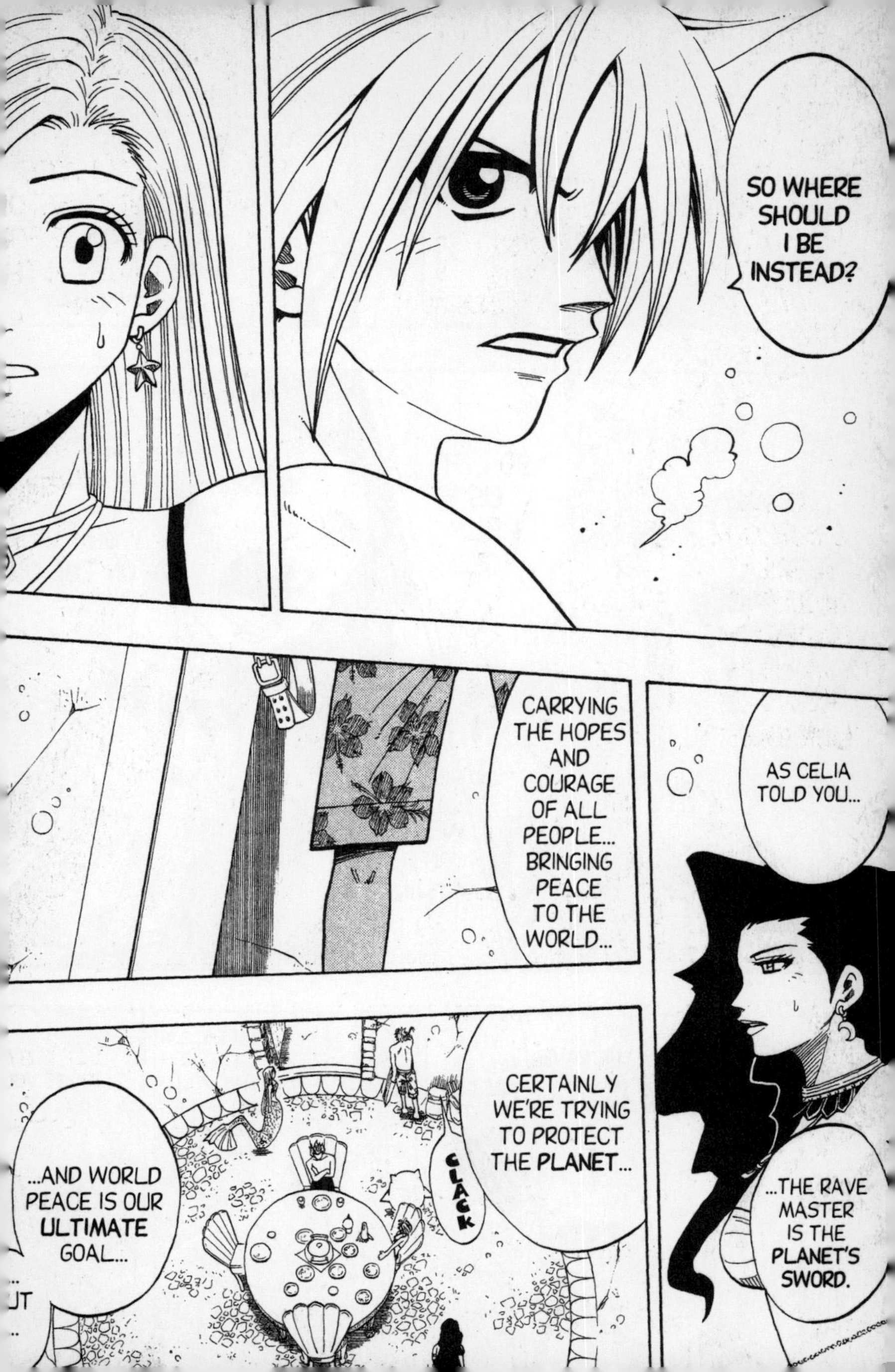
SO WHERE SHOULD I BE INSTEAD?
AS CELIA TOLD YOU...
...THE RAVE MASTER IS THE PLANET'S SWORD.
CARRYING THE HOPES AND COURAGE OF ALL PEOPLE... BRINGING PEACE TO THE WORLD...
CERTAINLY WE'RE TRYING TO PROTECT THE PLANET...
CLACK
...AND WORLD PEACE IS OUR ULTIMATE GOAL...

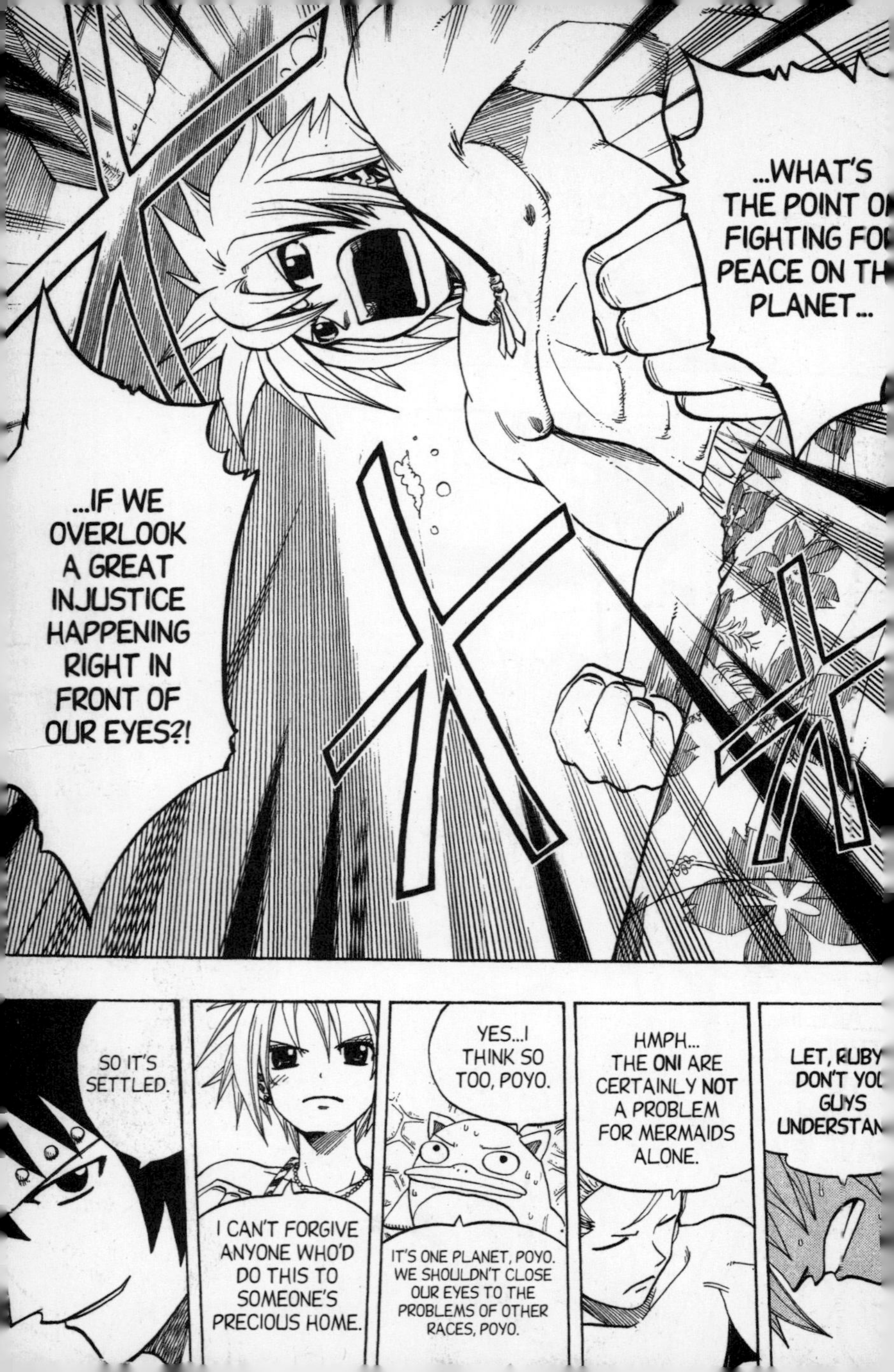
...WHAT'S THE POINT O FIGHTING FO PEACE ON TH PLANET...
...IF WE OVERLOOK A GREAT INJUSTICE HAPPENING RIGHT IN FRONT OF OUR EYES?!
LET, RUBY DON'T YO GUYS UNDERSTA
HMPH... THE ONI ARE CERTAINLY NOT A PROBLEM FOR MERMAIDS ALONE.
YES...I THINK SO TOO, POYO.
IT'S ONE PLANET, POYO. WE SHOULDN'T CLOSE OUR EYES TO THE PROBLEMS OF OTHER RACES, POYO.
I CAN'T FORGIVE ANYONE WHO'D DO THIS TO SOMEONE'S PRECIOUS HOME.
SO IT'S SETTLED.

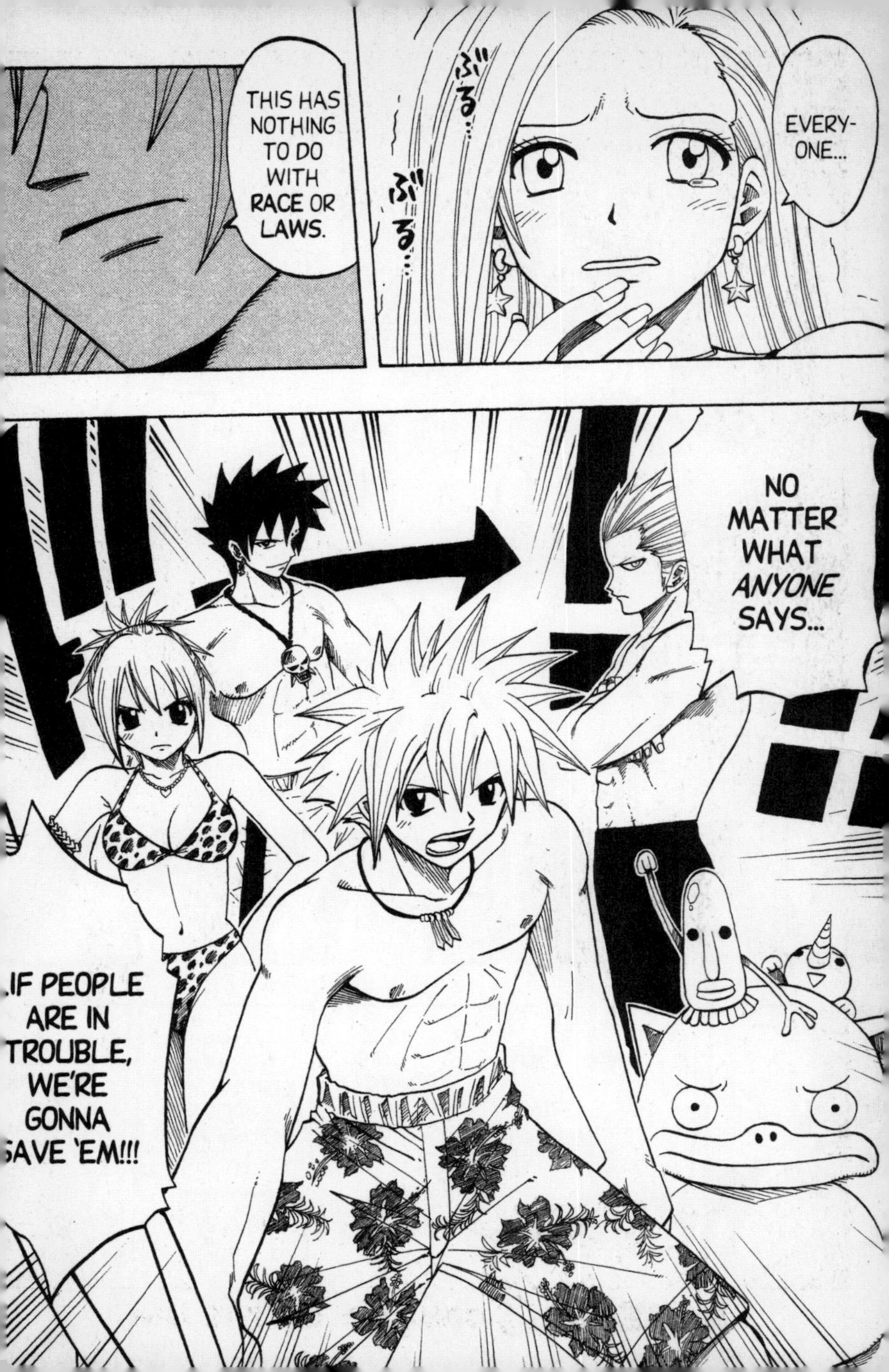
EVERY-ONE...
ぶる
ぶる
THIS HAS NOTHING TO DO WITH RACE OR LAWS.
NO MATTER WHAT *ANYONE* SAYS...
IF PEOPLE ARE IN TROUBLE, WE'RE GONNA SAVE 'EM!!!

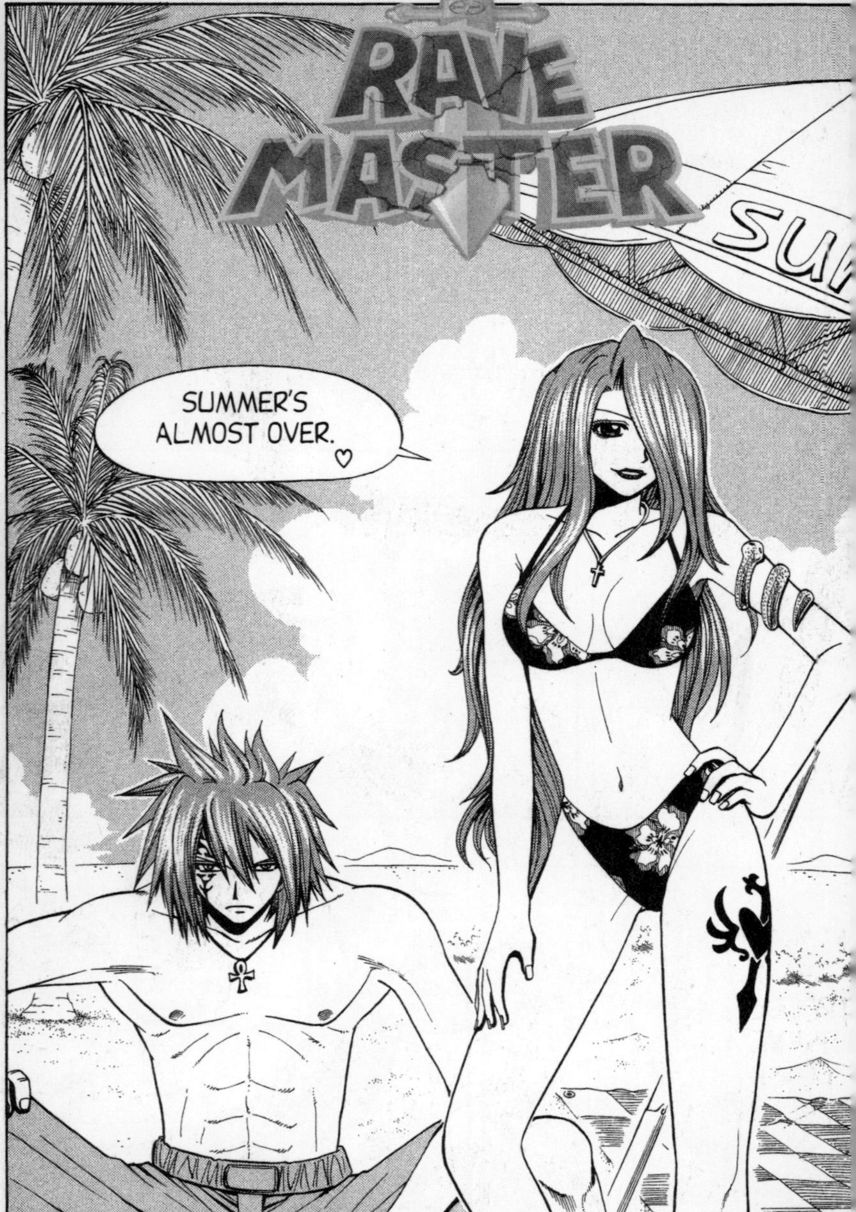
RAVE MASTER
SUMMER'S ALMOST OVER. ♡

RAVE:105 ✚ CRUELTY OF THE ONI

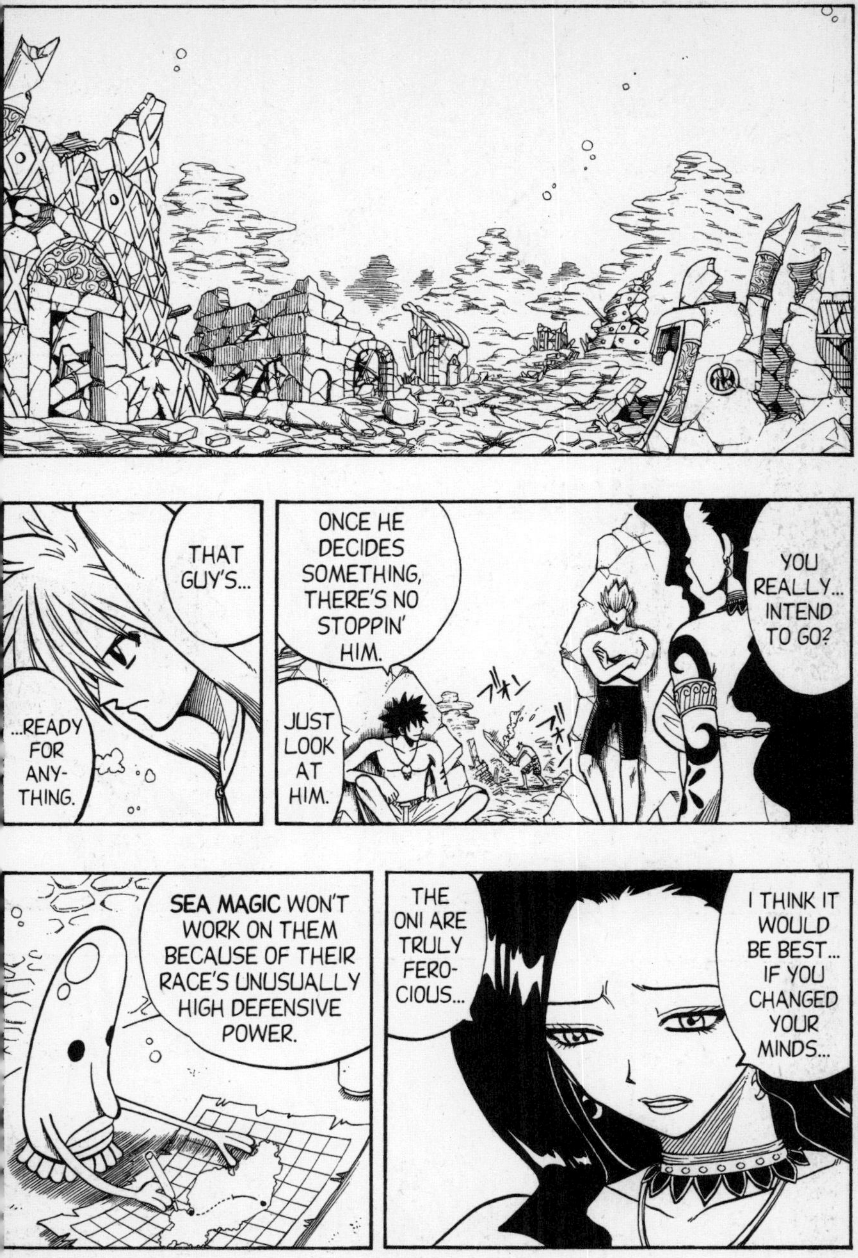

YOU REALLY... INTEND TO GO?
ONCE HE DECIDES SOMETHING, THERE'S NO STOPPIN' HIM.
JUST LOOK AT HIM.
ブオン
ブオン
THAT GUY'S...
...READY FOR ANYTHING.
I THINK IT WOULD BE BEST... IF YOU CHANGED YOUR MINDS...
THE ONI ARE TRULY FERO-CIOUS...
SEA MAGIC WON'T WORK ON THEM BECAUSE OF THEIR RACE'S UNUSUALLY HIGH DEFENSIVE POWER.

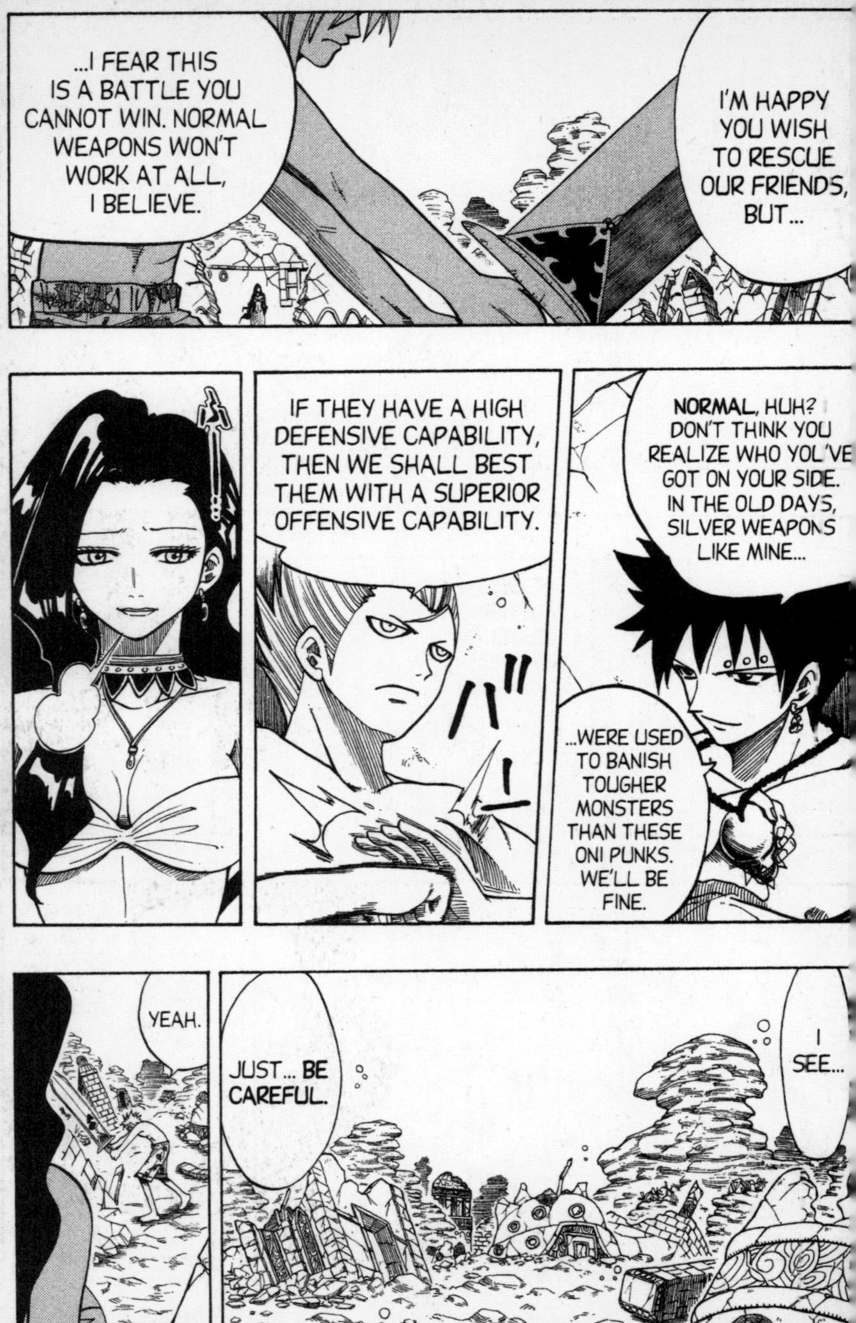
I'M HAPPY YOU WISH TO RESCUE OUR FRIENDS, BUT...
...I FEAR THIS IS A BATTLE YOU CANNOT WIN. NORMAL WEAPONS WON'T WORK AT ALL, I BELIEVE.
NORMAL, HUH? I DON'T THINK YOU REALIZE WHO YOU'VE GOT ON YOUR SIDE. IN THE OLD DAYS, SILVER WEAPONS LIKE MINE...
...WERE USED TO BANISH TOUGHER MONSTERS THAN THESE ONI PUNKS. WE'LL BE FINE.
IF THEY HAVE A HIGH DEFENSIVE CAPABILITY, THEN WE SHALL BEST THEM WITH A SUPERIOR OFFENSIVE CAPABILITY.
I SEE...
JUST... BE CAREFUL.
YEAH.

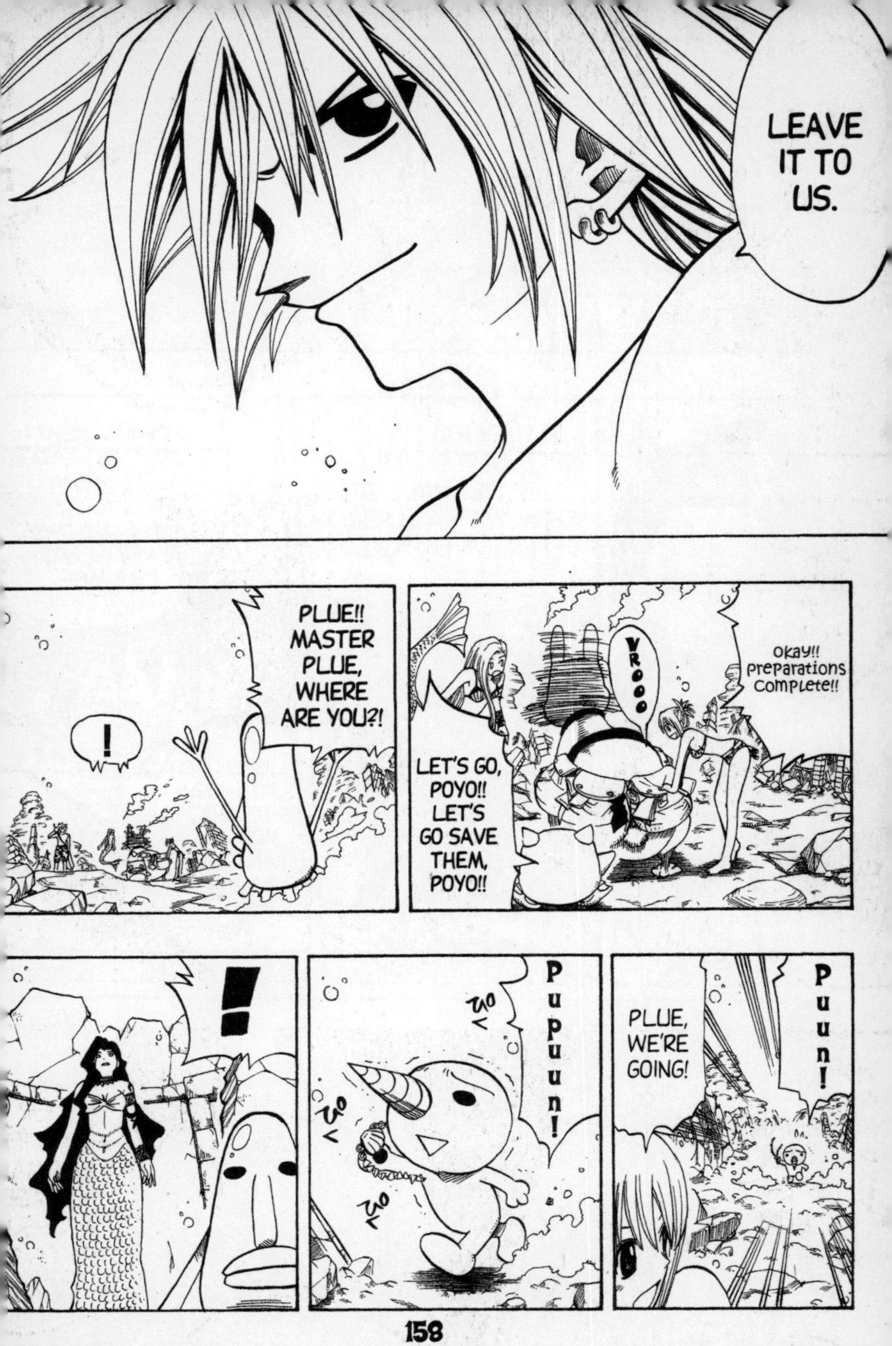
LEAVE IT TO US.
Okay!! preparations complete!!
VROOO
LET'S GO, POYO!! LET'S GO SAVE THEM, POYO!!
PLUE!! MASTER PLUE, WHERE ARE YOU?!
!
Puun!
PLUE, WE'RE GOING!
Pupuun!
!

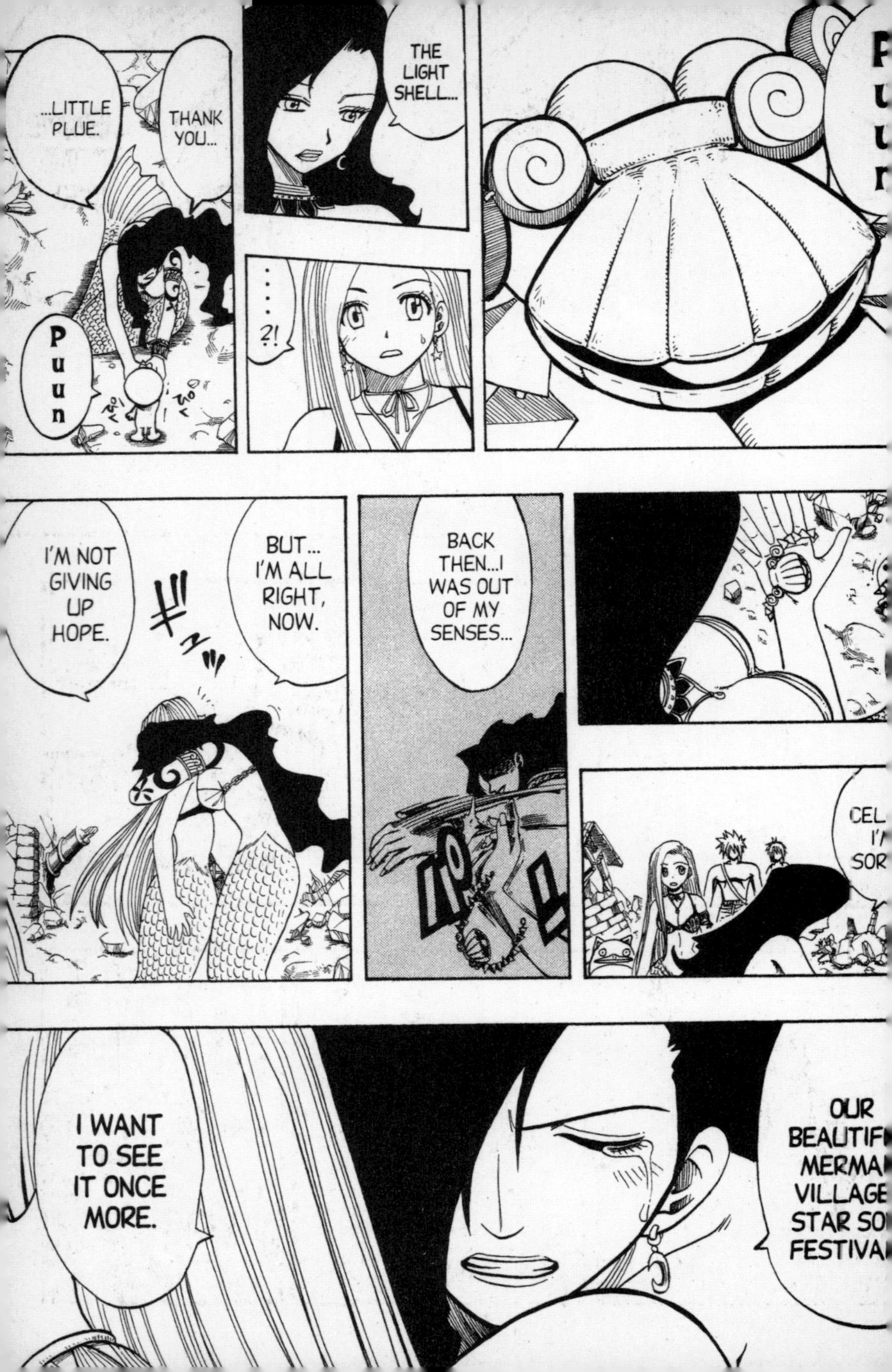
Puu
THE LIGHT SHELL...
...?!
THANK YOU...
...LITTLE PLUE.
Puun
CEL I' SOR
BACK THEN...I WAS OUT OF MY SENSES...
BUT... I'M ALL RIGHT, NOW.
I'M NOT GIVING UP HOPE.
OUR BEAUTIF MERMA VILLAGE STAR SO FESTIVA
I WANT TO SEE IT ONCE MORE.

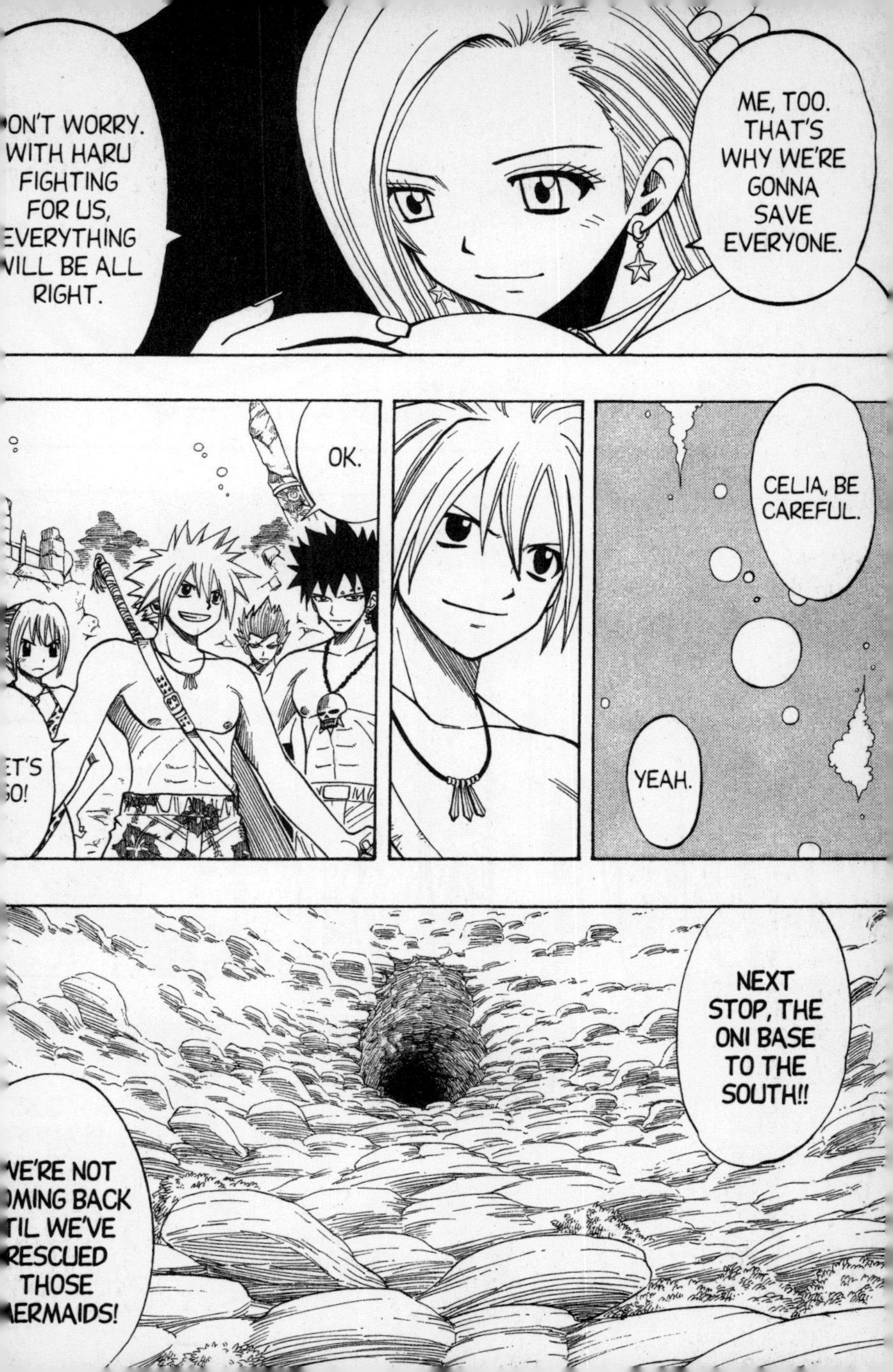
ME, TOO. THAT'S WHY WE'RE GONNA SAVE EVERYONE.
ON'T WORRY. WITH HARU FIGHTING FOR US, EVERYTHING VILL BE ALL RIGHT.
CELIA, BE CAREFUL.
YEAH.
OK.
ET'S GO!
NEXT STOP, THE ONI BASE TO THE SOUTH!!
VE'RE NOT OMING BACK TIL WE'VE RESCUED THOSE ERMAIDS!

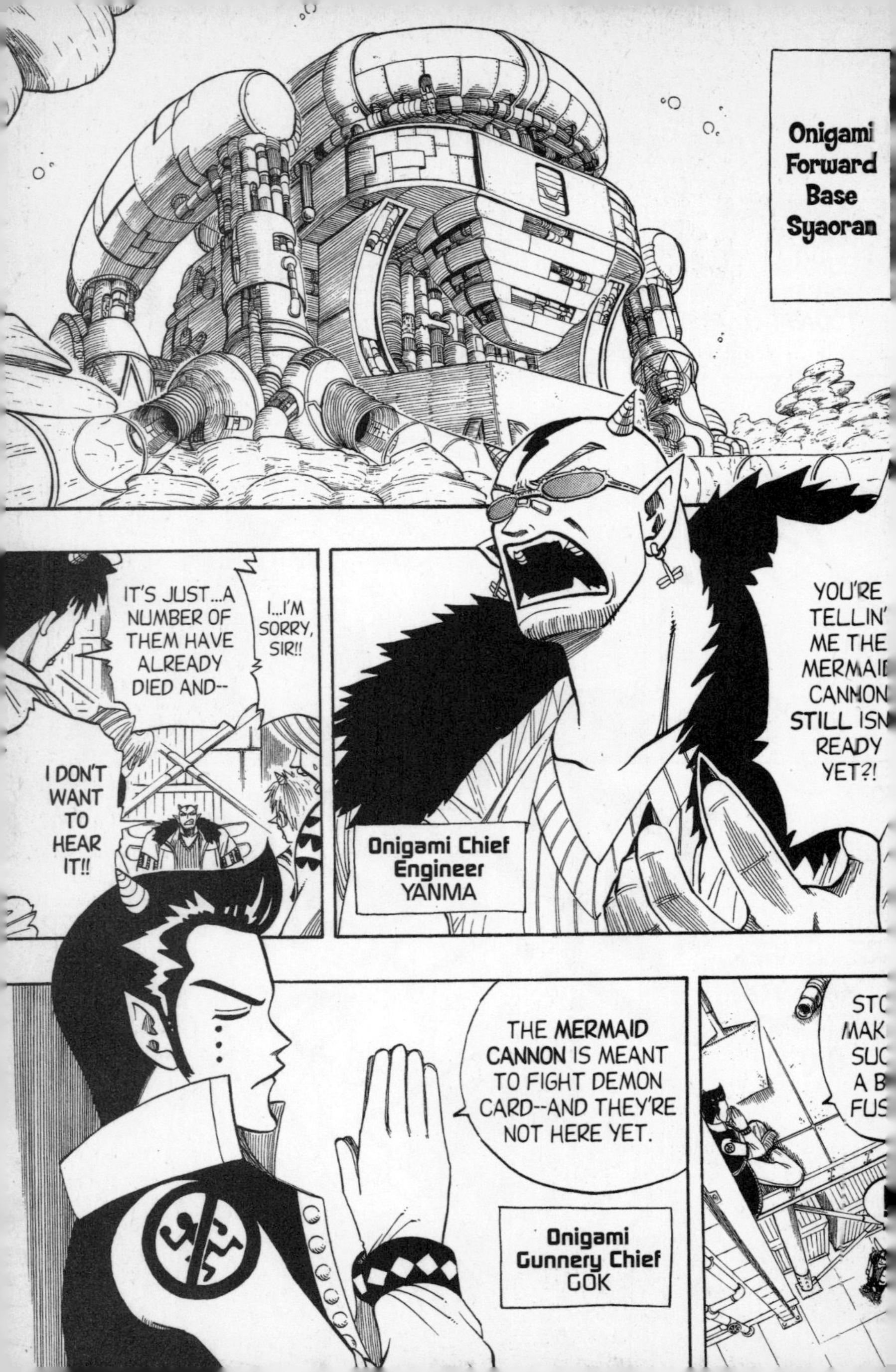
Onigami Forward Base Syaoran
YOU'RE TELLIN' ME THE MERMAID CANNON STILL ISN READY YET?!
Onigami Chief Engineer YANMA
I...I'M SORRY, SIR!!
IT'S JUST...A NUMBER OF THEM HAVE ALREADY DIED AND--
I DON'T WANT TO HEAR IT!!
THE MERMAID CANNON IS MEANT TO FIGHT DEMON CARD--AND THEY'RE NOT HERE YET.
Onigami Gunnery Chief GOK

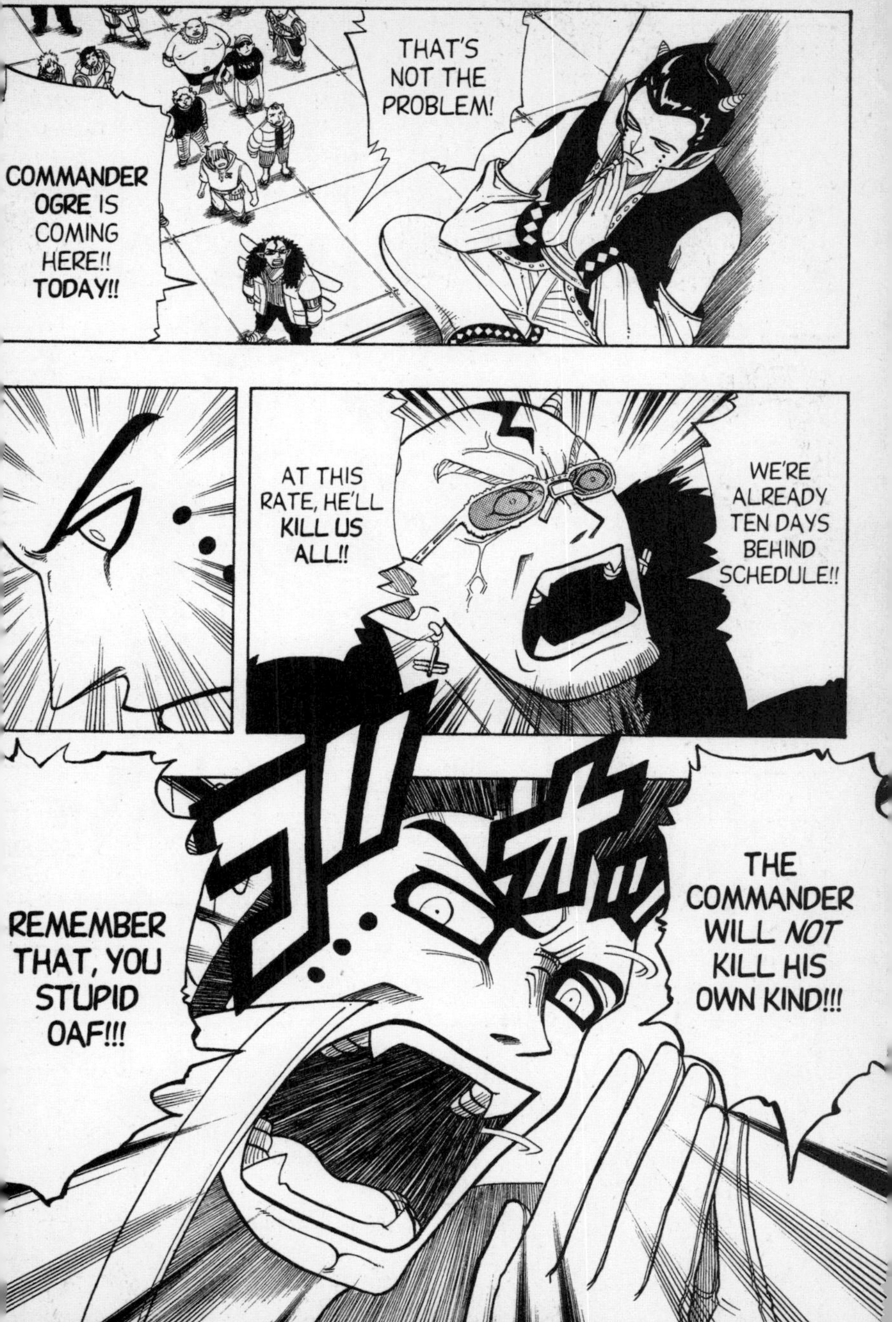
THAT'S NOT THE PROBLEM!
COMMANDER OGRE IS COMING HERE!! TODAY!!
WE'RE ALREADY TEN DAYS BEHIND SCHEDULE!!
AT THIS RATE, HE'LL KILL US ALL!!
THE COMMANDER WILL *NOT* KILL HIS OWN KIND!!!
REMEMBER THAT, YOU STUPID OAF!!!

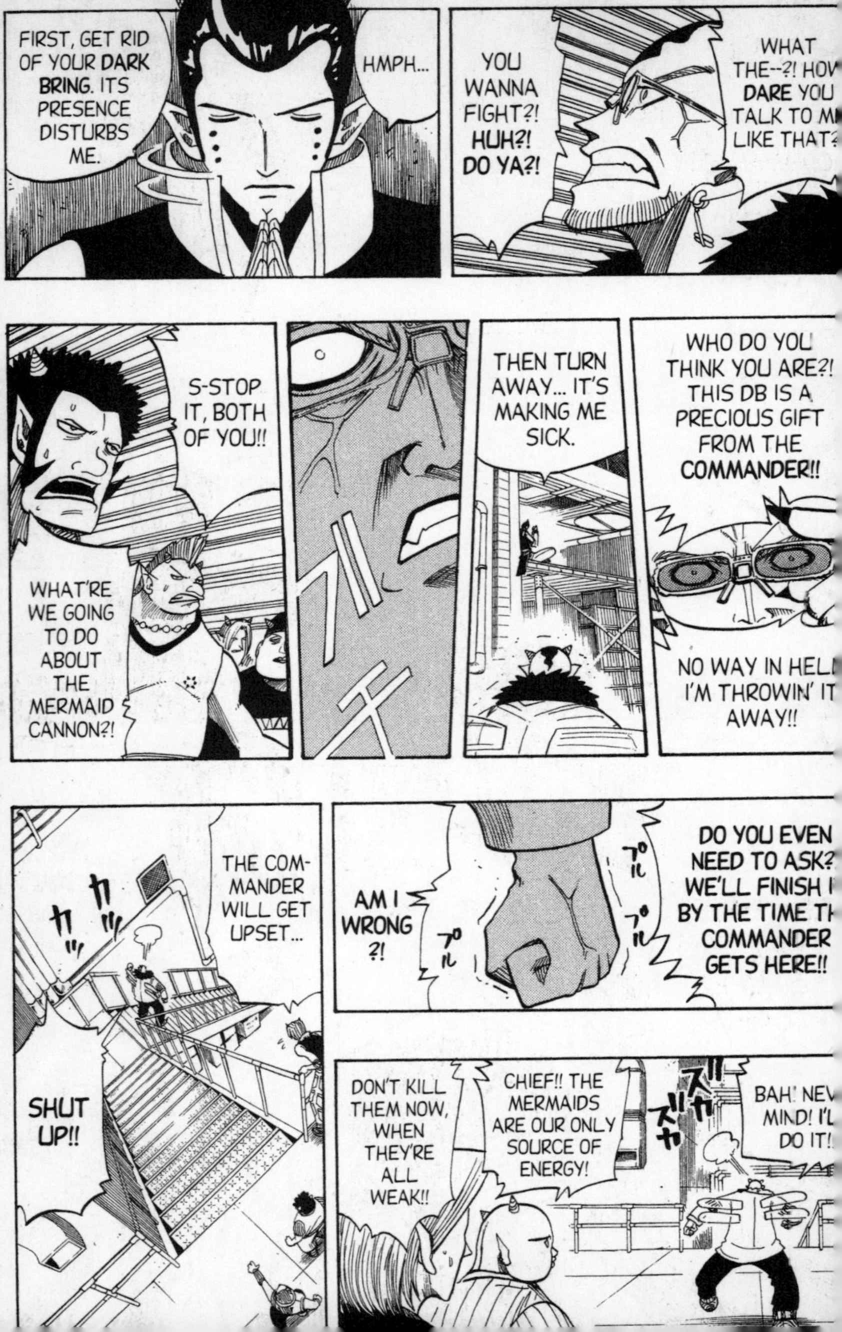
WHAT THE--?! HOW DARE YOU TALK TO ME LIKE THAT?
YOU WANNA FIGHT?! HUH?! DO YA?!
HMPH...
FIRST, GET RID OF YOUR DARK BRING. ITS PRESENCE DISTURBS ME.
WHO DO YOU THINK YOU ARE?! THIS DB IS A PRECIOUS GIFT FROM THE COMMANDER!!
NO WAY IN HELL I'M THROWIN' IT AWAY!!
THEN TURN AWAY... IT'S MAKING ME SICK.
S-STOP IT, BOTH OF YOU!!
WHAT'RE WE GOING TO DO ABOUT THE MERMAID CANNON?!
DO YOU EVEN NEED TO ASK?! WE'LL FINISH I BY THE TIME TH COMMANDER GETS HERE!!
AM I WRONG?!
BAH! NEV MIND! I'L DO IT!
CHIEF!! THE MERMAIDS ARE OUR ONLY SOURCE OF ENERGY!
DON'T KILL THEM NOW, WHEN THEY'RE ALL WEAK!!
THE COMMANDER WILL GET UPSET...
SHUT UP!!

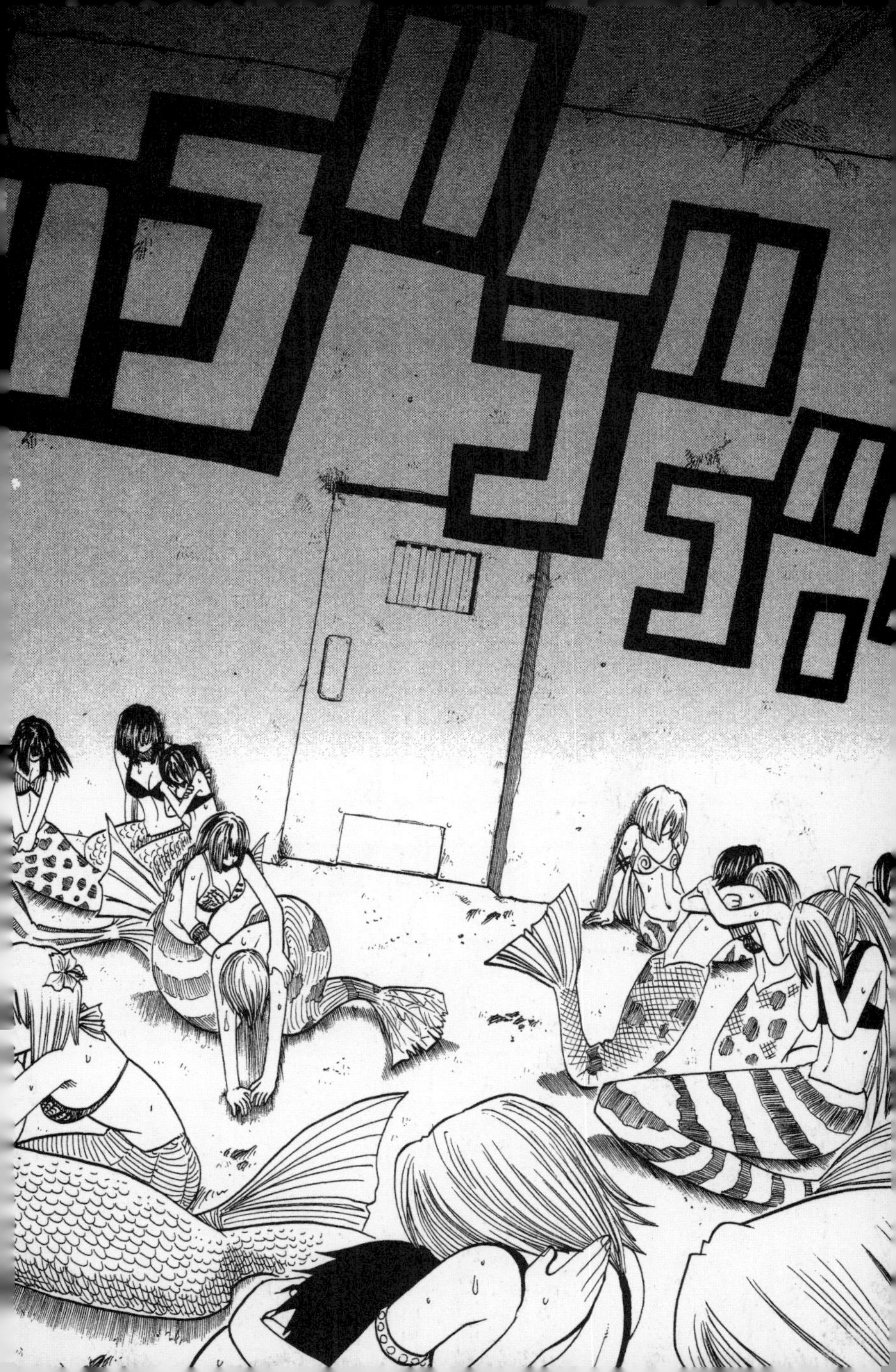

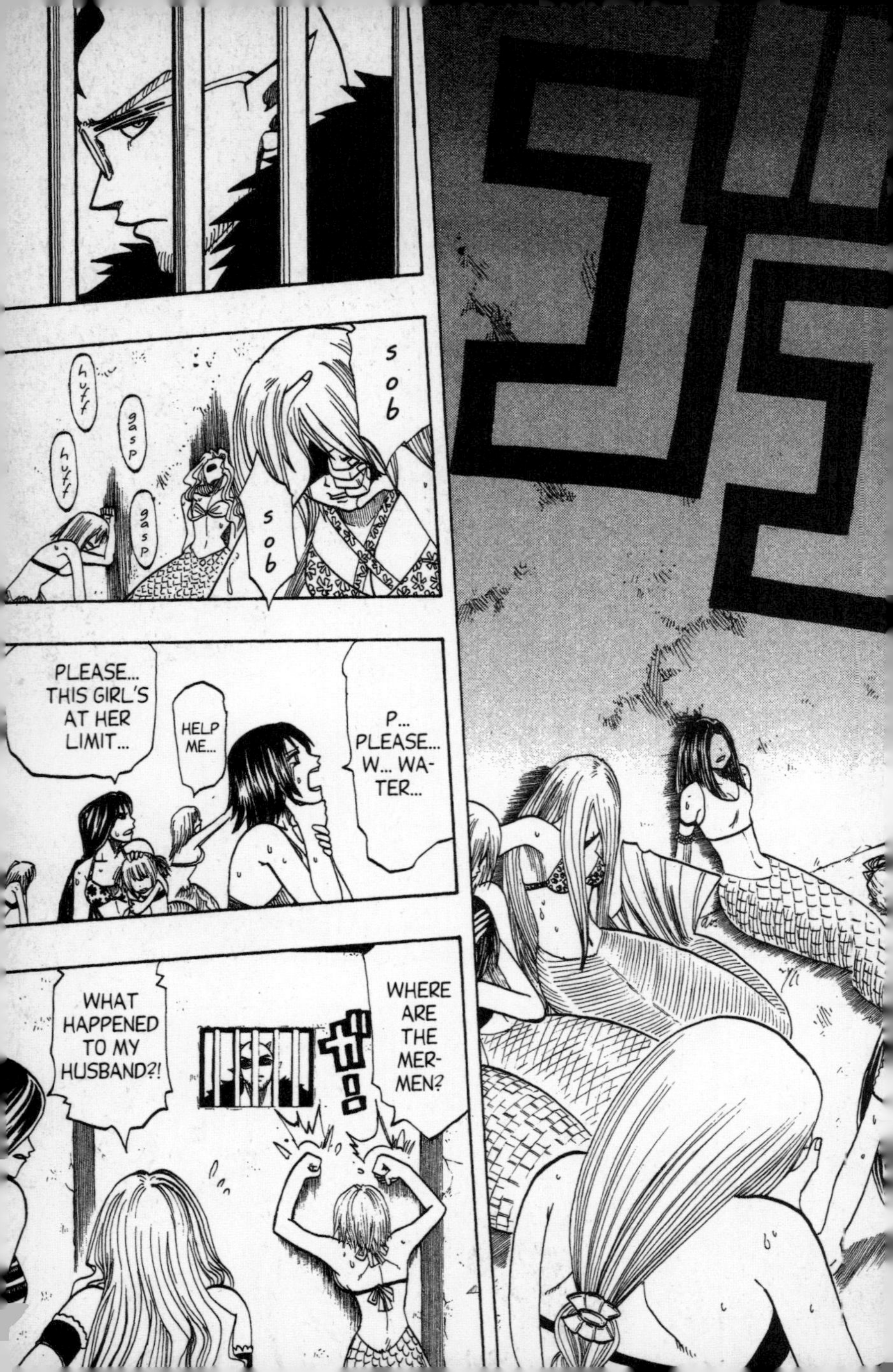
sob
sob
gasp
gasp
huff
huff
P... PLEASE... W... WA-TER...
HELP ME...
PLEASE... THIS GIRL'S AT HER LIMIT...
WHERE ARE THE MER-MEN?
WHAT HAPPENED TO MY HUSBAND?!

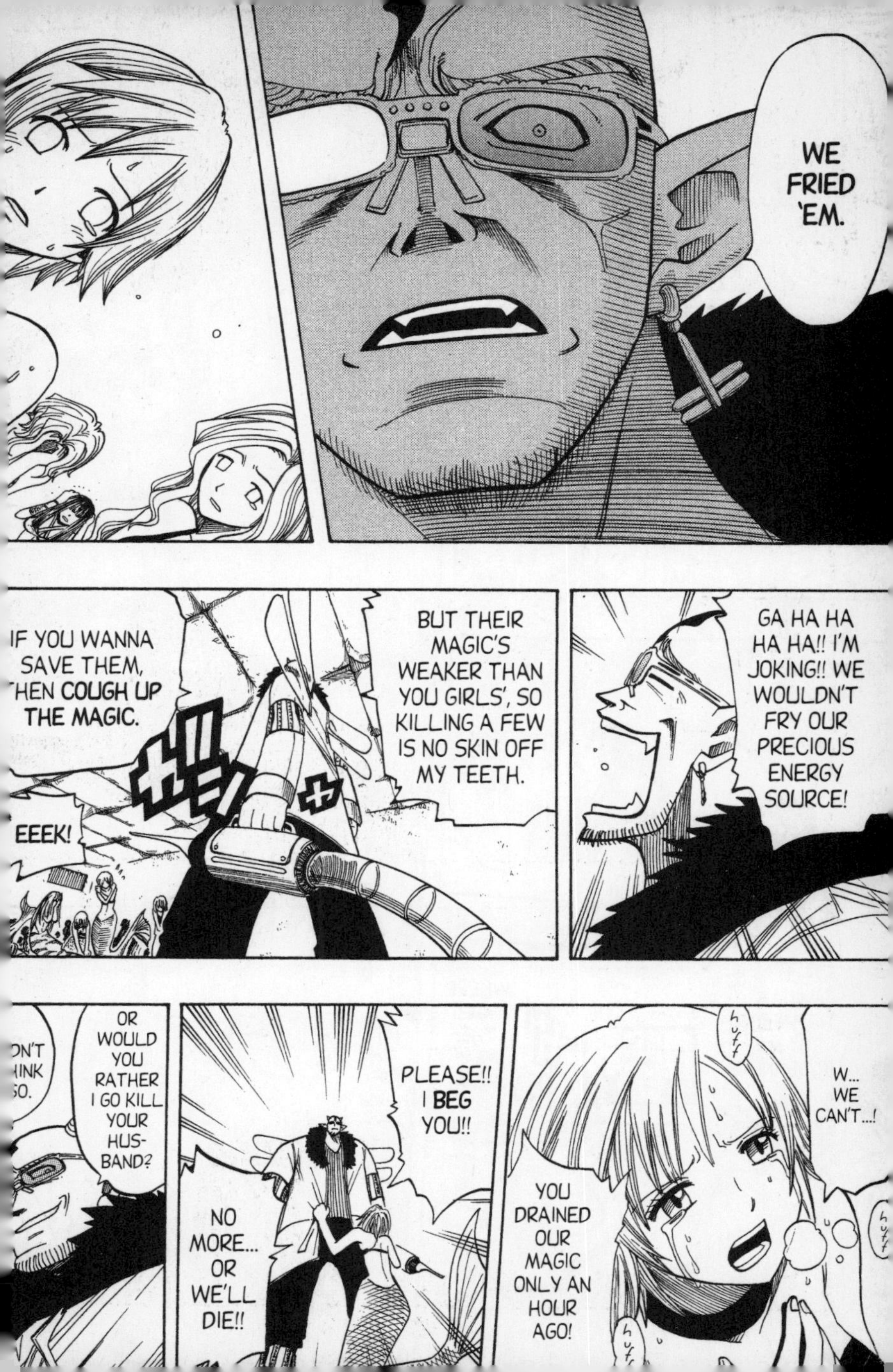
WE FRIED 'EM.
GA HA HA HA HA!! I'M JOKING!! WE WOULDN'T FRY OUR PRECIOUS ENERGY SOURCE!
BUT THEIR MAGIC'S WEAKER THAN YOU GIRLS', SO KILLING A FEW IS NO SKIN OFF MY TEETH.
IF YOU WANNA SAVE THEM, THEN COUGH UP THE MAGIC.
EEEK!
W... WE CAN'T...!
YOU DRAINED OUR MAGIC ONLY AN HOUR AGO!
PLEASE!! I BEG YOU!!
NO MORE... OR WE'LL DIE!!
OR WOULD YOU RATHER I GO KILL YOUR HUS-BAND?
N'T INK O.

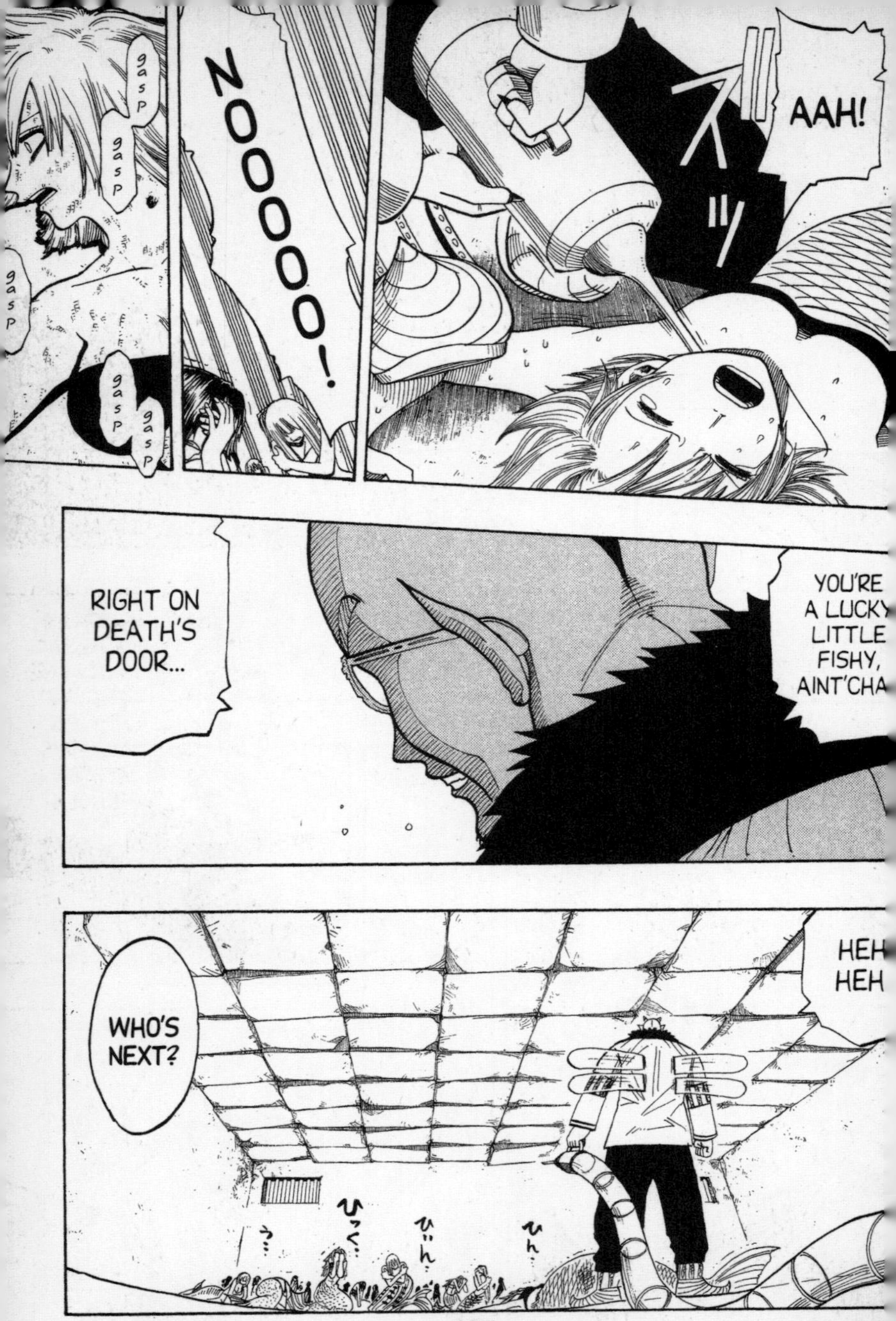
AAH!
NOOOOO!
gasp
gasp
gasp
gasp
gasp
YOU'RE A LUCKY LITTLE FISHY, AINT'CHA
RIGHT ON DEATH'S DOOR...
HEH HEH
WHO'S NEXT?
ひん…
ひぃん…
ひっく…
う…

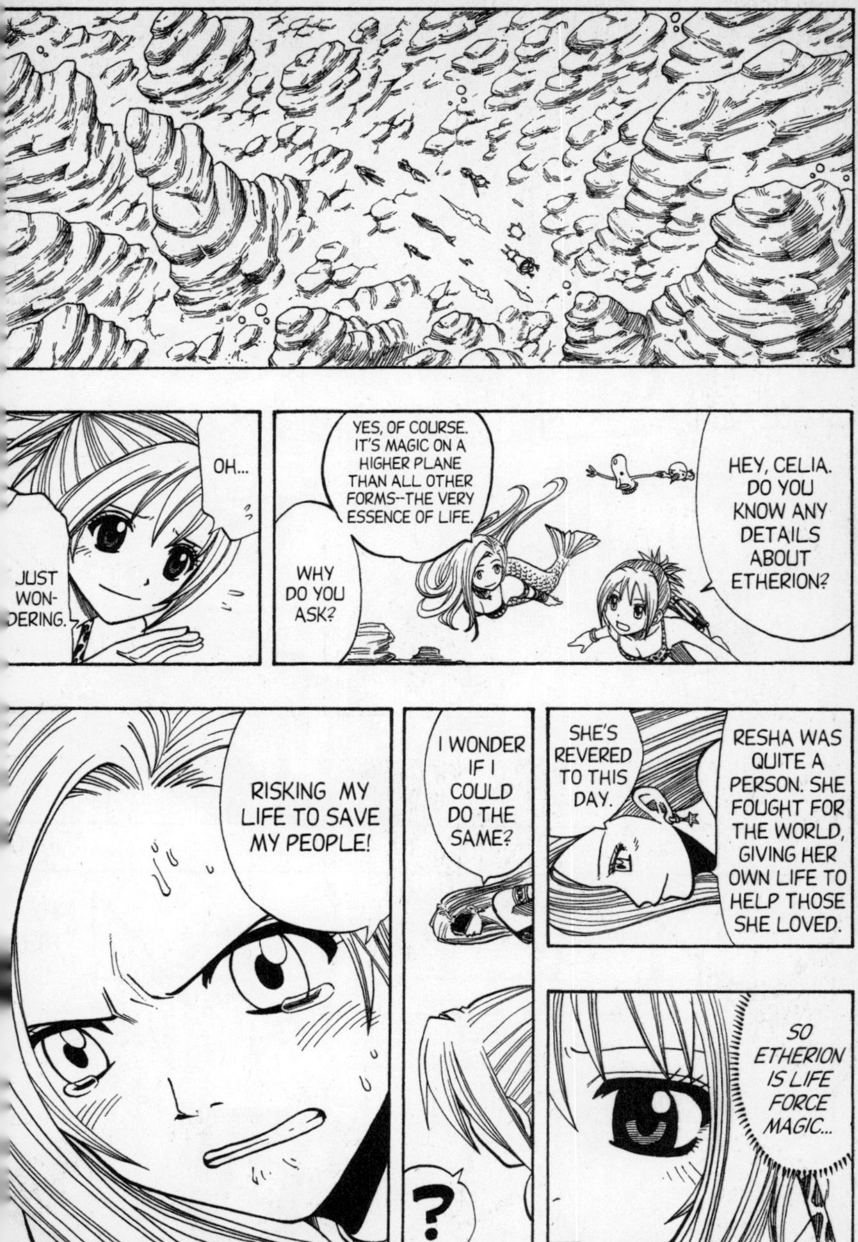
HEY, CELIA. DO YOU KNOW ANY DETAILS ABOUT ETHERION?
YES, OF COURSE. IT'S MAGIC ON A HIGHER PLANE THAN ALL OTHER FORMS--THE VERY ESSENCE OF LIFE.
WHY DO YOU ASK?
OH...
JUST WON-DERING.
RESHA WAS QUITE A PERSON. SHE FOUGHT FOR THE WORLD, GIVING HER OWN LIFE TO HELP THOSE SHE LOVED.
SHE'S REVERED TO THIS DAY.
SO ETHERION IS LIFE FORCE MAGIC...
I WONDER IF I COULD DO THE SAME?
?
RISKING MY LIFE TO SAVE MY PEOPLE!

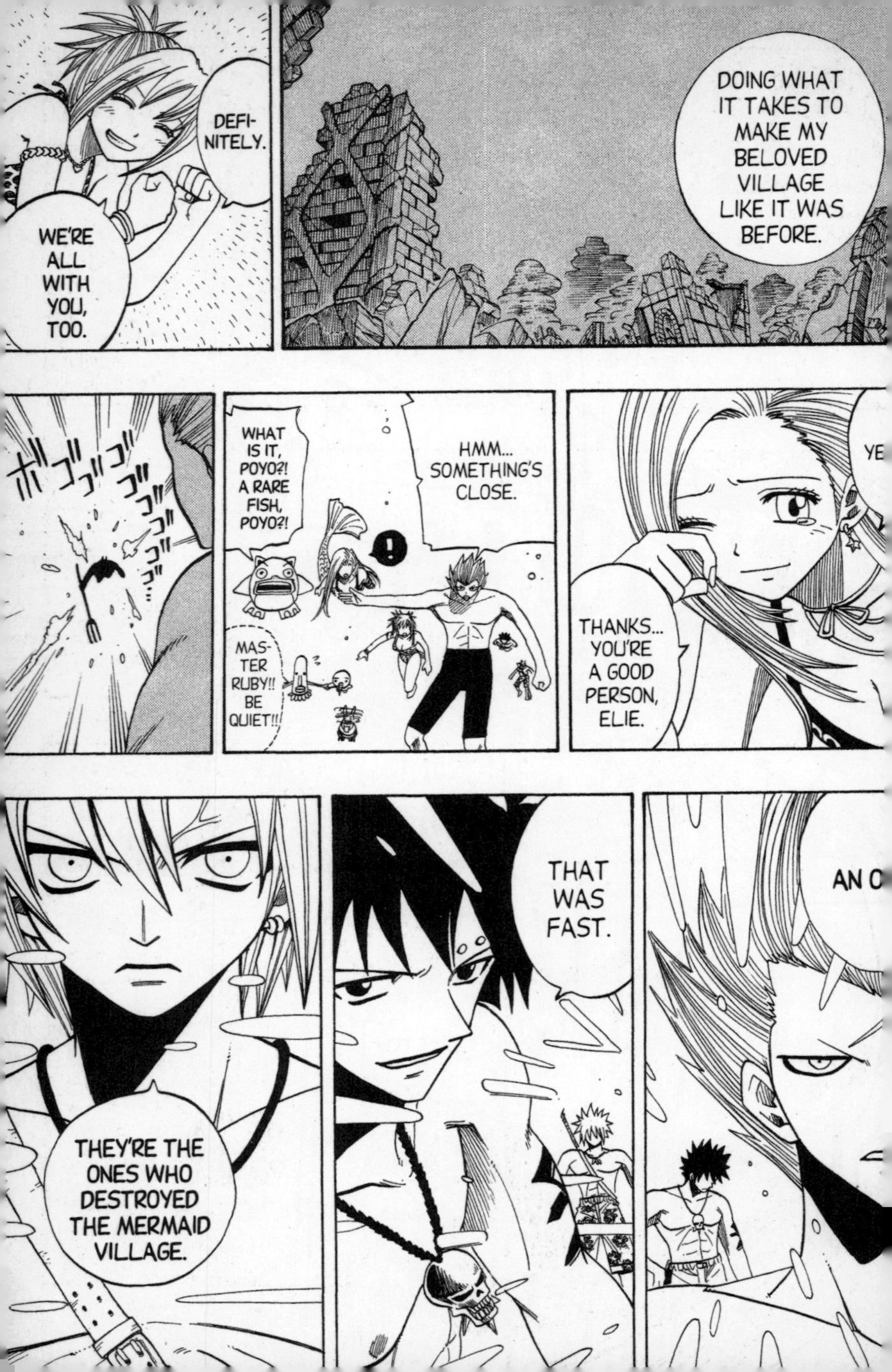
DOING WHAT IT TAKES TO MAKE MY BELOVED VILLAGE LIKE IT WAS BEFORE.
DEFINITELY.
WE'RE ALL WITH YOU, TOO.
YE
THANKS... YOU'RE A GOOD PERSON, ELIE.
HMM... SOMETHING'S CLOSE.
WHAT IS IT, POYO?! A RARE FISH, POYO?!
MASTER RUBY!! BE QUIET!!
AN O
THAT WAS FAST.
THEY'RE THE ONES WHO DESTROYED THE MERMAID VILLAGE.

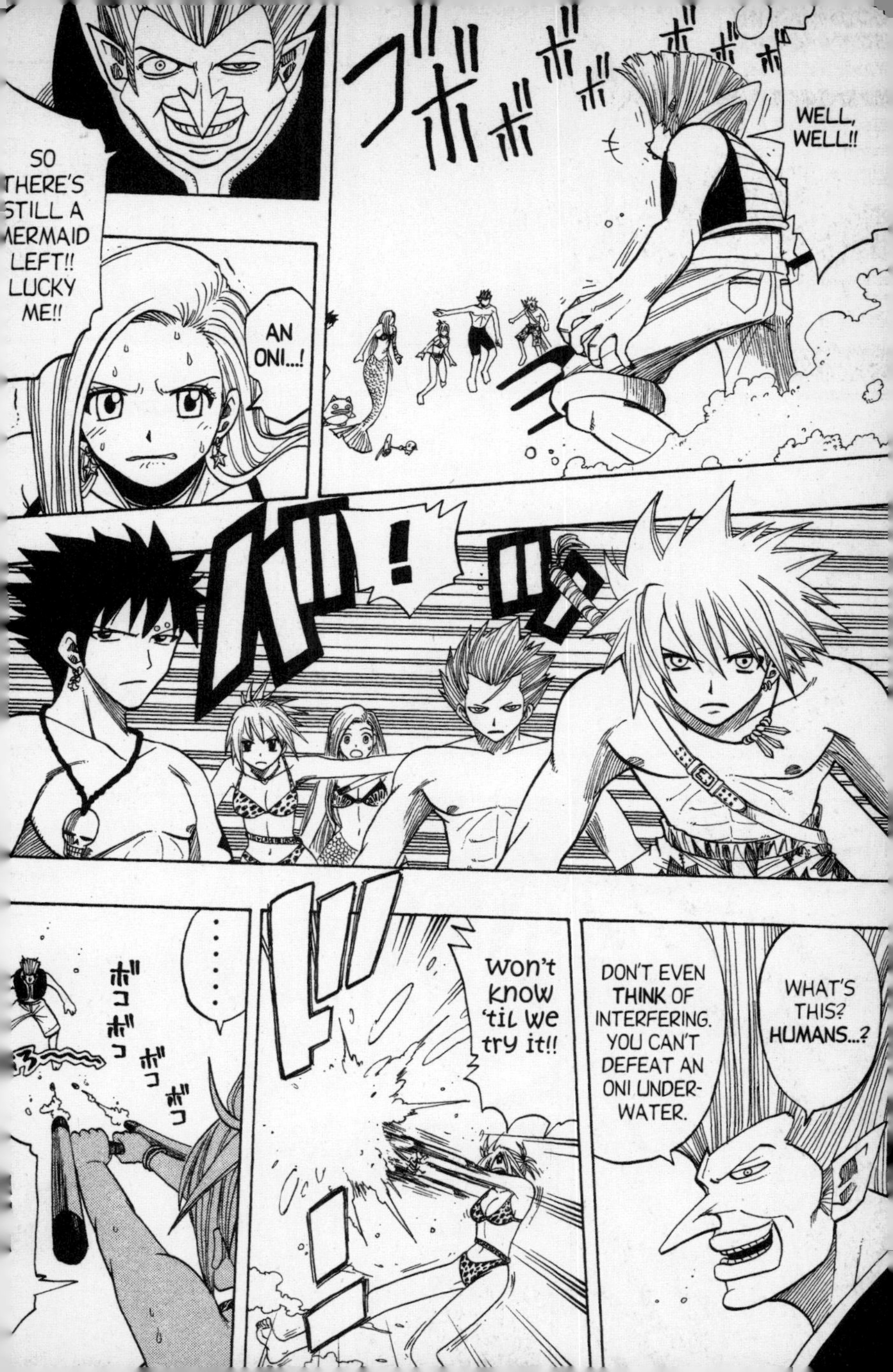

WELL, WELL!!
SO THERE'S STILL A MERMAID LEFT!! LUCKY ME!!
AN ONI...!
WHAT'S THIS? HUMANS...?
DON'T EVEN THINK OF INTERFERING. YOU CAN'T DEFEAT AN ONI UNDER-WATER.
Won't know 'til we try it!!
......
ボコボコ
ボコ
ボコ

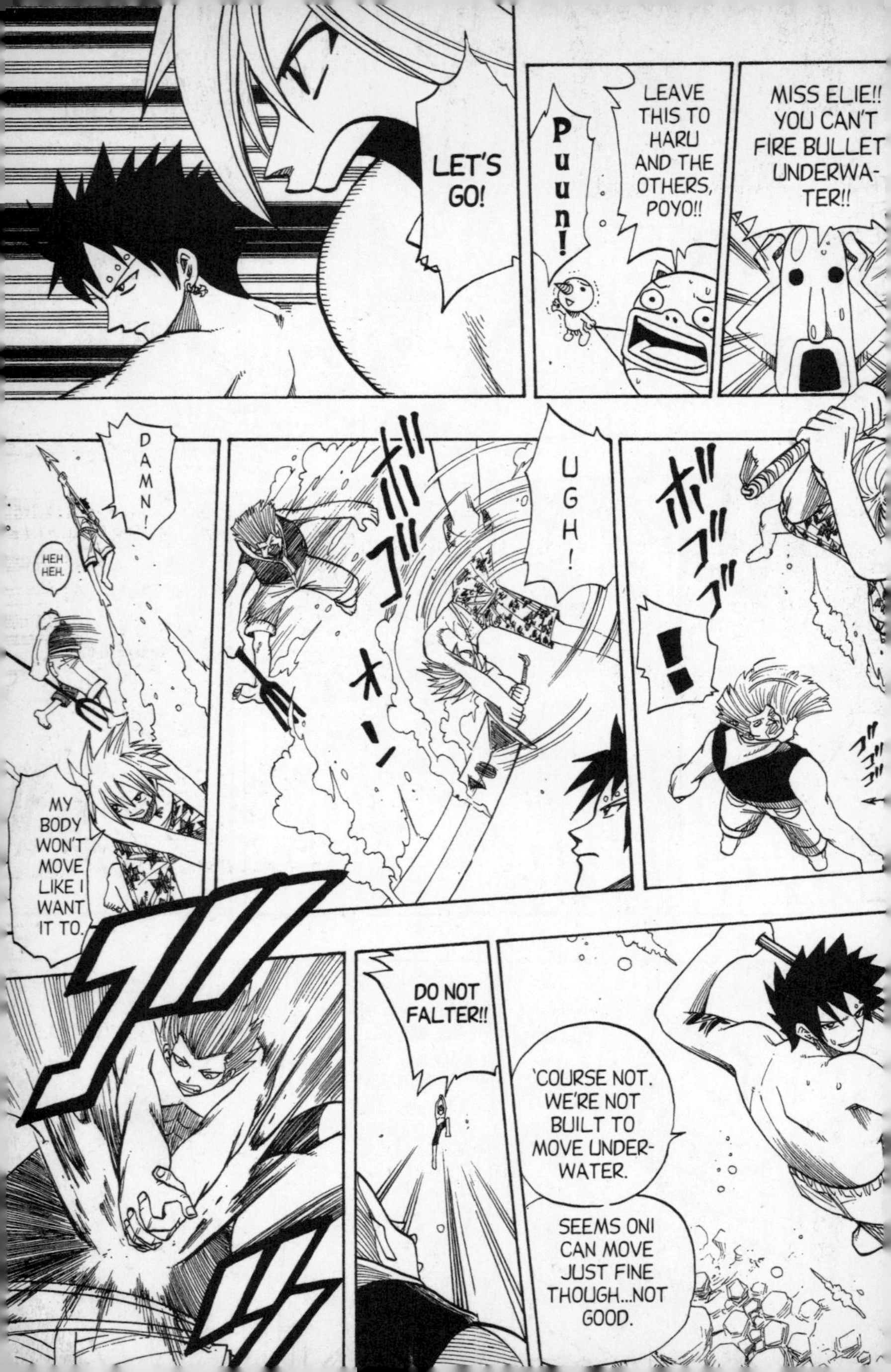
MISS ELIE!! YOU CAN'T FIRE BULLET UNDERWATER!!
LEAVE THIS TO HARU AND THE OTHERS, POYO!!
Puun!
LET'S GO!
!
UGH!
DAMN!
HEH HEH.
MY BODY WON'T MOVE LIKE I WANT IT TO.
'COURSE NOT. WE'RE NOT BUILT TO MOVE UNDERWATER.
SEEMS ONI CAN MOVE JUST FINE THOUGH...NOT GOOD.
DO NOT FALTER!!

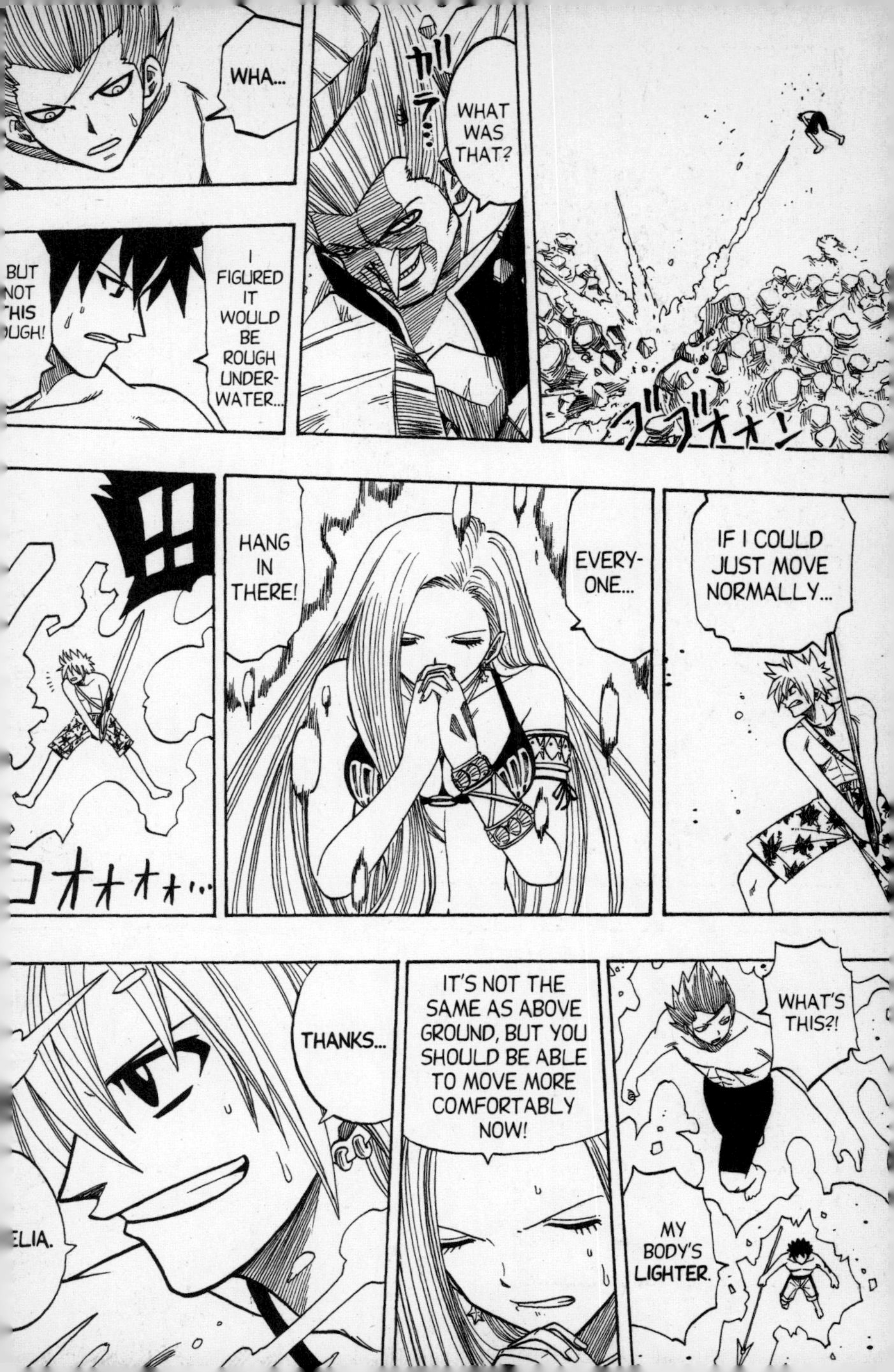
WHAT WAS THAT?
WHA...
I FIGURED IT WOULD BE ROUGH UNDER-WATER...
BUT NOT THIS
IF I COULD JUST MOVE NORMALLY...
EVERY-ONE...
HANG IN THERE!
WHAT'S THIS?!
MY BODY'S LIGHTER.
IT'S NOT THE SAME AS ABOVE GROUND, BUT YOU SHOULD BE ABLE TO MOVE MORE COMFORTABLY NOW!
THANKS...

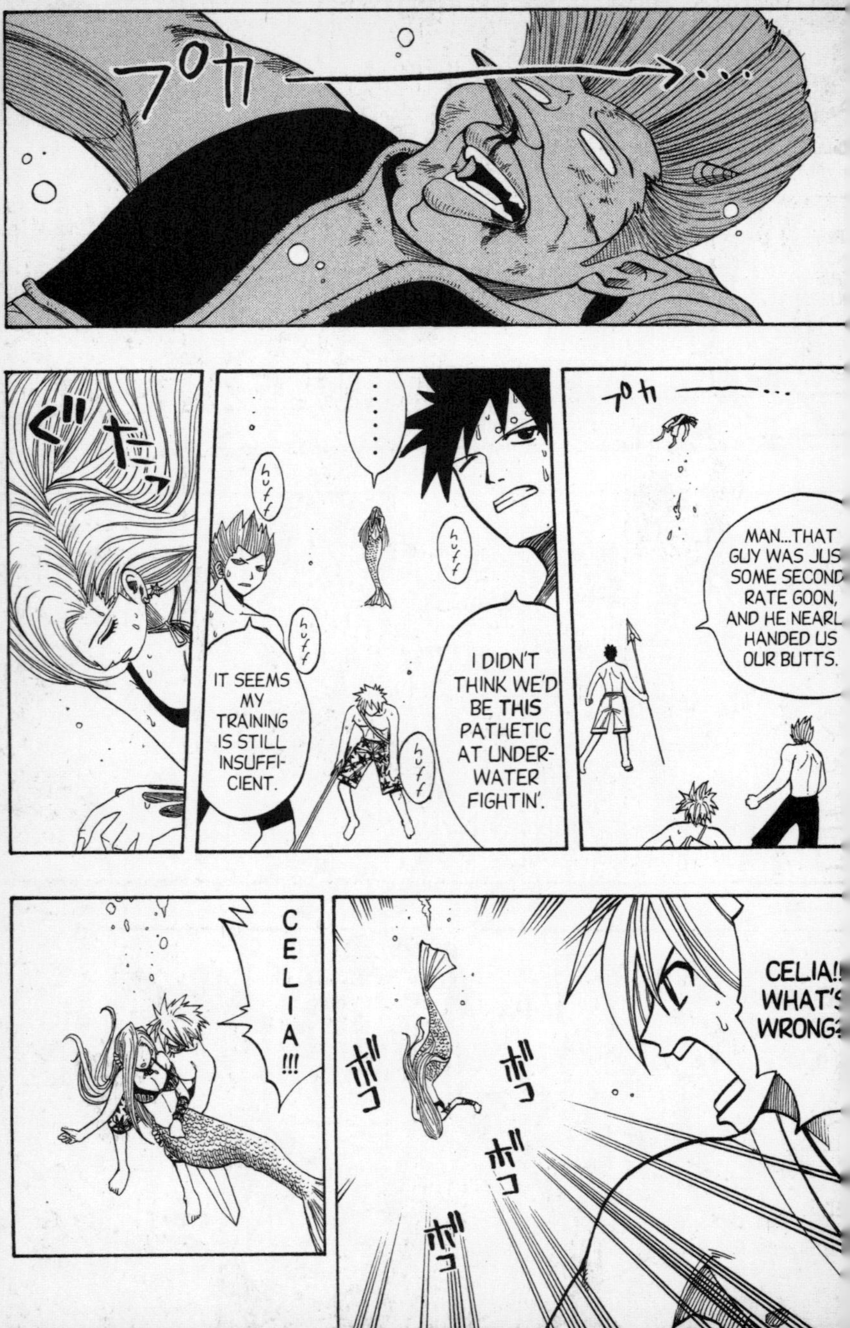

プカ―――…
プカ―――…
MAN...THAT GUY WAS JUS SOME SECOND RATE GOON, AND HE NEARL HANDED US OUR BUTTS.
......
huff
huff
I DIDN'T THINK WE'D BE THIS PATHETIC AT UNDER-WATER FIGHTIN'.
huff
huff
IT SEEMS MY TRAINING IS STILL INSUFFI-CIENT.
ぐたーっ
CELIA!! WHAT'S WRONG?
ボコ
ボコ
ボコ
ボコ
CELIA!!!

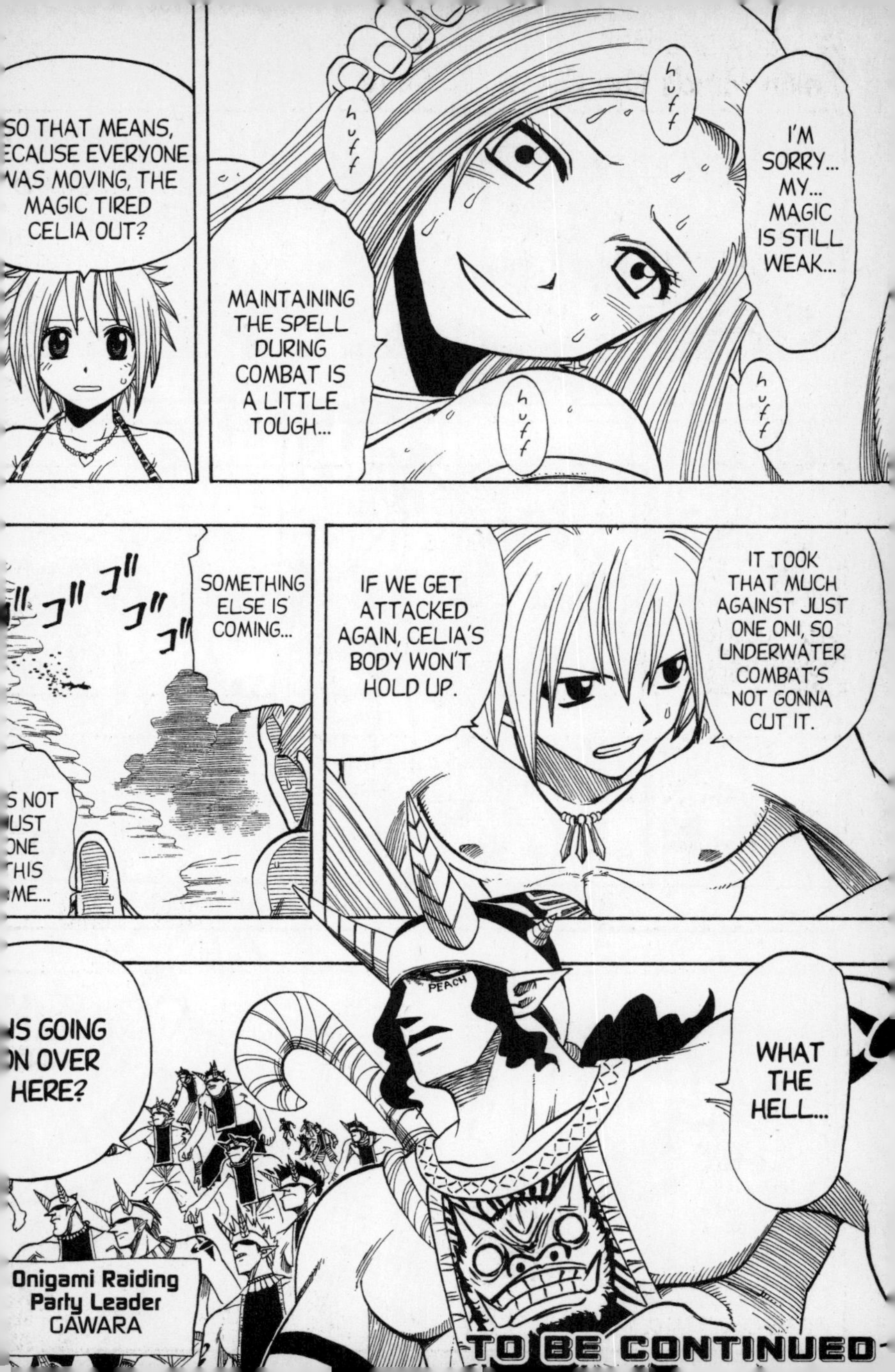
huff
huff
huff
I'M SORRY... MY... MAGIC IS STILL WEAK...
MAINTAINING THE SPELL DURING COMBAT IS A LITTLE TOUGH...
huff
SO THAT MEANS, ECAUSE EVERYONE WAS MOVING, THE MAGIC TIRED CELIA OUT?
IT TOOK THAT MUCH AGAINST JUST ONE ONI, SO UNDERWATER COMBAT'S NOT GONNA CUT IT.
IF WE GET ATTACKED AGAIN, CELIA'S BODY WON'T HOLD UP.
SOMETHING ELSE IS COMING...
ゴゴゴゴゴゴ
S NOT JUST ONE THIS ME...
WHAT THE HELL...
PEACH
S GOING N OVER HERE?
Onigami Raiding Party Leader GAWARA
TO BE CONTINUED

RAVE0077
Levin Minds the House 12: Song

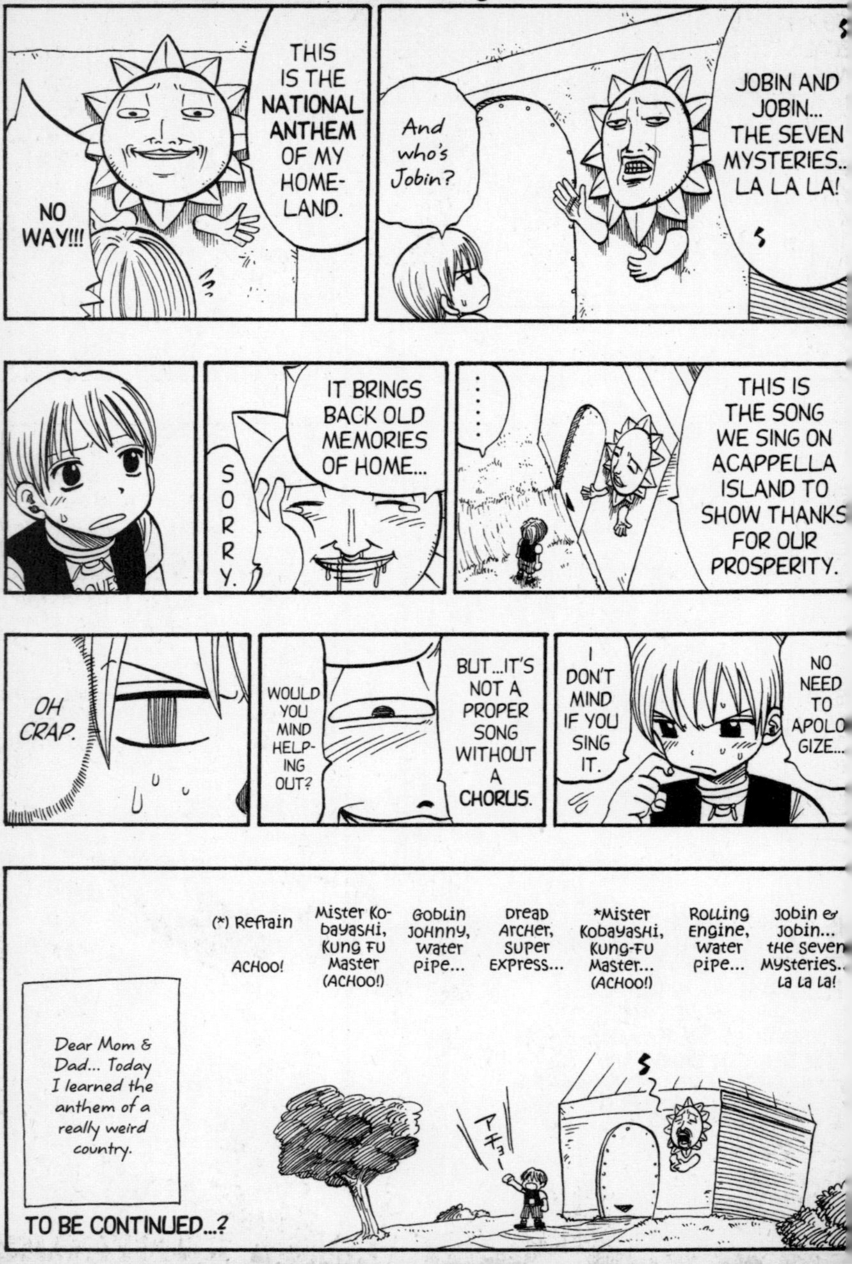

JOBIN AND JOBIN... THE SEVEN MYSTERIES.. LA LA LA!
And who's Jobin?
THIS IS THE NATIONAL ANTHEM OF MY HOMELAND.
NO WAY!!!
THIS IS THE SONG WE SING ON ACAPPELLA ISLAND TO SHOW THANKS FOR OUR PROSPERITY.
......
IT BRINGS BACK OLD MEMORIES OF HOME...
SORRY.
NO NEED TO APOLOGIZE...
I DON'T MIND IF YOU SING IT.
BUT...IT'S NOT A PROPER SONG WITHOUT A CHORUS.
WOULD YOU MIND HELPING OUT?
OH CRAP.
Jobin & Jobin... the Seven Mysteries.. La La La!
Rolling Engine, Water pipe...
*Mister Kobayashi, Kung-Fu Master... (ACHOO!)
Dread Archer, Super Express...
Goblin Johnny, Water pipe...
Mister Kobayashi, Kung Fu Master (ACHOO!)
(*) Refrain
ACHOO!
アチョー
Dear Mom & Dad... Today I learned the anthem of a really weird country.
TO BE CONTINUED...?

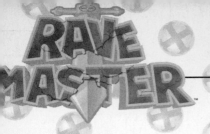

RAVE MASTER Fan Art

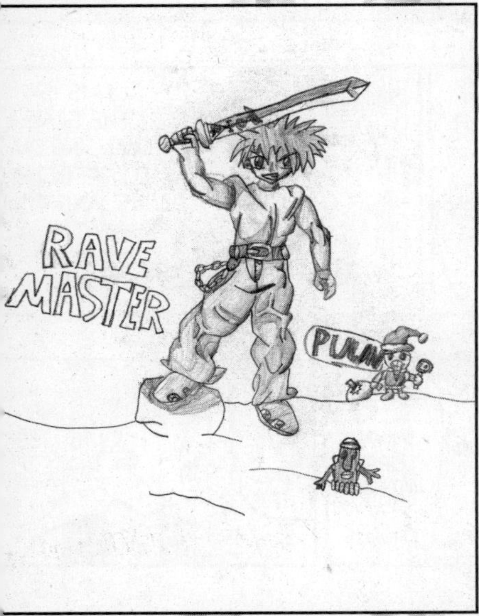
RAVE
MASTER

⬆ WITH A FIRM GRIP ON THE TEN POWERS, HARU LOOKS READY TO TAKE ON WHATEVER FOE AWAITS HIM, WHILE PLUE LOOKS LIKE HE'S ABOUT TO SWAP HIS TRADEMARK SUCKERS FOR CANDY CANES. AND I LOVE GRIFF'S SAFARI OUTFIT! WHAT A FUN PICTURE, BRENDEN!

BRENDEN C.
AGE 10
SANTEE, CA

HEY, ASPIRING MANGA ARTISTS! WANT TO SEE YOUR PICTURES IN PRINT? WELL, IF YOU THINK YOU CAN DRAW A COOL-LOOKING HARU, A SEXY ELIE OR A FUNNY PLUE, SEND 'EM THIS WAY! WE'LL PICK ONE LUCKY WINNER FROM EACH ROUND AND SEND THEM A SPECIAL PRIZE! WHAT DO HAVE TO LOSE? NOTHING!

HOW TO SUBMIT:

1) SEND YOUR WORK VIA REGULAR MAIL (NOT E-MAIL) TO:

RAVE MASTER FAN ART
C/O TOKYOPOP
5900 WILSHIRE BLVD.
SUITE 2000
LOS ANGELES, CA 90036

2) ALL WORK SUBMITTED SHOULD BE IN BLACK-AND-WHITE AND NO LARGER THAN 8.5" X 11". (AND TRY NOT TO FOLD IT TOO MANY TIMES!)

3) ANYTHING YOU SEND WILL NOT BE RETURNED. IF YOU WANT TO KEEP YOUR ORIGINAL, IT'S FINE TO SEND US A COPY.

4) PLEASE INCLUDE YOUR FULL NAME, AGE, CITY AND STATE FOR US TO PRINT WITH YOUR WORK. IF YOU'D RATHER US USE A PEN NAME, PLEASE INCLUDE THAT TOO.

5) IMPORTANT: IF YOU'RE UNDER THE AGE OF 18, YOU MUST HAVE YOUR PARENT'S PERMISSION IN ORDER FOR US TO PRINT YOUR WORK. ANY SUBMISSIONS WITHOUT A SIGNED NOTE OF PARENTAL CONSENT CANNOT BE USED.

6) FOR FULL DETAILS, PLEASE CHECK OUT HTTP://WWW.TOKYOPOP.COM/ABOUTUS/FANART.PHP

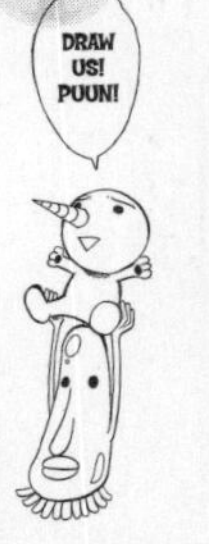
DRAW US! PUUN!

DISCLAIMER: ANYTHING YOU SEND TO US BECOMES THE PROPERTY OF TOKYOPOP INC. AND, AS WE SAID BEFORE, WILL NOT BE RETURNED TO YOU. WE WILL HAVE THE RIGHT TO PRINT, REPRODUCE, DISTRIBUTE OR MODIFY THE ARTWORK FOR USE IN FUTURE VOLUMES OF RAVE MASTER OR ON THE WEB WITHOUT PAYMENT TO YOU.

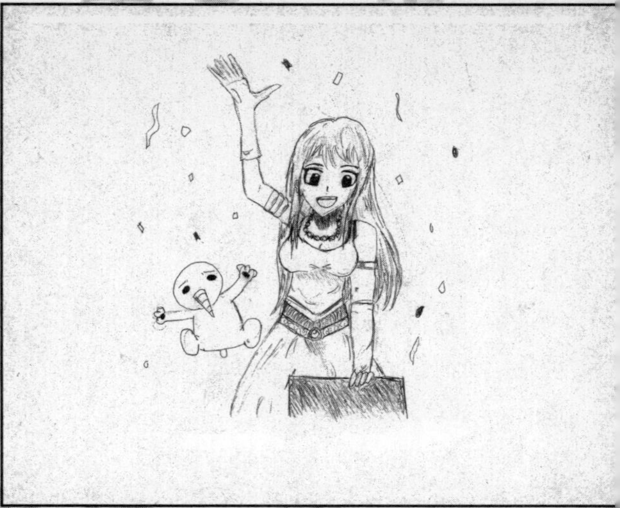

IS ELIE ACTUALLY WEARING A DRESS?! NO, THAT'S RESHA, CELEBRATING ALONGSIDE THE RAVE BEARER. THANKS FOR TAKING US BACK TO THE PAST WITH THIS PICTURE, STEPH. EXCELLENT WORK!

STEPH S.
AGE 14
BRENTWOOD, TN

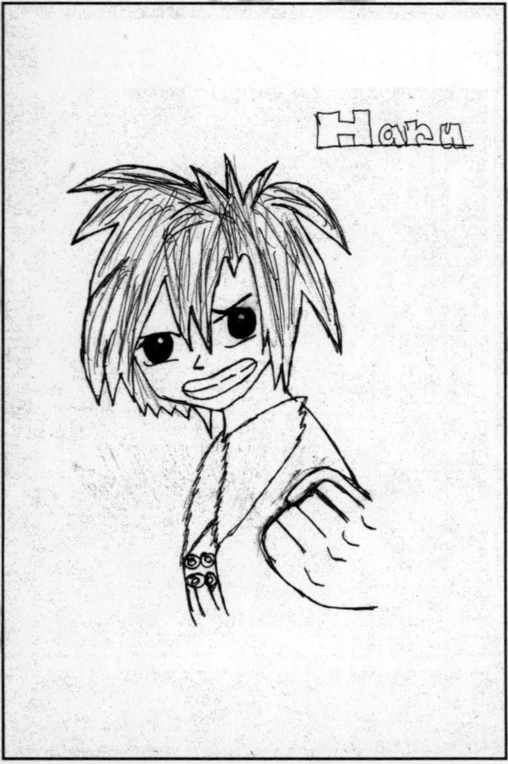
Haru

WITH HIS TEETH SET AND A LOOK OF DETERMINATION IN HIS EYES, HARU IS READY TO TRAVEL TO THE ENDS OF THE EARTH TO FIND STAR MEMORY FOR ELIE.

KAYLYN S.
AGE 13
WEST BLOCTON, AL

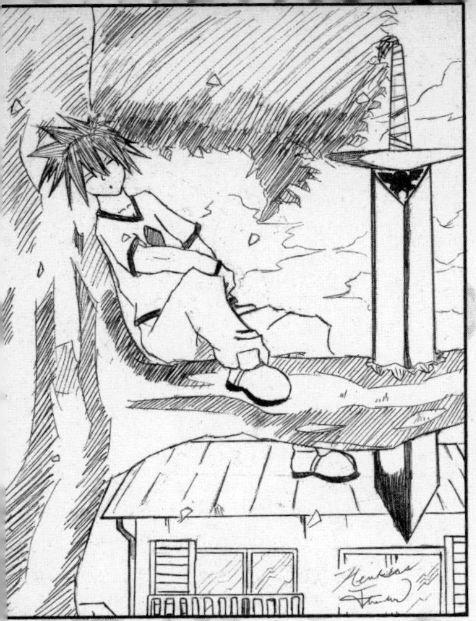

RIGHT ON, NICHOLAS! CONSIDERING HOW HARD HARU'S BEEN SEARCHING FOR THE MISSING RAVE STONES, IT'S ONLY NATURAL THAT HE'D BE A LITTLE TIRED. EVEN THE RAVE MASTER IS ENTITLED TO A LITTLE CATNAP!

NICHOLAS F.
AGE 14
SPRINGFIELD, VA

T JUST ME, OR DOES ELIE LOOK ANGRY ?E? I DON'T KNOW ABOUT YOU, BUT I SURE ULDN'T WANT TO BE ON THE OTHER END OF OSE TONFA BLASTERS. NICE WORK, SAGE!

SAGE M.
HOUSTON, TX

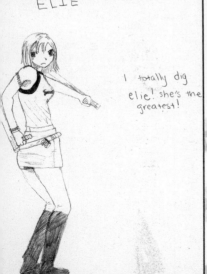

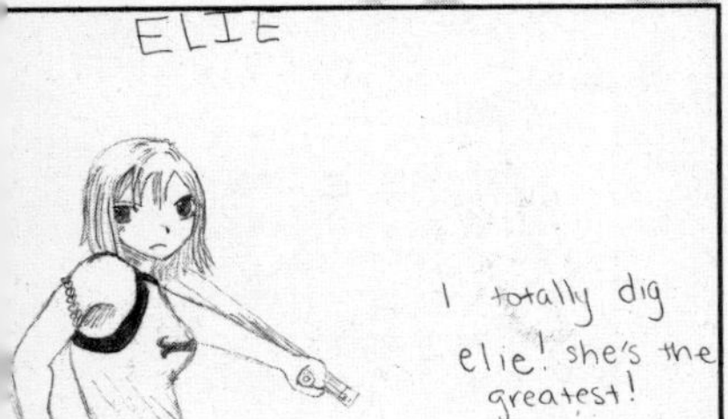
ELIE
I totally dig elie! she's the greatest!

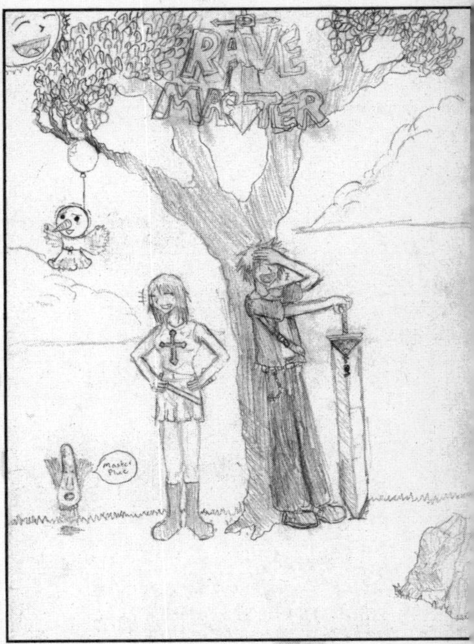
RAVE MASTER
Master Plue

IT'S NICE TO SEE THAT IN BETWEEN ALL THEIR FIGHTS WITH THE ORACION SIX, HARU AND ELIE STILL HAVE TIME TO ENJOY A GOOD LAUGH. POOR PLUE LOOKS LIKE HE COULD USE A HAND, THOUGH. THANKS FOR SENDING US THE COOL LOOKING COVER, RICHARD!

RICHARD I.
AGE 12
BRIGHTON, MI

Believer
Greetings from
Garage Island!

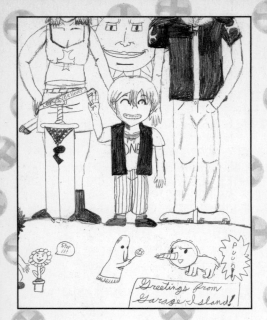

WITH ITS NECK-DOWN SHOTS OF HARU AND ELIE SET IN FRONT OF A GRINNING NAKAJIMA, I'D IMAGINE THIS PICTURE IS VERY CLOSE TO HOW LEVIN VIEWS THE WORLD. IS THAT CHINO REACHING OUT TO "BABY NAKAJIMA"? AND WHAT IS ELIE DOING WITH THE TEN POWERS? NICE WORK, NATALIE! WE HARDLY EVER SEE PICTURES OF LEVIN!

NATALIE D.
AGE 11
SAN DIEGO, CA

HOW LOW CAN HE GO? HOW LOW CAN HE GO?! I THINK THIS IS ONE CONTEST THAT PLUE MIGHT BE LOSING BY A NOSE. CHRISTOPHER'S PICTURE, HOWEVER, IS A WINNER!

CHRISTOPHER B.
AGE 13
CHINO, CA

LimBO contest
Go Master Plue
Limbo, ohhh do the Limbo

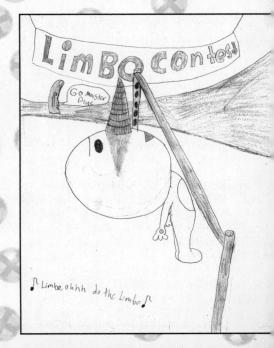

"AFTERWORDS"

WITH THIS VOLUME COMPLETE, RAVE MASTER IS NOW OVER 100 CHAPTERS STRONG!! YEEEAH, HOW EXCITING. LOOKING BACK, LOTS OF THINGS HAVE HAPPENED, BOTH FUN THINGS AND NOT-SO-FUN.

THE SUPPORT FROM ALL OF YOU READERS WAS A BIG HELP DURING THOSE DIFFICULT TIMES. PASSIONATE FAN LETTERS, LETTERS OF SUPPORT, LETTERS OF COMPLAINTS, POSTCARDS THAT ONLY HAD ONE WORD ON THEM...THEY ALL KEPT ME BOOSTED. THANKS SO MUCH!! I'M GOING TO KEEP AT IT, SO PLEASE KEEP UP THE ENCOURAGEMENT.

FUN TIMES! THERE'S JUST TOO MUCH TO TALK ABOUT CONCERNING THE MANGA, SO RATHER THAN EVEN TRYING TO FIT THAT ON ONE PAGE, I'M GOING TO TALK A BIT ABOUT MY PRIVATE LIFE.

I USUALLY TAKE A BREAK FROM DRAWING MANGA ON SATURDAY AND SUNDAY. IF I FINISH MY WORK EARLY I HAVE A DAY OFF ON FRIDAY, WHICH LETS ME HAVE A THREE-DAY WEEKEND!!

I HAVE LOTS OF HOBBIES, SO DURING MY BREAKS I DO EVERYTHING THAT I LIKE TO DO TO MY HEART'S CONTENT. I REALLY LOVE TO DRAW MANGA, BUT I TRY TO SPEND MY FREE TIME DOING OTHER FUN THINGS THAT I ENJOY. THAT SAID, I OFTEN FIND MYSELF DOODLING ON A SATURDAY OR SUNDAY, AND THE NEXT THING I KNOW, IT'S THE END OF THE DAY! THOSE SORT OF WEEKENDS ARE FAIRLY COMMON.

I'VE OFTEN BEEN ASKED WHAT I DO ON MY DAY OFF. THE ANSWER: **ANYTHING I WANT**! (LAUGHS) BOTTOM LINE IS THAT I JUST TRY TO ENJOY MYSELF.

I DON'T REALLY SLEEP ON MY DAYS OFF. SLEEPING IS A WASTE OF TIME. I GET ENOUGH SLEEP WHEN I'M DRAWING MANGA!! OOPS! IF I WRITE THAT, MY EDITOR WILL KILL ME! (LAUGHS) WHEN YOU WANT TO SLEEP, SLEEP!! WHEN YOU DON'T WANT TO SLEEP, DON'T SLEEP!! WHETHER YOU'RE DRAWING MANGA OR PLAYING AROUND, THAT'S THE BEST WAY TO APPROACH IT!!

UH...NOTHING I JUST WROTE SOUNDS THE LEAST BIT SANE, DOES IT? OH, WELL...

-HIRO MASHIMA

Yowza! How is the Rave Master going to get out of this?! Just a thought, but you might think about drawing the Ten Powers, Haru!

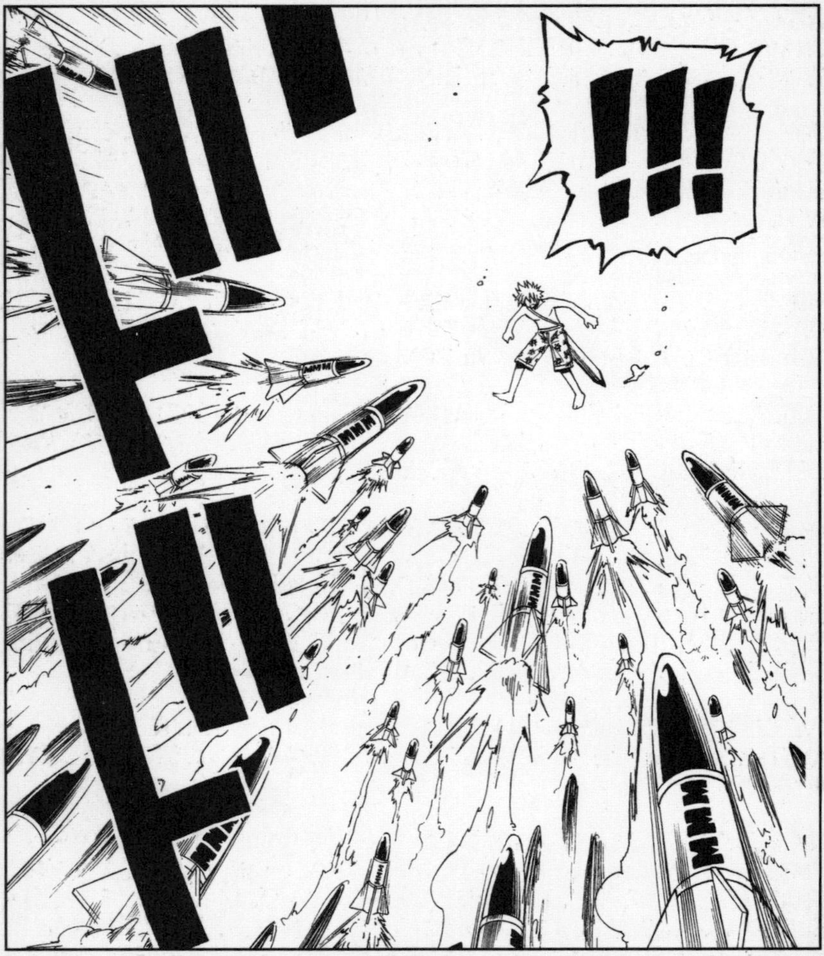
!!!

Haru and his companions have faced many enemies in their quest for the missing Rave Stones, but they've never fought a foe as cunning as the Onigami. They're battling on both land and sea in the next volume of Rave Master!

Rave Master Volume 14
Available April 2005

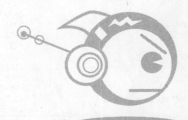

ALSO AVAILABLE FROM 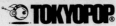 TOKYOPOP®

MANGA

.HACK//LEGEND OF THE TWILIGHT
@LARGE
ABENOBASHI: MAGICAL SHOPPING ARCADE
A.I. LOVE YOU
AI YORI AOSHI
ALICHINO
ANGELIC LAYER
ARM OF KANNON
BABY BIRTH
BATTLE ROYALE
BATTLE VIXENS
BOYS BE...
BRAIN POWERED
BRIGADOON
B'TX
CANDIDATE FOR GODDESS, THE
CARDCAPTOR SAKURA
CARDCAPTOR SAKURA - MASTER OF THE CLOW
CHOBITS
CHRONICLES OF THE CURSED SWORD
CLAMP SCHOOL DETECTIVES
CLOVER
COMIC PARTY
CONFIDENTIAL CONFESSIONS
CORRECTOR YUI
COWBOY BEBOP
COWBOY BEBOP: SHOOTING STAR
CRAZY LOVE STORY
CRESCENT MOON
CROSS
CULDCEPT
CYBORG 009
D•N•ANGEL
DEARS
DEMON DIARY
DEMON ORORON, THE
DEUS VITAE
DIABOLO
DIGIMON
DIGIMON TAMERS
DIGIMON ZERO TWO
DOLL
DRAGON HUNTER
DRAGON KNIGHTS
DRAGON VOICE
DREAM SAGA
DUKLYON: CLAMP SCHOOL DEFENDERS
EERIE QUEERIE!
ERICA SAKURAZAWA: COLLECTED WORKS
ET CETERA
ETERNITY
EVIL'S RETURN
FAERIES' LANDING
FAKE
FLCL
FLOWER OF THE DEEP SLEEP
FORBIDDEN DANCE
FRUITS BASKET

G GUNDAM
GATEKEEPERS
GETBACKERS
GIRL GOT GAME
GRAVITATION
GTO
GUNDAM SEED ASTRAY
GUNDAM WING
GUNDAM WING: BATTLEFIELD OF PACIFISTS
GUNDAM WING: ENDLESS WALTZ
GUNDAM WING: THE LAST OUTPOST (G-UNIT)
HANDS OFF!
HAPPY MANIA
HARLEM BEAT
HYPER RUNE
I.N.V.U.
IMMORTAL RAIN
INITIAL D
INSTANT TEEN: JUST ADD NUTS
ISLAND
JING: KING OF BANDITS
JING: KING OF BANDITS - TWILIGHT TALES
JULINE
KARE KANO
KILL ME, KISS ME
KINDAICHI CASE FILES, THE
KING OF HELL
KODOCHA: SANA'S STAGE
LAMENT OF THE LAMB
LEGAL DRUG
LEGEND OF CHUN HYANG, THE
LES BIJOUX
LOVE HINA
LOVE OR MONEY
LUPIN III
LUPIN III: WORLD'S MOST WANTED
MAGIC KNIGHT RAYEARTH I
MAGIC KNIGHT RAYEARTH II
MAHOROMATIC: AUTOMATIC MAIDEN
MAN OF MANY FACES
MARMALADE BOY
MARS
MARS: HORSE WITH NO NAME
MINK
MIRACLE GIRLS
MIYUKI-CHAN IN WONDERLAND
MODEL
MOURYOU KIDEN: LEGEND OF THE NYMPH
NECK AND NECK
ONE
ONE I LOVE, THE
PARADISE KISS
PARASYTE
PASSION FRUIT
PEACH FUZZ
PEACH GIRL
PEACH GIRL: CHANGE OF HEART
PET SHOP OF HORRORS
PITA-TEN
PLANET LADDER

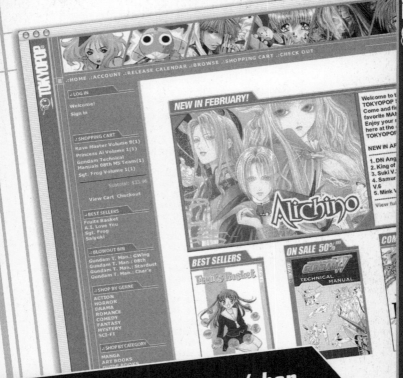
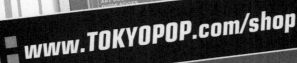

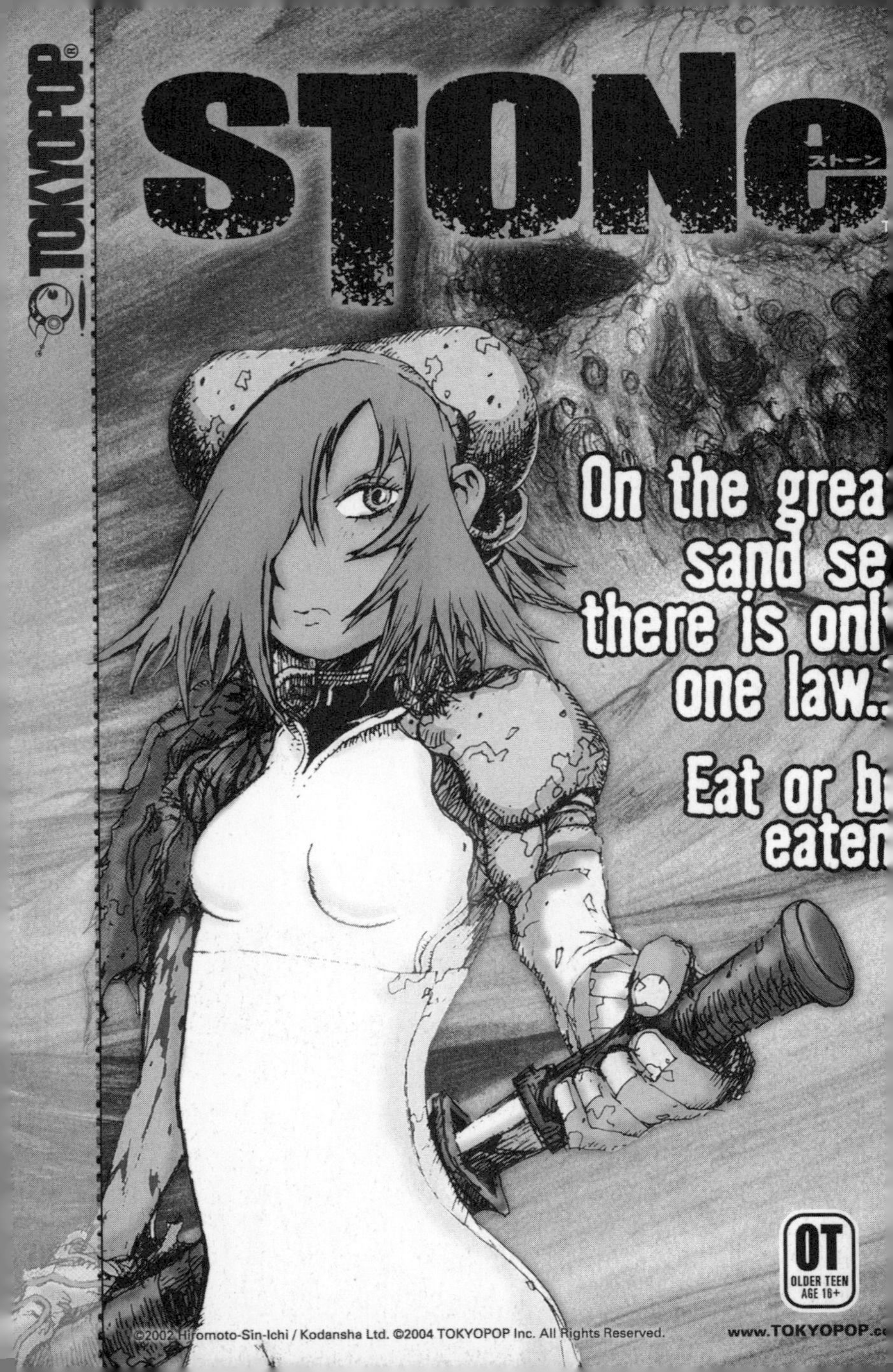
TOKYOPOP
STONe
ストーン
On the grea
sand se
there is onl
one law.
Eat or b
eaten
OT
OLDER TEEN
AGE 16+
©2002 Hiromoto-Sin-Ichi / Kodansha Ltd. ©2004 TOKYOPOP Inc. All Rights Reserved.
www.TOKYOPOP.c

WARCRAFT
THE SUNWELL TRILOGY

RICHARD A. KNAAK · KIM JAE-HWAN

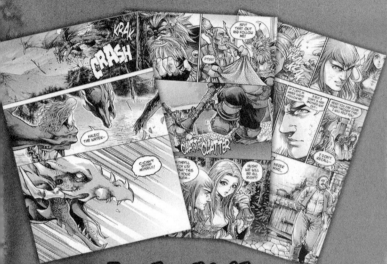

From the artist of the
best-selling *King of Hell* series!

It's an epic quest to save the entire High Elven Kingdom from the forces of the Undead Scourge! Set in the mystical world of Azeroth, *Warcraft: The Sunwell Trilogy* chronicles the adventures of Kalec, a blue dragon who has taken human form to escape deadly forces, and Anveena, a beautiful young maiden with a mysterious power.

T TEEN AGE 13+

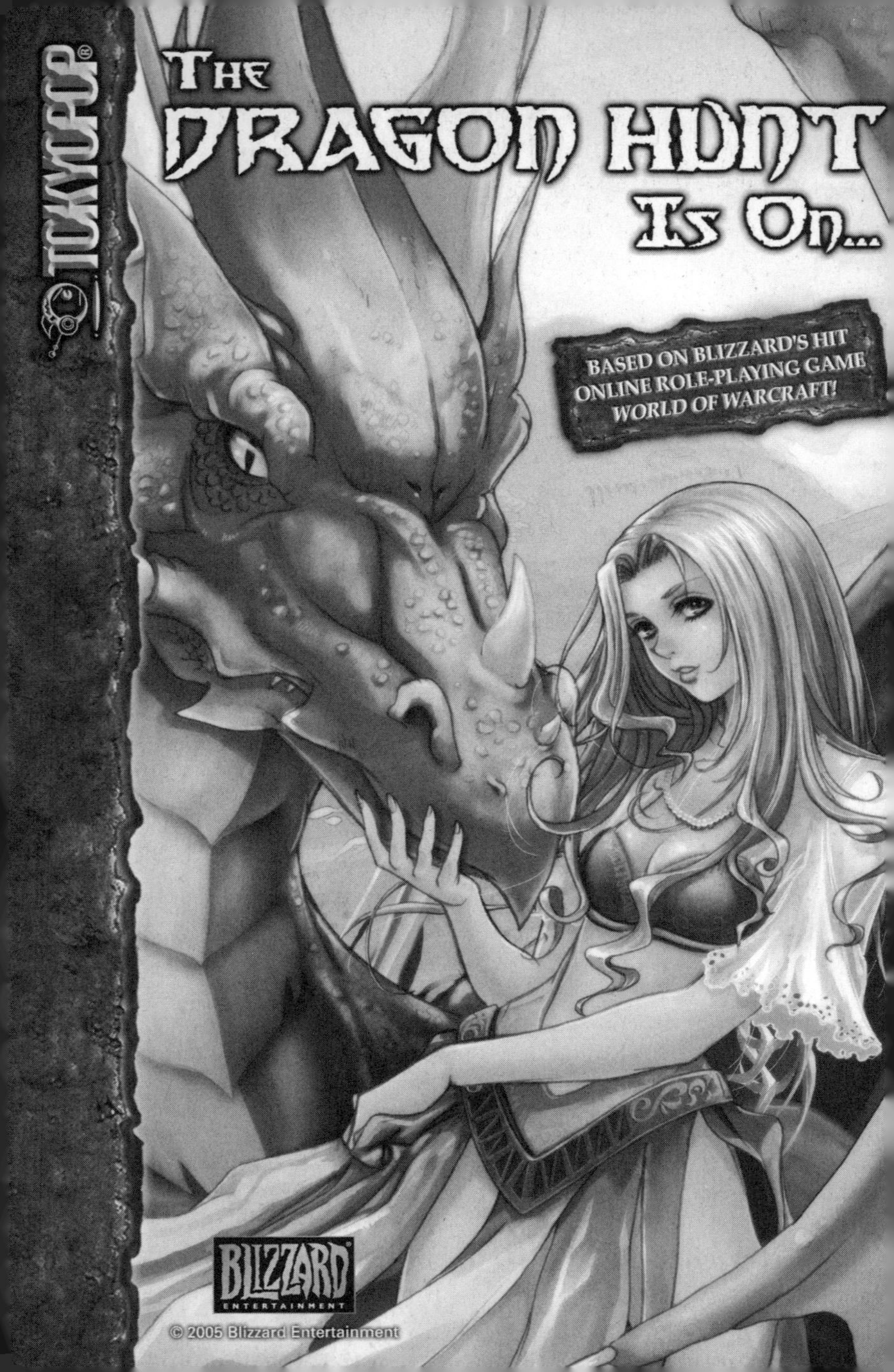
TOKYOPOP
THE DRAGON HUNT IS ON...
BASED ON BLIZZARD'S HIT
ONLINE ROLE-PLAYING GAME
WORLD OF WARCRAFT!
BLIZZARD ENTERTAINMENT
© 2005 Blizzard Entertainment

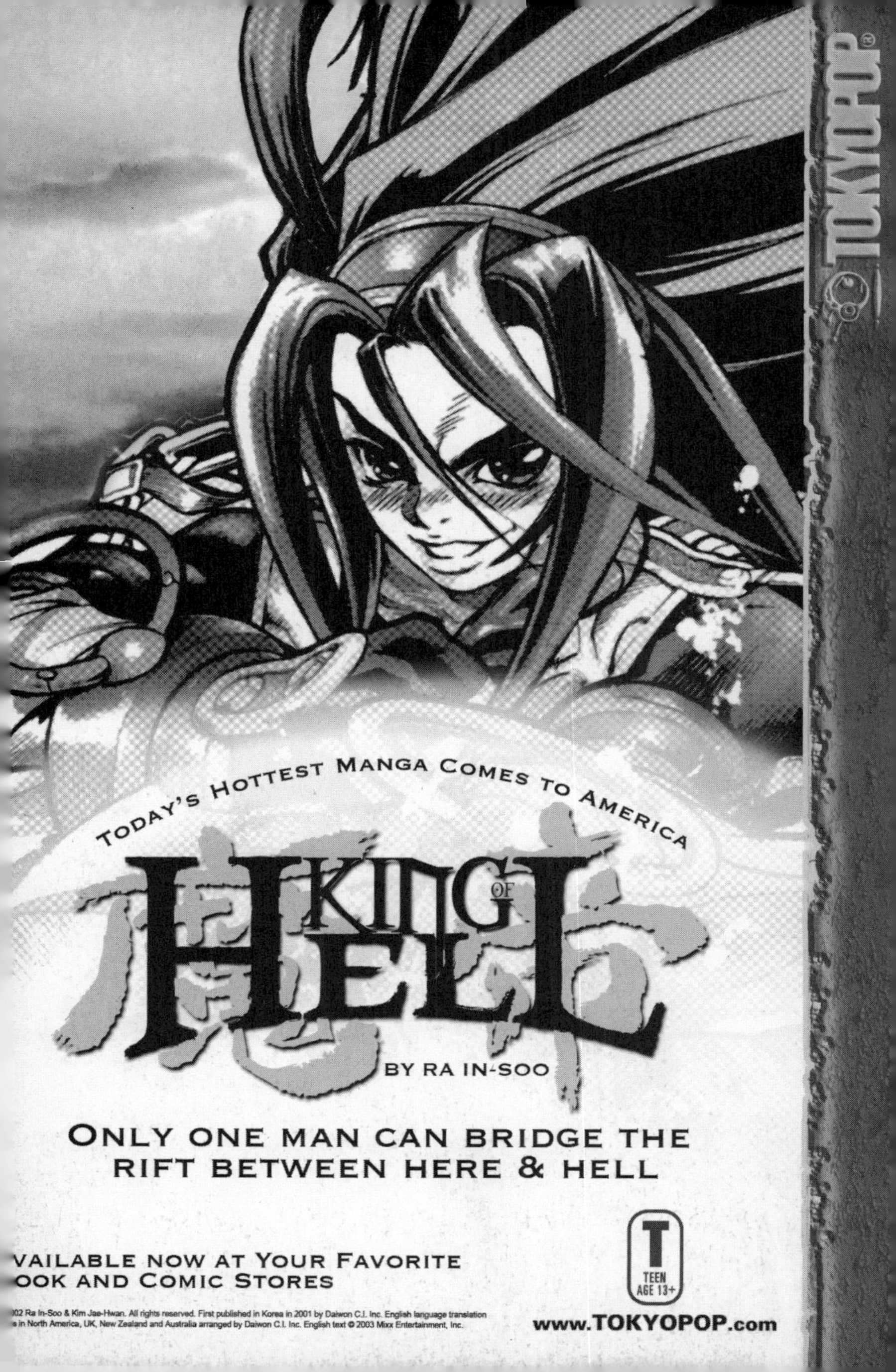
TOKYOPOP®
TODAY'S HOTTEST MANGA COMES TO AMERICA
KING OF HELL
BY RA IN-SOO
ONLY ONE MAN CAN BRIDGE THE RIFT BETWEEN HERE & HELL
VAILABLE NOW AT YOUR FAVORITE
OOK AND COMIC STORES
T
TEEN AGE 13+
02 Ra In-Soo & Kim Jae-Hwan. All rights reserved. First published in Korea in 2001 by Daiwon C.I. Inc. English language translation
s in North America, UK, New Zealand and Australia arranged by Daiwon C.I. Inc. English text © 2003 Mixx Entertainment, Inc.
www.TOKYOPOP.com

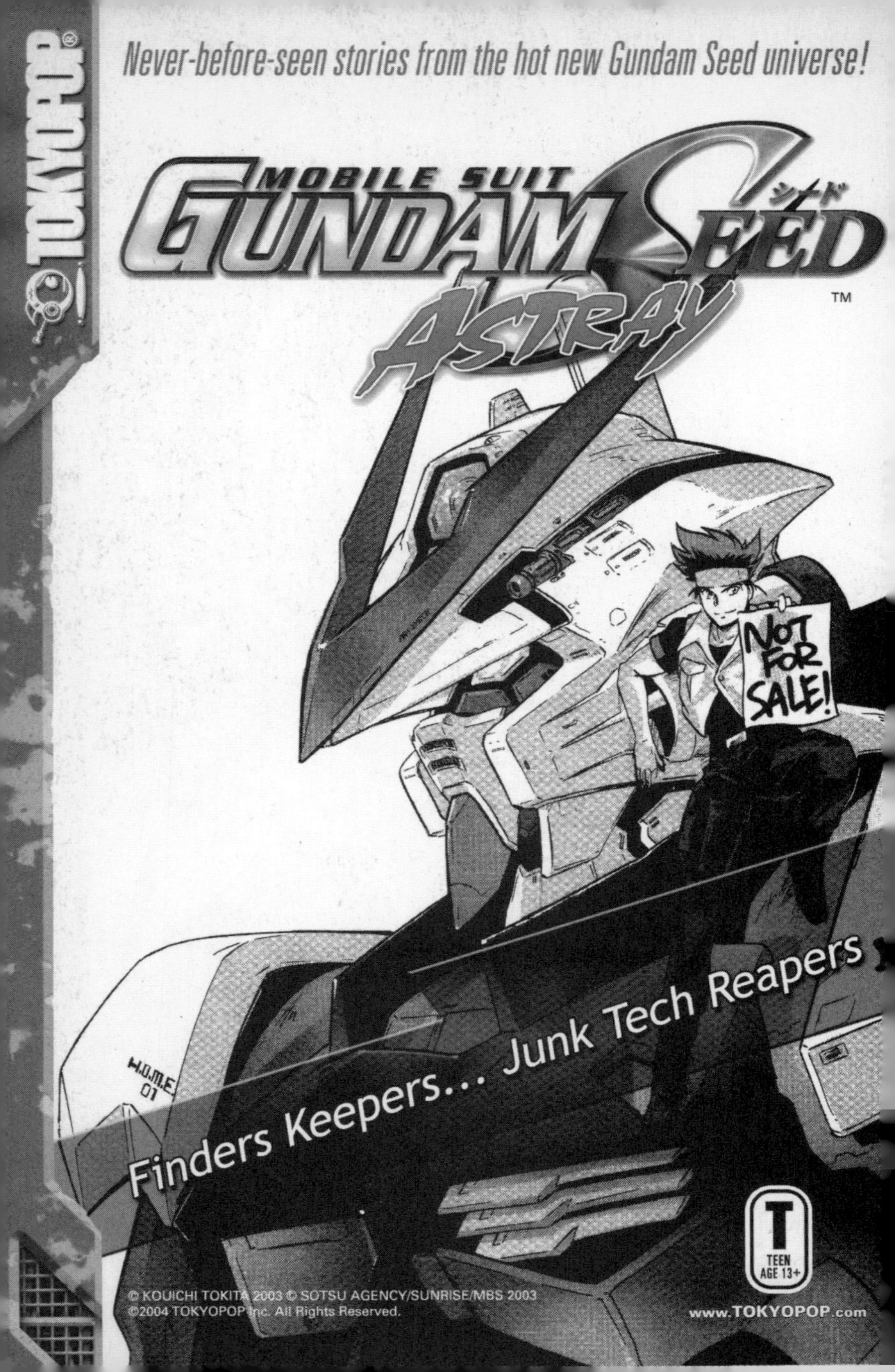

Never-before-seen stories from the hot new Gundam Seed universe!

MOBILE SUIT
GUNDAM SEED シード
ASTRAY ™

NOT FOR SALE!

Finders Keepers... Junk Tech Reapers

T TEEN AGE 13+

BASED ON THE HIT VIDEO GAME SERIES!

Suikoden™
III
幻想水滸伝

A legendary hero.
A war with no future.
An epic for today.

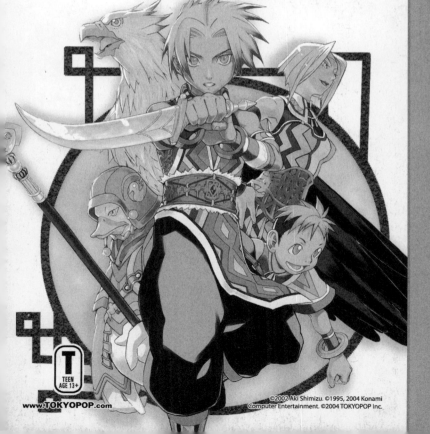

TOKYOPOP

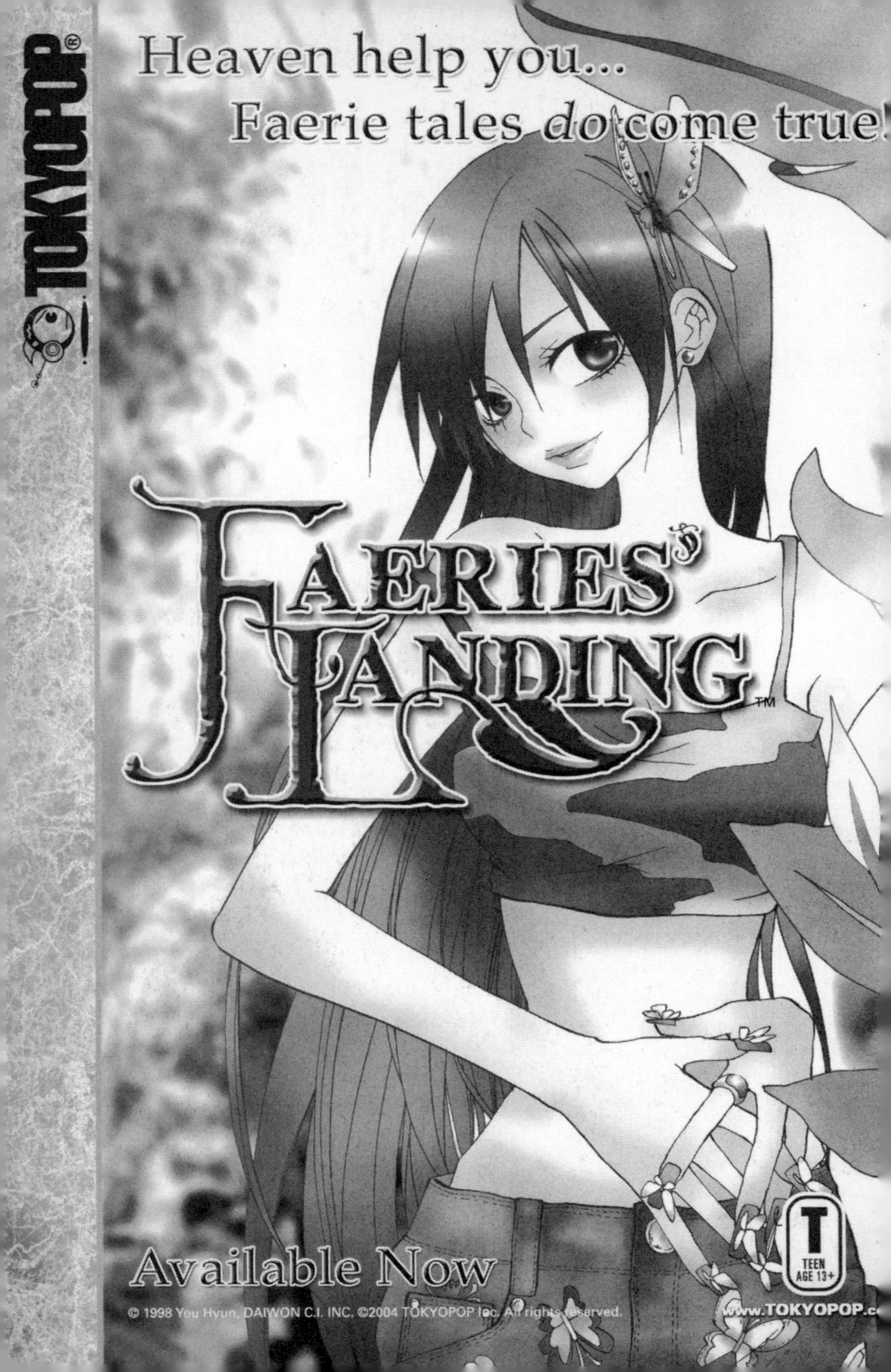
TOKYOPOP
Heaven help you...
Faerie tales *do* come true!
FAERIES' LANDING™
Available Now
T
TEEN
AGE 13+
© 1998 You Hyun, DAIWON C.I. INC. ©2004 TOKYOPOP Inc. All rights reserved.
www.TOKYOPOP.c

W9-DDN-180

STOP!

This is the back of the book.
You wouldn't want to spoil a great ending!

WITHDRAWN

This book is printed "manga-style," in the authentic Japanese right-to-left format. Since none of the artwork has been flipped or altered, readers get to experience the story just as the creator intended. You've been asking for it, so TOKYOPOP® delivered: authentic, hot-off-the-press, and far more fun!

DIRECTIONS

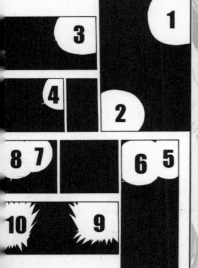

If this is your first time reading manga-style, here's a quick guide to help you understand how it works.

It's easy... just start in the top right panel and follow the numbers. Have fun, and look for more 100% authentic manga from TOKYOPOP®!

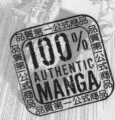